The Age of Apology

PENNSYLVANIA STUDIES IN HUMAN RIGHTS

Bert B. Lockwood, Jr., Series Editor

A complete list of books in the series is available from the publisher.

Published in association with United Nations University, which was established by the United Nations in 1972 as an international community of scholars engaged in research, postgraduate training, and the dissemination of knowledge in areas of concern to the United Nations and its agencies. Devoted to advancing human security and welfare, United Nations University focuses on issues of peace, governance, the environment, and sustainable development.

The Age of Apology

Facing Up to the Past

EDITED BY MARK GIBNEY,
RHODA E. HOWARD-HASSMANN,
JEAN-MARC COICAUD, AND
NIKLAUS STEINER

PENN

University of Pennsylvania Press

Philadelphia

Copyright © 2008 University of Pennsylvania Press

All rights reserved. Except for brief quotations used for purposes of review or scholarly citation, none of this book may be reproduced in any form by any means without written permission from the publisher.

Published by
University of Pennsylvania Press
Philadelphia, Pennsylvania 19104-4112

Printed in the United States of America on acid-free paper

10 9 8 7 6 5 4 3 2 1

A Cataloging-in-Publication Record is available from the Library of Congress.

ISBN-13: 978-0-8122-4033-7
ISBN-10: 0-8122-4033-2

Contents

Introduction: Apologies and the West   1
Rhoda E. Howard-Hassmann and Mark Gibney

PART I: LAW, ETHICS, AND THE THEORY BEHIND APOLOGIES

1. The Role of Apology in International Law   13
   Richard B. Bilder

2. Apology, Justice, and Respect: A Critical Defense of Political Apology   31
   Janna Thompson

3. Historical Injustice and Liberal Political Theory   45
   Michael Freeman

4. Apologies: A Cross-Cultural Analysis   61
   Alison Dundes Renteln

5. Elements of a Road Map for a Politics of Apology   77
   Jean-Marc Coicaud and Jibecke Jönsson

PART II: INTERNAL APOLOGIES BY STATES

6. When Sorry Is Enough: The Possibility of a National Apology for Slavery   95
   Eleanor Bright Fleming

7. The University and the Slaves: Apology and Its Meaning   109
   Alfred L. Brophy

vi   Contents

8. The Role of Apologies in National Reconciliation Processes:
   On Making Trustworthy Institutions Trusted   120
   Pablo de Greiff

9. Wrestling with the Past: Apologies, Quasi-Apologies, and
   Non-Apologies in Canada   137
   Matt James

10. Apology and Reconciliation in New Zealand's Treaty of Waitangi
    Settlement Process   154
    Meredith Gibbs

PART III: INTERNATIONAL APOLOGIES OF STATES

11. State Apologies Under U.S. Hegemony   171
    Carlos A. Parodi

12. "Deliver Us from Original Sin": Belgian Apologies to Rwanda
    and the Congo   187
    Paul Kerstens

13. Germany Faces Colonial History in Namibia: A Very Ambiguous
    "I Am Sorry"   202
    Leonard Jamfa

14. Words Require Action: African Elite Opinion About Apologies
    from the "West"   216
    Rhoda E. Howard-Hassmann and Anthony P. Lombardo

15. Colonialism, Slavery, and the Slave Trade: A Dutch
    Perspective   229
    Peter Baehr

16. Is Japan Facing Its Past? The Case of Japan
    and Its Neighbors   241
    Elizabeth S. Dahl

PART IV: APOLOGIES BY NON-STATE ACTORS

17. Papal Apologies of Pope John Paul II   259
    Michael R. Marrus

18. Rethinking Corporate Apologies: Business and Apartheid
    Victimization in South Africa   271
    Bonny Ibhawoh

PART V: THE WAR ON TERROR

19. Apology and the American "War on Terror"   287
    Mark Gibney and Niklaus Steiner

20. The Fourth Estate and the Case for War in Iraq: Apology
    or Apologia?   298
    Jonathan Marks

Notes   315

List of Contributors   321

Index   329

Acknowledgments   335

Introduction: Apologies and the West

RHODA E. HOWARD-HASSMANN AND MARK GIBNEY

We live in an age and a time that seeks to establish political truth, perhaps best exemplified by the creation of truth commissions in societies seeking to emerge from dictatorial pasts. Undoubtedly the most visible effort has been the Truth and Reconciliation Commission (TRC) in South Africa, which has sought to balance the need to examine the nature of apartheid rule against the exigencies facing this newly developing multiracial society. Similar efforts have been attempted in a host of other countries, albeit with varying degrees of success. There seems to be almost universal recognition that a society will not be able to successfully pass into the future until it somehow deals with its demons from the past.

The truth commission phenomenon has been a non-Western affair. The West has its own demons to exorcise, although recognition of this has materialized rather slowly. Still, Western states and institutions are beginning to deal with some of the harms that they have brought upon others. One means of doing this is to issue an apology. It would not be an exaggeration to say that apology has become the West's own version of the truth commission.

There has been much academic study of truth commissions, but specifically Western efforts to "come to terms" with the past have not yet attracted a great deal of academic attention, with some notable exceptions (Barkan 2000; Brooks 1999; Lazare 2004; Torpey 2003, 2006). The present volume builds on this work, but also offers a different approach. It focuses on more recent apologies, as well as those that have not received much academic attention and analysis. We also take a broad view of public apologies, including apologies by international organizations, business enterprises, and religious institutions as well as states. Beyond this, and taking a cue from Sherlock Holmes's observations about the barking habits of dogs, a non-apology might be as important to study as an apology. Thus, several chapters discuss the absence of or the refusal to apologize, what that might mean, and how it might be interpreted. Finally, the central theme of this volume is the West's relationship to the rest of the world, and the role that apology might (and should) play in the (re)ordering of this relationship.

The Meaning of Apologies

Historically in international affairs, no attention was paid to the principle that harms should be acknowledged. The dominant way of thinking was that the strong did whatever they wished, as reflected by Thucydides in the "Melian dialogue": "the strong do what they have the power to do and the weak accept what they have to accept." The apology phenomenon directly challenges this thesis: perhaps its most remarkable aspect is that powerful actors and institutions are apologizing to the relatively powerless. But what does this mean? Are apologies an indication or a representation of a new international order—both politically and insofar as they transform international law? Or are they fleeting in moment and insignificant in meaning? We hope this volume helps to answer such questions.

Several authors in this volume examine the relationship between apologies and the law. Richard Bilder's point of reference is the International Law Commission's newly completed Articles on State Responsibility. Taking issue with the work of Gibney and Roxstrom (2001), which had posited that state apologies might be fundamentally altering the law on state responsibility, Bilder argues that state apologies, by themselves, will do little to change customary international law. Bilder views apology more as a remedial tool, and a limited one at that.

While state responsibility remains unclear and underdeveloped, so does the law regarding corporate responsibility, ignoring the important Nuremberg precedent that corporations can be held responsible for violations of international law. In the absence of any meaningful legal restraints, corporate actors have been able to do business with all types of repressive governments, including the apartheid regime in South Africa. Bonny Ibhawoh considers how many of the corporations that did business with the white government in that country are now addressing their past actions. As with state responsibility, the larger question is whether these admissions of wrongdoing will have any real effect on the law governing corporate responsibilities.

Apologies as a Social Movement

The developments in international law enumerated above cannot completely explain the rapid proliferation of political apologies since 1995. Law follows society as much as it leads it. Since World War II, there have been changes in both religious and secular thought about relations between the powerful and the powerless. At the same time, new social movements, both within the West and internationally, have affected how people perceive oppression and how they remedy it.

The Second World War forced a change in religious thinking among Western Christians, who had to confront their own relative inaction as the Nazis murdered six million Jews. As Michael Marrus explains, in the 1960s Pope John XXIII inaugurated the Second Vatican Council, a wide-ranging discussion of Roman Catholic relations with other religions. As part of this exercise, the Catholic Church reconsidered its historic relationship to the Jews. During the war, some Catholics had been activist rescuers of Jews, and some Catholic leaders in some countries denounced their persecution. But the Vatican had not openly denounced Nazism or those who were or collaborated with Nazis. The debate about the role of the Catholic Church during the war simmered into the twenty-first century.

At this same time, a wider debate about the Church's role in colonial and postcolonial oppression of Third World peoples also took place. After a period of activism in such areas as Latin America—where, for example, Archbishop Romero of El Salvador was assassinated in 1980 because of his pro-poor activities—the Church became more conservative under the leadership of Pope John Paul II. Nevertheless, as Marrus tells us, by 1998 the Church had issued ninety-four apologies. Most were not apologies to direct victims of the Catholic Church, but were apologies to God for the way the Church, or members of the Church, had behaved. Many Protestant churches also debated Christianity's role in supporting repression, reflecting their new (if still religiously based) humanistic orientation.

This undertaking by religious faiths must be seen in the context of a much broader social movement that occurred in the 1960s and 1970s. In the United States, the civil rights movement was quickly followed by the women's liberation movement and later by the movement for gay and lesbian liberation. Each of these movements placed a premium on self-expression and awareness, but in addition, all demanded acknowledgment of harms done to the groups they represented. Partly as a spin-off of these new social movements, in the late twentieth century many social activists started to call attention to other groups that suffered violence and inequality but were essentially "voiceless." Children and the disabled were two such previously voiceless groups.

Indigenous peoples all over the world also began to assert their rights and demand acknowledgment of, and apology for, their past mistreatment. As Janna Thompson and Meredith Gibbs discuss, in both Australia and New Zealand, the descendants of white settlers were called to account for the crimes of their ancestors. Thompson uses the Australian example to consider the philosophical requisites for a sincere political apology. Gibbs tells us that, among other acts of reconciliation, both Queen

Elizabeth II and the prime minister of New Zealand apologized to the Maori people.

At the same time, many Western countries had to learn how to cope with more diverse populations, as immigrants and refugees from formerly colonized areas entered in large numbers and established communities that often seemed to be cut off from mainstream, white society. In 1988, for example, Canada adopted an official policy of multiculturalism. Other countries, more wary of "difference" and the possibility of a fractured citizenry, fought to integrate immigrants into the mainstream. One means to accommodate such minorities was to publicly apologize to them for their former mistreatment. As Matt James discusses, Canada apologized to Japanese Canadians for their blanket internment during World War II, as well as to other groups for other wrongs.

All these trends—social movements for liberation, indigenous demands for apology, and the politics of multiculturalism—stressed personal suffering and feeling. As a result, a new politics of recognition of "others," of minorities, emerged, as Michael Freeman discusses. Liberal theorists started to acknowledge that along with standard liberal goods such as equality and liberty, individuals also desire, even need, social recognition. In academic and policy discussion, a new focus on personal narratives began. Scholars and practitioners recognized that personal narratives were a strong route to empathy, the capacity to put oneself in others' shoes and understand what they had endured. Apologies were one means that states and other social institutions could use to show empathy to those they had harmed.

Some Caveats

This volume discusses many apologies offered by the "West," both to its own citizens and to others outside the borders of Western states. Some might think that the culture of apology presages a new era in national and international relations, in which former oppressors understand the gravity of their crimes, and sincerely attempt to make amends to their victims. In turn, it might be thought, in accepting these apologies victims will be relieved of some of their personal suffering. Both sides will be able to engage in collective reconstruction of social, political and personal relations.

The hope for such collective reconstruction was one of the underpinnings of the South African TRC. The commissioners of the TRC maintain that there are different kinds of "truth," that there is a narrative or social truth separate from a legal or forensic truth. This narrative truth, they claim, is an important aspect of reconciliation in so far as it develops a common historical narrative, a national story that brings all together in acknowledgement of past wrongs. This national acknowledgement, in turn, requires individual acknowledgement of harms committed. It also requires apology and forgiveness, so that individual acts of contrition and absolution can blend into a national act of reconciliation. Former perpetrators testifying before the TRC were encouraged to apologize to their victims. The victims, in turn, were sometimes subtly, or indeed even unwittingly, encouraged to forgive the perpetrators. Some commentators, observing this process, thought that there was too much focus in the TRC on the Christian idea of forgiveness. But the TRC also relied on an African concept, *ubuntu*, which emphasizes restorative justice, including restored relations between perpetrators and victims, over retributive justice. Another concern about the TRC, which also applies to the apologies we discuss, was whether individual apologies offered by perpetrators were genuine, or merely a blatant calculation of interest, a chance for perpetrators to get off by feigning sorrow. Those who confessed to political crimes and showed some repentance for them could be amnestied, while those who did not confess might later be tried and convicted in court. The incentives for false repentance were strong. This is a factor that ought to be noted in all studies of political apologies: they may merely be a new form of *realpolitik*. Much as states have always offered apologies to each other for accidents, such as Bill Clinton's apology to China for the NATO bombing of the Chinese Embassy in Belgrade during the Kosovo intervention in 1999, states and private actors now offer apologies to groups and individuals in the hope that they can thereby "close" the memory of an incident.

In any case, whatever the initial euphoria of reconciliation in South Africa might be, the long-term prospects of civil interaction in the public sphere will be influenced by much more concrete, material factors. One such factor is the continuing inequitable distribution of land between whites and blacks in Southern Africa that Robert Mugabe, president of Zimbabwe, used as an excuse for "land invasions" of white farms in the early twenty-first century. As Leonard Jamfa points out, there is fear of land invasions in Namibia, caused in part by resentment against white ethnic German landowners. The German government, sensitive to the threat against its co-ethnics, has issued a modified statement of apology for the 1905–8 genocide of the Herero people of Namibia. A political apology, then, might not be a sincere act of contrition so much as one in an arsenal of symbolic diplomatic moves.

Apologies for the past also raise the problems of intergenerational justice, which Eleanor Fleming and Al Brophy, among others, discuss. Fleming and Brophy consider whether apologies for past wrongs are owed to African Americans. What are the responsibilities of those living in the present, for the actions of their ancestors? And indeed, who are their ancestors? Brophy discusses his own successful attempt to persuade members of the University of Alabama to apologize because in the past, the university both used slave labor and permitted its members to own slaves. It may well be legitimate for officers of the University of Alabama to apologize for the actions of that institution's officers in the past; the institution itself is a continuous body. But who, if anyone, should apologize for the entire slave system in the United States? If the national government apologizes on behalf of its white citizens, as Fleming advocates, can that be considered sufficient? Perhaps individual descendants of slave-owners should also apologize to individual descendants of slaves. The "white" descendants of President Thomas Jefferson, for example, might apologize to his "black" descendants, to whom they are distantly related. Similarly, the white children of the racist South Carolina Senator Strom Thurmond might apologize to their much older black half-sister, the offspring of a liaison between the young Thurmond and a teenaged black maid in his parents' household. Although it would seem that such apologies would merely be private matters, without public import, they might nevertheless act as symbolic representations of the guilt of all American whites, since all, one might argue, benefit from the United States history of exploitation of blacks.

Yet it would seem that there is validity in an alternate point of view, suggesting that after several generations, historic injustices should be erased from consciousness, so that all citizens can go about their lives as equals. If, as a Mohawk proverb apparently has it, "It is hard to see the future with tears in your eyes," too much focus on the past prevents future betterment. The politics of memory can also result in a politics of bitterness, in which individuals whose ancestors were wronged await apologies from the descendants of those they believe committed those wrongs. It is easy for politicians to manipulate such bitterness.

Related to the question of intergenerational apologies is that of the fallacy of composition. Apologies between individuals may be meaningful, but this does not mean that apologies between groups or nations will necessarily have the same meaning. Apologies between individuals can result in restored relationships, even a degree of trust. Pablo de Greiff argues that apologies within nations might similarly result in "a thin civic trust" among citizens. But perhaps the more remote the apologizer, the less meaningful the apology. Can a representative of one group formally apologize to a representative of another group, in a manner that is meaningful to individuals?

If trust within nations is problematic even after apologies have been offered, trust among nations might be even more difficult to generate. Perhaps a thin sort of cosmopolitan trust can emerge from international apologies. But the likelihood of a genuine international apology is often complicated by its also being cross-cultural. What constitutes an apology in one society may not constitute it in another: indeed, genuine acts of contrition may be interpreted as hypocrisy, if local rituals of apology are not respected. Alison Renteln discusses the different ways apologies can be offered, but also the different ways they can be interpreted by the intended recipients. In some cultures, mere acknowledgment of a wrong might be accepted as an apology, or may be as far as the apologizer can go without losing too much face. In other cultures, words without action are meaningless, as Rhoda Howard-Hassmann and Anthony Lombardo discovered when discussing with elite Africans the social meaning of apology. If an apology is not offered in the socially correct manner, it might result in increased resentment. Finally, there is the problem of seeking forgiveness for the "unforgivable," one of the issues addressed by Jean-Marc Coicaud and Jibecke Jönsson.

To reiterate, this project is about the West and its own past. In focusing on the West, we are perhaps unduly deferential to the politics of resentment. There is much international resentment against the West for its past engagement in slavery, the slave trade, and colonialism: indeed, there is also much resentment against the West for neocolonialism and globalization. It is true that some countries of the West once bought and used slaves, and that some countries were once colonizers, as Peter Baehr discusses in his chapter on the Netherlands. There is much internal discussion in the Netherlands about apologies to former colonies, some Dutch citizens arguing that colonialism was beneficial, not anything to apologize for. Similarly, in Belgium, there is internal political conflict over apologies to that country's former colony, Congo. As Paul Kerstens explains, the decision to apologize can be as much about internal divisions between liberalizers and conservatives as about the "objective" need for an apology.

Another difficulty in the international discourse about apologies is that the West is not the only region of the world that has perpetrated harms against its own citizens, or against others. A small African reparations movement in the late twentieth century began to demand reparations for the slave trade from the West. Yet Arabs were also slave-traders, well into the twentieth century. Should Arab states then apologize to Africa, or to their own subordinate citizens of enslaved African descent? Within Africa, should Mauritanian slave-owners apologize to still-enslaved Mauritanians?

Another problem is what, exactly, constitutes the West? Extending the common notion, Elizabeth Dahl discusses the complicated question of Japanese apologies. During its period of imperialist aggrandizement in the first half of the twentieth century, Japan occupied South Korea and China. Among its other crimes, Japan engaged in biological experimentation on prisoners; used perhaps 200,000 captured women as sex slaves (euphemistically called "comfort women"), of whom 150,000 perished; and perpetrated a terrible massacre on civilians in the city of Nanking. Many survivors among the enslaved women have rejected Japan's attempt at acknowledgment, noting it is not accompanied by compensation from the Japanese state, but merely involves monies from a fund to which Japanese citizens can voluntarily contribute.

Finally, we must consider whether the politics of apology is not merely a cynical type of symbolic politics, meant to erase real injustices from public memory and exculpate their perpetrators. Carlos Parodi discusses how Latin American truth commissions are incomplete because they often ignore the United States involvement in the terrible atrocities of the second half of the twentieth century.

Mark Gibney and Niklaus Steiner consider the politics of President George W. Bush's "apology" for the tortures at the American-run Abu Ghraib prison in Iraq, revealed in 2004. Photographs taken by American soldiers scandalized the world with graphic images of sexual humiliation, beatings, and medieval torture. Such easy apologies as the type offered by Bush may merely permit elites to cover their errors, without dealing with real political problems. Similarly, if the American media apologize for their poor reporting of the Iraq invasion, as Jonathan Marks suggests they should, this will not remedy the problems of corporate-controlled mass media. Cynical apologies are likely to breed cynical responses. They are unlikely to result in that collective reconstruction of personal, social, and political relations that might be a positive outcome of a sincere apology, generously received.

We end this introduction, then, on a slightly uneasy note. Some authors in this volume consider the legal, philosophical, and anthropological meaning of Western apologies for historic wrongs. Others consider specific apologies already offered for wrongs committed from the turn of the twentieth century to the turn of the twenty-first. Yet others consider apologies sought but not yet offered. Our hope is that these apologies will have political consequences; that they will lessen the level of bitterness, anguish, and desire for revenge among victims; and that they will engender in perpetrators a genuine understanding of past harms and a genuine feeling of remorse. If all this happens, in some if not all cases, it will contribute to reconciliation and trust, both elements, we believe, that are crucial for democratic civic interaction. But weighed against this eventuality are hypocrisy, *realpolitik*, resentment, and cynicism. This is the cause of our unease, at the same time that we regard genuine political apologies as a hopeful sign for a more peaceful world.

Postscript

As this volume was being completed, Pope Benedict XVI was forced to issue a series of apologies for his inflammatory remarks depicting the Muslim faith as "evil and inhuman." Although not covered in this book, the episode helps underscore the central role apologies have come to play in world events.

References

Barkan, Elazar. 2000. *The Guilt of Nations: Restitution and Negotiating Historical Injustices*. New York: W.W. Norton.

Brooks, Roy L., ed. 1999. *When Sorry Isn't Enough: The Controversy over Apologies and Reparations for Human Injustice*. New York: New York University Press.

Gibney, Mark and Eric Roxstrom. 2001. "The Status of State Apologies." *Human Rights Quarterly* 23 (4): 911–39.

Lazare, Aaron. 2004. *On Apology*. New York: Oxford University Press.

Torpey, John C., ed. 2003. *Politics and the Past: On Repairing Historical Injustices*. Lanham, Md.: Rowman and Littlefield.

———. 2006. *Making Whole What Has Been Smashed: On Reparation Politics*. Cambridge, Mass.: Harvard University Press.

Part I
Law, Ethics, and the Theory Behind Apologies

Chapter 1
The Role of Apology in International Law

RICHARD B. BILDER

As oft-noted, there has recently been a striking and widespread resort to the use of public apologies in both intra- and international contexts. I want to discuss one facet of this phenomenon—the role of public apology in international law and the practical resolution of current and ongoing international relations problems. Thus, my focus will be primarily on official state-to-state and governmental apologies directed primarily at foreign audiences and relating to matters of current or relatively recent foreign relations or international concern. Among the questions I will address are

- How prevalent is the use of apology in the usual conduct of diplomatic practice and international relations and what are some current examples?
- What is the role of apology as a formal remedy in the international law regarding state responsibility and how does it relate to other legal remedies such as restitution, compensation, and satisfaction?
- Apart from their role as a formal remedy in international law, can apologies influence the development of customary international law or otherwise have legal consequences or affect international normative behavior and expectations?
- Why do the governments of states decide to apologize (or not apologize)?
- More broadly, what is the likely role of apology in resolving ongoing international grievances and disputes and does it deserve a more important place in our toolbox of international dispute settlement techniques?

Some Examples of Recent Apologies in International Relations

During the last several centuries there have been many instances of the use of formal state-to-state apologies as a means of resolving international differences—usually as a result of diplomatic negotiation but, in a few cases, of arbitral decision. The UN International Law Commission (ILC), in its various reports on its work concerning the international law regarding state responsibility, cites numerous examples of official state-to-state apologies or expressions of regret during this period—in particular, for conduct involving insults to the symbols of the state or government, attacks against diplomatic or consular representatives or other diplomatically protected agents, or attacks on diplomatic or consular premises, ships, or private citizens of the protesting foreign state (International Law Commission 1993). However, the role of apology in interstate relations has been somewhat problematic. Not infrequently, stronger states have coerced apologies from weaker states or peoples as expressions of dominance or means of humiliation.

A few examples may give a sense of the variety of contexts in which official international apologies have been given (or not given) or otherwise played a role in international diplomacy and dispute settlement in recent years.

The U-2 Spy Plane Incident. On May 1, 1960, just before the scheduled Paris Summit meeting between President Eisenhower and Premier Khrushchev, a U.S. U-2 spy plane, flying a covert intelligence-gathering mission over the Soviet Union, was shot down near Sverdlovsk in the Soviet Union and the pilot, Francis Gary Powers, was imprisoned. Khrushchev demanded an apology which Eisenhower was unwilling to give. In part because of this incident and the U.S. failure to apologize, the Paris Summit collapsed and mistrust between the two countries further developed, culminating in the 1962 Cuban Missile Crisis.

Attack on the U.S. Ambassador to Japan. Following an attempt on the life and the physical injury of the U.S. Ambassador in Tokyo in 1964, the prime minister and the foreign minister of Japan presented apologies to the U.S. ambassador and the Japanese minister of the interior resigned from office. In addition, Emperor Hirohito sent a delegate of his own to join members of the Japanese government in the presentation of apologies to the U.S. government.

Israel's Attack on the USS Liberty. On June 8, 1967, during the "Six-Day War," Israeli air force planes attacked an American intelligence ship, the U.S.S. *Liberty*, while it was off the Sinai coast, killing 34 Americans and wounding 171. Israel's ambassador called the attack a "tragic mistake" but contended that the "fog of war" was to blame, and that Israeli pilots had mistaken the *Liberty* for an Egyptian ship. President Johnson accepted Israel's explanation. The commander in chief of Israel's navy subsequently wrote that "We immediately accepted humanitarian responsibility, offered our apology and condolences and paid humanitarian reparations to the dead and the wounded in amounts set by the United States government" (Christol 2002: 172). The Israeli and U.S. governments finally resolved the diplomatic aspects of the incident by an exchange of diplomatic notes on December 17, 1980, without either country accepting responsibility.

The Pueblo *Incident.* In 1968, North Korean authorities seized the USS *Pueblo*, which it accused of gathering intelligence within North Korean territorial waters. In order to obtain release of the 82 officers and men of the vessel, the U.S. acceded to the North Korean government's insistence that the U.S. sign a document stating that it "shoulders full responsibility and solemnly apologizes for the grave acts of espionage committed by the U.S. ship" and "gives firm assurance that no U.S. ships will intrude again in the future into the territorial waters" of North Korea ("Release of Crew" 1969: 682). However, the U.S. at the same time made a statement declaring that the document it had signed was at variance with the true position of the U.S. that the ship had been illegally seized, "that the facts of the case call for neither an admission of guilt nor for an apology," and that the document was signed "to free the crew and only to free the crew."

The Rainbow Warrior *Affair.* In 1985 a team of French agents sabotaged and sank the *Rainbow Warrior*, a vessel belonging to the environmental organization Greenpeace International, while it lay in harbor in Auckland, New Zealand, resulting in the death of a Dutch crewman. Greenpeace had intended to use the vessel to protest the French conduct of nuclear tests at Mururoa Atoll in the South Pacific. The French agents were arrested, convicted, and sentenced to ten years each in New Zealand prisons. France and New Zealand discussed reparation but no settlement was reached. Eventually, the parties sought a ruling by the UN secretary general. In 1986, the secretary general ruled, *inter alia*, that "the Prime Minister of France should convey to the Prime Minister of New Zealand a formal and unqualified apology for the attack, contrary to international law, on the *Rainbow Warrior* by French service agents which took place on 10 July 1985" (26 *ILM* 1349 (1987)) and that the French Government should also pay New Zealand the sum of $U.S.7 million in compensation for the damage it has suffered.

President Clinton's Apologies to Rwandans and Guatemalans. In March 1998, President Clinton, visiting Kilgali, Rwanda, apologized to Rwandans for not "doing as much as we could have and should have done to try to limit what occurred in Rwanda in 1994" (Gibney and Warner 2000). In March

1999, President Clinton, visiting Guatemala, apologized for U.S. support for right-wing governments in Guatemala that killed tens of thousands of rebels and Mayan Indians in a 36-year civil war, and promised American support for national reconciliation.

NATO's Bombing of China's Belgrade Embassy. In May 1999, during NATO's air campaign against Yugoslavia regarding Kosovo, U.S. aircraft bombed the Chinese Embassy in Belgrade, killing several Chinese and eliciting an outraged protest by the People's Republic of China government. On May 8, 1999, NATO's North Atlantic Council issued a statement expressing "its deep regret for the tragic mistake" of the bombing of the Chinese Embassy in Belgrade. On May 10, 1999, President Clinton publicly apologized to the Chinese government, calling it "An isolated tragic mistake" ("NATO's Apology 1111"; "Clinton Apologizes" 1999). The U.S. subsequently paid a substantial sum to the Chinese government as compensation.

The LaGrand *Case (*Germany v. United States of America*).* Article 36 of the Vienna Convention on Consular Relations, to which both the U.S. and Germany are parties, provides that nationals of any parties must be notified of their right to communicate with their consular officials when they are detained by law enforcement officials in other states which are parties. The state of Arizona in the U.S. arrested, charged with murder, and later sentenced to death and executed two German nationals, the LaGrand brothers, without at any time informing them of their right to communicate with German consular officials. Germany protested and brought suit against the U.S. in the International Court of Justice (ICJ) claiming that the U.S. had violated its obligations under the Vienna Convention. In its 2001 opinion in the case, the ICJ held that the U.S. had breached its obligations to Germany. The Court noted that the U.S. had acknowledged that, in the case of the LaGrand brothers, it had not complied with its obligation to give consular notification and had presented its apology to Germany for this breach; the U.S. argued that Germany's entitlement to a remedy did not extend beyond such an apology. However, the Court considered that an apology was not sufficient in this case or similar cases where foreign nationals had not been advised without delay of their rights under the Convention and had been subjected to prolonged detention. Germany had not requested material reparation for injury to itself or the LaGrand brothers, but sought a general assurance of nonrepetition, which the Court found was met by certain U.S. commitments regarding notification in the future.

The Ehime Maru *Incident.* On February 9, 2001, a U.S. submarine, the U.S.S. *Greenville,* while surfacing, collided with and sank a Japanese fishing research vessel, the *Ehime Maru*, resulting in the deaths of a number of young students training on the vessel. Immediately following the incident, U.S. Admiral Fallon, a special envoy of President George W. Bush, hand-delivered a letter to Japanese authorities expressing the United States apologies and regrets; the commanding officer of the submarine, Commander Waddle, presented his "most sincere regrets to the people of Japan"; and the U.S. secretary of state phoned the Japanese foreign minister to express his regrets. However, relatives of the victims said they would not accept an apology unless it was made in person. Shortly after the incident, Commander Waddle expressed his desire to visit Japan to apologize. It was reported at that time, however, that the U.S. navy, along with the commander's lawyers, were preventing him from doing so since it might dilute their legal position in negotiations for compensation. In December 2002, Commander Waddle did go to Japan, met and expressed condolences to the family of one of the victims, and offered a "heartfelt apology" to four surviving students. Most of the victims agreed to an American offer of compensation. Some relatives said that an apology was a condition of reaching a settlement.

Many other recent examples of official international apologies or demands for such apologies might be given.

Apology as a Formal Remedy in International Law

In contrast to many (at least Western) national legal systems, international law recognizes apology as a formal remedy for violations of international law. However, its role is generally exceptional and subordinate or auxiliary to the role of other remedies such as restitution or the provision of monetary compensation.

The role of apology as a remedy for internationally wrongful conduct is most recently and authoritatively described in the UN International Law Commission's Draft Articles on Responsibility of States for Internationally Wrongful Acts (hereafter "the Articles"), which the Commission, after several decades of study and debate, finally adopted and referred to the UN General Assembly in 2001 (Crawford 2002). As the ILC's Commentaries to the Articles explain, the Articles seek to formulate, by way of codification and progressive development, the basic rules of international law concerning the responsibility of states for their internationally wrongful acts. The emphasis of the Articles is on the so-called secondary rules of state responsibility—that is, the general conditions under international law under which a state will be considered responsible for wrongful acts or omissions and the legal consequences which flow therefrom. The Draft Articles do not attempt to define the primary or substantive rules of international law which define the content of the international obligations the breach of which gives rise to state responsibility.

The broad structure of the Draft Articles, as here relevant, may be briefly described. In general, every internationally wrongful act of a state—that is, conduct attributable to a state which constitutes a breach of its international obligation—entails the international responsibility of that state (Articles 1 and 2). A responsible state is under a duty to continue to perform the obligation breached (Article 29); to cease the wrongful act and, if circumstances require, to offer appropriate assurances and guarantees of non-repetition (Article 30); and, finally to make full reparation for the injury (including both material and moral damage) caused by its internationally wrongful conduct (Article 31). Full reparation for the injury caused by the wrongful act can take the form of restitution, compensation or satisfaction, either singly or in combination (Article 34). The responsible state is, first, under an obligation to make restitution—that is, to reestablish the situation which existed before the wrongful act was committed, provided that restitution is not impossible and does not involve a burden out of proportion to the benefit deriving from restitution instead of compensation (Article 35). However, to the extent that the damage caused by the wrongful act cannot be made good by restitution, the responsible State is under an obligation to compensate for the damage caused thereby (Article 36). Finally, insofar as the injury caused by a wrongful act cannot be made good by restitution or compensation, Article 37 of the Articles requires the responsible state to give "satisfaction"—which may include a formal apology—for the injury caused by the wrongful act.

More specifically, Article 37, *Satisfaction*, provides:

1. The State responsible for an internationally wrongful act is under an obligation to give satisfaction for the injury caused by that act insofar as it cannot be made good by restitution or compensation.
2. Satisfaction may consist in an acknowledgment of the breach, an expression of regret, a formal apology or another appropriate modality.
3. Satisfaction shall not be out of proportion to the injury and may not take a form humiliating to the responsible State.

The ILC, in its Commentary on Article 37, while noting that the remedy of satisfaction for nonmaterial injury "is well-established international law," also comments that "satisfaction is not a standard form of reparation, in the sense that in many cases the injury caused by an internationally wrongful act of a State may be fully repaired by restitution and/or compensation" and that it has a "rather exceptional character" in that it is only in those cases where restitution and compensation have not provided full reparation that satisfaction may be required.

The ILC Commentary on Article 37 comments, with respect specifically to "apology," that

(7) Another common form of satisfaction is an apology, which may be given verbally or in writing by an appropriate official or even the head of State. . . . Requests for, or offers of, an apology are a quite frequent feature of diplomatic practice and the tender of a timely apology, where the circumstances justify it, can do much to resolve a dispute. In other circumstances an apology may not be called for, e.g., where a case is settled on an *ex gratia* basis, or it may be insufficient. In the *LaGrand* case the Court considered that "an apology is not sufficient in this case, as it would not be in other cases where foreign nationals have not been advised without delay of their rights . . . and have been subjected to prolonged detention or sentenced to severe penalties."

In a recent discussion of the ILC articles on reparations, Professor Dinah Shelton notes that the ILC articles are based primarily on a theory of remedial justice—to rectify the wrong done an injured party and correct injustice by restoring the *status quo ante*—rather than on possible alternative theories such as punishment, deterrence or restorative justice and reconciliation (Shelton 2002: 844).

In sum, it is evident that the role of apology as a formal remedy in international law, at least as currently viewed, is limited. First, its function is seen as primarily reparational and supplementary—essentially a "fallback" remedy if more adequate ways of seeking to restore the *status quo ante* the wrongful conduct in question, such as restitution or compensation, are not available or appropriate. Second, the ILC Commentary makes clear the Commission's distrust of apology as a remedy and its concern that demands for apology may be misused as a means of humiliation. Indeed, there is little indication in the ILC Commentary or various reports that the Commission seriously considered the broader possible role or relevance of apology as an instrument of dispute-management, reconciliation, or restorative justice.

Customary International Law, Treaty Interpretation, and Estoppel

As Mark Gibney and Erik Roxstrom point out in "The Status of State Apologies,"

state apologies might play a . . . direct role in terms of the development of the law of state responsibility. Statements by high level officials—such as apologies—may, under certain circumstances, constitute evidence of state practice and therefore 1) contribute to the formation of customary international law; 2) constitute a source of interpretation for the purpose of determining the content of obligations arising from treaty law; and 3) serve as a unilateral declaration that is at least binding on the state that issued the apology. (Gibney and Roxstrom 2001: 915)

Let me briefly comment on each of their points. First, as they indicate, an apology may, in appropriate circumstances, serve as evidence of the existence of a customary rule of international law. Customary international law results from a general consistent practice of states following them from a sense of legal obligation. In its recent study of formation of customary international law, the International Law Association's committee on this subject stated:

(1) ... a rule of customary international law is one which is created and sustained by the constant and uniform practice of states and other subjects of international law in their international relations, in circumstances which give rise to a legitimate expectation of similar conduct in the future.
(2) If a sufficiently extensive and representative number of states participate in such a practice in a consistent manner, the resulting rule is one of "general customary international law. (International Law Association Committee 2000: 8)

It is usually said that, to establish the existence of a customary rule of international law, it is necessary to show both that: (1) the conduct in question (which can be either acts or omissions to act) amount to a settled practice—that is, a practice which is generally uniform, extensive and representative in character (the so-called "objective element"); and (2) that this pattern of state conduct evidences a belief on its part that this practice is required by international law—that is, that the states concerned believe that they are conforming to what amounts to a legal obligation to engage (or not to engage) in that conduct (the so-called "subjective element" or *opinio juris sive necessitatis*). Unlike obligations established by international agreements, which are generally binding only on those states which, through their express consent, have become parties to the agreement, a rule of customary law is binding on all states without the need for evidence of their express consent.

It is generally accepted that state practice can be manifested, not only by physical acts, but also by verbal acts such as diplomatic or other official policy statements. Consequently, it is clear that an official state apology, as a "speech-act," may, in appropriate circumstances, constitute an instance of a particular state's practice which can contribute to, or evidence, a broader settled practice of states regarding the conduct for which the apology is made. Perhaps more significant, an official apology may, by its language or context, also acknowledge that the apologizing state regards its conduct—either its act or failure to act—as wrongful under international law, thereby manifesting its belief that the violated norm is obligatory (the *opinio juris*). Certainly, the U.S. apology for the bombing of China's Belgrade Embassy or France's apology for the blowing up of the *Rainbow Warrior* in Auckland harbor acknowledged that this conduct violated applicable international law, thus reinforcing the customary (and treaty) law prohibitions on the use of force involved. Indeed, even an apology which essentially seeks to excuse or justify the conduct in question as not in terms violating a customary rule may implicitly serve to affirm the existence and validity of the rule.

The Role of Apology in International Law   21

However, in assessing the possible effect of a state's apology on the formation or reinforcement of a purported rule of customary international law, certain cautions may be in order. First, it may be clear from the language or context of the apology that the apologizing state does not, in fact, regard its conduct as violating any obligatory rule of customary international law, because it either does not acknowledge or expressly or impliedly disclaims the existence of such an alleged norm, or because (as in the case of U.S. apology in the *Pueblo* incident) it disputes the facts that would bring its conduct within the ambit of such a norm. Moreover, a state's apology may, due to its language or context, be ambiguous as to whether that state in fact regards its conduct as violating an obligatory rule of customary rule. As Gibney and Roxstrom appear to suggest, it is only "authentic" apologies—ones that genuinely and unequivocally recognize the existence of particular rules—and, indeed, perhaps also meet other criteria of "authenticity"—that can, in theory, have this custom-formative effect (Gibney and Roxtrom 2001). For example, as Gibney and Roxstrom also recognize, it is not clear whether President Clinton, by his apologies, really intended to acknowledge that the U.S. had violated legal—as contrasted with moral—obligations towards Rwanda and Guatemala; presumably, he did not intend to imply that the U.S. was financially responsible for the extensive injuries and monetary loss suffered by those countries and their peoples. Consequently, I am less sanguine than these two authors that President Clinton's statements, even if taken together with subsequent practice such as NATO's intervention in Kosovo, lend significant weight to establishing international norms sanctioning unilateral humanitarian intervention or prohibiting assistance to oppressive regimes.

Moreover, even if a state apology is regarded as "counting" as a single example of the existence of the practice and sense of obligation relevant to establishing a particular alleged customary rule, the question remains as to the weight to be given that instance in establishing the existence of a broadly applicable customary rule. Thus, while a coerced apology, an apology by a state with little interest or involvement in the conduct regulated by alleged customary norm, or an apology by some minor state official in a limited or informal setting may all theoretically "count" as instances of state "practice," they will likely have only very limited significance or persuasive authority as evidence of the alleged norm. And, it must again be emphasized that a particular apology evidences, at best, only one state's practice, whereas it is necessary to show a fairly uniform and representative practice on the part of a number of states to persuasively establish the existence of a general customary rule.

It is also important to recognize that, just as an apology may conceivably serve as evidence of the practice and *opinio juris* necessary to establish an obligatory customary rule, a state's refusal or failure to apologize for particular conduct also constitutes "practice" and may manifest a belief that the conduct involved is *not* inconsistent with any customary norm, thus serving as evidence of the *nonexistence* of the alleged norm. This might particularly be the case where an apology has been expressly sought by another state but the state engaging in the protested conduct refuses to offer such an apology.

Second, as Gibney and Roxstrom suggest, an apology by one of the parties to an international agreement may help to inform or confirm the interpretation of an obligation established by that agreement. Article 31, paragraph 3 of the Vienna Convention on the Law of Treaties, generally acknowledged as codifying the customary law of international agreements, provides, *inter alia*, that in interpreting a treaty:

3. There shall be taken into account, together with the context:
    (a) any subsequent agreement between the parties regarding the interpretation of the treaty or the application of its provisions;
    (b) any subsequent practice in the application of the treaty which establishes the agreement of the parties regarding its interpretation. . . .

An apology by a party specifically acknowledging that its conduct has failed to conform with particular obligations of an international agreement might arguably constitute, or at least be analogous to, such a subsequent agreement or practice and thus be considered as confirming the interpretation of the agreement as creating the obligation the apologizing state acknowledges having breached. Thus, the U.S. apology to Germany in the *LaGrand* case for Arizona's failure to notify the LaGrand brothers when they were arrested of their right to communicate with German consular officials, as Germany insisted was required by the Consular Convention, clearly evidences and establishes the two countries' now common interpretation of those obligations under the convention.

Third, as Gibney and Roxstrom again suggest, an apology may have legal consequences even apart from the possible effect of the apology on customary or treaty law. For example, an official apology acknowledging or representing that particular conduct is required by international customary law, especially if relied on by a particular other state or states, may arguably be held to "estop" the apologizing state from later denying the existence of that rule as applicable in their relations. That is, the apologizing state's statement, intended to induce reliance, may be held to require that the apologizing state subsequently conduct itself in accordance with the norm it purported to recognize. Again, even if the U.S. apology in the *LaGrand* case was regarded as not establishing an agreed interpretation by Germany and the U.S. regarding the meaning of the Convention's consular notification provisions, it would clearly be very difficult for the U.S., in any future dispute with Germany, to suggest that those provisions had some different meaning. Moreover, as Gibney and Roxstrom again suggest, there is international authority (albeit somewhat controversial) indicating that official unilateral statements, such as an official state apology, may in some circumstances be given legal effect. This might presumably be true, in particular, of a formal apology which represents or promises that the apologizing state will act, or cease to conduct itself, in certain ways in the future. Thus, in the 1974 *Nuclear Test* case (*Australia and New Zealand v. France*), involving France's conduct of nuclear tests in the atmosphere on a French island in the South Pacific, the International Court of Justice held that certain unilateral statements by French authorities indicating that they would no longer conduct nuclear tests in the atmosphere in the South Pacific had binding legal effect, and on that basis mooted and dismissed the case.

Finally, even if an apology is not of such a character as to entail formal legal consequences, it may arguably still have some normative effect in shaping expectations concerning state behavior. International law and international relations scholars have recently become increasingly interested in the phenomenon of so-called "soft law"—nonbinding or informal collaborative actions or instruments which, while not intended to be legally obligatory, may nonetheless normatively influence how states believe they should conduct themselves. Indeed, "soft law" may in some circumstances evolve over time into "hard" customary or treaty law. Certainly apologies, such as President Clinton's apologies concerning Rwanda and Guatemala may—as Gibney and Roxstrom suggest—have at least this kind of informal effect on the development of international normative expectations regarding the appropriateness of humanitarian intervention or the giving of assistance to repressive regimes.

In sum, apology may conceivably affect the formation or reinforcement of customary international law, the interpretation of treaties, or perhaps estop a state from challenging the existence of an alleged rule for the violation of which it apologized. However, whether a particular apology can arguably be considered to have such effects, and the weight it will likely be accorded in this respect, will depend on many factors—the particular context and circumstances under which the apology is made, its wording and content, the official level at which it is rendered, and so forth. Moreover, in practice, most state-to-state apologies regarding matters of current foreign relations concern probably relate to and serve to reinforce relatively clear and firmly established international norms—such as prohibitions relating to the use of force, the protection of diplomats and diplomatic premises, or compliance in good faith with treaty obligations—rather than involving and contributing to the development and acceptance of new norms.

Why Do Governments Apologize (or Not Apologize)?

States—or more accurately, their governments or ruling elites—would not apologize if they did not think that apologies served their national or governmental interests. Depending on circumstances, state-to-state or governmental apologies serve a variety of state interests and purposes, which may, however, differ from those usually served by interpersonal apologies.

What are some reasons why a state government might choose to apologize?

First, we should recognize that a government may decide to apologize to the government or people of another state because it genuinely believes that this is the right thing to do. That is, a government or official, reflecting the view of many or most of the state's citizens, may: (1) truly believe that its acts or omissions, accomplished through its agents, have been wrongful and caused harm to another state or its citizens; (2) be genuinely sorry for and regret that conduct; and (3) wish to make amends to, be forgiven by and restore good relations with the other state and its people. And this apology may in fact reach the people who were injured, be accepted by them, and result in forgiveness, reconciliation, and a resumption of good relations. This model of state-to-state apology is obviously closely analogous to that of an authentic and successful interpersonal apology. Indeed, a government may have a very practical interest in maintaining a reputation as a decent, just and law-abiding country, not only as a matter of maintaining its own people's favorable self-image, but because a state's reputation may significantly affect its ability to gain internal and external support for its policies and accomplish its goals. As with interpersonal apologies, the useful functions of such an authentic state-to-state apology can include: (1) demonstrating remorse for the wrongful or harmful action or inaction and respect for the wronged state and any victims; (2) negating any intent to cause harm; (3) preventing escalation of the dispute; (4) providing a basis for settlement negotiations; (5) repairing the damaged relationship and affecting reconciliation; and (6) affirming relevant international norms and international community interests. The U.S. (and Commander Waddle's) apologies in the 2001 *Ehime Maru* incident may approximate this model.

Second, a government may apologize in compliance with the binding judgment of an international court or of an arbitral tribunal, as in the *Rainbow Warrior* case. Here, the apology simply implements a judicially ordered remedy of "satisfaction," and the apology may, but need not, be authentic. The reaffirmation of the relevant norm, labeling of the apologizing state's conduct as wrongful and vindication of the wronged state results primarily from the judicial tribunal's decision rather than from any initial belief or conclusion of the apologizing state itself. Implementation of the judgment requiring an apology settles the legal dispute, strengthens the relevant norm and may have some future deterrent effect, but may or may not satisfy those injured and resolve underlying grievances or differences.

Third, it is conceivable—though I believe unlikely—that a government might render an apology for particular conduct in hope that its apology will contribute to establishing or reinforcing some desired customary law rule or treaty interpretation. That is, the state's apology may be intended primarily to signal and communicate to another state or the international community that it has changed its position with respect to the legality or appropriateness of such conduct; remedial, redemptive or restorative consequences of its apology may have no or only secondary importance in its decision to apologize.

Fourth, a government may make a *pro forma* apology simply as an accepted, low-cost, and time-honored way of resolving or defusing an incident or contretemps involving some relatively minor invasion of another state's rights or interest. As previously indicated, many state-to-state apologies are for conduct ostensibly violating another state's "sovereignty," "honor" or "dignity"—for example, insults to its flag, minor violations of its territory, insults to or injury to its diplomats and so forth. Absent apology, the "wronged" state may feel compelled, perhaps by public sentiment, to defend its "honor" by retaliating, thus risking escalation of the situation. Japan's apology for the 1964 attack in Tokyo on the U.S. ambassador and NATO's and President Clinton's 1999 apologies for the bombing of China's Belgrade embassy are perhaps examples. In such cases, the apology may be less an expression of genuine remorse than of political expediency—a face-saving technique or ritual through which both states can move on and put the incident behind them.

Fifth, a government may deliberately attempt to use apology as a tactic for seeking to avoid or mitigate the consequences of its intentionally wrongful conduct. That is, it may decide to risk doing what it wants, then say it is sorry, and hope to get away with it, assuming that the wronged and injured state will find it more difficult to justify retaliation in the face of even a hypocritical apology. Former U.S. undersecretary of state Richard Armitage is quoted as saying: "I learned one lesson that never served me wrong: that forgiveness is easier to get than permission" (Mann 2004: 55).

Sixth, a government may apologize simply because it is coerced to do so and has no other practical option. This may be the case even if it believes it has done nothing wrong and that the other state is bullying it into apologizing in order to humiliate it. That is, the apology is forced upon the apologizing government as a symbolic surrender and token of its powerlessness and inferiority. As indicated, the International Law Commission was well aware that apology had historically often been used for this purpose and consequently included apology as a formal remedy in its Draft Articles only with some reluctance. Interestingly, in the 1968 *Pueblo* incident, North Korea—the weaker state—forced the U.S.—the stronger state—to apologize as a condition of North Korea's release of the *Pueblo*'s crew. Clearly, North Korea had no illusion that the U.S. apology would be authentic or result in restoration of Korean-U.S. relations; its purpose in requiring the apology was simply to humiliate and embarrass the U.S.

Finally, a government's—or a particular official's—apology or expression of regret may be intended primarily as a public relations gesture, directed primarily at a domestic or international audience other than the state or people actually wronged and designed to gain public approval—currently, perhaps, by the government's participation in a supposedly now fashionable "culture of contrition." This cynical perspective is reflected in Jay Rayner's satiric novel, *The Apologist*; the novel's protagonist is so good at expressing remorse and begging forgiveness that he is hired as its chief apologist by the fictional "UN Office of Apology and Reconciliation," with the job of going around the world saying how "sorry" the UN is for a variety of present and past injustices and atrocities (Rayner 2004). Certainly, there has been some skepticism expressed as to the sincerity and motivation of at least some of the current rash of apologies.

But it may also be useful to suggest some reasons why the government of a state may decide *not* to apologize.

First, a government may refuse to apologize because it genuinely does not believe that it has done anything to apologize for. Thus, it may challenge the alleged facts involved or the existence of an international norm it is alleged to have violated, or it may argue that its conduct was in any event excused or justified. For example, both the U.S. in the *Pueblo* incident and Israel in the *Liberty* incident took this position.

Second, a government may refuse to apologize because it is concerned that an apology may be regarded as an admission of its responsibility in the matter and thus weaken its legal position and possibly expose it to liability in future negotiations or litigation. Certainly, foreign office legal advisers will always see this as a concern. Alternatively, the government may decide to make a "safe" or "partial" apology or statement of "regret," being careful to make sure that its statement is so phrased as to not be capable of being construed as an admission of responsibility. And it may also ensure that any payment it may make for the harm caused is described solely as an *ex gratia* or "humanitarian" payment rather than as compensation or reparation. Again, the Israeli government, in its expressions of regret in the *Liberty* incident, was careful to make clear its position that the attack was an accident—a reasonable and excusable mistake on its part—for which it believed the U.S. at least shared responsibility.

Third, a government may conceivably be concerned that an apology will lend support to a particular customary rule or treaty interpretation it opposes. For example, President Eisenhower's refusal to apologize to the Soviet Union in the U-2 incident may have been partly because the U.S. was then proposing an "open skies" policy which would recognize a right of overflight for arms control inspection purposes. Apart from other political considerations, its apology might have weakened its efforts to establish such an international legal "right."

Fourth, a government may refuse to apologize because, under the circumstances, it regards such an apology as demeaning, suggesting weakness and damaging to its international prestige or honor, or because it fears domestic criticism or political cost if it makes such an apology. This may particularly be the case where the proposed apology is to an enemy or rival power.

Finally, a government may refuse to apologize, even if it believes it has acted wrongfully, simply because it sees no political need to do so and no disadvantage from not doing so. Thus, a powerful state may see no reason to apologize to a much weaker state or to a state with which it has no desire to maintain good relations.

Apologies and Foreign Relations

Despite the supposed emergence of a "culture of apology," I suspect that apology will continue to play only a relatively limited role in the adjustment of most present-day international incidents and differences. It is true, of course, that we have recently seen a striking number of state apologies for long-past historical injustices—although these "apologies" are often worded primarily as expressions of general regret rather than as genuine admissions of fault and responsibility and are rarely coupled to commitments to effective reparation. However, I see little evidence that diplomats or international lawyers are more inclined now to resort to apology as a way of resolving current international grievances and disputes than they have been in the past.

Certainly, apology has been and remains a useful—perhaps significant—tool in the diplomats' and international lawyers' dispute-settlement toolbox and there are clearly many situations where it can be very helpful in resolving international difficulties and differences. As previously noted, the diplomatic ritual of a *pro forma* apology has, in particular, long been an accepted method of defusing awkward and potentially troublesome incidents—particularly those involving supposed insults to another state's honor, dignity, or "sovereignty," or incidents involving unintentional, mistaken or unauthorized actions or omissions resulting in relatively limited harm to another state's nationals, property, or interests. As we have seen, in such cases, apology permits the government of the wronged state to maintain that its honor and interests have been respected, and for the two states to put the matter behind them and move on. However, it seems still the case that, with respect to more significant disputes, apology alone is rarely enough. In the more serious incidents, while apology may often comprise a component of settlement, the eventual resolution of the matter will typically require more concrete forms of reparation and adjustment, such as restitution, the payment of money damages, and assurances of nonrepetition.

Of course, much of this is speculation. There not a great deal of empirical data concerning either the use or consequences of apology in diplomatic practice and international affairs, and many questions remain unanswered. Are state-to-state governmental apologies really successful in resolving grievances and disputes? Do they have the effect of diminishing or increasing demands for monetary compensation? Do the people injured really know about these governmental apologies and feel better and more forgiving because of them? Do apologies really affect reconciliation between countries and peoples? Does it really make any difference whether such apologies are or not authentic? Do the answers differ as among different kinds of transgressions and perhaps different cultures? And what accounts for the recent surge in government and other apologies for historical injustices? Hopefully, studies such as those for this volume will cast light on some of these questions.

Should we try to increase the role of apology in international law and diplomacy? There are currently various proposals by U.S. lawyers and academics—particularly those interested in issues of restorative justice—designed to increase the availability and role of apology as a dispute settlement technique and remedy within the U.S. legal system (Latif 2001; O'Hara and Yam 2002). These commentators suggest that there are a variety of situations—for example, motor vehicle accidents, alleged medical malpractice, victim-offender mediation, and alternative dispute settlement generally—where apology might resolve the matter, avoid or at least facilitate the settlement of litigation, or otherwise help to achieve reconciliation. However, under existing U.S. law, potential defendants may be reluctant to apologize for fear that the apology will be taken as an admission of responsibility, exposing them to liability. Consequently, reformers have, *inter alia*, proposed legislation providing that certain kinds of "safe-harbor" apologies cannot be used as admissions of liability; they have thus far succeeded in obtaining such legislation in Massachusetts, Texas, and California. Might similar efforts to encourage resort to apology in an international context be likely to find favor?

I doubt that most states would currently find such proposals of interest. First, governments now seem generally content with the present range of available dispute settlement techniques and may see no particular need for—or interests to be served by—an increased resort to apologies. Second, as we have seen, there are many reasons why governments are reluctant to apologize; concern for exposure to potential legal liability is only one of these reasons. Third, as indicated, the International Law Commission's recently completed Draft Articles on State Responsibility, adopted after many years of study and debate and presumably reflecting the prevailing current attitudes of both governments and the "invisible college" of international lawyers, clearly opt for a primarily remedial and reparation-oriented model of justice, relegating "satisfaction" and apology to a relatively secondary role; it seems unlikely that the international legal or diplomatic community will soon be eager to reconsider this approach.

Certainly, the possibility of using apology as a means of resolving international differences remains readily available to governments and they should be alert to situations where apology can be appropriate and helpful. Hopefully, current apologies for historical injustices will in fact help to heal long-held resentments and bring about a measure of reconciliation. But, I suspect that, in the near term at least, apology is likely to remain only a secondary and auxiliary technique for the resolution of most current international incidents and disputes.

References

Christol, A. Jay. 2002. *The Liberty Incident: The 1967 Israeli Attack on the U.S. Navy Spy Ship.* Dulles, Va.: Brassey's.

"Clinton Apologizes Anew for Embassy Bombing." 1999. Associated Press, May 10.

Crawford, James, ed. 2002. *The International Law Commission's Articles on State Responsibility: Introduction, Text and Commentaries.* Cambridge: Cambridge University Press.

Gibney, Mark and Erik Roxstrom. 2001. "The Status of State Apologies." *Human Rights Quarterly* 23 (4): 911–39.

Gibney, Mark and Daniel Warner. 2000. "What Does It Mean to Say I'm Sorry? President Clinton's Apology to Guatemala and Its Significance for International and Domestic Law." *Denver Journal of International Law and Policy* 28: 223–33.

International Law Commission. 1993. "Report of the International Law Commission on the Work of Its Forty-Fifth Session." *International Law Commission Yearbook* 2 (2).

International Law Association Committee on the Formation of Customary General International Law. 2000. *Final Report of the Committee on Statement of Principles Applicable to the Formation of General Customary International Law.* London: ILA London Conference.

Latif, Elizabeth. 2001. "Apologetic Justice: Evaluating Apologies Tailored Toward Legal Solutions *Boston University Law Review* 81 (1): 289–320.

Mann, James. 2004. *The Rise of the Vulcans: The History of Bush's War Cabinet.* New York: Viking Penguin.
"NATO's Apology to China." 1999. *New York Times*, May 9.
O'Hara, Erin Ann and Douglas Yam. 2002. "On Apology and Consilience." *Washington Law Review* 77: 1121–92.
Rayner, Jay. 2004. *The Apologist.* London: Atlantic Books.
"Release at Panmunjon of Crew of USS Pueblo." 1969. *American Journal of International Law* 63: 682–85.
Shelton, Dinah. 2002. "Righting Wrongs: Reparations in the Articles on State Responsibility." *American Journal of International Law* 96 (4): 833–56.

Chapter 2
Apology, Justice, and Respect:
A Critical Defense of Political Apology

JANNA THOMPSON

A political apology is an official apology given by a representative of a state, corporation, or other organized group to victims, or descendants of victims, for injustices committed by the group's officials or members. For some political leaders apology has become a standard way of coming to terms with past injustices and victims' demands for redress. But official apology is by no means an uncontroversial or universally accepted practice, and its present popularity may not last. There is no agreement on what a political apology means, whether it is meaningful at all, when it should be offered, whether it is possible or appropriate to apologize for injustices of the more distant past, whether offering political apologies is an adequate way of dealing with injustices, and what relation they have to reparative justice.

Most, if not all, nations have committed injustices, to people inside or outside their borders. But political leaders have been very circumspect about what they apologize for, and some refuse to apologize at all. Prime Minister Howard of Australia resisted pressure to issue an official apology for injustices to Aborigines. Present generations, he said, should not be expected to take responsibility for crimes committed in the past (Howard 1997). Former U.S. President Bill Clinton was willing to apologize to Native Hawaiians for U.S. violation of their sovereignty (Barkan 2000) and to the people of Guatemala for the role of the U.S. in repression and political violence (Gibney and Roxstrom 2001). But he regarded it as inappropriate to apologize for slavery—though some members of Congress wanted him to do so (Brooks 1999). Prime Minister Blair expressed regret for British failures during the Irish potato famine, but did not apologize to citizens of African or Middle Eastern countries for wrongs committed during British colonial rule (Blair 1997). One might conclude that political leaders are willing to apologize only when they think that there will be no serious political or legal repercussions.

Many commentators on political affairs are skeptical about political apologies. McLaughlin calls official apologies, "symbolic and meaningless gestures" made by leaders who have no intention of avoiding similar acts in the future (McLaughlin 1997). And not all victims of injustice are keen on receiving them. The Aboriginal leader Patrick Dodson thinks that the only meaningful act that an Australian government could perform is to guarantee the rights of indigenous Australians in the Australian Constitution (Dodson 2000: 269). Other Aboriginal leaders think that apology is a useless symbolic act which non-Aboriginal Australians want because it would make them feel better, but which won't do anything to solve the problems of Aboriginal communities.

I resist such skepticism. It could be the case that all or most state apologies issued so far are meaningless or inadequate. But it doesn't follow that the practice of political apology must be meaningless or without value. I will first argue that apology is not only morally important but also central to reparative justice. I will then discuss some of the conceptual and moral problems associated with political apologies and how they can be overcome. Finally, I will provide an example of what a political apology must be like if it is to count as genuine.

Apology and Reparative Justice

An apology is a speech act—that is, an action performed by an appropriate person saying appropriate words on an appropriate occasion (Austin 1962). The meaning of a speech act is what it conveys to its intended audience: what the speaker through performing the action is giving this audience an entitlement to believe or do. In the case of apology, the person performing the act is conveying the following to his or her victim (Davies 2002).

1. That she acknowledges that she has committed a wrongful act against the victim and takes responsibility for it;
2. That he feels remorse for his deed;
3. That she undertakes to avoid similar transgressions against the victim in the future.

The apologizer is giving the victim an entitlement to trust that these things are true, and in the case of a genuine apology, trust is not misplaced. A genuine apology can have many good effects. It has the power, says Tavuchis (1991), to rehabilitate the individual and restore social harmony; it promotes reconciliation and can prevent trespasses from becoming obstructions to social relationships. However, these desirable effects should be distinguished from the meaning of apology as a speech act. If a person's *only* reason for making an apology is to restore harmonious relationships or make people feel better, then he can be accused of insincerity. And a person can regard it as appropriate to apologize even if the good effects are not likely to eventuate. Nevertheless, that apologies sometimes can restore good feelings and trusting relationships is obviously a reason for valuing the practice of apology.

A view of apology which stresses its reconciliatory role seems either to put it outside the realm of justice or to give it only an auxiliary role in an account of justice as reparation. Most definitions of reparative justice do not mention apology. According to Roberts (2002) and Nozick (2001), reparative justice requires that victims be restored to the situation they were in before the injustice took place (so far as possible) or that they receive compensation equal to the value of what they have lost. Gaus thinks that apology, forgiveness and mercy are important acts, but that they take place outside the framework of justice (Gaus 1991: 72). Waldron regards apology and other symbolic acts as appropriate responses to injustice, but separates them from justice as reparation or compensation for harm done (Waldron 1992). As Bilder notes in his chapter, The International Law Commission of the UN presents apology as a means of giving satisfaction in cases where justice in the form of restitution or compensation is not possible, thus giving it a subordinate, auxiliary role in an account of justice among nations.

Apology may be morally important even if it plays little or no role in reparative justice. Remembrance, says Waldron, is important to the identity of individuals and communities.

> To neglect the historical record is to do violence to this identity and thus to the community that it sustains. And since communities help generate a deeper sense of identity for the individuals they comprise, neglecting or expunging the historical record is a way of undermining and insulting individuals as well. (Waldron 1992: 6)

If an injustice has been done to a group, then this becomes part of their historical identity, and perpetrators ought to respond in a way that respects the meaning history has for the victims. Apology and other symbolic acts are important, Waldron believes, because they acknowledge the importance of the victims' understanding of the past.

But this account fails to explain why apology—as distinct from other acts of acknowledgment or remembrance—is so important. We could show respect for the historical record by simply acknowledging that the injustices happened, by listening to the narratives of the victims or by giving them the opportunity to grieve. But apology is different from these acts. The moral importance of showing respect for a history, and the people whose history it is, doesn't explain why apology, rather than some other symbolic or caring act, is the moral response that ought to be made by the perpetrators of injustice.

The problem stems from the view that apology, as an act of reconciliation, must lie outside the central requirements of reparative justice. Boxill regards apology, or something like it, as essential to reparation, not separate or subordinate. Injustice, whatever form it takes, always involves disrespect for the victim; thus, reparation must include "an acknowledgment on the part of the transgressor that what he is doing is required of him because of his prior error" (Boxill 1972: 118). Boxill does not call this apology, but apology fulfils this function and also does other things that seem required if the perpetrator intends to make amends for the lack of respect that was intrinsic to his wrongdoing. According to Govier and Verwoerd, "the power and importance of apology lie in its potential to offer to victims a *moral recognition or acknowledgement of their human worth and dignity*" (Govier and Verwoerd 2002, emphasis original). An apology, so understood, is intrinsically an act of respect. It not only conveys to the victim of an injustice that the perpetrator takes responsibility for what he has done. It is an act of contrition addressed to the victim by the perpetrator, and as such demonstrates respect.

Apology, according to this account, is not something extraneous to reparative justice. It is not a good-hearted but non-obligatory gesture. It is not an alternative or substitute for reparation in the form of restitution or compensation. It is a necessary component of reparative justice itself, at least for acts of deliberate wrongdoing or negligence, even when justice also requires restitution or compensation. Regarding apology as part of reparative justice answers to the harm that injustice causes to the dignity of the victims. The objective of reparation, as stated by Nozick and Roberts, cannot be accomplished by returning to victims property or opportunities that they lost through an injustice. Such returns do not compensate for the failure of respect intrinsic to wrongdoing. But a wrongdoer can make recompense for his failure of respect through an act that demonstrates respect by conveying to the victim his remorse, acceptance of responsibility for the wrong and a commitment to respectful behavior in the future.

The Problems of Political Apology

Apology is essential to reparative justice itself, and thus has obvious moral importance. However, the definition of apology offered in the last section assumes that the wrongdoer is a person offering an apology to another person or persons. In the case of a political apology, a leader, or some other official, offers apology on behalf of the state or some other organization to victims, whether individuals or groups. The obvious question is how states (or other collectivities) can satisfy the requirements of genuine apology. Three main difficulties must be overcome to defend political apologies against skepticism. The first is the problem posed by Prime Minister Howard: how can existing citizens or their representatives take responsibility for wrongs committed by their predecessors? The second is explaining how a collectivity like a state can be remorseful or contrite. The third is explaining how states can commit themselves to avoid wrongdoing in future.

States consist of their citizens; thus, one way to explain how a state can fulfil requirements of genuine apology is to refer to citizens' attitudes and their ability to act collectively. Govier in her explanation of how groups can forgive takes this course (Govier 2002, chap. 5). Since forgiveness and apology are closely related speech acts, her approach can be adapted to an explanation of how groups can apologize. Groups, she thinks, can make genuine apologies, first, because structured groups, like states, have decision-making processes and can act as agents. When their members deliberate and make decisions, members' desires and goals become the desires and goals of the group. Second, groups have feelings in so far as members respond to things that affect the group with outrage, hatred, shame, pride, or sorrow. If members feel remorseful about injustices that their group has committed, then an official who apologizes expresses this collective remorse. As collections of individuals, groups can forgive, according to Govier, and they should also be able to apologize.

Nevertheless, when applied to states, and other large, complex organizations, Govier's approach encounters obvious difficulties. Members of states are not likely to be of one mind or heart. Some citizens may feel remorse for acts committed by their state, but many will not. Some will want their leaders to offer an apology, but some will not, and many will be indifferent. Most of the apologies offered by leaders (if not all) were probably not an expression of the sentiments of a majority of citizens. We must either conclude that these apologies were not genuine—the leaders were not expressing the feelings of the citizens—or that general or widespread feelings of remorse are not necessary for political apologies.

Govier's approach also encounters the problem of explaining how a collectivity can apologize for injustices of the distant past, committed before all or most citizens were born, came to maturity, or arrived in the country. It is true that some citizens feel shame, or even guilt, when learning about injustices committed in their nation's past. But many do not, and it is not obvious that their lack of feeling is morally reprehensible. More important, we need to explain why feelings of shame about the deeds of our national predecessors, however widespread, give us, through our leaders, the entitlement to apologize. We did not have a hand in committing the injustice, and standard theories of responsibility and entitlement insist that participation in committing an injustice is necessary for responsibility, and that being a victim of injustice is a prerequisite for having an entitlement to reparation (Feinberg 1968). Govier addresses this difficulty when she considers whether people who were not actual victims of injustice are entitled to forgive. She argues that those who suffer the effects of the injustice as secondary or tertiary victims have an entitlement. But strictly speaking, according to the standard account of collective responsibility and entitlement, these secondary and tertiary victims should only be able to forgive the injustice done to them: that is, the injustice of not ameliorating the long term effects of the original injustice.

This discussion suggests that it is not easy to make sense of political apologies if we model them on apologies made by individuals or make them depend on the acts and sentiments of individuals. In his treatment of political forgiveness, Digeser leaves out the condition often assumed to be intrinsic to forgiveness, that forgivers must free themselves from resentment and other negative feelings. Political forgiveness, he thinks, should be conceived as a public act, carried out by the appropriate official, of forgiving a debt where both the forgiver and the person or group to which the act is directed understand both the message that the debt has been forgiven and that an invitation has been issued to restore a relationship (Digeser 2001: 4). Presumably, the same approach can be taken to political apologies by removing the second requirement of apology (which insists that the apologizer must be remorseful) and defining a political apology as a public act, carried out by the appropriate official, that acknowledges and takes responsibility for an injustice committed (or allowed) by officers of the state, and commits governments to avoid such injustices in the future.

The question remains whether apology without sentiment makes sense. Relieving a debt, at least a material debt, does not require any particular motivation, but apology does seem to need a morally relevant driving force. And remorse, or at least the conviction of agents that they have an obligation to make up to their victims for moral turpitude, seems to be necessary to drive apology. Why else should we think that agents ought to demonstrate to their victims that they take responsibility for a wrong? Why else should we think that they have a special obligation to avoid similar wrongs to them in future?

However, let us concede that political apologies do not require remorse. The problem remains how officials can forgive or apologize for injustices of the more distant past. Monetary debts and credits can be passed from one generation to another, or from present to succeeding officials of a state or corporation. So it does make sense to suppose that debts accrued in the past can now be forgiven by the successors of those to whom the debts were originally owed. But the sins of fathers and mothers are not supposed to become the moral debts of children—at least according to ideas about responsibility in a liberal democratic society. So it remains unexplained how citizens or their political representatives get the right to forgive or apologize for a wrong done to or by their ancestors or predecessors.

We might circumvent this problem by insisting that a structured organization like a state is an agent in its own right—an agent whose existence transcends the lives of individuals who make it up. Though Blair and other citizens of the United Kingdom bear no responsibility for the potato famine, "the government of the United Kingdom did exist in the nineteenth century, and [its] apology makes sense because its policies helped to bring about the famine that so severely affected the Irish people" (Govier and Verwoerd 2002: 6). The implication is that a state as an agent in its own right should take responsibility for its past deeds, including those which occurred before the lifetimes of present citizens. If it has committed an injustice, then it ought to apologize. The problem is that the moral agency of the state depends on its members' accepting certain responsibilities. We have to suppose that citizens have a collective duty to ensure that their state acts appropriately and to bear the resulting burdens. But the existence of such a duty needs justification. When people join a corporation they voluntarily accept the requisite responsibilities. However, membership of a state is not generally a matter of consent, and the responsibilities and burdens of membership require justification, which, according to many philosophers, is not easy to supply (Simmons 1979).

Putting this difficulty aside, it remains to consider whether states as agents can truly take responsibility for wrongs and commit themselves to avoid wrongdoing in the future. Political realists insist that states are bound to act for strategic reasons, not from moral principle. If so, apologies of state are always self-interested and never genuine. The cynicism of many political commentators about political apologies seems to have its source in the realist view. But it is not necessary to be a political realist to doubt whether states can fulfill the requirements of apology. State decisions are generally the resultant of several forces. The real agents, the individuals who make political decisions, have various, and often different, reasons for advocating a particular policy.

Clinton apologized to Guatemalans for the harm done by U.S. intervention in their political affairs. Suppose that this apology came about as the result of the following process. Some of his advisors favored acts that would change political relations with Guatemala and other countries in the region. They had in mind a U.S. congressional inquiry into past injustices, as well as other policies designed to show that the U.S. was serious about facing up to the past, and they wanted Clinton to announce these initiatives in his speech. But other advisors didn't want any policy changes and reasoned that it would be detrimental to U.S. interests to rake up the past. Others thought an apology might improve relations with Guatemala but didn't want to give anyone the idea that this signaled a major shift in U.S. policy. In the end it was decided that Clinton should make a low key apology; and whether anything followed from it would be determined by further political contestation.

What this (not improbable) story shows is that acts of state are to be explained by power plays, conflicts of interests, and the compromises that lie behind them. This explanation of acts of states and other organizations undermines the idea that they can be regarded as persons in a moral sense: agents capable of acting consistently and responsibly over time. But this means that a state cannot be expected to satisfy the requirements of apology—especially not the requirement that it commit itself to avoid wrong in the future. Perhaps particular politicians are able to make such commitments for the term of their office. But their policy is subject to reversal as soon as other people take power. This consideration, as much as the realist view of the state, leads to the conclusion that states cannot make genuine apologies.

However, skeptics exaggerate the problem. States *are* able to make and keep long-term commitments. They are able to follow rules and can rightly be criticized for not doing so. If this were not so, international law would be impossible and treaties would be meaningless. If states can make treaties and accept obligations of reparation, then they should also be able to make genuine apologies. However, an explanation is needed of how these things are possible—given that policies of states and other organizations are determined by conflicting and continually changing interests and opinions of leaders and members. The explanation should connect the obligations of a state and the moral or legal obligations that its citizens do, or should, accept. In particular, it should provide an account of why citizens ought to take responsibility for wrongs committed by their state—including wrongs of the distant past—and why they are morally entitled to make commitments concerning the future which bind their successors as well as themselves (and why their successors are morally obligated to keep them).

Political Apology and Transgenerational Commitments

Political apologies require that states (and other structured organizations) be transgenerational polities in which members pass on responsibilities and entitlements from one generation to another. Its citizens, through their representatives, must take responsibility for its past injustices, including those of the more distant past, and must be able to make commitments which their successors are also bound to fulfill. They must regard themselves as obliged to participate in and maintain a practice that enables citizens to discharge the responsibilities and fulfil the commitments associated with apology. Only if this practice exists, or if it can be brought into existence, are genuine political apologies possible.

Individuals who identify with their state are predisposed to accept national obligations without question. They do not need a justification for taking on the burdens of their national history. But not all citizens are patriotic, and even patriots are likely to have different ideas about obligations. In justifying the requirements of a transgenerational polity, we will be on firmer ground if we can explain why individuals, whether patriotic or not, should accept them.

From the point of view of individual members, it is obviously desirable that their political society pass on obligations and entitlements from one generation to another. Long-term commitments promote political stability and individual security. They also contribute to moral relationships. To the extent that individuals value their membership in states and other organizations, they are bound to value a practice which entails respect for transgenerational associations and for the interests of individuals, past, present, and future, that are bound up with their continued existence. They will not only want practices which enable members to make long term commitments. They will think that making such commitments is morally important, given the interests and values of individuals. But long-term commitments require existing citizens, through their representatives, to impose moral demands on future members. If commitments of their predecessors are to be trusted, then future citizens will have to regard themselves as morally obligated to keep promises that they had no say in making. Present citizens have a moral entitlement to impose such obligations on future citizens only if they have reason to believe that in making such commitments they are operating in the framework of a practice that requires them to take responsibility for the commitments made by past citizens and the injustices that they have committed (Thompson 1992, chaps. 1, 2). Those who think that they are entitled to impose demands on future people must be prepared to assume the responsibilities intrinsic to a transgenerational polity.

The practices by means of which citizens in a transgenerational polity pass on obligations from one generation to another often involve official acts of government. Treaties in many countries are approved by a parliamentary body and are made into law—thus making it more likely that they will be honored by future as well as present governments and citizens. Governments sometimes hold official inquiries to determine how an injustice of the past occurred and what should be done about it. But in the last analysis, the ability of a state to make commitments and take responsibility for the past depends on the moral attitude of citizens and leaders: whether they accept the obligations and responsibilities that the practices entail. This means that they not only have to regard it as important that their state keeps its commitments and fulfils its responsibilities. They also have to be able and willing to recognize circumstances in which their state should make commitments or should take responsibility for a past injustice.

A transgenerational polity is able to satisfy the first and the third conditions of a genuine apology. It can acknowledge responsibility for past injustices and make a commitment to avoid such injustices in the future. Citizens or leaders may not feel remorse for injustices that they are not personally responsible for committing. But this particular sentiment is not required so long as citizens are motivated by the existence and value of their transgenerational practices. Apology, unlike forgiveness of monetary debts, requires an appropriate moral motivation, but in the case of political apologies it seems enough that citizens recognize the moral importance of fulfilling transgenerational obligations. In particular, they should recognize the responsibility of their state, as a transgenerational polity, to recompense victims for a history of injustice and disrespect.

That a state, as a transgenerational polity, can make a genuine apology does not mean that any state has ever done so. Until matters are clarified, there is going to be no stable, adequate practice of political apology. In the next section I contribute to this clarification by considering what it would take for the Australian state to make a genuine apology to Aborigines.

How to Make a Genuine Political Apology

In 1992, when he was Australian prime minister, Paul Keating gave a speech in Redfern, a suburb of Sydney where many Aborigines live, which acknowledged past injustices to Aborigines.

> We took the traditional lands and smashed the traditional way of life. We brought the diseases. The alcohol. We committed the murders. We took the children from their mothers. We practised discrimination and exclusion. It was our ignorance and our prejudice. (Keating 1992)

This was a strong speech. Nevertheless, it did not amount to a political apology. This is not because Keating did not use the words "We apologize." An act of apology does not depend on a particular form of words. But the Aborigines attending the proceedings were simply present as members of an audience; they were not a representative group to whom an apology could be made. Non-Aboriginal Australians were also not prepared for an event of any particular significance. Keating undoubtedly discussed his speech with other members of his party, but he did not discuss it with other political leaders or explain to the Australian people why an act of contrition was necessary. So even though the speech was given by the prime minister, it was construed as representing his opinion or the opinion of his political party. And so it proved. For the succeeding prime minister not only failed to endorse Keating's words, but expressed opposition to the point of view that lay behind them, which he described as a "black armband view of history" (Howard 1996). As these later events confirmed, there was no assumption when Keating made his speech that any official commitment was being made.

When Howard refused to make an official apology, some Australian citizens signed a statement of apology by adding their names to books of signatures made available in public places. Supposing that a majority of citizens had signed these books, this would still not have amounted to a political apology. It is not enough that most citizens are apologetic. The act must be an institutional one, and so must be the commitment that a genuine act of apology requires. These negative examples, along with the requirements of apology discussed in the last section, suggest that a genuine political apology for injustices done to Aboriginal communities and their members should have the following features.

1. Its content and the way it is presented—the ceremony that surrounds it, who performs the role of apologising and the other roles that the ceremony demands—should be endorsed by victims and their representatives. Indeed, as Meredith Gibbs also argues in her chapter, it would be desirable if the victims or their representatives have a role in determining the nature of the apology and how it is presented.
2. Its content and the way it is presented should, so far as possible, be endorsed by people who belong to the nation responsible for the wrong. It cannot be expected that all citizens will endorse an apology, but an effort can be made to promote public discussion of the issues, particularly in forums where victims and members of the perpetrating group can interact. It would be desirable if the apology were approved by Parliament and delivered by an official who is regarded as being above politics (the governor general, in the case of Australia).
3. The government should take steps to demonstrate that the injustice and the sufferings of the victims have become embedded in the official history of the nation, and this historical account should be something that the victims can endorse. This could be done by including an account of the injustices in school textbooks, putting up plaques and monuments, presenting the story of the injustice in public exhibitions, and so on.
4. The government should demonstrate its commitment to ensuring

that the nation will not commit similar wrongs to the victims or their descendants in the future. Embedding an account of the injustice in the nation's official history contributes to that goal. But it might also do so by compensating the victims—an act that not only mitigates some of the harm done but also sets a precedent in law or government practice, thus bringing into existence a disincentive against further offenses. Or in the case of injustices committed against Aboriginal communities, an obvious way of guarding against future wrongs would be to make a treaty—thus embedding recognition, along with certain guarantees, in law or in well understood and respected political practices.

A political apology, according to this account, is a major undertaking, not an everyday event. There is good reason why this should be so. First, an official apology is supposed to constitute a watershed in the history of relations between two peoples or between a government and a group of wronged individuals. It is supposed to separate a past of injustice and indifference from a future of just dealings and respect. To be such a watershed it has to be a memorable public event—a historical landmark. If it is to have this significance, it has to stand out from the flood of political events that are featured in newspapers one day and disappear from public view the next. It has to acquire the status of a national symbol. This is why a political act of apology requires preparation, ceremony, and subsequent actions; saying the words is a small part of the proceedings. Thus governments and citizens should be circumspect about what apologies they should make. Political apology should not be offered too often.

The second point is that an apology of state requires the participation of both victims and wrongdoers, or their representatives, at three stages. First it requires that the parties reach a common understanding of the injustice—something that is likely to require considerable public discussion. Second, there has to be an agreement about how and under what circumstances the apology should be presented; and third there has to be negotiation about what should follow from the apology, including other acts of reparation. Participation is required because an apology must be, above all, a demonstration of respect for the existence, point of view, and interests of the other party. One of the most serious wrongs done to Aborigines during the course of European settlement was the refusal of British officials and colonial governments to acknowledge their sovereignty, law, or rights over land. No treaties or agreements were made with Aboriginal communities. So an apology offered to Aborigines for the injustices of the past, if it is to be properly respectful, would have to acknowledge and show respect for their communities, their law and their desire to maintain these things.

The third point is that genuine apology has to involve a commitment that binds future governments and citizens and that ensures, so far as it is in the power of leaders and citizens to do so, that the commitment will be kept by future as well as present people. The future-directed aspect of apology means that those who advocate it are not in opposition to people who call for a treaty or a constitutional act of recognition. A treaty may be the best way to ensure that the commitment is kept.

The description of apology I have given is the expression of an ideal. Apologies have different purposes, and one that does not have all the above features may nevertheless serve an important function. Some victims of injustice simply want their suffering and loss to be officially acknowledged. They are not demanding anything more. Nevertheless, an apology that approaches the ideal could have profound implications for relations between Aboriginal and non-Aboriginal Australians. It could signal and make possible a change in the course of Australian history and national consciousness.

I have focused on a particular case, but my account can be applied to others. Other nations have committed injustices to those within their borders; and their citizens and leaders have been motivated to acknowledge and make recompense through apology and other acts. In international relations, where rivalries between states play such a large role, skepticism about apology seems more plausible. However, Gibney and Roxstrom (2001) suggest that a practice of apology, even when less than ideal, can have positive effects by encouraging nations to be aware of the harm that they can do to outsiders. And if the practice is available, there is always a chance that over time it might come to be taken more seriously as an instrument of international relations.

Let us engage in a fantasy about what that might mean. Suppose there are rival nations which have in the past committed injustices against each other. Because of this history, the citizens of each feel aggrieved and long for revenge. But acts of revenge simply fuel the hatred both sides have for each other and motivate further acts of revenge. The cycle of violence and counterviolence has been going on for a long time, and it seems that it will go on indefinitely into the future. Suppose that leaders and a significant number of people on each side recognize that they are prisoners of a history which dooms them and their descendants to a repetition of violence and suffering. What they need is a symbolic act that has the power to change the course of history and bring the violence to an end. For a symbolic act of apology to have such power, the stage must be set by a process of negotiation and reconciliation. But if such negotiation is possible, then a mutual and genuine apology—each side taking responsibility for the injustices their nation has done and pledging to avoid similar injustices in the future—could be the act that makes all the difference between a tragic future and one that contains more hopeful possibilities.

References

Austin, John. 1962. *How to Do Things with Words.* Oxford: Clarendon Press.
Barkan, Elazar. 2000. *Guilt of Nations: Restitution and Negotiating Historic Injustice.* New York: W.W. Norton.
"Blair Apologises to Ireland for Potato Famine." 1997. *Daily Telegraph,* June 2.
Boxill, Bernard. 1972. "Morality of Reparation." *Social Theory and Practice* 2: 113–22.
Brooks, Roy L. 1999. "Not Even an Apology." In *When Sorry Isn't Enough: The Controversy over Apology and Reparation for Human Injustice,* ed. Roy L. Brooks. New York: New York University Press.
Davies, Paul. 2002. "On Apology." *Journal of Applied Philosophy* 19 (2): 169–75.
Digeser, Peter E. 2001. *Political Forgiveness.* Ithaca, N.Y.: Cornell University Press.
Dodson, Patrick. 2000. "Lingiari: Until the Chains Are Broken." In *Reconciliation: Essays on Australian Reconciliation,* ed. Michelle Grattan. Melbourne: Bookman Press.
Feinberg, Joel. 1968. "Collective Responsibility." *Journal of Philosophy* 65 (21): 674–88.
Gaus, Gerald. 1991. "Does Compensation Restore Equality?" In *Compensatory Justice,* ed. John W. Chapman. New York: New York University Press.
Gibney, Mark and Erik Roxstrom. 2001. "The Status of State Apologies." *Human Rights Quarterly* 23 (4): 922–23.
Govier, Trudy. 2002. *Forgiveness and Revenge.* London: Routledge.
Govier, Trudy and Wilhelm Verwoerd. 2002. "The Practice of Public Apologies: A Qualified Defense." http://www.ijr.org.za/sa_mon/art_pgs/gov_verwoed.PDF
Howard, John. 1997. Opening Address to the Australian Reconciliation Convention, Melbourne, May 26. http://www.austlii.edu.au/au/other/IndigLRes/car/1997/4/pmspoken.html
Howard, John. 1996. Speech delivered October 30, 1996. In Mark McKenna, "Different Perspectives on Black Armband History." Research Paper 5, Australia Department of the Parliamentary Library. Information and Research Services, 1997–98. http://www.aph.gov.au/library/pubs/rp/1997-98/98rp05.htm#BLACK
Keating, Paul. 1992. "Australian Launch of the International Year for the World's Indigenous People." December 10. http://apology.west.net.au/redfern.html
McLaughlin, Martin. 1997. "Blair and the Potato Famine." *Socialist Equality,* June 14. http://www.socialequality.org.uk/potato.shtml
Nozick, Robert. 1974. *Anarchy, State, and Utopia.* New York: Basic Books.
Roberts, Rodney C. 2002. "Justice and Rectification: A Taxonomy of Justice." In *Injustice and Rectification,* ed. Rodney C. Roberts. New York: Peter Lang.
Simmons, A. John. 1979. *Moral Principles and Political Obligations.* Princeton, N.J.: Princeton University Press.
Tavuchis, Nicholas. 1991. *Mea Culpa: A Sociology of Apology and Reconciliation.* Stanford, Calif.: Stanford University Press.
Thompson, Janna. 1992. *Taking Responsibility for the Past: Reparation and Historical Injustice.* Cambridge: Polity Press.
Waldron, Jeremy. 1992. "Superseding Historic Injustice." *Ethics* 103 (1): 4–28.

Chapter 3
Historical Injustice and Liberal Political Theory

MICHAEL FREEMAN

The Ethics and Politics of Apologies

Apologies are very familiar. Even children have some understanding of them. Yet they are complex social phenomena. They can have many purposes and many outcomes. An apology can be accepted and a line drawn under the episode that the apology completes. An apology may be rejected because the wrong for which the apology is offered is too great: an apology for genocide might be inappropriate, for example. It may be rejected because it seems insincere. It can also be rejected unfairly: if the wrong is slight, and the apology genuine, rejection may be ungracious. Apologies can be individual or collective. I can apologize to you for missing an appointment; an airline can apologize to its passengers for a flight delay. The most familiar apologies are everyday events, and it is likely that the rules governing them are culturally variable.

States do not often apologize, but sometimes they do. The Realist theory of international relations would say that states apologize only when it is in their interest to do so, but this only prompts us to ask why they should consider it to be in their interest. States, like individuals and other collectivities, have an interest in their reputation and in having a favorable self-image. Such interests might lead them to apologize; this would be more likely if the apology had a practical benefit, such as improving trade relations with another country. Realism suggests, however, that states' willingness to acknowledge responsibility for past wrongdoing is likely to be limited. A common reason for the reluctance of states (and other bodies) to apologize is fear of large claims for financial compensation.

Apologies may be used as a diplomatic tool, as Realism would suggest. Svetozar Marović, president of Serbia and Montenegro, has apologized for the siege of Sarajevo. Many Bosnians reportedly received this apology with cynicism. In September 2003 Marović had made a similar apology to the people of Croatia for the crimes perpetrated during the 1991–95

Serb-Croat war. That apology had been reciprocated by the president of Croatia, Stipe Mesic (*Guardian*, November 14, 2003). This indicates that apologies may be useful diplomatic devices to smooth relations among elites without being significant moral events for most people.

Sometimes it is not clear who should apologize to whom. At the sixtieth anniversary of the Warsaw uprising of August 1944, the Polish prime minister, Marek Belka, asked the British government to apologize for its failure to send aid during the uprising (Aris 2004). The British government admitted that it could have done more but stopped short of an apology (Smith 2004). It is generally agreed that the Allies responded inadequately to the Warsaw uprising (Davies 2004), yet apology appears too strong a gesture to meet the requirements of this complex situation.

A systematic account of political apologies should answer several questions. When are apologies appropriate? Are apologies enough when the wrong done is serious? If they are not, what else is required? What is the role, if any, of financial compensation? If financial compensation is appropriate, should it be paid to the victims or their heirs, or in the form of community development? To what extent, if any, are states and their peoples responsible for the wrongdoing of their predecessors? Can states accept apologies on behalf of victims? Does the present concern with apology identify certain people as "victims," and thereby violate their dignity? Should we forget about apology, and concentrate on justice? How are apology and justice related to forgiveness and reconciliation?

Apology and Justice

"Justice," John Rawls famously said, "is the first virtue of social institutions" (Rawls 1972: 3). How is the concept of "apology" related to that of "justice"? To answer this question, we need to distinguish different types of justice. Recent political theories of justice have been mainly concerned with *distributive* justice. Theories of distributive justice often endorse the concept of "human rights" as providing minimal protection and powers for all. The discussion of "apology" refers us to the ideas of *restitutive*, *reparative*, or *restorative* justice. These forms of justice (similar but not identical to each other) are closely related to *retributive* justice that seeks to establish appropriate punishment for wrongdoing. The various forms of justice may, however, not be mutually compatible. Restitutive justice—returning property wrongfully taken or paying equivalent compensation—may not yield just distributions of wealth. Distributive justice may wrongly ignore the claims of restitutive justice. The concept of human rights is primarily a distributive concept, emphasizing the obligation to accord to all their due here and now, and gives restitution at best a secondary place.

Human rights advocates often supplement their commitment to distributive justice with strong support for retributive justice. Human rights violations, in this view, are crimes, and those who commit them ought, if convicted after a fair trial, to be punished. "Impunity"—the failure to punish human rights crimes—is believed to be an important cause of violations. Punishment is therefore doubly justified: it is right in itself and it has the consequence of reducing human rights violations. In the extensive recent literature on "transitional justice," however, there has been considerable disagreement as to whether retributive justice does contribute to the protection of human rights. Some see it as necessary to establish respect for the rule of law; others as at best one element in the complex, pragmatic politics of transition (Wilson 2001; Zalaquett 1992). The "international community" seems to have inconsistent attitudes to "impunity": they have been keen to have trials for Pinochet, the former Yugoslavia and Rwanda, but have supported the "truth and reconciliation" project in South Africa that has accorded immunity to most of the criminals of apartheid.

Within the theory of distributive justice, apologies may seem permissible, even desirable, but insufficient, since they distribute little value, except perhaps (and importantly) respect. Within the theory of retributive justice, apology may seem at best marginal, and at worst a distraction from justice. Apology and punishment are not incompatible in principle, but may be difficult to combine in practice. However, since the relations among distributive, restitutive, and retributive (not to speak of reparative and restorative) justice are quite controversial, we can say no more than that apology may play a role in justice, but it will have to take its place in a complex and contested field of moral considerations.

Political Theory and Historical Injustice

Western political theory has been largely "ideal" and unhistorical. The theories of Burke, Hegel, and Marx are exceptions, but they had difficulty in deriving prescriptions from their historical analyses without either smuggling ideal theories back in or making spurious appeals to historical necessity. Theories of justice from Plato to Rawls have been concerned mainly with describing ideally just societies that exist outside history. Natural-law and Utilitarian theories generate conceptions of justice that ignore or at best marginalize historical injustices. The concept of "human rights" is usually located in the natural-law tradition, and consequently shares the failure of that tradition to take historical injustice seriously. Natural-law theories typically acknowledge, in passing, that many injustices—such as those of colonialism and slavery—were committed in the past, but they generally give priority to creating a more just future over rectifying historical injustices.

Liberal theory traditionally had at its center an entity known as the "individual," the "person," or the "self." Liberalism's concern has been with the fundamental rights and freedoms of this entity. Communitarian political philosophers have criticized this concept on the ground that it is ontologically empty. Real selves, they maintain, are socially constructed, and are constituted by social beliefs, norms, and values. Liberals respond that, insofar as selves are socially constructed, this refutes neither the reality nor the fundamental moral importance of human autonomy. It is indeed the foundation of human dignity. The concept of human rights is usually thought to presuppose this liberal line of argument. To connect the concept of human rights to that of the rectification of historical injustice, however, it may be necessary to accept the truth in communitarianism. The individual self is constituted in part by *memory*. Identity depends on memory. Memory is individual and collective: I remember my individual experiences and also participate in shared memories of my nation. Memory is, of course, fallible. The recognition of collective memory and identity is consistent with the recognition of individual human rights. Some communitarians sentimentalize collective memories and identities, or ignore their dark side. Liberals do not, or certainly should not, do so.

The relation between collective memories and *obligations* is more problematic. David Miller has argued that collective national memories entail obligations to the nation. Our ancestors, he says, made sacrifices for us, and this entails obligations on our part to the nation (Miller 1995). If a collectivity, such as a nation or a state, has an obligation to apologize for or otherwise to rectify a historical injustice, I may share that obligation as a member of the nation or as a citizen. However, if the wrongdoing state is not a democracy, the obligations of its people are less clear. If it is a democracy, the obligations of those who did not vote for the government and/or actively opposed the wrongful policy are also in question. Individual obligation to contribute to reparation for the injustice committed by collectivities may be based on the fact that individuals *identify* with the collectivity (which should be distinguished from supporting all its actions) and/or on the *benefits* that they derive from membership of the collectivity. Both these grounds of obligation are problematic. The *empirical* basis of identification and benefit may be doubtful, and is likely to be variable, and the *normative* argument from the facts of identity and benefit may be quite controversial.

Ton Van den Beld has argued that the concept of human rights presupposes an individualist moral ontology that seems inconsistent with the concept of collective responsibility. It is difficult to see how innocent individuals can be responsible for injustices committed before they were born. If, however, we accept that our personal identity is socially constituted as a narrative continuity, an individual might bear responsibility for collective injustices in the absence of individual guilt, because of an association with the collective that is responsible for the injustice. Van den Beld concludes that innocent individuals are not guilty of injustice to which they did not contribute, but they may nevertheless have reason to accept responsibility for the actions of the collectivities of which they are members (Van den Beld 2002). Igor Primoratz suggests that citizens may be responsible for the actions of their state, especially in a democracy in which the people are supposed to be sovereign. The imperfections of actual democracies are constraints on what citizens can do, but not excuses for doing nothing. If citizens may be responsible for the wrongful actions of their governments, the obligation of apology and restitution may be wider than is commonly thought (Primoratz 2002).

Janna Thompson holds that individuals as citizens can incur obligations as the result of the commitments or actions of their predecessors. Thompson combines Miller's "identity" argument with the benefit argument. Nations, she argues, have historical continuity, and the wealth of some nations has been built on past injustices to others. She believes that there are pragmatic as well as moral reasons for repairing past injustices. The international practice of treaty-making has both moral and practical merits, and it can persist only if the commitments of one generation are honored by later generations. The continuity of nations and their obligations is the basis of international relations. Collective commitments entail obligations to make reparation for injustice. This obligation is both backward- and forward-looking. The obligation is that of *citizens*, not *descendants*; it is political not biological. These obligations may conflict with liberal individualism, democratic decision-making and with other obligations, especially obligations of justice to present and future generations (Thompson 2002).

Liberal theories of justice, such as Rawls's, tell us what an ideal distribution of goods would look like, here and now. They say little about rectifying past wrongs. Robert Nozick's "historical" theory of entitlements tells us what "just holdings" are, based on just past holdings and just transfers of goods. It allows for the rectification of past wrongs (that is, unjust transfers, such as theft), although the theory is strictly individualistic, and does not recognize the significance of "identity," culture, or collective rights, unless these are derived from the free agreement of individuals. According to Nozick's theory, Thompson's transgenerational communities might themselves be unjust. However, even in his own terms, Nozick failed to develop a theory of rectification. Perhaps this was because the theory is an "ideal" theory, and its application to the real world is consequently unclear (Nozick 1974). Although Nozick's theory appears to be better suited than Rawls's to deal with the rectification of past wrongs, because justice is conceived diachronically and not synchronically, it has two serious defects. The first is that, since just holdings are holdings derived justly from previous just holdings, just holdings must be traceable through an unbroken line of just transfers to an original just holding. There is, however, no uncontroversial way to identify *this* original position.

The second problem arises only if we have solved the first. Suppose that we can identify an original just distribution of goods. Suppose further that we can track all subsequent transfers, and note which were just and which unjust. Now we have to rectify the unjust transfers. The merit of this approach is that it generates the question we want to answer: how ought we to rectify past injustices? Yet we would now encounter another challenge. In the literature on reparations, it is usually taken for granted that compensating for wrongs in the distant past would be absurd: no-one demands that the Italian government apologize for the injustices perpetrated by the Roman empire. Yet Nozick's theory would strictly require that all such wrongs be rectified. This may lead to the conclusion that Nozick's theory is absurd. But we have no theory that tells us why Tony Blair was obliged to apologize for the Irish famine of 1846, but not for the massacres carried out by Cromwell in 1649–50. Apologies seem theory-free. This leaves it to intuition to tell us when apologies are called for. And this may lead to disagreement, which will threaten to undermine the "healing" features of apologies, and cynicism when apologies are just another tool in the diplomatic bag. The Miller-Thompson notion of transgenerational continuity, whatever its merits, cannot identify discontinuities in an uncontroversial manner.

Max du Plessis argues that Western demands that former colonies respect human rights are weakened by the failure of former slave-trading and slave-owning states to apologize for these past injustices. Reparations for slavery might be regarded as a legitimate part of the human rights movement. He suggests that Rawls's "principle of redress" could ground reparations for historical injustice, but Rawls does not say so, and, if he had, his theory would raise the problems that Nozick's does. Thompson's argument that the international law of treaties generates transgenerational obligations cuts both ways, because international law recognizes no obligation to rectify wrongs that were not *illegal* at the time they were committed. Du Plessis argues for rectification now because it would promote human rights now, rather than, as Thompson argues, on the ground that we have present obligations to rectify the injustice that our predecessors committed (Du Plessis 2003).

The contemporary world is beyond question unequal, and, by most theories of justice (including those of both Rawls and Nozick) unjust. Past wrongs have played a major role in making it so. The failure to rectify the injustices associated with Western imperialism, for example, and the difficulty we have in identifying who owes what to whom, underlie many of the current controversies, not only about reparations for slavery and colonialism, but also over the supposed "right to development," minority rights, multiculturalism, and the rights of indigenous peoples. It is rarely recognized that the problems under discussion—such as, for example, special rights for religious minorities—are the product of historical injustice. The literature on minority rights and that on reparations for past injustice appear not to be on speaking terms. It may be, however, that the sets of problems that they deal with are interrelated, and that relating the analyses in these two fields will advance both.

Will Kymlicka has criticized the liberal conception of human rights, for example, on the ground that it cannot provide equal citizenship for all. The structure of contemporary liberal societies unjustly disadvantages certain groups, such as indigenous peoples, and, he maintains, certain collective rights are necessary to implement the *liberal* principle of the equal right to justice. Those whose culture is socially dominant can defend their culture without special rights. Those whose culture is subordinate or marginal cannot do so. This inequality in the conditions of citizenship is unjust. In this situation equal rights entail special rights (Kymlicka 1995). While Kymlicka defends a liberal theory of minority rights, James Tully has criticized the "monological" character of liberal constitutionalism, and argued that it should be replaced, in a multicultural society, by intercultural dialogue (Tully 1995). Liberals fear that multiculturalism is a thin disguise for the defense of illiberal practices, including the violation of human rights. It is sometimes unclear whether multiculturalists and communitarians are prepared to make human rights concessions to cultural difference. Critics of liberalism argue that not all cultures endorse liberal values, and to impose them on reluctant cultures is liberal imperialism or "liberal Jacobinism" (Chaplin 1993; Parekh 2000). To the liberals, the multiculturalists are, more or less, cultural relativists, and therefore willing to sell out universal human rights (Barry 2002). To the advocates of multiculturalism, interculturalism or minority rights, the liberals are insensitive to, or stubbornly unwilling to recognize the importance of, culturally based, unjust inequalities (Parekh 2000, 2002).

The parties to this debate about liberal democracy and multiculturalism emphasize historical injustice surprisingly little. References are occasionally made to colonialism, but usually to argue that current inequalities reflect the inequalities of colonial times, not to discuss reparations for past wrongs. The concern of the multiculturalists is with *culture* and current inequality, not with apology or reparation. Kymlicka argues both that human rights are *insufficient* to provide justice to cultural minorities and that they may be used to aggravate injustice to such groups. Although his theory appears to be motivated by a concern with the historical injustice done to indigenous peoples and other minorities, it is a neo-Rawlsian theory with a collectivist twist rather than a theory of rectification of historical injustice.

We have, therefore, three theoretical approaches to liberalism, human rights and historical injustice. The first, "classical" approach, defended by Brian Barry and Jack Donnelly (2003), says that justice requires full respect for human rights and equal citizenship in a democracy. Collective rights should be viewed with suspicion, because they may easily threaten individual human rights. This approach does not rule out reparations, but they are marginal to its concerns. The second approach, defended by Kymlicka, holds that the "classical" approach is not genuinely egalitarian, because it fails to recognize structural inequalities in society based on cultural hierarchies. Although these cultural hierarchies are the product of historical injustice, this approach defends collective rights for subordinate groups on the ground of a group-sensitive, neo-Rawlsian, liberal conception of justice, and not on the ground of the rectification of historical injustice.

The third approach, represented by Parekh and Tully, argues that "classical" liberalism bears the marks of its imperial past in its failure to recognize the worth of minority cultures that may not be fully liberal. This approach is more historical and somewhat more "communitarian" than the other two. Reason is said to be "historically situated" and culture to be necessary to self-respect and a good life. It rejects neither liberal values nor human rights, but places collective, cultural values in the balance against them. It emphasizes intercultural "dialogue," but leaves unclear whether the protection of human rights is a necessary condition for such dialogue. It is a theory of intercultural justice that recognizes the validity of non-liberal cultures. It accuses "classical" liberalism of cultural arrogance and a refusal to recognize cultural difference that has historically led to violence and oppression. Barry underestimates precisely what Kymlicka and Tully emphasize: the imperialist ghost in the liberal-democratic machine (Tully 2002; Parekh 2000, 2002). Although Tully and Parekh seem, like Kymlicka, to be motivated by a concern with historical injustice, this plays little role in their theories, which advance principles of culture-sensitive justice, in which reparations are absent, though not necessarily ruled out. Unjust cultural inequalities have historical origins, but the injustice is said to lie in the contemporary inequality, not in the historical origins.

Barry defends the "classical" position against what he regards as its fashionable, but dangerously misguided, multiculturalist critics on the ground that liberal justice should not be watered down or distorted by sentimental responses to past wrongs. The guilty conscience of post-imperialist white liberals may undermine the defense of justice and human rights. The rectification of historical injustice requires an ahistorical theory of justice. Some multiculturalists take insufficient account of the rights of certain categories of individuals, such as women and children, who have been victims of historical injustice, and remain victims of present injustice. The "classical" position is vulnerable, however, to at least three objections. The first is that liberal justice is justice among *persons*, and the interests of persons are, to an important extent, historically and culturally constituted. Justice therefore requires an understanding of cultural commitments. Monological liberal theory excludes the need for this understanding. Understanding does not entail approval, but disapproval without understanding is not valid. Understanding cultures requires taking account of historical injustice. The second objection is that historical injustice can have harmful effects on present persons who were not its direct victims by inculcating social attitudes that continue to accord them less than equal respect. Unacknowledged past wrongs can distort parties' perceptions of each other and of themselves. Victims may internalize their morally inferior status, while violators may have a distorted sense of their moral superiority. Such asymmetry in social relations makes justice impossible (Tan 2004). The third objection is that contemporary, synchronic justice is given priority over restorative or restitutive justice and the rectification of past wrongs. Difference-blind liberalism, say its critics, suffers from an amnesia that overlooks crimes of the past in designing social policies for the present. The strategic advantage of thinking about reparations is that it recalls the past, and thereby contributes to the design of just policies in the present (Valls 2004).

Barry defends a form of liberal justice that includes a commitment to human rights and consequently opposes arbitrary discrimination. He maintains that this offers justice to all members of cultural minorities. Camille Paglia takes a similar view in the debate over apologies and reparations. The issue of apology, she says, shows the bankruptcy of what she calls "liberal identity politics" (Barry would deny that identity politics can be liberal). Identity politics sharpens racial consciousness; apologies are "empty gestures," and what is required is substantive reform. African Americans should be treated as fellow-citizens and not as former slaves. "Western imperialism is not the serpent that brought evil into paradise. The obsession with slavery—abolished here [USA] nearly a century and a half ago—is itself a form of enslavement" (Paglia 1999: 353–54). It would clearly be wrong to consider African Americans *only* as former slaves. However, the contemporary problem of racism cannot be adequately understood except as a product of Western imperialism. Understanding and acknowledging historical injustice is not a form of enslavement; it is a form of liberation (Kelly 2002: 62–71).

The "classical" liberal theory of justice, therefore, can recognize that wrong ought to be rectified so far as possible, but is reluctant to recognize special rights for minorities that have suffered historical injustice on the ground that this would violate the principle of equal rights. Samuel Freeman has pointed out, however, that the Rawlsian theory of distributive justice—which identity-based special rights might violate—is an *ideal* theory. In liberal theory, he argues, some departure from the liberal ideal of fair equal opportunity is permissible in less than ideal circumstances to rectify past and present discrimination, and when it would promote the conditions of equality needed for a just society (Freeman 2002). The debate over liberalism and multiculturalism suffers from a failure to distinguish between ideal and non-ideal theory. It may be that Barry's ideal theory would differ from that of Parekh and Tully, who believe that culture constitutes identity, and that identity is a necessary element in an adequate theory of justice. Yet Barry applies his liberal theory to the world as it is, and it is plausible to suggest that the world that we have is marked by past injustices in a way that requires us to take questions of apology, recognition, and reparations seriously.

Rectifying Historical Injustices

The task for the theory of human rights, therefore, is to reconcile the liberal theory of justice, which is the principal justificatory basis of human rights, with a theory of redress for past injustice. Roy Brooks has suggested that necessary conditions of a just claim for collective redress are (1) an injustice has been committed; (2) the victims can be identified as a distinct group; (3) the current members of the group continue to suffer harm; (4) the past injustice is causally connected to the present harm (Brooks 1999: 3–11).

Some believe that the discourse of "reparations" stirs up old animosities and, in so doing, makes future justice more difficult. It is better to concentrate on justice now for all than "payback" for past wrongs (Smith 1999: 370). Jeremy Waldron suggests that "drawing a line under" the past may be an offense against the victims: literally adding insult to injury. *Acknowledging* the past, telling the truth to the best of one's ability, and admitting injustices done, recognizes the dignity of survivors and those whose identity is linked with them. The sentiment that bygones should be bygones may allow dominant groups to be unjustifiably self-congratulatory and victim-groups unjustly undervalued. In this sense, historical memory may be necessary, not only to identity, but to justice. Financial reparations may serve as acknowledgement and apology, and their symbolic value may be more important than their material value (Waldron 1992).

If forgetting past injustice is itself unjust, what is an *adequate* response to past injustice? Waldron argues that rectifying historical injustice raises several difficult problems. The most obvious problem is that the relevant evidence may be unclear. A less obvious problem is that of counterfactual knowledge. If A steals the property of B, A should normally return the property or pay appropriate compensation. However, if the theft occurred generations ago, it may be impossible to return it now or to calculate what it would have been worth had it not been stolen. The counterfactual value of the unstolen property is unknowable because it depends on the (untaken) free decisions of the original, rightful owners. This problem is aggravated by what Waldron calls "the contagion of injustice." If A stole B's land generations ago, the stolen land may lower property values, and C may benefit from this. C is an innocent beneficiary of an injustice: does C have an obligation of reparation? There is also a problem of *expectations*. Suppose A stole B's land generations ago. The descendants of A and B do not know this, and have built lives on the expectation that their present holdings are just. If historical research reveals the original theft, is it just to frustrate B's expectations, and A's, in order to rectify the original injustice? Where land is stolen, and it has enduring symbolic value, then a present group may have the right to some form of reparation, even if return of the land is impracticable and/or morally questionable.

Waldron suggests, finally, that what justice requires for the rectification of past wrongs depends on *circumstances*. If A stole B's land generations ago, and A's descendants are now starving while B's are not, then to require A's descendants to compensate B's might be unjust and even violate their economic and social human rights. Waldron argues that historical injustice may be *superseded* if circumstances change. He concludes that, if doing justice now conflicts with repairing historical injustice, doing justice now should trump reparative justice. This does not mean that rectifying past injustice is never appropriate, but that entitlements that fade with time, counterfactuals that are impossible to verify, and injustices that are overtaken by circumstances complicate the simple principle that, if something was wrongly taken, it must be right to give it back. The proposition that the justice of reparations might depend on the *consequences* of paying them may offend those who hold anti-consequentialist conceptions of justice, but it cannot easily be dismissed. Germany was made to pay reparations after the First World War, and this may have weakened the Weimar democracy with disastrous consequences (Steel 2003).

It is generally agreed that the victims of serious human rights violations are entitled to reparations. It is less clear, however, what this entails. A simple view is that, if A has wronged B, A should restore B to the condition B was in before the wrong was committed. But this is logically impossible. Whatever A does, B is now a wronged person, and no reparation can change that. Further, certain wrongs—such as murder or torture—have no "equivalent" reparation. Practical assistance and financial compensation may sometimes be better than nothing, but they do not necessarily "repair" the wrong.

Richard Goldstone has argued that *full justice* is impossible after gross human rights violations because there are too many victims and too many perpetrators. Amnesia is impossible, and attempts to forget past wrongs lead to resentment on the part of the victims that could be mobilized for future human rights violations. Generalization about appropriate policy responses is also impossible, because such responses must take account of pragmatic circumstances, and these are highly variable (Goldstone 1998: ix–x). This creates formidable problems for the crime-and-punishment model of retributive justice. This deals primarily with the perpetrators of human rights violations, although it does not ignore the victims, who may have a right to (retributive) justice. Ben Chigara has indeed argued that granting amnesties to human rights violators constitutes a violation of the human rights of the victims (Chigara 2002). Criminal trials of human rights violators affirm the rule of law, but they are not well-suited to giving a voice to the victims in a sympathetic environment, to setting the violations in their historical context, to allocating reparations to victims, or to reconciliation. Truth commissions are now widely thought to be able to do things that trials cannot—tell a wider truth, give more voice to victims, recognize and validate their suffering and the injustice of it, and recommend reparations—but they have their limits, including those of time and other resources, and their contribution to reconciliation has been doubted. Although criminal trials can be, and have been, combined with truth commissions, they are incompatible insofar as amnesties provide an incentive to perpetrators to tell their part of the truth. Truth commissions also raise the problem that they may name alleged human rights violators without the protections of due process of law (Minow 1998; Hayner 2002).

Some victims' rights seem clear: for example, the right of torture victims to medical aid. This has a cost, of course, and this may be borne by those who were innocent of the crimes. Since citizens have a general responsibility to contribute to the public good, including the support of the most vulnerable, this seems a clear case in which successor governments and their citizens have an obligation to bear the cost of human rights violations of their predecessors. If medical aid is appropriate, financial aid might also be so. This raises various problems: needs may outstrip resources; they may compete with other legitimate social programs; inadequate compensation may add insult to injury, yet a small amount of compensation may be acceptable as a symbol of apology. Some believe that social development programs, carried out with the participation of the victims, may be the best option when resources are limited.

Martha Minow suggests that sincere apology can rehumanize the dehumanized relation between perpetrator and victim, but cannot by itself rectify wrongs. Insofar as this is possible at all, it requires constructive, practical, forward-looking measures for a more just society (Minow 1998). Thompson argues that reparation for historical injustice may be a public good for which at least some rights might properly be sacrificed (Thompson 2002: 92). This view is in some tension with Waldron's account of the "supersession" of historical injustice, although the two views differ in emphasis, and are not necessarily mutually inconsistent. Waldron considers situations in which the demands of justice now might outweigh "fading" claims of the past, whereas Thompson deals with the obligations of the present generation to claims for the reparation of historical injustice. This difference of emphasis has theoretical significance, however. Waldron seeks to incorporate a weakish form of reparative justice into a post-Rawlsian, liberal conception of distributive justice. Thompson grounds the obligation of reparative justice in a neo-Burkean conception of transgenerational continuity. She generates a stronger obligation of reparation, but on the basis of a theory that values collectivities such as nations and families that are less harmonious than Waldron's liberalism with a strong conception of human rights. This reinforces the argument that there is a tension between the liberal conception of human rights and the "communitarian" conception of reparative justice to collectivities.

Retributive justice looks mainly to the perpetrators of human rights crimes. Restitutive and reparative justice looks to the victims. *Restorative* justice seeks to heal society. Some, especially in the Christian tradition, look to *forgiveness* as the basis of reconciliation and reconstruction, but forgiveness is personal, and may be too much to expect, and perhaps not even appropriate, when human rights violations have been extreme (Garrard 2002).

Conclusions

The rise of the West, and its domination of the rest of the world, involved various injustices associated with slavery, colonialism and racial discrimination. These injustices may persist in economic, political and cultural inequalities, although the causal connections are difficult to identify. The "universal" idea of human rights has been criticized as a manifestation of this Western domination or because it hides it. Sincere apologies may be part of the process of healing old wounds, but only if combined with measures to achieve global justice.

Pablo de Greiff has argued that reparations contribute to the constitution of a new political community, and are therefore political rather than judicial (de Greiff 2004). Massive and systematic human rights violations overwhelm national and international juridical frameworks. International human rights law provides for compensation in some cases, but this involves various problems: full restitution is often impossible; it is often difficult to quantify losses; resources are likely to be scarce; there may be political opposition to reparations. There are dangers in raising unrealistic expectations. The rights of victims should be combined with other claims of justice. The recognition and rectification of historical injustices are, however, necessary to equal citizenship and equal justice in the present. The rule of law and the discourse of human rights are not likely to create a stable, just society if due recognition and fair reparation are not given to the victims of past injustice. Reparations should be forward-looking as the constitutional moment in transitional societies. Contrary to the view of certain "classical" liberals, such as Brian Barry, this form of recognition is necessary to liberal justice.

Reparation should also be distinguished from development; both are desirable, but their justificatory bases are quite different. Reparation may also come into conflict with democracy, which may substitute development for reparation at the expense of the victims of past injustice (de Greiff 2004; Hamber 2004). In Uruguay, there was a democratic vote for impunity. In Argentina, Chile and South Africa, the use of truth commissions with extensive impunity has achieved little reconciliation. There is a tension between the demands of international human rights law and democracy in the reconstruction of damaged societies. The failure to enforce human rights may lead to injustice for victims and weaken the stability of the new society, but rigid legalism may undermine the political determination of complex demands of different types of justice.

State apologies may be an aspect of the age of human rights. They may recognize past wrongs and contribute to future reconciliation and justice. They can, however, be cynical moves, and thereby generate cynicism. *Pace* some liberal theorists, apologies and reparations may be necessary to justice now. Historical injustice contaminates the present. Waldron demonstrates some of the complexities of combining the rectification of past wrongs with the pursuit of present justice. De Greiff rightly sees this as a political process. Yet, in this field, democracy can be at odds with reparative justice. It may be, as Wilson argues, that international human rights law acts as an important constraint on democracy in transitional societies in which the rule of law is still in question. Barry and Donnelly defend liberal democracy against the temptations of cultural relativism. Their theories require supplementation, however, by a theory of reparative justice. Thompson makes a strong case for this, while Waldron warns us to find a fair balance between rectifying past wrongs and doing right in the present and the future. There is a consensus that we have an obligation to combine justice to the victims of past wrongs with the restoration and reconstruction of society. Apology is good, if sincere, but not enough. Certain prevalent conceptions of justice and human rights are good, but not enough. Putting together the best package of rectification, human rights, democracy and development is a complex task that, as Goldstone has rightly said, defies generalization. The task of political theory is to clarify issues, identify mistakes, and point out options. It is not to offer recipes.

References

Aris, Ben. 2004. "Schröder Apologises to Poles for "Immeasurable" War Time Suffering." *The Guardian* (London), August 2.
Barry, Brian. 2002. "Second Thoughts—and Some First Thoughts Revived." In *Multiculturalism Reconsidered: "Culture and Equality" and Its Critics*, ed. Paul Kelly. Cambridge: Polity Press.
Brooks, Roy L. 1999. "The Age of Apologies." In *When Sorry Isn't Enough: The Controversy over Apologies and Reparations for Human Injustice*, ed. Roy L. Brooks. New York: New York University Press.
Chigara, Ben. 2002. *Amnesty in International Law: The Legality Under International Law of National Amnesty Laws*. Harlow: Longman.
Chaplin, Jonathan. 1993. "How Much Cultural and Religious Pluralism Can Liberalism Tolerate?" In *Liberalism, Multiculturalism and Toleration*, ed. John Horton. Basingstoke: Macmillan.
Davies, Norman. 2004. *Rising '44: The Battle for Warsaw*. London: Pan Books.
de Greiff, Pablo. 2004. "Justice and Reparations." Paper presented at the international conference, Reparations: An Interdisciplinary Examination of Some Philosophical Issues, Queen's University, Kingston, Ontario, February 6–8.
Donnelly, Jack. 2003. *Universal Human Rights in Theory and Practice*. 2nd ed. Ithaca, N.Y.: Cornell University Press.
Du Plessis, Max. 2003. "Historical Injustice and International Law: An Exploratory Discussion of Reparation for Slavery." *Human Rights Quarterly* 25 (3): 624–59.
Freeman, Samuel. 2002. "Liberalism and the Accommodation of Group Claims." In *Multiculturism Reconsidered: "Culture and Equality" and Its Critics*, ed. Paul Kelly. Cambridge: Polity Press.
Garrard, Eve. 2002. "Forgiveness and the Holocaust." In *Pardoning Past Wrongs*, ed. Eve Garrard. *Ethical Theory and Moral Practice* (special edition) 5 (2): 147–65.
Goldstone, Richard J. 1998. Foreword. In Martha Minow, *Between Vengeance and Forgiveness: Facing History After Genocide and Mass Violence*. Boston: Beacon Press.
Hamber, Brandon. 2004. "Reparations as Symbol: Narratives of Resistance, Reticence and Possibility in South Africa." Paper presented at the international conference, Reparations: An Interdisciplinary Examination of Some Philosophical Issues, Queen's University, Kingston, Ontario, February 6–8.
Hayner, Priscilla B. 2002. *Unspeakable Truths: Facing the Challenge of Truth Commissions*. New York: Routledge.
Kelly, Paul. 2002. "Defending Some Dodos: Equality and/or Liberty?" In *Multiculturalism Reconsidered: "Culture and Equality" and Its Critics*, ed. Paul Kelly. Cambridge: Polity Press.
Kymlicka, Will. 1995. *Multicultural Citizenship: A Liberal Theory of Minority Rights*. Oxford: Clarendon Press.
Miller, David. 1995. *On Nationality*. Oxford: Clarendon Press.

Minow, Martha. 1998. *Between Vengeance and Forgiveness: Facing History After Genocide and Mass Violence.* Boston: Beacon Press.
Nozick, Robert. 1974. *Anarchy, State, and Utopia.* Oxford: Blackwell.
Paglia, Camille. 1999. "Ask Camille: Camille Paglia's Online Advice for the Culturally Disgruntled." In *When Sorry Isn't Enough: The Controversy over Apologies and Reparations for Human Injustice,* ed. Roy L. Brooks. New York: New York University Press.
Parekh, Bhikku. 2000. *Rethinking Multiculturalism: Cultural Diversity and Political Theory.* Basingstoke: Macmillan.
———. 2002. "Barry and the Dangers of Liberalism." In *Multiculturalism Reconsidered: "Culture and Equality" and Its Critics,* ed. Paul Kelly. Cambridge: Polity Press.
Primoratz, Igor. 2002. "Michael Walzer's Just War Theory: Some Issues of Responsibility." *Ethical Theory and Moral Practice* 5 (2): 221–43.
Rawls, John. 1972. *A Theory of Justice.* Oxford: Oxford University Press.
Smith, David. 2004. "Warsaw Uprising Veterans Demand Britain Says Sorry." *The Guardian* (London), August 1.
Smith, Mary E. 1999. "Clinton and Conservatives Oppose Slavery Reparations. In *When Sorry Isn't Enough: The Controversy over Apologies and Reparations for Human Injustice,* ed. Roy L. Brooks. New York: New York University Press.
Steel, Ronald. 2003. "The Missionary." *New York Review of Books,* November 20.
Tan, Kok-Chor. 2004. "Colonialism, Reparations and Global Justice." Paper presented at the international conference, Reparations: An Interdisciplinary Examination of Some Philosophical Issues. Queen's University, Kingston, Ontario, February 6–8.
Thompson, Janna. 2002. *Taking Responsibility for the Past: Reparation and Historical Justice.* Cambridge: Polity Press.
Tully, James. 1995. *Strange Multiplicities: Constitutionalism in an Age of Diversity.* Cambridge: Cambridge University Press.
———. 2002. "The Illiberal Liberal: Brian Barry's Polemical Attack on Multiculturalism." In *Multiculturalism Reconsidered: "Culture and Equality" and Its Critics,* ed. Paul Kelly. Cambridge: Polity Press.
Van den Beld, Ton. 2002. "Can Collective Responsibility for Perpetrated Evil Persist Over Generations?" *Ethical Theory and Moral Practice* 5 (2): 181–200.
Valls, Andrew. 2004. "Is There a Case for Black Reparations?" Paper presented at the international conference, Reparations: An Interdisciplinary Examination of Some Philosophical Issues. Queen's University, Kingston, Ontario, February 6–8.
Wilson, Richard. 2001. *The Politics of Truth and Reconciliation in South Africa: Legitimizing the Post-Apartheid State.* Cambridge: Cambridge University Press.
Waldron, Jeremy. 1992. "Superseding Historic Injustice." *Ethics* 103 (1): 4–28.
Zalaquett, José. 1992. "Balancing Ethical Imperatives and Political Constraints: The Dilemma of New Democracies Confronting Past Human Rights Violations." *Hastings Law Journal* 43: 1425–38.

Chapter 4
Apologies: A Cross-Cultural Analysis

ALISON DUNDES RENTELN

Since the 1990s, there has been a remarkable trend toward governments apologizing for gross violations of human rights, sometimes to their own citizens and other times to governments for mistreating the citizens of another country.[1] However, what has not been questioned is whether apologies have the same meaning in all societies. This essay explores the cross-cultural significance of apologies by drawing on literature in various fields. In doing so, it will identify cross-cultural differences in the conceptualization and use of apologies. Without a clear transcultural concept of apology and without an understanding of its usage in different societies, it is not possible to determine the efficacy of apologies as a remedy for human rights violations. The larger point is that while apologies may be desirable in many circumstances, they must not take the place of restitution.[2] One might argue, then, that an apology is necessary but not sufficient to address serious human rights violations. This means that while there is some benefit to a state apology, it is ultimately insufficient in and of itself to ensure that justice is achieved.

The Concept of Apology

Many writers treat the apology as a mechanism for restoring a wrong. It is a speech act uttered by a wrongdoer to acknowledge responsibility for the offense and to request forgiveness. (Tavuchis 1991: 17). Olshtain defines apology as "a speech act which is intended to provide support for the hearer who was actually or potentially malaffected by a violation X" (1989). By making a verbal apology, the speaker demonstrates a willingness to be "humiliated" to some extent and admits to fault and responsibility. There is a crucial link between the concept of apology and the concept of face: "Hence the act of apologizing is face-saving for the H (hearer) and face-threatening for the S (speaker)" (Olshtain 1989: 121).

Some raise the question as to whether an apology must be sincere to count as an apology.[3] Work on the strategic use of apologies calls into question the sincerity with which they are often made. American scholars often seem preoccupied with the question of whether apologies are sincere, although this is not always considered crucial in other cultures.[4] In American culture, there is even a genre of folklore known as "feigned apologies." This apology is made sarcastically by the offended party, who should actually be the recipient of the apology, as a way of censuring the original offender: "For example, if someone is rudely interrupted, he might say: 'I'm sorry if the middle of my sentence interrupted the beginning of yours'" (Dundes 1967).

While some view the apology as an alternative to the payment of monetary damages, others consider restitution itself as a symbolic form of apology.[5] While apology and restitution are not mutually exclusive, it is unclear whether the payment is widely regarded as being part of the notion of an apology.

The question is whether the general concept of apology is transcultural, and if it is, whether it has the same elements in all societies. Existing scholarship makes it difficult to determine this.

Cross-Cultural Research on Speech Acts

There has been a longstanding debate in sociolinguistics about whether there are universal rules to language. The works of philosophers like Austin and linguists like Brown and Levinson are usually cited to support the claim that there are universal patterns to languages (Hill et al. 1986). Others, however, have questioned this presumption.[6] Anna Wierzbicka, who has done some of the best work in this area, notes the "astonishing ethnocentrism" in studies of speech acts (Wierzbicka 1985b). She challenges scholars' use of patterns in the English language to generalize about language rules across the globe:

Consider, for example, the following assertion (Clark and Schunk 1980: 111). When people make requests, they tend to make them indirectly. They generally avoid imperatives like *Tell me the time*, which are direct requests, in preference for questions like *Can you tell me the time?* or assertions like *I'm trying to find out what time it is*, which are indirect requests. It is clear that the authors based their observations on English alone; they take it for granted that what seems to hold for the speakers of English must hold for "people generally." Throughout this paper, I will try to show that statements such as the one quoted above are based on an optical illusion: it is not people in general who behave in the way described, it is the speakers of English." (Wierzbacka 1985b: 145)

When trying to document the "cultural logic" of language systems, the terminology must be precise and specific. Wierzbicka makes this point, noting the tendency of Western scholars to refer to Anglo-Saxon cultural norms as "direct" or "blunt" and to Non-Western norms as "indirect." Her own study showed that English norms, as compared with Polish norms, favor indirectness. Yet, what this suggests is that this characterization of "indirectness" is virtually meaningless. Drawing on Wierzbicka's insights, a number of doctoral dissertations have taken as their starting point the notion that one must investigate rules governing language use in their cultural context (Mulamba 1991; Wagner 1999; Bataineh 2004; Svina 2002).

Not only are there methodological questions about the transcultural application of linguistic terms, there are also different connotations to phrases even within the same language group. For example, Dell Hymes has observed that British "thank you" differs from American "thank you" (1971). Whereas this phrase in American English connotes an expression of gratitude, in England it also has come to mean a way of marking the end of certain interactions. Coulmas (1981) adds that in Australian English it can mean a verbalized punctuation when it occurs three times in succession. A conductor sells a ticket and says thank you when handing over the ticket; the passenger in turn says thank you upon receiving the ticket; and finally, the conductor says thank you again.

Humor is also markedly different. One riddle illustrates cultural variation in humor:

There was an international convention being held in one of the large New York city hotels. During one of the breaks, an Englishman was wandering around the lobby and began talking to a bellhop (hotel porter in English usage). During the conversation the bellhop said, "I have a riddle for you: I am the son of my father and the father of my son. Who am I? The Englishman thought for a while and then said "Blimey, you've really got me stumped on that one. I give up. Who are you?" The bell hop replied "I'm me!" The Englishman broke up: "By George, that's really good, extremely funny." A few months later the same Englishman was back in England and talking with some of his colleagues there, telling of his trip to America. "While I was in America I really heard a funny one. I bet you can't figure this one out.: "I am the son of my father and the father of my son. Who am I?" His friends thought for a while and they finally said that they couldn't figure it out. So he quickly replied, "Well, strange as it may seem, I am a bellhop in the lobby of a New York hotel." (Dundes 1987: 154–55)

This text illustrates that the Englishmen misremembers American folklore, revealing a different sense of humor and also a cross-cultural misunderstanding.

Another way of demonstrating how a single speech act can vary across cultures comes from research on compliments. Nessa Wolfson's (1981) essay "Compliments in Cross-Cultural Perspective" reveals that different societies have divergent traditions with respect to paying compliments. For instance, Athabaskan Indians' joking behavior about American compliments reveals that they are embarrassed by what they regard as excessive complimenting in American culture (Basso 1979). This research on "cultural ways of speaking" shows that clashes between interactional styles can lead to cross-cultural miscommunication. Words do have meaning, but words do not exist in a vacuum. Rather, they must be viewed within their contextual setting. Unfortunately, much of the scholarly literature on apologies has ignored the context in which apologies have been given—as well as those in which apologies have been received.

Cultural Divergence in Apologizing

Although fascinating work exists on the cross-cultural use of apologies, it tends to concentrate on strategies of language use, how frequently apologies are made in a given society, and the difficulty of grasping rules for apologies for those learning to speak a new language.[7] Some studies compare and contrast usage across groups. Evidently, Spanish speakers apologize more than English speakers and Hebrew speakers apologize the least often.[8] Unfortunately, there is a dearth of information on broader cultural differences concerning apologies.[9] Moreover, as Aaron Lazare notes, despite widespread interest in the status of apologies in different societies, no comprehensive treatment of the subject exists (Lazare 2004).

One of the more intriguing sources on the subject is a doctoral dissertation completed in 2004, which provides a comparative analysis of American and Jordanian use of apology strategies. The main finding is that

> Jordanians used more types of the expression of remorse to the extent that the researcher felt their responses were exaggerated at times. Although both Jordanians and Americans used the statement of remorse, accounts, and reparation as their primary apology strategies, they differ in the use of the other strategies. Unlike Americans, Jordanians used the strategy of promising not to repeat offense more than compensation in an attempt to talk their way out of the offense instead of paying for what they had done. They also used two strategies that were not seen in Americans' responses, namely invoking Allah's (God's) name and using proverbs and sayings; . . . while Jordanians blamed others more than themselves for the offense in question, Americans blamed themselves and others almost equally. (Bataineh 2004: 193–94)

Although Bataineh's study offers some insights as to different uses of apologies by the speaker or wrongdoer, it does not consider the extent to which the hearer or victim accepts the apology. This, however, is typical of comparative studies of apologies.

Another difficulty is that there are different forms of apology within the same society. Hang Zhang (2001) notes that there are six different levels of apology in the Chinese language. In Japanese culture, there are multiple forms of apologizing including "quasi-apologies," "preventive apologies," "grateful apologies" and others (Mizutani and Mizutani 1987; Coulmas 1981; Sugimoto 1999). Another difficulty associated with identifying speech acts in Japanese and in English is that some apologies that are appropriate in the former would be construed as expressions of gratitude in the latter (Coulmas 1981). Furthermore, from the Japanese point-of-view, apologies serve not only to address past misconduct but also to anticipate future transgressions.

One comparative analysis of apologizing behavior reveals that Japanese prefer more direct and more extreme apologies accompanied by compensation whereas Americans' apologies were somewhat less direct and less extreme, and Americans often explained their behavior rather than simply admitting to it (Barnlund and Yoshioko 1990). Another study concluded that the Japanese believe they should apologize for members of their group, which includes a broader social network than Americans who include only self, spouse (only when the person is incapacitated), small children, and pets (Sugimoto 1999).

As the literature on cultural differences in apologizing tends to compare two groups, it does not allow one to draw any real conclusions of a global nature. Much of the literature summarizes interviews in which subjects are asked to explain their reasons for apologizing. It attempts to show that different social contexts call for apologies in different societies (Shigeta 1972; Lipson 1994). However, a few significant scholarly contributions deserve special mention for their insights into the comparative analysis of apologies.

In an important cross-cultural consideration of apology, "The Social Contexts of Apology in Dispute-Settlement: A Cross-Cultural Study" (1986), Leticia Hickson contends that: cultures differ in the extent to which their members stress apology as a redressive technique and proceeds to advance this argument with a case study from Fiji. As part of her analysis of apologies as a reconciliation ritual, she offers three hypotheses: (1) apology is an important dispute resolution mechanism in hierarchical societies; (2) the apology plays a prominent role in such societies because of the tendency for disputes to be characterized as challenges to one's position in the status hierarchy; and (3) apology serves as a means of avoiding punishment because it defuses anger. This is a key point:

In hierarchical societies . . . even if the offended individual's anger is not completely assuaged by the tribute offered in an apology, the social pressure on an individual to respond to a show of humility and deference with tolerance and forbearance means that the offender's apology is certain to be accepted and punishment avoided. (Hickson 1986: 286–87)

Hickson begins with the premise that apology is clearly associated with a hierarchical social structure, and attempts to test the strength of this relationship. Her conclusion is this:

cultural emphasis on apology in dispute resolution reflects a more general interpersonal response or strategy within that culture. Apology is essentially a diplomatic, or politic, act; that is, it is a way in which one can secure one's own interests by being sensitive to and responsive to the interests of another. It is an act in which one acknowledges oneself to be at the mercy of another and often exploits this subordinate position. (1986: 290)

Her analysis emphasizes the ways in which apology functions to restore interpersonal relations. She explicitly mentions that the person offering the apology is in a subordinate position and seeks to exploit this position.

Hickson expected to find a positive relationship between the use of apology and responsibility training. She suggests that the failure to find such a relationship occurred because those coding the data had different ways of defining responsibility. Another factor is variation in the content of apologies across cultures. She provides the example of Iran where apologies are frequent but include an excuse designed to absolve the offender of responsibility and to lay blame on a third party who led the alleged offender astray. In Japan, the apology includes a statement to the effect that the offender was powerless to control his actions. Even in the U.S., where there is a tendency to shun apologies, when they are made they are often accompanied by excuses for the offense, as the apologizing party oftens seeks to shift blame or responsibility to the offended individual.

Apologies in Japanese Culture

A great deal of the literature on apologies focuses on their prevalence in Japanese culture. Although most accept that there is a Japanese proclivity toward apology, some attempt to downplay this tendency (Ohbuchi 1999; Dudden 2002). The leading scholar on Japanese apologies, Naomi Sugimoto, regards apologies as a distinctive Japanese behavioral pattern central to social life. She conducted a study comparing Japanese and U.S. etiquette manuals, which found that whereas most Japanese books had an entire chapter devoted to apologies, only one American book did (Sugimoto 1999). Evidently, apologies assume such a great importance in Japanese culture that in the Japanese version of Little Red Riding-Hood, the wolf has to ask for forgiveness via an apology (Lanham and Simura 1967).

The importance of apologies in Japanese society is reflected in practices observed in the legal system. Judges have been known to refuse to allow defendants to leave their courtrooms unless they offer an apology (Haley 1998). When defendants do apologize, some receive little or no punishment as a result of performing the culturally requisite behavior. John Haley explains:

Confession, repentance, and absolution provide the underlying theme of the Japanese criminal process. At every stage, from initial police investigation through formal proceedings, an individual suspected of criminal conduct gains by confessing, apologizing, and throwing himself upon the mercy of the authorities. (Haley 1982: 269)

A commonly cited incident illustrates the failure of Americans to grasp this requirement. Two American soldiers were prosecuted for the sexual assault of a Japanese woman. On the advice of their Japanese attorney, the defendants paid her $1,000 and obtained a letter from her stating that she had been fully compensated and that she absolved them of responsibility. As the woman left Japan with another U.S. soldier, the attorney argued that his clients were denied a fair trial because they were prosecuted solely on the basis of an affidavit and had no way to cross-examine her. When the judge asked if the defendants had anything to say, they replied: "We are not guilty, your honor." Unimpressed by their refusal to accept responsibility for their conduct, the judge imposed the maximum sentence. Although the attorney was knowledgeable about American law, he had not considered that the Americans would not realize they were expected to apologize (Haley 1982).

With respect to civil matters, apologies are thought to reduce the likelihood of lawsuits. For example, after the 1982 Japan Air Lines crash in Tokyo Bay, the president of the airlines met with victims and families. The apology and payment of compensation evidently obviated the need for litigation (Wagatsuma and Rossett 1986; Haley 1998).

These data raise the question of whether the "omnipresence" of apologies in Japanese culture makes a state apology more or less significant. The frequency of apologies could render them trivial, or it could show the acceptance of this mechanism of resolving conflicts. Commentators sometimes note that even though apologies between individuals are common in Japan, paradoxically the government has been reluctant to offer public apologies.[10]

While much scholarship concentrates on apologies in interpersonal relationships, other work examines state-to-state apologies (Er 2002). Differing understandings of the rules governing apologies are clear in interstate relations. For instance, when the *USS Greenville*, a nuclear submarine off the coast of Hawaii, accidentally attacked the *Ehime Maru*, killing nine members aboard, this resulted in a serious cultural misunderstanding. Although President Bush apologized to Japan the day after the accident and Secretary of State Colin Powell apologized to the Japanese foreign minister, the American responsible, Commander Scott Waddle, was slow to apologize. When he eventually did so, it was not regarded as meaningful. His first apology, a letter conveyed through his attorney, was not deemed a full apology in Japanese. When Waddle resigned as part of an effort to minimize his punishment, this infuriated the Japanese, who wanted an apology from him—not as an individual, but as a member of the U.S. navy.

Subsequently, Waddle wrote a book in which he claimed that his navy lawyer prevented him for making a prompt apology because of concerns over liability. Ironically, the U.S. had to pay a settlement of $13.9 million to the families of those killed, possibly higher than it would have been had Waddle apologized and resigned immediately.

Ambivalence Toward Apologies in the U.S.

In the United States, apologies are strongly discouraged because of the litigious nature of American society. Lawyers typically discourage their clients from making apologies to avoid liability on the part of their clients. Because saying "I'm sorry" could require paying damages, individuals in car accidents are warned by insurance agents not to make an apology. Some scholars who recommend use of alternative dispute resolution (ADR) have claimed that apologies should be made in this context because it helps the injured party heal. They realize, however, that this policy could be costly, and have, therefore, advocated the adoption of rules of evidence that would render apologies made in ADR inadmissible in court (Neckers 2002). Some states have, in fact, enacted apologies exemption laws to prevent the introduction of this evidence.

Another difficulty with encouraging greater use of apologies is that strategic use of apologies arguably robs them of their moral power, at least from the American perspective.[11] Americans do not regard apologies as valid if they are not sincere, heartfelt or voluntary (Joyce 1999).[12] Hence, if they are used to avoid litigation and the payment of damages, they may not be genuine (Brown 2004). One scholar put it eloquently when he said:

> When the performer of apology is protected from the consequences of the performance through carefully crafted statements and legislative directives, the moral thrust of apology is lost. The potential for meaningful healing through apologetic discourse is lost when the moral component of the syllogistic process in which apology is situated is erased for strategic reasons. (Taft 2000: 1155)

Questions Concerning the Conceptualization of Apologies

To determine whether the apology is a meaningful transcultural concept, it is advisable to juxtapose this idea with other moral notions. For example, some have suggested that there is a relationship between the apology and "saving face." That is, the apology is a social mechanism that permits the repair of damage to reputation. However, this may not help create a universal understanding of apology inasmuch as the concept of "face" is complicated and may not be useful outside the context of Chinese culture and those Asian societies that have been influenced by it (Hu 1944; Ho 1976).

Some try to link the concept of face with biological data on blushing: "the very act of being embarrassed can itself serve as an apology, providing a visual sign that the person acknowledges responsibility for the untoward act" (Edelmann 1994: 240). While some individuals who realize that their conduct is inappropriate may feel embarrassed, not all of them will make an apology. Whether one accepts this line of arguments depends on whether one conceptualizes an apology as a speech act requiring a verbal utterance.

Others maintain that the apology may serve different purposes in "guilt" societies as opposed to "shame" societies. This distinction emphasizes individual internalization of the recognition of a norm violation for the former and concern about the impact of the transgression on the group for the latter. It is unclear to what extent, if at all, this distinction elucidates the relative importance of apologies in different cultures.

Some writers emphasize the importance of making an apology and promising not to repeat the mistake. Whether an apology requires an explicit promise not to engage in the proscribed behavior is not obvious. If there is a connection between state apologies and avoidance of future misconduct, this would lend more credence to those who applaud officials for making apologies.

The Trend Toward State Apologies

Even if there are cultural variations in the meaning of apologies, toward the end of the twentieth century states in different regions offered apologies for atrocities committed by their governments. State apologies became possible in part because of the widespread adoption of laws authorizing the disclosure of government misdeeds. For example, Freedom of Information Act requests led to the release of documents that exposed government misconduct. Access to information makes it possible to expose governmental abuses for which political leaders may feel compelled to offer apologies.

Another factor that may explain the trend is that individuals had a greater expectation that states would be held accountable. Related to this expectation of state accountability is a desire to set the historical record straight, which requires that a state acknowledge responsibility for perpetrating human rights abuses (Graff 2004). The controversy surrounding the public issuance of a state apology can lead to an educational process that can be highly beneficial.

Even though there is a widespread assumption that the trend is a desirable development, it is possible that apologies may not satisfy the desire for justice. More data are needed to determine how apologies are viewed in different cultural contexts. Without proof that apologies are acceptable as a means of dealing with human rights violations, there are reasons to think state apologies may be inadequate to the task of responding to historic injustices. I turn now to these concerns.

Difficulties with State Apologies

The analysis of apology as a mechanism of dispute settlement reveals that it may be an illusory means of resolving a conflict. The purpose of offering an apology is to repair an injury, thereby restoring social equilibrium. One serious difficulty with this approach to redressing an individual's grievance against a state is that in reality there is no way to restore such a balance. That is, the state will also wield much more power than the individual. So, whereas an apology between one individual and another or between one state and another of comparative power could result in some form of equilibrium, this is inconceivable in the relationship between a state and an individual.

If a state apology is offered as an alternative to the payment of monetary damages, then it may appear to be an empty gesture. Victims of gross violations of human rights deserve reparations as well as an apology. To the extent that governments expect to avoid paying compensation by merely apologizing, this is a development that deserves to be questioned.

Those who have suffered terrible human rights violations certainly want the historical record to show that they were not at fault. Victims should not be stigmatized because they were tortured or victims of mass rapes. And yet it is too easy for governments to shirk their responsibilities by offering meaningless apologies.

One problem is that the empirical data do not reveal the extent to which the public is satisfied with apologies in different societies. It is unknown whether or not those injured regard apologies as a valid means of settling disputes. The trend to greater use of apologies has occurred without regard to whether or not they satisfy a social need for justice.[13]

Another question is whether state apologies can accomplish the goal of restoring group harmony. The scholarship on apologies makes mention of the connection between the apology and the "social goal of maintaining harmony between the S and H" (Olshtain 1989). Yet, this could simply be a tool of pacifying an oppressed and disgruntled citizenry. In her compelling work *Harmony Ideology* (1990), Laura Nader argues that the obsession with harmony masks a political strategy to suppress dissent: "Harmony ideologies may be used to suppress peoples by socializing them toward conformity in colonial contexts, or they may be used to resist external control." Furthermore, she argues, state use of alternative mechanisms of dispute resolution should be viewed with suspicion because siphoning cases away from legal institutions thereby avoids setting precedents that can be used against the government in subsequent cases (at least in common law systems).

Apologies and Forgiveness

Another important issue is the relationship between apologies and forgiveness (Tavuchis 1991). In her brilliant analysis, Martha Minow explains the relationship in these terms: "Nevertheless, forgiveness, while not compelled by apology, may depend upon it (Minow 1991: 114). She goes on to say: "Apologies explicitly acknowledge wrongdoing and afford victims the chance both to forgive or to refuse to forgive" (Minow 1998: 116). Similarly, Aaron Lazare emphasizes the connection when he refers to the "causal relationship between apology and forgiveness" (Lazare 2004: 247).

Yet, like the notion of apology, it is by no means clear that forgiveness itself is a universal concept. Nevertheless, it is conceivable that the basic notion of accepting responsibility for individual or group wrongdoing and requesting that the injured party or group absolve them of this responsibility is found in other belief systems. The problem is that existing scholarship on comparative religious ethics makes it difficult to determine how widespread the concept of forgiveness is.

Some scholars maintain that forgiveness is part of three major world religions: Christianity, Islam and Judaism. Schimmel (2002) makes this point, acknowledging, however, that the circumstances under which it is considered appropriate to forgive differ. According to Schimmel, whereas repentance is not a necessary precondition for divine forgiveness in Christianity, it is for these other religions. The idea of repentance is relevant to this analysis because apologizing is one stage of the process of repentance:

> We should know, though, that our repentance for the wrongs we have done to others can be emotionally and morally valuable for us and them. In our culture, and in many others, there is an expectation that if we hurt others we should apologize, whether or not we are asked to do so. Sincere apologies are stepping stones to healing and reconciliation. (Schimmel 2002: 148–49)

Yet Schimmel's assertion that many societies expect apologies for wrongdoing is not supported by data. Other statements he makes about apologies are also suspect. For instance, he claims that "Apologies are best made by the offender to his victim, face-to-face." This is inconsistent with studies suggesting that gaze aversion varies by culture (Edelmann and Iwawaki 1987).

Some commentators make reference to the concept of forgiveness in Islam (Moucarry 2004; Sardar 2000). Carol Schersten LaHurd notes the frequent mention of the idea:

The concordance to the Arabic text of the Qur'an shows over sixty uses of *ghafara*, "to forgive" (most describe the activity of God) and over forty of *istaghfara*, "to ask forgiveness." More significantly the Qur'an describes God as "All-Forgiving" [Ghaffaar] more than 100 times. (LaHurd 1996: 288)

With respect to person-to-person relations, she contends that forgiveness is valued in this context as well. For example, although the death penalty is the punishment for murder, a family may accept compensation or blood money instead of demanding an execution.

While government officials deserve praise for offering apologies that acknowledge responsibility for atrocities, the determination of whether they are purely symbolic or substantive depends on the extent to which victims take satisfaction in them. Although some victims may find it difficult to forgive representatives of the government who were not themselves the perpetrators, insofar as the state inherits the obligations of predecessor states, it is the social construct of the state that must be forgiven. As Mark Amstutz astutely remarks: "forgiveness is important because it provides a basis for political reconciliation" (Amstutz 2005: 87).

If reconciliation requires acknowledgment of the wrong before requesting forgiveness, then offering apologies even to victims who are dead may be worthwhile. State apologies appear to serve as public confessions that serve multiple purposes:

The public confession is a way of letting the community know that you are truly remorseful and would have apologized and asked forgiveness from your victim if only he were still alive. Moreover, since many offenses against others are breaches of communal norms, the public confession is a declaration of acceptance of the community's norms. (Schimmel 2002: 156)

Are Reparations Preferable?

This critique of apologies may rely on an ethnocentric assumption that the payment of money damages to victims is a better response than state apologies. Some, however, have called into question the notion that restitution itself is entirely satisfactory. According to one legal scholar, there is a hidden, more insidious, side to reparations. First, the money is inevitably an inadequate sum when one considers the nature of the injustice. Second, the payment of reparations to one group—for example, Japanese Americans who were interned—may generate inter-ethnic conflict when meritorious claims by others—for example, African Americans requesting reparations for slavery—fail. Finally, when governments pay reparations, they do not address deeper structural social problems like racism (Yamamoto 1998).

In some contexts, those who have suffered an injustice would prefer an acknowledgement that the government committed a wrong (Govier and

Verwoerd 2002). For instance, as Turkey has never acknowledged the Armenian genocide, an apology by the Turkish government to Armenians would have tremendous significance. The Prime Minister of Australia was criticized for offering only a personal apology rather than a national apology to the "Stolen Generations" of indigenous people (Augoustinos, Lecouteur, and Soyland 2002). In a lawsuit documented in *A Civil Action*, the mother (and lead plaintiff) whose son died from leukemia wanted an apology, not money (Latif 2001). Some of the "comfort women" in Japan declined to accept payments initially because they sought an official apology along with legal compensation (Field 2005).

Yet it is not always the case that reparations are preferable to apologies; the judgment as to what remedy is best depends on circumstances. Moreover, the cultural context where human rights violations have taken place will shape the perception of the appropriate state response.

There is, however, no reason why state apologies cannot go hand-in-hand with reparations. Or as Mark Amstutz, one of the leading scholars in the realm of restitution, has argued,

> The increasing use of apologies by public officials has perhaps cheapened their impact, especially since tangible reparations rarely support such declarations. If apologies are to serve as instruments of public repentance, the public expressions of contrition must be reinforced by acts of restitution and promises that future wrongdoing will not be repeated. (Amstutz 2005: 245 n. 41)

It is problematic, then, when states attempt to use the apology as a means of avoiding being held accountable in other ways.

Conclusion

Even though scholars discuss the apology as though this term has the same meaning in every society around the world, this presumption of universality is unwarranted given the lack of available data. Until comparative research is undertaken to determine the extent to which apologies are used and the meaning they have for peoples in different regions, one cannot decide whether state apologies for human rights violations are viable. The dearth of empirical data on cross-cultural status of apologies leaves us in a sorry state.

References

Amstutz, Mark R. 2005. *The Healing of Nations: The Promise and Limits of Political Forgiveness*. Lanham, Md.: Rowman and Littlefield.

Augoustinos, Martha, Amanda Lecouteur, and John Soyland. 2002. "Self-Sufficient Arguments in Political Rhetoric: Constructing Reconciliation and Apologizing to the Stolen Generation." *Discourse & Society* 13 (1): 105–42.

Barnlund, Dean C. and Miho Yoshioka. 1990. "Apologies: Japanese and American Styles." *International Journal of Intercultural Relations* 14: 193–205.
Basso, Keith H. 1979. *Portraits of "the Whiteman": Linguistic Play and Cultural Symbols Among the Western Apache.* Cambridge: Cambridge University Press.
Bataineh, Rula Rahmi. 2004. "A Cross-Cultural Study of the Speech Act of Apology in American English and Jordanian Arabic." Master's thesis, California State University, Dominguez Hills.
Bautista, Maria Lourdes S. 1979. "Apologies, Compliments, Directives, and Probes in Philipino Radio Dramas: An Exploratory Analysis of Philippine Speech Acts." *Philippine Journal of Linguistics* 10: 45–62.
Blum-Kulka, Shoshana, Juliane House, and Gabriele Kasper, eds.. 1989. *Cross-Cultural Pragmatics: Requests and Apologies.* Norwood, N.J.: Ablex.
Brown, Jennifer Gerarda. 2004. "The Role of Apology in Negotiation." *Marquette Law Review* 87: 665–73.
Choi, Dai-Kown. 2000. "Freedom of Conscience and the Court-Ordered Apology for Defamatory Remarks." *Cardozo Journal of International and Comparative Law* 8: 205–24.
Clark, Herbert H. and Dale H. Schunk. 1980. "Polite Responses to Polite Requests." *Cognition* 8: 111–43.
Cordella, Marisa. 1991. "Spanish Speakers Apologizing in English: A Cross-Cultural Pragmatics Study." *Australian Review of Applied Linguistics* 14 (2): 115–38.
Coulmas, Florin. 1981. "'Poison to Your Soul': Thanks and Apologies Contrastively Viewed." In *Conversational Routine: Explorations in Standardized Communication Situations and Prepatterned Speech,* ed. Florin Coulmas. The Hague: Mouton.
Dudden, Alexis. 2002. "The Politics of Apology Between Japan and Korea." In *Truth Claims: Representation and Human Rights,* ed. Mark P. Bradley and Patrice Petro. Rutgers, N.J: Rutgers University Press.
Dundes, Alan. 1967. "Some Minor Genres of American Folklore." *Southern Folklore Quarterly* 31: 31–32.
———. 1987. "Misunderstanding Humor: An American Stereotype of the Englishman." In Dundes, *Cracking Jokes: Studies of Sick Humor Cycles and Stereotypes.* Berkeley, Calif.: Ten Speed Press. 154–55.
Edelmann, Robert J. 1994. "Embarrassment and Blushing: Factors Influencing Face-Saving Strategies." In *The Challenge of Facework: Cross-Cultural and Interpersonal Issues,* ed. Stella Ting-Toomey. Albany: State University of New York Press.
Edelmann, Robert J. and Saburo Iwawaki. 1987. "Self-Reported Expression and Consequences of Embarrassment in the United Kingdom and Japan." *Psychologia* 30.
Er, Lam Peng. 2002. "The Apology Issue: Japan's Differing Approaches Toward China and South Korea." *American Asian Review* 20 (3): 31–54.
Field, Norma. 1995. "The Stakes of Apology." *Japan Quarterly* 42 (4): 405–18.
Fraser, Bruce. 1981. "On Apologizing." In *Conversational Routine: Explorations in Standardized Communication Situations and Prepatterned Speech,* ed. Florian Coulmas. The Hague: Mouton. 259–71.
Fuentes-Mascuñana, Evelyn. 1998. "An Exploratory Analysis of the Speech Act of Apology and Its Associated Socio-Cultural Factors." *Silliman Journal* 39 (1): 6–26.
Gill, Kathleen. 2000. "The Moral Functions of an Apology." *Philosophical Forum* 31 (1): 11–27.
Govier, Trudy and Wilhelm Verwoerd. 2002a. "The Promise and Pitfalls of Apology." *Journal of Social Philosophy* 33 (1): 67–82.

———. 2002b. "Taking Wrongs Seriously: A Qualified Defence of Public Apologies." *Saskatchewan Law Review* 65: 139–62.
Graff, E. J. 2004. "All Apologies." *Radcliffe Quarterly* 89 (2): 10–13.
Haley, John O. 1982. "Sheathing the Sword of Justice in Japan: An Essay on Law Without Sanctions." *Journal of Japanese Studies* 8 (2): 265–81.
———. 1998. "Apology and Pardon: Learning from Japan." *American Behavioral Scientist* 41 (6): 842–67.
Hickson, Letitia. 1986. "The Social Contexts of Apology in Dispute Settlement: A Cross-Cultural Study." *Ethnology* 25 (4): 283–94.
Hill, Beverly, Sachiko Ide, Shoko Ikuta, Akiko Kawasaki, and Tsunao Ogino. 1986. "Universals of Linguistic Politeness: Quantitative Evidence from Japanese and American English." *Journal of Pragmatics* 10 (3): 347–71.
Ho, David Yau-fai. 1976. "On the Concept of the Face." *American Journal of Sociology* 81 (4): 867–84.
Hu, Hsien Chin. 1944. "The Chinese Concepts of 'Face'." *American Anthropologist* 46 (1): 45–64.
Hymes, Dell H. 1971. "Sociolinguistics and the Ethnography of Speaking." In *Social Anthropology and Language*, ed. Edwin Ardener. London: Tavistock.
Joyce, Richard. 1999. "Apologizing." *Public Affairs Quarterly* 13: 159–73.
Kim, Duk-Young. 2001. "A Descriptive Analysis of Korean and English Apologies with Implications for Interlanguage Pragmatics." Doctoral dissertation, University of Florida.
LaHurd, Carol Schersten. 1996. "'So That the Sinner Will Repent': Forgiveness in Islam and Christianity." *Dialog* 35: 287–92.
Lanham, Betty B. and Masao Simura. 1967. "Folktales Commonly Told American and Japanese Children: Ethical Themes of Omission and Commission." *Journal of American Folklore* 80 (315): 33–48.
Latif, Elizabeth. 2001. "Apologetic Justice: Evaluating Apologies Tailored Toward Legal Solutions." *Boston University Law Review* 81 (1): 289–320.
Lazare, Aaron. 2004. *On Apology*. Oxford: Oxford University Press.
Lipson, Maxine. 1994. "Apologizing in Italian and English." *International Review of Applied Linguistics in Language Training* 32 (1): 19–39.
Minow, Martha. 1998. *Between Vengeance and Forgiveness: Facing History After Genocide and Mass Violence*. Boston: Beacon Press.
Mizutani, Osamu and Nobuko Mizutani. 1987. *How to Be Polite in Japanese*. Tokyo: Japanese Times.
Moucarry, Chawkat. 2004. *The Search for Forgiveness: Pardon and Punishment in Islam and Christianity*. Leicester: Inter-Varsity Press.
Mulamba, Kashama. 1991. "Apologizing and Complaining in Ciluba, French, and English: Speech Act Performance by Trilingual Speakers in Zaire." Ph.D. dissertation, Ball State University.
Nader, Laura. 1990. *Harmony Ideology: Justice and Control in a Zapotec Mountain Village*. Stanford, Calif.: Stanford University Press.
Neckers, Bruce W. 2002. "The Art of the Apology." *Michigan Bar Journal* 81 (1): 10–11.
Ohbuchi, Ken-Ichi. 1999. "A Social Psychological Analysis of Accounts: Toward a Universal Model of Giving and Receiving Accounts." In *Japanese Apology Across Disciplines*, ed. Naomi Sugimoto. Commack, N.Y.: Nova Science Publishers.
Olshtain, Elite. 1989. "Apologies Across Languages." In *Cross-Cultural Pragmatics: Requests and Apologies*, ed. Shoshana Blum-Kulka, Juliane House, and Gabriele Kasper. Norwood, N.J.: Ablex.

Sardar, Ziauddin. 2000. "I, a Muslim, forgive the Pope, but . . . " *New Statesman*, March 20.
Schimmel, Solomon. 2002. *Wounds Not Healed by Time: The Power of Repentance and Forgiveness*. New York: Oxford University Press.
Shigeta, Midori. 1972. "Ambiguity in Declining Requests and Apologizing." In *Intercultural Encounters with Japan*, ed. John C. Condon and Mitsuko Saito. Tokyo: Simul Press.
Sugimoto, Naomi. 1999a. "Norms of Apology Depicted in U.S. American and Japanese Literature on Manners and Etiquette." In *Japanese Apology Across Disciplines*, ed. Naomi Sugimoto. Commack, N.Y.: Nova Science Publishers.
———, ed. 1999b. *Japanese Apology Across Disciplines*. Commack, N.Y.: Nova Science Publishers.
Suszcynska, Malgorzata. 1999. "Apologizing in English, Polish, and Hungarian: Different Languages, Different Strategies." *Journal of Pragmatics* 31 (8): 1053–65.
Svina, Elena. 2002. "The Influence of American English on Russian Apologies." Master's thesis, University of California, Dominguez Hills.
Taft, Lee. 2000. "Apology Subverted: The Commodification of Apology." *Yale Law Journal* 109 (5): 1135–60.
Tavuchis, Nicholas. 1991. *Mea Culpa: A Sociology of Apology and Reconciliation*. Stanford, Calif.: Stanford University Press.
Trouillot, Michel-Rolph. 2000. "Abortive Rituals: Historical Apologies in the Global Era." *Interventions* 2 (2): 171–86.
Tukatsu, Masumi and Manabu Takechi. 1995. "The Eclipse of Showa Taboos and the Apology Resolution." *Japan Quarterly* 42 (5): 419–25.
Wagatsuma, Hiroshi and Arthur Rossett. 1986. "The Implications of Apology: Law and Culture in Japan and the United States." *Law and Society Review* 20 (4): 461–98.
Wagner, Lisa. 1999. "Towards a Sociopragmatic Characterization of Apologies in Mexican Spanish." Ph.D. dissertation, Ohio State University.
Weyeneth, Robert R. 2001. "The Power of Apology and the Process of Historical Reconciliation." *Public Historian* 23 (3): 9–38.
Wierzbicka, Anna. 1985a. *Cross-Cultural Pragmatics: The Semantics of Human Interaction*. Berlin: Mouton de Gruyter.
———. 1985b. "Different Cultures, Different Languages, Different Speech Acts: Polish vs. English." *Journal of Pragmatics* 9 (2–3): 145–78.
Wolfson, Nessa. 1981. "Compliments in Cross-Cultural Perspective." *TESOL Quarterly* 15: 117–24.
Yamamoto, Eric K. 1998. "Racial Reparations: Japanese American Redress and African American Claims." *Boston College Law Review* 40 (1): 476–523.
Zhang, Hang. 2001. "Culture and Apology: The Hainan Island Incident." *World Englishes* 20 (3): 383.

Chapter 5
Elements of a Road Map for a Politics of Apology

JEAN-MARC COICAUD AND JIBECKE JÖNSSON

The expectations put upon apology, as well as the stakes involved, are high. Acknowledging a wrong, admitting guilt, taking responsibility, recognizing suffering, but also seeking to reverse victimization, reestablish trust, empower the powerless, and end cycles of resentment, are some key elements in the process of apology. These elements have emerged as all the more important in recent decades, if not years, with the issue of apology becoming a significant sign post of national and international politics, as a way to recognize and attempt to amend past wrongs.[1]

The following pages aim to consider the complexities of apology and unpack the notion by touching on three main aspects. First, and very briefly, the issue of time, and how apology connects the present with the past. Second, what apology, from a theoretical point of view, aims to achieve for the issuer, the receiver (the primary victim), their relationship, as well as for society at large. Third, and finally, while recognizing the contribution that it can make to reconciliation, the questions that apologies leave unanswered, if not unaddressed.

Apology and Time: The Past Meets the Present

It is a constant refrain of those who want to evade accountability for past wrongs to argue that the past is a self-contained reality, disconnected from the present. In this context, it is said that the past is best left behind. In contrast, apology rests upon a unified understanding of time. The possibility and the need for an apology presupposes not only that the past and present are connected, that the past continues in and has bearing on the present, but also that it shapes the future. And the more this continuum is denied, the more the past will haunt the present, and its pathologies persist (Rousso 2002).

Attempts to come to terms with the past are an implicit indication of how human rights extend over time. Of course, what is right, and therefore what is viewed as a violation, evolves throughout history. What is conceived as a wrong today may not have been so yesterday. The historicity of law and of the culture of right is an illustration of this reality. However, by seeking accountability for wrongs committed far in the past, the mechanism of apology recognizes and gives a certain a-temporality (which amounts to a form of transcendence) to human rights, even when these were only recently formally recognized and institutionalized in the body of law.

The growing importance of the individual and of the rights of the individual in recent decades has reinforced this state of affairs. Norms of human rights have been instrumental in the emergence of the individual as an actor and a rights bearer. That the universal respect of human rights has increasingly become a benchmark of good governance has opened the door to the possibility of condemning present, but also past, violations. To this adds the evolution of political conditions in the past twenty years or so. Victims, families or representatives of victims have increasingly called upon norms of human rights to challenge states nationally and internationally. Unable to continue to overlook their wrongdoings, states have been forced to adopt a more self-critical attitude and the offering of an apology has emerged as the minimal right thing to do.

Unpacking Apology

In this section three sets of questions are addressed. First, what is an apology? What does the offering of an apology entail, and what does it imply to be on the receiving end? Moreover, what is the significance of the relationship created between the issuer and the receiver of the apology? Second, what are the expected benefits of an apology, especially when it is accepted? Third, how to assess apology at the collective or political level, as opposed to the individual?

Apology: The Issuer, the Receiver and Their Relationship

At the most basic level, apology can be defined as a written or spoken expression of regret, sorrow and remorse for having wronged, insulted, failed and/or injured another. It is an act, speech or writing, that implies a certain relationship between someone who has caused another pain (the wrongdoer, who becomes the issuer), and someone who has been wronged (the victim, who becomes the receiver).

For the offering of apology to have a real value, it is essential that the remorse conveyed is genuine. In itself, this somehow requires a sense of guilt, the acute feeling and consciousness of having wronged someone. As Karl Jaspers indicates in his study on German guilt following the Holocaust, guilt unfolds at various levels. Although they are intimately related, it is useful to distinguish between them. In this perspective, Jaspers argues that guilt takes the forms of criminal guilt (as a result of rights violations), political guilt (following criminal actions conducted by political leaders in the name of the state), moral guilt (based on the assumption that acts are ultimately the products of morally responsible individuals), and metaphysical guilt (expressing the betrayal of the solidarity that exists between all fellow human beings and which makes all co-responsible for any occuring injustices) (Jaspers 2002). While criminal and political guilt are meant to be treated with exterior tools, namely, legally imposed punishment and political accountability, what Jaspers identifies as moral and metaphysical guilt has to be dealt with first and foremost from the inside. Following self-assessment and self-understanding, it is penance and humility that can bring renewal. At stake here is the ability of the perpetrator to come to terms with his responsibility in the wrong committed, and to reconcile with himself (and others).

If the issuer of the apology is important, even more important is the receiver of the apology. Archbishop Desmond Tutu, who served as the chairman of the South African Truth and Reconciliation Commission (TRC), gives a striking illustration of this by recalling the testimony of a black woman to the TRC that describes how her husband was tortured to death by policemen. The woman made it clear that no commission or government could forgive on her behalf. "Only I, eventually could do it. And I am not ready to forgive, or for forgiveness." In other words, although apology calls for someone to issue it, until the individual to whom it is directed is willing to receive and accept it, apology remains incomplete; a message that fails to reach its addressee. Thus, the fate of the apology and that of the one issuing the apology depends upon the victim's willingness to accept it.

Provided that the person to whom the apology is offered is open to receive it, the process of apology is made of three defining elements. First, the receiver has to recognize being wronged. This is not always without difficulty as victimization can go so deep and be so painful that the victim is blinded to the violation inflicted. Second, the actor responsible for the wrong has to be identified. Putting a face and a name on the wrongdoer and the inflicted trauma helps validate a sense of victimhood that is not directed against oneself, that is to say, that is not self-destructive. Third, the apology empowers the victim. From being on the receiving end of a wrong, the apology has now put the victim in a somewhat commanding position.

An apology is a reciprocal act that depends on the relation between the issuer and the receiver, one asking for forgiveness while making a promise, the other receiving the offering and, if not forgiving, then at least being open to try and do so. This parallels the fact that it takes two to experience a wrong; one committing it and another suffering from it. As such, the relationship between the issuer and the receiver of the apology serves as a reenaction of the past, but this time as a way to come to terms with the wrong which has been committed. And it is from the positive outcome of this relationship, with the issuer genuinely apologizing and the receiver being as much as possible willing to accept it, that the benefits of the apology can be drawn.

The Personal and Social Benefits of Apology

More specifically, and more systematically, what are the personal and social benefits of apology? Although the two dimensions work hand in hand and consequently are difficult to dissociate in practice, the imperative of clarity requires at least a theoretical distinction between benefits at the personal and social level.

On the personal level, a distinction between the inter and intra-personal aspect has to be made. When apology goes forward successfully, the relationship between the wrongdoer and the victim is improved. Indeed, an apology tries to open a dialogue to give way to some sort of accomodation and sharing experience which, assuming that the apology is sincere, contributes to ease antogonistic feelings. Moreover, by helping to make sense of the wrong, an apology is part of an explanatory scheme that introduces a form of mutual understanding. In the best scenario, the deflation of tension between the wrongdoer and the victim leads to a mutual trust.

Nevertheless, this does not mean that all is well in the interpersonal relationship. For the victim, pain (psychological and/or physical) may persist, allowing resentment toward the wrongdoer to be present and likely to surface on occasions. As for the issuer of the apology, the fact that the apology is accepted, although it may reduce the sense of guilt, does not (and should not) eliminate it. A sense of awkwardness is therefore prone to be a permanent feature of the interpersonal relationship.

The improvement of the relationship between the issuer and the receiver tends to be proportional to the intrapersonal benefits that apology brings to both. Because, while a successful apology is about reconciling the wrongdoer and the victim with one another, it is also, and ultimately, more about reconciling with oneself. This is true to the point that for an apology to have a substantial and lasting positive impact as a whole, greater importance has to be given to the latter. In other words, reconciliation with one another is only tentative until one has reconciled with oneself. The fact that the interpersonal benefits of apology are low when after the apology the wrongdoer and the victim essentially continue to be at war with and within themselves, serves as a case in point.

As alluded to before, this does not imply that at the intrapersonal level a successful apology has the power to turn back the clock as if nothing had ever happened. Once the wrong has taken place, a state of innocence has been lost, which not even the best of apologies can reverse. However, the dynamic of apology is an opportunity to aim for a state of mind in which the light and carefree character of innocence can be replaced by a sense of gravity and humility. The gain attached to this change is not to be underestimated. When an apology is succesful, the awareness of, and sensitivity to, vulnerability that springs from acknowledging that the evil of wrondoing and being wronged is a concrete possibility, creates both for the wrongdoer and the victim an opportunity to improve their ability to better be present to themselves. In the process, the capacity to connect better with one another, and with reality in general, is opened. In this perspective, apology can allow the wrongdoer and the victim to break away from their respective self-centeredness and put them on the path of understanding better how responsibility toward others is part and parcel of responsibility toward oneself.

We can see how the benefits for the past and the present translate into future social benefits. Helping to prevent a possible reversal of roles between the wrongdoer and the victim serves the social environment in the long run. A successful apology gives the victim the option of not reproducing the wrong by hindering unaddressed pain from translating into resentment that risks leading the victim to take matters into his or her own hands. As such, apology can prevent society from becoming a succession of "cycles of hatred" (Minow 2003). These cycles are all the more dangerous and destructive considering that, in the structure of the social environment, they are part and parcel of a blurred demarcation between the wrongdoer and the victim, as well as between paranoia and reality, in the context of which the wrongdoer sees him or herself as a victim.[2] As a whole, this not only hinders a reversal of the initial wrong, but it also impedes a strong sense of empathy and compassion for others and encourages more antagonistic relations and deeds.

From Individual Apology to State Apology

The first state apology offered in the twentieth century was by Germany, when signing the Treaty of Versailles at the end of World War I. However, it was a reluctant apology, limited to a forced signing of a treaty accepting responsibility and granting reparations without expressing a real sense of guilt or remorse. One world war later, Germany issued another apology, but this time more genuinely recognizing the damage caused. Since then, Germany has apologized on a variety of occasions for its war crimes. A handful of states followed in Germany's footsteps, apologizing for the war and genocides, some by paying reparations, others by speaking remorseful words, some by both. Till this day, claims for reparations and apologies are considered and debated. One well-known example is the still disputed issue of "comfort women" who were forced into sexual slavery by the Japanese Imperial Army prior to and during World War II.

But the need to come to terms with the past has, if anything, accelerated since World War II. Throughout the 1980s, a number of states shifted from dictatorships, in which basic liberties had been regularly violated, to democratic governments. Latin America is often identified as the region setting the precedent, followed by newly independent states created as a result of the collapse of the Soviet Union, and African countries which went through their own tumultuous transition in the aftermath of the Cold War. With these changes, the scope and range of ethical, legal and political difficulties of transition from dictatorship to democracy came to be increasingly realized. The problem of impunity became more and more of an issue, not only to new states but also to those still burdened by their colonial and world war pasts. As a result, states and the international community invested much time and effort into developing mechanisms with which to deal better with abusive and criminal pasts. Apologies became one of the tools for addressing the past.

It should come as no surprise that there is a complex relationship between apology, justice and politics, including moral, legal, and philosophical issues. The complexity of this matter is furthered by the fact that a state apology can never replace an apology offered by an individual. The differences between the encompassing level of the state and the level of the individual have an impact on apology. Consequently, beyond the straightforward nature of apology and the benefits that it generates, it is necessary to touch upon the problems that apology leaves within the political context.

Challenges for Apology in a Political Environment

There are three types of issues that are especially challenging for apology in the political context. First, there is the question of issuing a political apology for the unforgivable. This concerns the possibility of issuing an apology, as well as the possibility of receiving it, at the national and international level. Second, there is the trapping, or hijacking, of apology by political considerations using apology as a means to avoid accountability. Third, and finally, there is the issue of apology in a culturally pluralist world, within and among nations.

Political Apology and the Unforgivable

Not all wrongs are equal. Some are graver than others. Not surprisingly, the level of difficulty of apology varies with the degree of gravity of the wrong. The less serious the wrong, the easier to issue and receive an apology; the greater the wrong, the more difficult to apologize. In addition, it is not as if the value of apology is the same regardless of the level of the wrong, in fact, quite the contrary. Despite the fact that it is never worthless, the value of apology grows with the extent of the wrong. But then, if, as Jacques Derrida puts it, the value of apology is at the highest when the challenge is at the highest, when it is confronted with the impossible, namely to issue and accept an apology for an unforgivable wrong (Derrida 2001), the following question arises: how to ask for forgiveness, how to apologize for, and how to forgive a crime that is unforgivable?

In this regard, crimes against humanity represent the ultimate "unforgivable." Crimes against humanity are indeed unlike any other crime, murder included. These are crimes that go beyond hurting a personalized individual to attack and deny an entire group of people the right and even essence of being human. The unforgivable nature of crimes against humanity is that they challenge the humanity of being human. While the notion of crimes against humanity is the expression of a conscience and conceptualization of right and wrong which owe much to the commitment of democratic values to human rights, the fact that it defines the outer limit of evil sets it apart. For this reason more than any other, since the end of World War II crimes against humanity have served as the horizon of international justice, gaining meaning since the introduction of this concept in the Statute of the Tribunal of Nuremberg in 1945.

The first question to ask is this: is it possible—is it decent—to issue an apology for crimes against humanity? In a way, the sheer inhumanity of the crime, the lack of proportionality between the crime and anything else, makes the issuing of an apology somewhat absurd, if not obscene. For an apology, regardless of whether or not it hopes, let alone expects, to be accepted, presupposes that the issuer is not entirely disconnected from the intended receiver. In addition, it seeks to help the perpetrator to reintegrate, if only in the margins, the human community as well as his or her own humanity. But precisely, is it not true that the crime committed, while now making the victim more than ever a preeminent member of the human community (especially as someone to whom the greatest injustice has been committed, and to whom therefore the greatest justice is due), is also what has removed in a fundamental manner the perpetrator from the human experience and by and large forecloses his or her right to be part of it again? In these circumstances, if the perpetrator truly wishes to express remorse, perhaps asking him or her to adopt a state of genuine and uncomfortable guilt-ridden silence (because seen by all) might be a better way to express penance and remorse. After all, it is not sure that the relief that apology brings to the victim is substantial enough to justify the comfort that it brings to the perpetrator. In other words, when confronted with the unforgivable, could it be that the best apology for the perpetrator would be one amounting to being the captive of his or her crime, to remain, without the release of explicit public contrition, ceaselessly tormented by it?

The challenge of apology in the context of the unforgivable is equally difficult on the side of the victim. Although it falls upon the victim to accept the apology and to forgive, this is based on an assumption that is rarely at work after crimes against humanity, namely that the victim is in the position to forgive the unforgivable. Yet, what makes the unforgivable unforgivable is that it is merciless for the victim. The unforgivable is so because most of the time it prevents the victim from receiving and accepting the apology. This makes it extraordinarily challenging. Indeed, after a crime against humanity has been carried out, either the victims are no longer alive, consequently, not physically able to forgive, or the crime by annihilating the human capacity of those who survived to feel empathy for the perpetrator, puts forgiveness beyond reach. Surely, a third party can be called upon to represent the victims and act on their behalf. In fact, this is one of the engines of apology understood within the dynamic of reconciliation. But as the South African example referred to earlier indicates, no third party has *stricto sensu* the right to forgive. While the commemoration and memorialization of the victims help to address this problem, it does not solve it. As such, the difficulty of apology vis-à-vis the unforgivable is greater than the one of punishment and (material) reparation. Because these do not require the cooperation of the victim (the presence of the victim is not needed, rather, it is enough that there once was a victim for punishment and reparation to take place), they are less problematic to implement. Yet this is not to say that they have the capacity to establish a sense of proportionality between them and the crime.

The third way in which the unforgivable character of the crime undermines the possibility of apology is more political. It unfolds at two levels. First, the unforgivable transcends what politics can offer. Because society and life in society must go on, politics, when it is committed to recognize that a major wrong has been committed and refuses to simply forget, endorses the responsibility to seek and negotiate reconciliation among victims and perpetrators, as well as with the past. As a third party, political leaders and institutions are simply not in the position to truly forgive (or apologize for that matter). At best, reconciliation is prone to be tentative, especially since it has to be negotiated as shown in the South African granting of amnesty in exchange for reconciliation (Krog 2000). A second difficulty in the political environment is the dependency of apology upon power. Regardless of what it achieves, making apology part of the reconciliatory agenda requires a sovereign force that has the ability to decide that an apology is needed and has the resources to pursue it. This is parallel to the fact that to acknowledge a crime and a need for punishment, the backing of power is necessary. But such power is neither easy to find, nor to mobilize. The truth of the matter is that historically, by and large, such power has been and continues to be elusive. This is not surprising considering that enrolling power in the service of justice presupposes reversing a long duration of history in the context of which power to abuse has more often than not led to an abuse of power. As it tends to amount to an indictment of established powers, there is much reluctance to do so. A case in point is how the United Kingdom in the context of the United Nations Conference Against Racism in Durban in early September 2001, refused to accept the issuing of an apology of the European Union for the transatlantic slave trade. This not only shows that it is difficult to have power supporting the possibility of apology even in the case of crime against humanity, but also that power is eager to evade accountability and, if possible, manipulate apology to its advantage.

Apology and the Risk of Its Political Devaluation

Beyond the challenge of apologizing for the unforgivable, there are more difficulties associated with apology in the political context. These are by-products of the value of apology. What makes apology valuable is indeed what opens it to being politically denatured. In this regard, apology is particularly vulnerable to various types of misuse and the dangers that they entail: though intended as a mechanism of accountability, apology might well contribute to circumventing accountability; while meant to support the recognition and purging of a crime, apology might lead to the normalization of crime; and, although designed to facilitate the return to relatively normal and healthy life, apology risks to reinforce alienation.

Political Apology and Evading Accountability

Apology does not in itself present the whole picture of accountability, but a significant part of it. The fact that in a functioning system of justice it is appreciated that the wrongdoer, in addition to being punished, apologizes for the crime, illustrates this state of affairs. So does the recourse to apology in situations where other means of justice are unavailable, such as when the rule of law is lacking or when the direct perpetrator is unavailable. The downside of this positive role of apology is nevertheless that apology can be called upon to evade accountability. It only takes to posture apology to betray it.

Performing a ceremonial apology without genuinely apologizing is one form in which apology has been politically miscarried over the years. One reason for this is the fact that the apologizer is oftentimes not the same party who committed the transgression in the first place. When combined with a narrow pursuit of the state interest, this leads to a practice of apology that is more geared toward political gains than toward a sincere attempt to apologize. Apologizing without apologizing, taking responsibility without taking responsibility, amounts to trying to have it both ways. To this day, Japan (perhaps, some argue, feeling more sorry for itself than for the crimes that it committed in the course of its imperial adventures) has been accused of playing this game in the Asian context. Because of their ambiguity, often, Japanese apologies have been unable to project sincerity. This plays a role in the difficulty for the region to put the past behind.

Using apology in a non-apologetic manner in order to hold onto power is another way for politics to hijack apology. It builds upon the powerful mode of legitimization offered by apology as a promise of a new beginning. Needless to say, such power is especially useful in periods of national or international crisis, be it when political institutions and leaders have to deal with a particular wrong or in situations of regime transition. By trying to indict the wrong, the recourse to apology gives "lettres de noblesse" (patents of nobility) to power and helps to establish or reestablish its legitimacy. The incentive to follow this path is all the stronger considering that political legitimacy, at the national and international level, now largely depends upon the upholding of democratic norms, which includes politically acknowledging the wrongs committed. Apology as a tool of legitimization allows political actors to reach out and reassure the support of both citizens and states. Unfortunately, this does not guarantee legitimization through apology to always be the expression of a sustained commitment to change, let alone of change itself. Experience shows that, more often than not, recourse to apology can be a way to buy time only to return to business as usual afterward. Surely, it is not possible to extend the credit line *ad infinitum*. When repeated too many times, it ceases to have a legitimizing effect. Rather than being a reason for hope, this may be an additional cause for despair.

Apology and the Normalization of Crime

With the undermining of the legitimizing power of apology can come another form of evasion of accountability, namely that of the normalization of crime. This is all the more damaging in light of the fact that apology has the objective to do the contrary. Nevertheless, when the use and reuse of apology fails to generate change, when the use and reuse of apology fails to enhance in an indisputable fashion the sense of responsibility and the imperative to abide by it, a banalization of crime, if not in principle, at least *de facto*, is encouraged. Apology that fails to bring change, amounting to a sanction-free, and therefore futile, recognition of a wrongdoing somewhat reminiscent of an attitude coined in French as "responsable mais pas coupable" (responsible but not culpable), gives rise to cynicism toward politics. In this scenario, at best, the expectations of what political actors can do are likely to be lowered. At worst, it is not only the political establishment but politics itself that runs the risk of being viewed as rotten to the core, and consequently hopeless. When this is true, apology, designed to be a victim-oriented mechanism within the restorative justice approach, has turned against the victim.

APOLOGY AND THE POLITICAL ALIENATION OF RIGHTS

The denaturing of apology is furthered in the political world when it is inhabited by a paternalistic attitude toward the victim. Ultimately, this reflects the reluctance in a more general manner to recognize the victim's rights as those of an individual beyond the crime itself. The critical need for apology to convey a sense of respect for the victim is a good starting point to understand this issue. It amounts to the fact that for apology to contribute to restore the victim's self-respect as well as respect from others, apology has to relate to the victim with respect. In other words, to bring back that self-respect and respect from others which the crime undermined, apology has to project to the victim, as well as to onlookers, that the apology is itself respectful of the victim. Moreover, the greater the crime, the greater the need for the apology to be respectful. Short of this, apology simply fails to be part of restorative justice. It even doubles the victim status. Adding insult to injury, it introduces, on top of the initial wrong, the additional wrong of disregard for the victim.

But, of course, for apology to be respectful of the victim, and to recognize the victim as a victim, it has to consider the victim worthy of respect. This can seldom be seen in a nondemocratic context. But it is not easy to achieve in a democracy either. To be sure, in the democratic world, where each individual is said to have value and where the value of each is said to be equal regardless of race, religion, gender, and social and economic conditions, respecting the individual and the victim is meant to be the norm. The purpose of law, as an expression and tool of democratic values, is to ensure that the rights of each individual are acknowledged and implemented and that, based on this, due respect is given to the victim when these have been violated. Reality, however, is quite different. While values, norms, and laws of democracies design lines of inclusion and of equality, they do not get rid of exclusion and hierarchy. The toll that it takes on the social, economic, and political justice of society as a whole varies with the level and particular conditions of democracy in these states. Nevertheless this toll can never be minimized.

Political Apology in a Pluralist Environment

The third type of challenge for apology in a political context is that it takes place in a culturally diverse world, both within and beyond borders. In this regard, two issues particularly catch the attention: the Western-driven phenomenon of political apology; and apology as a reconciliation tool across cultures.

Western and non-Western apology: It is true that in recent years apology has mainly been a Western-induced phenomenon. Compared to the relative willingness of states from the West to apologize for crimes committed domestically and internationally, non-Western countries appear reluctant to come forward for their wrongs.

Yet Western powers have no high moral ground to expect from apologizing. In fact, political apology from the West comes with a certain ambiguity. While it is a good thing that Western powers apologize, they do so because they committed massive crimes. The inclusive and humanistic values associated with apology cannot be dissociated from the exclusionary and predatory behavior that they try to redress. In addition, that the West is at times willing to apologize does not imply that it is open to apologize for all wrongs committed. The West is selective, tackling only those cases that it can afford to address. While Western powers have yet to apologize for the transatlantic slave trade, they are even further from apologizing for colonization, let alone for neocolonialism. As a result, Western apology amounts to a low form of accountability, as displayed in the refusal of the West to relinquish its commanding position. More than anything else, it wants to have it both ways. Following Mark Gibney and Erik Roxstrom, we could say: "it wants credit for recognizing and acknowledging a wrong against others, but it also wants the world to remain exactly as it had been before the apology was issued" (Gibney and Roxstrom 2001: 935). Thus, Western political apologies show that the West is, to this day, faithful to its history of the past 500 years or so, oscillating between right and wrong, in a tamed, cynical, or righteous manner without being able to choose one over the other. Its moral success continues to be trapped in its moral failure.

This is not to say that non-Western countries are exonerated for their uneasiness about political apology. The fact that non-Western countries have often been on the receiving end of Western power in modern history is no excuse for them not to be forthcoming about their own criminal record, within and beyond borders. As the saying goes, two wrongs do not make a right. There is no cultural reason for the non-Western world not to apologize. Although apology can be traced back to Western Christianity and humanism, it is by no means a Western invention. Non-Western homegrown apologetic mechanisms exist and their importance cannot be mistaken.

Political apology in the midst of cultures and international accountability: The variety of methods called upon to address the criminal past in a cultural plurality is indicative of how challenging it can be to apply a given normative framework of apology to environments that do not share the cultural premises of that framework. Moreover, there is the issue of accountability at the international level.

The minority of states that have addressed their painful past have chosen different ways to do so. Take for instance South America, where almost all populations were afflicted by state repression and terror during the 1970s, but where states dealt with their history of injustices differently. While Argentina decided to hold human rights trials, Chile, much like South Africa, went for everything to be known but not for everything to be prosecuted (Pion-Berlin 1994; Shriver 1995). Why is it that in Chile the work of the country's truth commissions resulted in a nationally televised *apology* whereas in Argentina legal prosecutions were undertaken? Surely, whether a country decides to apologize after mass violations of human rights is connected with circumstances attached to the gravity of crimes. Yet, each time, the modalities of transitional justice are adopted first and foremost by factoring in constraints and possibilities such as the balance of power of actors in that specific cultural context.

It is never easy for apology to be issued at the right moment in time, nor to be issued in the most effective way, especially not in an international setting. This challenge is well displayed in the context of the transitional justice policies underwritten by the United Nations. Indeed, the fact that since the early 1990s the UN has been increasingly involved in post-conflict reconstruction led it, in the various aspects of restorative justice, to try to find a balance between its usually rather context-free methods (as a universal organization prone to rely on "one size fits all" approach) and the imperative to adjust to the local needs of the region and people affected by war (United Nations 2004). Its mixed track record in Bosnia, Kosovo, East Timor, Rwanda, and elsewhere illustrates how difficult this is to achieve.

The inability of the United Nations to save civilian populations caught in the midst of conflicts has also brought apology to the fore as part of global accountability. Following the failure to protect the Muslim Bosnians placed under its responsibility in Srebrenica and to stop the genocide in Rwanda, the many reports assessing what had gone wrong gave Secretary-General Kofi Annan the opportunity to issue some sort of apology (United Nations 1999a,b). In the Srebrenica report, he declared: "it is with the deepest regret and remorse that we have reviewed our own actions and decisions in the face of the assault on Srebrenica.... No one regrets more than we the opportunities for achieving peace and justice that were missed. No one laments more than we the failure of the international community to take decisive action to halt the suffering and end a war that had produced so many victims" (1999a). On the occasion of the publication of the report on Rwanda, he stated that "All of us must bitterly regret that we did not do more to prevent it [the genocide]. . . . On behalf of the United Nations, I acknowledge this failure and express my deep remorse" (1999c). Compared to the past, this marked a certain progress. Yet it should be noted that simply expressing regret and remorse falls short of issuing a real apology and taking responsibility for the wrong committed. Thus, nowhere in the documents, reports or statements do the terms "apology" or the expression "I apologize" appear. In addition, even if a proper apology had been offered to the victims of Srebrenica and Rwanda, one has to admit that it would have represented a rather meager form of overall accountability for the UN (and its member states).

Conclusion

Apology, although a small part, is still an important part of justice. Surely, there can be justice without apology. Yet apology, if well conducted (for the right reasons and in the right ways), can also be a significant conduit for justice. The recognition that it brings to the wrong/crime helps the victim to reconcile with oneself and, in the process, with others and the world. The reason why this is, is also why apology is currently given such importance. It has to do with the power of apology, a fairly simple tool in the end, when applied successfully. It is a matter of humanization. For the same reason that dehumanization is the most powerful tool of war, humanization is the most powerful tool of reconciliation. Apology is one of the ways in which humanization is attempted.

As such, the inner peace that apology helps to bring to the victim turns out to be a tool of outer peace, of social peace. Its contribution to inner (psychological) security translates into outside security for society at large. It is in this that the political benefit of the moral value of apology resides. Because of this, and assuming that it does not on its own represent the whole picture of justice and that the challenges and trappings of its use in a political context are not overlooked, apology has to be cultivated and encouraged as much possible.

This chapter is dedicated to Henry Rousso. The authors thank Jean-Marie Chenou for his research assistance, and Ramon Ray for comments on parts of the text.

References

Burrin, Philippe. 2005. *Nazi Anti-Semitism: From Prejudice to the Holocaust.* New York: New Press.

Derrida, Jacques. 2001. *On Cosmopolitanism and Forgiveness.* New York: Routledge.

Gibney, Mark and Erik Roxstrom. 2001. "The Status of State Apologies." *Human Rights Quarterly* 23 (4): 911–39.

Jaspers, Karl. 2002. *The Question of German Guilt.* New York: Fordham University Press.

Krog, Antjie. 2000. *Country of My Skull: Guilt, Sorrow, and the Limits of Forgiveness in the New South Africa.* New York: Three Rivers Press.

Mamdani, Mahmood. 2001. *When Victims Become Killers: Colonialism, Nativism, and the Genocide in Rwanda.* Princeton, N.J.: Princeton University Press.

Minow, Martha. 2003. *Breaking the Cycles of Hatred: Memory, Law and Repair.* Princeton, N.J.: Princeton University Press.

Pion-Berlin, David. 1994. "To Prosecute or to Pardon? Human Rights Decisions in the Latin American Southern Cone." *Human Rights Quarterly* 16 (1): 105–30.

Rousso, Henry. 2002. *The Haunting Past: History, Memory, and Justice in Contemporary France.* Philadelphia: University of Pennsylvania Press.

Shriver, Donald W., Jr. 1995. *An Ethic for Enemies: Forgiveness in Politics.* Oxford: Oxford University Press.

United Nations. 1999a. *Report of the Secretary-General Pursuant to General Assembly Resolution 53/35: The Fall of Srebrenica.* New York: United Nations.

———. 1999b. *Report of the Independent Inquiry into the Actions of the United Nations During the 1994 Genocide in Rwanda.* New York: United Nations.

———. 1999c. Statement of the Secretary-General on Receiving the *Report of the Independent Inquiry into the Actions of the United Nations During the 1994 Genocide in Rwanda.* December 16. http://www.un.org/News/ossg/sgsm_rwanda.htm

———. 2004. *The Rule of Law and Transitional Justice in Conflict and Post-Conflict Societies.* New York: United Nations.

Part II
Internal Apologies by States

Chapter 6
When Sorry Is Enough: The Possibility of a National Apology for Slavery

Eleanor Bright Fleming

Personal Reflections

My grandmother is the "rememberer" of our family. At our house, the past is very much alive. She reminds us grandchildren that we are but four generations from slavery. She tells the stories of our ancestors who worked in Tennessee. She asks us to imagine what life must have been like for them, without freedom. She encourages us to hold dear to the hope that kept them alive then, and which still keeps our family going. She describes the lands of Marshall County, and the farms of the family that owned our family.

Recently, while tracing our family history, our cousin met with a descendent of the family who owned our family. This descendant apologized for her family's enslaving our family. Almost 140 years after our ancestors were set free from bondage, a descendant of their owners apologized. Why in the contemporary moment, when there are no living slaves or slave-owners, would someone feel the need to offer an apology, acknowledge a wrong, and accept responsibility to try to make right the wrongs of the past? Is this an isolated story, or does it have a greater resonance for the United States?

The question whether the United States should pay descendants of African slaves reparations forces the nation to confront its unresolved past of slavery. Proponents of reparations argue that the government and some private individuals owe Blacks for slavery and its legacy of racial inequality and oppression. Opponents counter that since there are no living slaveholders or slaves, calls for reparation lack any legal footing. Both sides frame the debate about reparations in terms of victims and perpetrators, instead of actual wrongs that occurred. Reparation is a question of justice, specifically how a nation can resolve a traumatic past. Reparationists have argued, in lawsuits against corporations and most strongly in Randall Robinson's *The Debt*, that the nation owes a "social debt" for the atrocities of slavery (Robinson 2000). However, money cannot serve as a proxy for the crimes against humanity and violations of dignity and self-respect inflicted on African slaves. By itself, money does not make amends for the past. It reduces to property the ancestors whose memory reparationists invoke to support their arguments.

I argue that national apologies are especially important to the politics of a democratic polity. When the practice of a democratic polity has violated the dignity of its own citizens, the nation ought to restore their dignity. It must make the relationships right between the nation and its citizens. I analyze U.S. apologies made to its own citizens, and consider the possibility of a national apology for slavery. Slavery was a crime against humanity that violated the dignity of African slaves, and made a farce of America's experiment with democracy. The nation ought to atone for its past by apologizing to present-day African Americans who carry on their ancestors' claims for justice.

If American citizens see the past of slavery as a violation of humanity, and understand themselves as democrats who value human rights and respect the dignity of individuals, they ought to embrace a national apology as the best possible democratic solution to make amends for the past. For a nation to make amends for slavery and racial inequality, the apology must mark a beginning, not an ending. Thus, this chapter explores how a national apology can help the nation not only to face its own past, but also to create new democratic possibilities for the future.

Reparations for Slavery

Despite the early promise in Major William T. Sherman's 1865 Special Field Order to compensate newly freed slaves with "a plot of not more than (40) forty acres of tillable ground" (Winbush 2003: 326), calls for monetary reparations for slavery received little attention until the modern reparations movement. That movement began with the 1969 speech by the radical activist James Forman, entitled "The Black Manifesto." Forman argued that the nation's White religious establishment owed monetary reparations to Blacks for the oppression of slavery. Viewing monetary reparations as the first step in his quest to "build a socialist society inside of the United States" (Forman 1969), he wanted to use reparations to repair the damage done to American society by racism, capitalism, and imperialism.

After "The Black Manifesto," few scholars (see Schuchter 1970) wrote in depth on reparations, or placed the idea under critical scrutiny. One notable exception was Yale legal scholar Boris Bittker. He tried "to bring the concept of black reparations out of its ghetto" (Bittker 1973: 7) and offered arguments for reparations using a theory of legal responsibility or liability. He argued that reparationists should move beyond slavery, largely because of the time lapse since the original injury occurred, and instead make the case for reparations based on violations of the equal protection clause of the Fourteenth Amendment to the Constitution. By moving the reparations argument away from "correct[ing] ancient injustice" (Bittker 1973: 7), Bittker focused on redressing segregation.

Reparationists paid little attention to Bittker's suggestions until the 1988 apology and reparations to Japanese Americans interned during World War II. Legal scholars (e.g., Magee 1993) then turned to how Bittker framed reparations in the context of American law. Instead of focusing on Forman's initial claim that the White religious establishment should pay reparations, they placed the burden on the federal government. Robert Westley combined Forman and Bittker's arguments to suggest that a private trust be established to benefit all Blacks, as compensation for the government's role in slavery and the violation of Black rights during segregation. Westley contended that group reparations ought to be used to confront racism, because "Blacks have been and are harmed as a group [and] . . . racism is a group practice" (Westley 1998: 469).

Implied in Westley's (1998) argument is the idea that reparation "makes Blacks whole for the losses they have endured." I question what this wholeness means. How can Blacks be made whole, when throughout their history in the United States, they were never whole? What does reparation seek to repair? I propose a solution to reparations not in terms of repair but in terms of atonement; that is, making the past right by eliminating the systems of inequality that permitted slavery and segregation. Westley concludes that he wants group reparations to give Blacks "their chances at public happiness . . . the same as that of any white citizen who currently takes this concept for granted because the public so utterly 'belongs' to him, so utterly affirms his value, his humanity, his dignity and his presence." I argue that the nonmonetary means of reparations that Westley opposes can bring about this "public happiness" by atoning for the past and restoring dignity to the victims' ancestors.

Though Westley provided the most significant scholarly account of reparations, his work has not received as much attention as Robinson's *The Debt*. Robinson, a political activist, succeeded in mainstreaming the idea of reparations, and became the key articulator of reparations for the Reparations Coordinating Committee, of which he is a leading voice. Robinson argues that the government and some private institutions (read here as White America) owe a "social debt" to Black America for the unpaid labor of African slaves, and for slavery's legacy of racial and economic inequality. Like Westley, Robinson envisions reparations as a private trust that will provide educational and economic empowerment of Blacks, as well as "make the victim whole."

I wonder to which victim Robinson refers. Robinson believes that African slaves and their descendants are the only victims of slavery and segregation. This is an obvious but incomplete understanding. America as a collective of people and democratic ideals should also be included as a victim. The act of enslaving Africans, using them to build a nation, and then denying them the dignity and equality that they deserved by virtue of their humanity, made a mockery of all the democratic ideals that the nation and its citizens profess. By counting the nation as the embodiment of democratic ideals among the victims, Robinson could make his argument that by recognizing and acknowledging its role in slavery, the nation can become whole. Thus, he could move his focus from monetary reparations for Blacks toward atonement. A national apology would lay the foundation to bring citizens together to resolve the past, and create a new future for American democracy, in which race would not divide citizens.

Reparationists often argue that monetary compensation will bring honor and respect to the memory of their African ancestors. In effect, they use monetary settlement of a social debt as a proxy to repair the damages to dignity suffered by their ancestors. By using money to restore the damage to the dignity of African slaves who were robbed of their humanity and treated as property, reparationists return their ancestors to property. This is especially true of the reparations class action lawsuit filed against FleetBoston, Aetna, and CSX (*Deadria Farmer-Paellmann v. FleetBoston Financial Corporation, Aetna Inc. and CSX* 2002). While the suit invokes the memory of African slaves, and uses the violation of their human rights as part of the legal case, it ignores those slaves' humanity. It looks to financial compensation to right the damages of slavery.

If the goal of the reparations movement is to honor the dignity of African ancestors, reparations is the wrong term. Reparation suggests that contemporary African Americans are entitled to compensation for the labor of past slaves. But we cannot trade human dignity for financial gain or monetary redistribution. Resolving the nation's past of slavery requires that reparationists restore human dignity, and push for a kind of atonement and national repentance that is based on respect for the dignity of all individuals. In this way, reparationists ought to be committed to creating an American democracy that respects human dignity.

A move beyond reparations can see victims beyond African slaves and Black Americans injured under segregation. It can take into account the harm that racial inequality does to all members of the nation. By thinking in terms of atonement, reparationists can overcome the shortcomings of their efforts that opponents from David Horowitz (2002) to Glenn Loury (2000) have been quick to point out: there are no living slave owners, and by placing all the blame on White America, reparations divide Americans rather than uniting them.

Another Approach: Human Dignity and Expiation

Reparation does not focus on a future possibility for the nation and its race relations, but attempts to make a commodity of a past injustice. I move away from reparations and toward expiation. Expiation means atonement; it means to make amends and bring together in peace two individuals who were once divided. When applied to the nation's past of slavery, expiation suggests that the nation and all of its citizens take steps to admit the wrongs of their past and become as one.

Because slavery and segregation institutionalized a system of racial inequality that destroyed the humanity and dignity of both Blacks and Whites, expiation does not suggest monetary compensation for the wrong. Rather, it considers the possibility of a national apology for slavery, to acknowledge the wrong of the past and to respect Americans' common humanity and dignity in future political practices. In this process of making amends for the past, what began as an effort of Black Americans to have the wrongs against them recognized and rectified through reparations becomes a project that has a lasting impact in shaping the future of the United States and all its citizens. Thus, the act of making amends for the past of slavery is about more than forty acres and a mule. Its focus is on uncovering what American democracy can be when the nation recognizes and respects the dignity of all people.

Human dignity is one of the theoretical underpinnings of human rights. Human rights and human dignity go hand in hand: the Preamble to the 1948 Universal Declaration of Human Rights links the two closely, opening with the statement that "recognition of the inherent dignity and of the equal and inalienable rights of all members of the human family is the foundation of freedom, justice and peace in the world."

Human dignity provides a foundation to human rights by emphasizing the rights, duties, and entitlements that go along with the social and political individual; at least, this is the story from the liberal tradition (Howard 1995). In the biblical tradition, human dignity does not imply "something inherent in the human being," but a God-given humanity with man made in the image of God (Ritschl 2002). Human dignity includes a respect for humanity and individuals as agents of God, possessing a bit of that divinity in addition to their humanity. Dignity carries with it not only a duty to respect, but also responsibility to uphold both one's own dignity and the dignity of others (Safrai 2002).

Dignity and respect ought to be the foundation for both justice and democratic practice. There is also a transgenerational concern that democratic citizens assume. While they inherit the benefits of citizens, they also take on certain obligations. Because I recognize the value of my humanity and see the dignity that I have also in you, I protect both my dignity and yours by making sure that you are protected and provided for, just as I am. This perspective couples dignity both with our own rights, and with our responsibilities to others. The key concern is no longer about monetary debts carried over from the past, but about atoning for past and present practices of racial inequality that damage the dignity of people. Arguments for atonement move forward even though there are no living slaves or slaveholders. Bringing the people of the American polity together around their shared humanity, and uniting around their dignity, not dividing over their differences, pays the "social debt." In this way, the unresolved past remains alive and is brought to bear in the contemporary moment, not to make Americans whole or to restore a people who never were, but to mark the beginning of a people who are because of who they were (Tutu 1999).

Dignity and its articulation in human rights allow for atonement with an apology. The act of an apology sets into motion making amends for a wrong. With one party saying to another, "I am sorry," an apology brings a sense of humanity and respect to a situation where both had been violated. The party offering the apology recognizes the humanity in the party whom they have offended "by acknowledging their wrongdoing, accepting responsibility for their act, expressing regret, and promising not to repeat the act" (Tavuchis 1991: vii). The expression of regret is an act of respect to the offended party. In accepting the apology, the offended party sees the humanity of the apologizer and has their own humanity reflected back to them.

If Americans see the past of slavery as a violation of humanity, and see themselves as democrats who value human rights and the dignity of individuals, the dignity perspective should lead us to atone for our past with apologies. An apology should come from the nation and its leaders to African Americans, representing their ancestors who suffered damages to their dignity under slavery and the subsequent systems of racial inequality. With this apology, the nation and all of its citizens recognize the wrongs sanctioned by the federal government. While it may be important for individuals and certain institutions to acknowledge specific wrongs, the emphasis here is on collective responsibility and collective atonement. The point is not for individual Americans—recent immigrants or descendants of slave-owners—to seek out Blacks and make formal, heartfelt, and sincere apologies. The key is ownership of the past of a nation to which an individual belongs—recognizing that in the not so distant history of the United States, Africans were enslaved and crimes against humanity were sanctioned by the government, with a legacy of white racial supremacy that continued after slavery. As citizens share a common bond as Americans and accept the rights and liberties that come with that citizenship, they also carry the legacies and unresolved history of the nation, which are tied to their citizenship. In this way making an apology for the past wrongs of the nation is part of the collective responsibility that comes with citizenship.

Following the example of President Reagan's formal apology to interned Japanese Americans, an apology for slavery must acknowledge the wrong that was done. It must also create a political and social space to atone for that wrong, with some kind of repentance through racial reconciliation. Given the amount of work that an apology requires, this apology must be not a matter of evoking White guilt. Instead, it must make an effort to move forward in a concerted effort toward reconciliation and racial healing. Sincerity should be measured not by the "heart condition" of the individuals offering the apology, but by the chain of events following from it. The apology lays the groundwork for the creation of a social bond: the nation becomes open to honest dialogue on race and inequality. The apology is the first step in the process of the nation's expiation: eliminating the institutional structures that permitted social inequalities, particularly violation of human dignity.

Models for the United States

The case of Australia's Aboriginal Stolen Generations highlights the possibilities that lie in an apology. From the late nineteenth century to the 1970s, the Australian government removed Aboriginal children from their families and sent them to state institutions, or had them adopted by White families in an effort to "civilize" them and eliminate systematically the Aboriginal culture. Families were broken, and children grew up in some of the worst institutions conceivable. Aboriginal communities were disrupted, and all chances for development and growth were destroyed (National Sorry Day Committee 1997).

In May 1995, the Australian Federal Government directed the Human Rights and Equal Opportunities Commission (HREOC) "to investigate the past and present separation of aboriginal children from their parents and communities, the need for any changes in current laws and practices, and principles relating to compensation." The HREOC conducted hearings in every state capital, and in many regional and smaller communities, encouraging individuals to come forth and share their experiences of being forcibly removed (HREOC 1997) The HREOC also emphasized the legacy of this past (Tjalaminu, Dixon and Gidgup 1999). The result of the Commission was the 1997 report *Bringing Them Home*, which argued that "forcible removal was an act of genocide contrary to the United Nations Convention on Genocide ratified by Australia in 1949" (Human Rights and Equal Opportunity Commission 1997). By ratifying the Genocide Convention, Australia had brought it to bear on its domestic policies.

The HREOC called on all Australians to heal the wound that affected contemporary Australians, whether they were harmed by the past, or considered responsible for it. The responsibility for the past falls on the state and its citizens. Since the Commission's report, all State and Territorial Parliaments except that of the Northern Territory have formally apologized for the Stolen Generations. With representatives of the Stolen Generations sharing their stories, much has been done "to restore dignity of those whose dignity was trampled on by the removal policies" (National Sorry Day Committee 1997). More important, "several Indigenous leaders have said that, since these apologies, there has been a noticeably greater understanding of, and concern for, the problems which their people face in areas such as health and employment." Thus this discussion of reparations has opened up possibilities for justice. Justice is not limited to making right the wrongs of the past, but can also address present inequalities.

Although state and territorial governments have apologized, the federal government has refused to apologize and to consider compensation. In December 1997, Senator John Herron, Minister for Aboriginal and Torres Strait Islander Affairs, presented a package of $63 million in "practical assistance" in response to the HREOC report, yet by May 2000, only $13 million had been spent. Explaining the government's reluctance to apologize, Senator Herron in 1998 said:

The government does not support an official national apology. Such an apology could imply that present generations are in some way responsible and accountable for the actions of earlier generations, actions that were sanctioned by laws of the time, and that were believed to be in the best interest of the children concerned. (cited in Collins 1998)

However, in an act of "acknowledgement, unity, and commitment," a grassroots effort invited "the whole Australian community to join in a Journey of Healing" (National Sorry Day Committee 1997). The Sorry Day Committee called for a National Sorry Day on May 26, 1998. Recommended in *Bringing Them Home*, the Sorry Day marked "a day when all Australians can express their sorrow for the whole tragic episode, and celebrate the beginning of a new understanding . . . as a means of restoring hope to people in despair." In the frame of universal human dignity, the Sorry Day was a visible and symbolic way for Australians to accept the obligation to repair their past, regardless of the opinion of the Federal Government. Dr. Mick Dodson, coauthor of *Bringing Them Home*, said:

We're all Australians and we call this place home. Let us rejoice in our diversity and difference because it's they that will ultimately enrich us as peoples. So let us begin this journey, a journey of healing, healing the body, the soul, our hearts and the spirit of our nation. (Dodson 2000)

One of the clear consequences of the day was significant progress in national healing. By encouraging citizens to engage in serious dialogue on the nation's past, the day helped to restore the dignity of many survivors of the Stolen Generations (Head 1998). The Stolen Generations movement did not sacrifice the dignity of survivors for monetary reparations. The movement brought the two objectives of reparations together not to settle a "social debt" but to begin the process of healing across groups.

While the ideas of collective responsibility and collective atonement were important for how the Stolen Generations movement addressed their calls to repair the past, these are also important for the politics of apology. Because apologies depend on states' acknowledging their responsibility for a wrong, state officials often do not want to accept that responsibility, as was case in Senator Herron's explanation of the government's reluctance to apologize. Yet former prime minister Malcolm Fraser believed that an apology is essential (Fraser 2003):

We can't undo the past, but we can, in an apology, recognize the fact that many actions in the past did a grave injustice to the Aboriginal population of Australia. We have a commitment to recognize that and other past injustices in walking together into a new future. (Kuzner 2001)

For him, collective responsibility required an apology. Reparationists must not trade apologies for monetary compensation. Apologies are needed and are the prime objectives of most reparations efforts: acknowledging a wrong and committing oneself to make the wrong right.

Reconciliation in Canada, discussed in this volume by Matt James, shows how a nation can repair its past with its aboriginal communities (CBS News 2002). The Canadian government policy toward its aboriginal people had been "to eradicate Indian culture from the Canadian nation," especially by establishing residential schools for Indian children. In 1998 the Canadian government, the pope, the archbishop of Canterbury, and the head of the United Church Synod of Canada all apologized. Noting this apology, executive director of Canada's Aboriginal Healing Foundation Mike DeGagné believed that "the Australian government should follow Canada's example and say sorry to its indigenous population" (CNews 2001). He argued that "saying sorry, like the Canadian government did in January 1998, would be a 'critical place' to start for reconciliation in Australia," and continued that "It would be awkward to begin a process of reparations . . . without a pre-acknowledgment that something happened." While in the case of the Stolen Generations, the debate over apologies stems from whether the state should acknowledge collective responsibility for the past, in the Canadian case apologies have an entirely different meaning. A state apology marks the beginning of reparations. For Australia, as well as in the case of slave reparations in the

U.S., the inability to offer an apology for the Stolen Generations may stem from "fearing a drawn-out and expensive compensation process similar to what has happened in Canada."

Apologies in the United States

Though reconciliation in Australia and Canada is not complete, the governments have issued statements that begin to accept responsibility for the past. By contrast, the United States government and state officials have been extremely reluctant to acknowledge the role of the U.S. government in slavery, or to recognize the effects that slavery and racial inequality have on contemporary society. An apology is needed to begin reconciliation by acknowledging a wrong, and the legacy of that wrong. Such was the case in the reparations for the internment of Japanese Americans. For slavery, though, apologies have been slow to come. In 1995 the Southern Baptist Convention passed a resolution to apologize to Blacks for racism (Southern Baptist Convention 1995) and in 2000 Aetna, Inc., apologized for selling policies insuring slaves as property (Rowe 2002). Yet the federal government has not taken any formal steps toward reconciling its past, though many argue that in freeing the slave and extending civil rights to Blacks, the government has apologized. However, this is not enough, for these legislative efforts gloss over the past, failing to remedy it.

In the United States, apologies are not without precedent. In 1988, Congress offered a formal apology to the Japanese Americans who were interned in the United States during World War II. In 1990, Congress apologized to uranium miners, people affected by nuclear tests in Nevada, and their families. In 1993, Congress offered a formal apology to native Hawaiians for the role the United States and U.S. citizens played in the overthrow of the government of the Kingdom of Hawaii 100 years earlier (Hall 1999: 351). The apology to native Hawaiians acknowledged a distant past. The victims and perpetrators were more than likely dead, yet the federal government still acknowledged the wrong.

To this list, we can add the 1997 apology for the syphilis study conducted in Tuskegee. For forty years, beginning in 1932, the federal government sponsored a study to examine the effects of syphilis on Black men, without telling them they were infected with the disease: 399 poor black sharecroppers in Macon County, Alabama, were told that they were being treated for "bad blood" but were denied treatment for syphilis and deceived by physicians of the United States Public Health Service. The Tuskegee Syphilis Study Legacy Committee argued that "as the highest elected official of the United States, the President should offer the apology for the Study which was conducted under the auspices of the United

States government" (Tuskegee Syphilis Study Legacy Committee 1996). To the eight survivors and the families of the victims, President Bill Clinton apologized on behalf of the federal government and the American people:

> The United States Government did something that was wrong—deeply, profoundly, and morally wrong. It was an outrage to our commitment to integrity and equality for all our citizens. . . .What was done cannot be undone. But we can end the silence. We can stop turning our heads away. We can look at you in the eye and finally say on behalf of the American people, what the United States Government did was shameful, and I am sorry. (Clinton 1997)

According to Fred Gray, the victims' attorney, although the apology arrived sixty-five years later, it was just as important for the nation as it was for the victims. He said, "It is very important for our government, as powerful as it is and as influential as it is, and with all of the resources behind it, there had come a time when it simply needed to do what the President did today is make an outright confession and ask for forgiveness, and that's what occurred" (PBS News 1997).

A closer look at President Clinton's apology reveals more than mere acknowledgment of past wrongs. Clinton also repented in ways that Gray suggested. He asked that the nation not just say the words of an apology, but consider the ramifications of the past in light of the nation's professed ideals: "remembering that shameful past that we can make amends and repair the nation," "remembering that past that we can build a better present and a better future." In asking the nation to remember, the apology initiates a process of atonement. It recognizes and acknowledges a wrong, makes a confession, and performs an act of penance to make the relationship between Blacks and the government right (by building a memorial at Tuskegee and establishing a center for bioethics in research and health care). An apology, then, cannot merely acknowledge wrongdoing, but is a "first step toward healing the wounds inflicted" (Tuskegee Syphilis Study Legacy Committee 1996).

In July 2003, President George W. Bush offered the latest in a number of "near apologies" for slavery, following a similar apology made earlier by President Clinton (Clinton 1998). Unlike apologies made for the internment of Japanese Americans or the Tuskegee syphilis experiments, Bush's "near apology" for slavery acknowledged its evils, yet did not accept the nation's responsibility. Quoting President John Adams, Bush recognized slavery as "an evil of colossal magnitude" (Bush 2003). While he recounted America's "journey toward justice," he stopped short of apologizing for slavery. The problem that the United States faces in its apology for slavery is the fear of the unknown. What happens after the apology?

Conclusion: The Apology for Slavery

The act of apology sets in motion making amends for a wrong. When one party says to another, "I am sorry," the apology brings a sense of humanity and respect to a situation where both humanity and respect had been violated. The party offering the apology recognizes the humanity in the party whom they have offended Respect is given to the offended party with the expression of regret. In accepting the apology, the offended party sees the humanity of the apologizer and hopefully their own humanity reflected back to them.

If Americans see slavery as a violation of humanity, and see themselves as democrats who value human rights and the dignity of individuals, they should atone for their past with apologies. An apology should come from the nation and its leaders (either the president or the Congress). The apology should be made to African Americans, representing their ancestors who suffered damages to their dignity under slavery and the systems of racial inequality that followed. With this apology, the nation and all its citizens recognize the wrongs sanctioned by the federal government. The embrace of the dignity perspective, coupled with atonement for not repairing the past, may make possible a struggle for dignity, along the lines of the social movements of the 1960s. Thus, we move from the politics of apology, where the focus is on the federal government's making the first step in the process of atonement, to a political struggle. In this political struggle, groups whose dignity has been violated and overlooked come together to fight for recognition and protection of their dignity. In such a grassroots social movement, the struggle for dignity would attack violations on all fronts, including race, class, gender, and sexual orientation. It would bring about atonement from the bottom up. The apologies begin with individuals coming together on the model of Australia's Sorry Day to recognize their shared dignity. They would then use that momentum to effect larger political changes on matters from homelessness and a living wage for workers, to parity in primary public education. By focusing on dignity and bringing together different marginalized peoples, this movement may initiate the creation of a social bond as well as the democratic politics of dignity.

References

Bittker, Boris. 1973. *The Case for Black Reparations.* New York: Random House.

Bush, George W. 2003. "President Bush Speaks at Goree Island in Senegal." July 8. http://www.whitehouse.gov/news/releases/2003/07/20030708-1.html

CBS News. 2002. "Killing the Indian." *60 Minutes II*, April 10. www.cbsnews.com/stories/2002/04/09/60II/printable505725.shtml

Clinton, William C. 1997. "Remarks by the President in Apology for Study Done in Tuskegee." May 16. http://clinton4.nara.gov/textonly/New/Remarks/Fri/19970516-898.html

———. 1998. "Remarks at the Kisowera School in Mukono, Uganda." March 24. http://clinton4.nara.gov/Africa/199803243374.html

CNews. 2001. "Australia Should Apologize to Aboriginals, Says Head of Canadian Foundation." August 15. http://www.skicanadamag.com/CNEWSCanadiana01/0815_australia-cp.html

Collins, Bob. 1998. "Statehood, Reconciliation and Good Health." http://www.australianpolitics.com/states/nt/collins.shtml

Deadria Farmer-Paellmann v. FleetBoston Financial Corporation, Aetna Inc. and CSX. 2002. http://news.findlaw.com/hdocs/docs/slavery/fpllmnflt032602cmp.pdf

Dodson, Mick. 2000. "Corroboree 2000." May 27. http://www.austlii.edu.au/au/orgs/car/media/Dr%20Mick%20Dodson.htm

Forman, James. 1969. "The Black Manifesto." In *Black Manifesto: Religion, Racism, and Reparations*, ed. Robert S. Lecky and H. Elliott Wright. New York: Sheed and Ward.

Fraser, R. Hon. Malcolm. 1999. Apology Must Be First Step." *Sydney Morning Herald*, April 8.

———. 2003. Speech. May 26. http://www.alphalink.com.au/~rez/Journey/fraserspeech.htm

Hall, Tony P. 1999. "Defense of Congressional Resolution Apologizing for Slavery." In *When Sorry Isn't Enough: The Controversy over Apologies and Reparations for Human Injustice*, ed. Roy Brooks. New York: New York University Press.

Head, Mike. 1998. "The Politics of Australia's 'National Sorry Day'." World Socialist Web Site, June 2. http://www.wsws.org/news/1998/jun1998/aust-j2.shtml

National Sorry Day Committee. 1997. "Healing the Stolen Generations." www.alphalink.com.au/~rez/Journey/qna.htm

Horowitz, David. 2001. "Ten Reasons Why Reparations for Blacks is a Bad Idea for Blacks?—and Racist Too." Frontpagemagazine.com, January 1. http://www.frontpagemag.com/Articles/ReadArticle.asp?ID=1153

———. 2002. *Uncivil Wars: The Controversy over Reparations for Slavery*. San Francisco: Encounter Books.

Howard, Rhoda. 1995. *Human Rights and the Search for Community*. Boulder, Colo.: Westview Press.

Human Rights and Equal Opportunity Commission (HREOC). 1997. *Bringing Them Home: Report on the National Inquiry into the Separation of Aboriginal and Torres Strait Islander Children from Their Families*. Sydney: HREOC, April. http://www.austlii.edu.au/au/special/rsjproject/rsjlibrary/hreoc/stolen/

Kretzmer, David and Eckert Klein, eds. 2002. *The Concept of Human Dignity in Human Rights Discourse*. The Hague: Kluwer Law.

Kuzner, Scott. 2001. "Seeking Justice for Australia's Aborigines." Sidebar in David Masci, "Reparations Movement," *CQ Researcher* 11 (June 22).

Lancaster, Donald Aquinas, Jr. 2000. "Slavery and Segregation: A Property Law and Equitable Analysis of African American Reparations." *Howard Law Journal* 43: 171–212.

Loury, Glenn C. 2000. "It's Futile to Put a Price on Slavery." *New York Times*, May 29.

Magee, Rhonda V. 1993. "The Master's Tools, from the Bottom Up: Responses to African-American Reparations Theory in Mainstream and Outsider Remedies Discourse." *Virginia Law Review* 79: 863–916.

National Sorry Day Committee. 1997. Australian National Sorry Day. http://www.austlii.edu.au/au/special/rsjproject/sorry/index.htm

PBS News. 1997. "An Apology 65 Years Late." *NewsHour with Jim Lehrer.* Transcript, May 16. http://www.pbs.org/newshour/bb/health/may97/tuskegee_5-16a.html
Ritschl, Dietrich. 2002. "Can Ethical Maxims be Derived from Theological Concepts of Human Dignity?" In *The Concept of Human Dignity in Human Rights Discourse*, ed. David Kretmer and Eckart Klein. The Hague: Kluwer Law.
Robinson, Randall. 2000. *The Debt: What America Owes to Blacks*, New York: Dutton.
Rowe, John W. 2002. "Aetna Offers an Apology for Policy on Slavery." Associated Press, March 10. http://www.aetna.com/news/2002/slavery_reparations_issue.html.
Safrai, Chana. 2002. "Human Dignity in a Rabbinical Perspective." In *The Concept of Human Dignity in Human Rights Discourse*, ed. David Kretzmer and Eckary Klein. The Hague: Kluwer Law.
Schuchter, Arnold. 1970. *Reparations: The Black Manifesto and Its Challenge to White America*. Philadelphia: J.B. Lippincott.
Southern Baptist Convention. 1995. Resolution on Racial Reconciliation on the 150th Anniversary of the Southern Baptist Convention. http://www.sbc.net/resolutions/amResolution.asp?ID=899
Tavuchis, Nicholas. 1991. *Mea Culpa: A Sociology of Apology and Reconciliation.* Stanford, Calif.: Stanford University Press.
Tjalaminu, Mia, Graeme Dixon and Ron Gidgup. 1999. "The Stolen Ones." *New Internationalist* 311 (April).
Tuskegee Syphilis Study Legacy Committee. 1996. Final Report, May 20. http://www.med.virginia.edu/hs-library/historical/apology/report.html
Tutu, Desmond Mpilo. 1999. *No Future Without Forgiveness*. New York: Doubleday.
Verdun, Vincent. 1993. "If the Shoe Fits, Wear It: An Analysis of Reparations to African Americans." *Tulane Law Review* 67: 597–668.
Westley, Robert. 1998. "Many Billions Gone: Is it Time to Consider the Case for Black Reparations?" *Boston College Law Review* 40: 469–76.
Winbush, Raymond A. 2003. *Should America Pay: Slavery and the Raging Debate on Reparations*. New York: HarperCollins.

Chapter 7
The University and the Slaves: Apology and Its Meaning

ALFRED L. BROPHY

Hidden behind the grand president's mansion on the campus of the University of Alabama are several small brick buildings. They are nondescript and today are used for storing garden tools. Yet in the years before the Civil War they housed slaves. For, until federal troops arrived in Tuscaloosa on April 4, 1865, and freed them, slaves were owned by the university.

Such is the hidden connection between race and the university that many people think that blacks were not present on the campus until Vivian Malone and James Hood enrolled with the help of Nicholas Katzenbach and the National Guard in June 1963. But blacks were present at the university before students arrived in 1831 (Clark 1995). One of the University's first acts was the purchase of a slave, Ben, who worked building the campus. And now the University of Alabama's faculty senate has apologized for the antebellum faculty's use of slave labor and for the role of the faculty in punishing slaves. This essay explores the case for apology and the conflict over the apology. It is a case study of what we may expect from an institution's apology.

Slaves and Slaveholders on the University of Alabama Campus

The connections between the University of Alabama and slavery are many. The university owned one slave from 1828 to 1834, maybe none until 1838, a second in 1842, more thereafter, perhaps many more by the early 1860s. Records are incomplete (Sellers 1953). Most often when there was work to be done by slaves, the university rented slaves from Tuscaloosa residents. Slaves appeared frequently on the campus. Often they were brought by students. At least once, slaves appeared on campus as a place of refuge. When some fugitive slaves were found hiding in Franklin Hall, the university investigated whom they belonged to and apparently returned them.

Several faculty members owned slaves—some of them owned a significant number of slaves—and they rented out their slaves. Basil Manly, who served as president of the university from 1837 to 1855, owned 38 (Fuller 2000: 265). English Professor Landon Cabell Garland brought three wagonloads of slaves with him when he and his family moved from Virginia. The University's historian, James Sellers, makes the story of the move from Randolph Macon College, where Garland was teaching literature, to the University of Alabama, into a story of what was once called the moonlight and magnolia school—a story about the South that mythologized the beautiful landscape at the expense of the realities of life. Sellers adopted this description of Garland's biographer.

> Dr. Garland was very fond of his slaves. When he and his wife were married, a special gift bestowed upon them by their parents was the choice of slaves for their servants. In the course of years, however, the number of slaves increased from three to sixty. Nevertheless, "Old Master"'s black women folk wanted to stay with him and refused to be sold to owners of their husbands, as Dr. Garland had prospered. His policy ... had always been to keep families as nearly intact as possible; consequently, he bought the women's husbands. (Sellers 1953: 79)

In 1855 Garland became president of the university. On the eve of the Civil War he delivered a trio of lectures at the YMCA on proslavery thought (Sellers 1953).

Slaves made the bricks that went into buildings; they worked the grounds and buildings around the campus. They carried water, serviced the dormitories, worked in the dining halls. One slave, Sam, who was rented by the university, worked as a laboratory assistant for Professor F. A. P. Barnard, a brilliant young science professor, president of Columbia University after the war and the namesake of Barnard College. President Manly recorded in his diaries frequent conflict with Sam. Once, Sam "behaved very insolently to Thos. G. Grace, and refused to measure or receive a load of coal which Grace had brought. By order of the Faculty, he was chastised, in my room, in their presence. Not seemingly humbled, I whipped him a second time, very severely" (Manly 1840). And when slaves died, they were occasionally buried on campus. Until the summer of 2004, those graves were unmarked. However, a monument at the University cemetery now commemorates the graves.

Plaques and other commemorative devices elsewhere on campus memorialize the era of slavery and Civil War. There is a granite monument to Confederate veterans outside the library. There are also plaques on the library's exterior commemorating Confederate veterans, as well as a plaque commemorating the reparations paid for the era of slavery and civil war. A plaque outside Clark Hall notes that it is named after the trustee who chaired the committee that oversaw the 46,000 acres of land given to the University, "in reparation for the 1865 destruction of the campus by Federal troops." Such is the nature of reparations for the era of slavery and Civil War.

Several buildings on campus are named after prominent slaveholders. There is Morgan Hall, built in 1910 and named after Alabama senator John Tyler Morgan, who led the battle to obtain federal funds in reparation for the university's destruction in 1865 by Union forces. Morgan might also be remembered as a leader of the Alabama Secession Convention. who said something along the lines of, the best thing we could do is to go to Africa and bring back as many Africans as possible and turn them into slaves. There are also halls named after the two slaveholding presidents, Garland and Manly.

Then there is Nott Hall, named after Josiah Nott, who founded a medical school in Mobile in the late 1850s. He was a polygenesist—that is, in his writings on proslavery thought he explored the idea that blacks and whites have a separate origin (Nott 1854). His ideas provided intellectual machinery to support the slave system. Those are some of the physical connections of slavery to the campus; there are also important intellectual connections.

Proslavery Thought at the Antebellum University of Alabama

The early history of the university, which opened in 1831, was one of reverence for Enlightenment ideas of reason. In the late 1820s and early 1830s, James G. Birney, who later ran for president on the Liberty Party, was a trustee of the university. He was responsible for hiring many of the early faculty, including Henry Tutwiler, who had been educated at the University of Virginia. Birney and Tutwiler actively promoted the American Colonization Society in Tuscaloosa, and Birney wrote some antislavery essays in Tuscaloosa. One important, though underappreciated, story is that Tuscaloosa had a tradition of exploring radical views at least into the mid-1830s. Then, as happened elsewhere in the south in the 1830s, that changed. In 1835, alumnus Alexander Meek wrote that Birney was "the most deluded of abolitionist fanatics" (Quist 1998: 318). In 1836, the Philomathic Society, one of the two literary societies at the university, expelled Birney from honorary membership. The society cited Birney's "espousal and endeavors to propagate opinions which militate and are at direct variance with the rights of the South, the peace of society, and the perpetuity of our government" (Sellers 1953: 179–80). Birney and Tutwiler had once supported the termination of slavery through colonization. Their views represent an alternative view of Alabama—of what might have been. In November 1837, Basil Manly departed from his South Carolina pulpit to assume the presidency of the University of Alabama. Manly is a critical figure in understanding the intellectual history of the antebellum south. He was seemingly ubiquitous: in the pulpit of the First Baptist Church in Charleston, South Carolina during the nullification controversy; leading southern Baptists out of the American Baptist Convention in 1845; swearing in Jefferson Davis as president of the Confederacy at the start of the Civil War.

Manly did much that was positive at the university. He was a proponent of the democratization of education. He was one of those antebellum educators who believed in the promise of education. He brought order to the university, created a grand campus (with the assistance of slaves' labor, of course), and brought some excellent faculty.

The problem came with the content of that education, for, while Manly supported many people learning, the lessons he taught were of obedience to the status quo. They were lessons that confirmed the worldview of his students, which fit neatly with the demands of the powerful. In a series of sermons and lectures, he taught his audiences that slavery is the natural order of things. He delivered lectures on ants and bees, to illustrate the natural order that exists in society—constant warfare, conflict over property, hierarchy of some working for others. In his correspondence with Brown University president Francis Wayland, Manly expanded on the virtues of slavery (Manly 1850). Manly's 1845 sermon on the "Duties of Masters and Servants" makes slavery out to be a positive good, something that, in the words of his biographer, "made slaves happy and industrious and masters prosperous and beneficent" (Fuller 2000: 214). Manly became a frequent target of abolitionists for his statement that he believed that Southerners supported the right to sell slaves at will—and that "however great the trial to my feelings in other respects, I have none as to the rights of property" (Fuller 2000: 222).

The Meaning of Apology

Given this history, the faculty senate considered an apology in the spring of 2004. The current faculty are the intellectual successors to those antebellum professors who owned slaves, used them, supervised their discipline, and spoke widely in favor of slavery. The senate apologized to the memory of those enslaved by the university, to the people brutalized, to those who worked without pay on this campus, as well as those whose names we will never know who suffered in part because this university failed to oppose the slave system. Apology is part recognizing the past and giving closure to it. It is part of making the campus more welcoming to African American students. Part of it is also opening a serious dialogue about what the university's current identity is and ought to be.

The questions, what good comes of this talk of the past, and why there should be an apology, are critically important. For the apology has significant implications for how we think about the past and its current meaning. Novelist Ralph Ellison wrote about the ways that history is important, yet ignored by Americans in his essay "Going to the Territory" (1995). By "pushing significant details of our experience into the underground of unwritten history, we not only overlook much which is positive, but we blur our conceptions of where and who we are" (Ellison 1995: 595). The past does not stop having meaning just because we do not talk about it. In Ellison's magical phrasing, "our unwritten history looms as . . . obscure alter ego [of written history], and although repressed from our general knowledge of ourselves, it is always active in the shaping of events."

The apology reminds us of our complex history. That history demonstrates that African Americans have a much richer history at the university than we remember. That past is important to those who have been left out of history's mainstream. It is an important part of remembering their contributions and honoring them.

There are lessons in the apology for us now. The university supported, indeed reinforced, the accepted power arrangements of the antebellum era. One lesson is that it is easy, but also dangerous, for university officials to accept the power structure. The university's role should be to question, not accept ideas of the powerful. Our identity ought to be of a university that honors and includes the entire community (Brophy 2004). An apology can be part of the process of reconciliation. And we can assist in providing a lesson to the local community about our shared past, as we have a common discussion. One other lesson of the apology is that universities are particularly important places to seek redress. The sentiments of the campus community may make them more receptive than many other institutions to the case for apology. Moreover, there are other things that the community can do to correct our imbalanced history. For example, a common way of changing names is by changing use. As Ralph Waldo Emerson said, "Colleges and books only copy the language which the field and work-yard made" (Emerson 1837/1983: 62). We can call the buildings what we will, and they will, after sufficient time, be known by that name. So if students think we should honor someone other than President Manly we can rename Manly Hall by calling it by another name. Perhaps we can call it Luna Hall, in honor of one of the women slaves owned by Professor F. A. P. Barnard and who labored on the campus. Luna Hall will, eventually, become the name of the hall, no matter what the university's maps label that building.

The Arguments Against Apology and Their Meaning

Much of the cultural significance of the apology appears in the arguments against the apology. The campus debate over apology became one of the leading news stories in the state in March and April 2004. It was on the front page of virtually every newspaper in the state and was a topic of intense discussion on radio and television programs throughout the state. The intensity of the discussion and opposition suggests just how meaningful the battle over memory of the era of slavery is for Alabamians. We are fortunate that so many people wanted to talk about the apology, for it provided an opportunity to revisit the memory of slavery and its meaning (Grahn-Farley 2004).

Those opposing apology advanced a series of reasons for doing so. Often the opposition was emotional and based on anger. Such was the response of a vice-president of Laureate Education, who wrote about the apology, "I am sick and tired of the African Americans making excuses based on the 'slavery era.'" Similarly, one anonymous poster wrote of the apology, about his anger at integration at liberal Southern universities:

No surprise here. Our Southern universities have been transforming into clones of Berkeley for a long time now. The only reason for a young Southron [sic] to attend one of these cesspools now is to undermine it. I admit that I still go to University of Georgia football games, but I take a good hot shower when I get home because after seeing all the miscegination, [sic] and the general deconstruction of our beloved Southland I feel like I've been raped.

A post to a story in the student newspaper, the *Crimson White*, wished for a return of a politician like Governor George Wallace, who would, presumably, deny requests for apology or reparations: ""I admire George Wallace—probably the last statesman this country has seen. If only the men we elect today had the courage of Governor Wallace. He'd give these money-grubbing reparation morons exactly what they deserve—nothing. Call that racism? I call it common sense" (Clark 2004). Another anonymous post threatened violence. He wrote, "Send Brophy to my house. I'll teach him about slavery. Jesse Jackson wannabe."

The responses that provided reasons against the apology more specifically fall into several broad categories:

1. The current generation is not responsible for prior crimes and an apology is, therefore, meaningless.
2. An apology dishonors the memory of the university or the South more generally, or at least distorts the role of slavery in the university's history. The request for apology might also force Alabamians into giving an apology when they do not want to give one, or it attaches moral blame to Alabamians who have no culpability and are, themselves, oppressed.
3. It causes more harm than good, because it opens old wounds and causes further conflict.

4. An apology is not sincere; it is designed for political purposes or to obtain publicity.

Those rationales tracked the national debate over apologies for slavery. The apology, while centered on one institution, opens up a host of issues related to continuing culpability, the meaning of apologies to those making them and those receiving them, and the cultural war over how we remember the past and what, if anything, we should do about it.

At base the first reason—that there is no responsibility—says that we may inherit traditions and the benefits of those traditions, but that we have no responsibility for the crimes of the past. This appeared in a lot of forms. In its most radical form, it was that slavery was not so bad; perhaps even there was never anything to apologize for. One opponent of the apology argued that the slaves were happy with slavery:

> Sorry folks, but the slaves would disagree with you, even those of you who say that slavery was evil and unconscionable. Just a casual browsing of the Federal Government's "Slave Narratives" will show many slaves that were quite happy in their position in society, and even those who preferred it and admitted that they wouldn't mind returning to those days. Don't believe me? READ the Slave Narratives. It [sic] is online. You will be surprised at how little truth there is to the general "Uncle Tom's Cabin" version of slavery. Apologize? If you want to. But first make sure you know what you are talking about, Mr. Brophy and Ms [Lisa] Dorr. I just don't think the real slaves would care much either way.

For there is a well-engrained belief in the moonlight and magnolia myths of the antebellum south—the place of happy slaves working on the plantation and making their cultivated masters wealthy. Such a story is often mixed with misinformation about the nature of slavery itself.

But leaving aside whether there was culpability in the past, opponents claimed that the current generation is not responsible for (or seemingly a beneficiary of) slavery. Often the statements of lack of culpability were accompanied by statements about the need to remember history.

The second argument—that the apology distorts the University's culpability—rests on an argument about the presence of slavery elsewhere in the United States and in human history. For some argued that the University of Alabama had no particular culpability for slavery: slavery was part of society at the time; others owned slaves in the South at the time. The argument quickly moved beyond the university. The South was not alone in supporting slavery, for slavery has been nearly ubiquitous in human history. A sort of equal protection argument is invoked to say, "we're not so bad. Other people were also bad." The argument is that unless every society that held slaves is held liable, then none can be.

Opponents of the apology want to move on and they think the university is not responsible for the crimes of the university in the past. A music professor who was the most prominent faculty opponent of the apology argued that those asking for an apology, like history professor George Williamson, are

"visitors in a foreign land," strongly predisposed to maintain that alien perspective, establish moral authority, and control the agenda to their perpetual advantage. Dr. Williamson has already warned us "not in your lifetime, nor in the lifetime of your children, nor in the lifetime of your grandchildren . . . can we move on and let the past be past.

In fact, the desire to be freed from responsibility is the central feature of the opposition. The music professor feared "that we may be led down the garden path to admitting fundamental flaws, incurable weakness and permanent unworthiness of citizenship."

The *Montgomery Advertiser* questioned the value of an apology at the present time, noting that neither slaves nor slave owners are still alive:

It is worth asking whether an apology in 2004 can have any real meaning. If this were 1904, when former slaves and former slaveowners still lived, perhaps that question would not be asked, but this debate is taking place a century later. (*Montgomery Advertiser* 2004)

The *Advertiser* thought that, because there are no living slaves or slaveholders, there is no culpability and no harm. For "No one living today can plausibly claim to suffer now because slavery existed in Alabama 140 years ago, nor can anyone living today plausibly claim to benefit now for the same reason."

So the opponents rallied a series of arguments, which tended to dispel the University's liability and to demand that we stop talking about the past. There were fears that the apology was unneeded, divisive, or, in the words of an editorial in Auburn University's student newspaper, a "Big Mistake" The apology is seen also, however, as an attack on Southern heritage. This is part of the culture war (Goldfield 2002; Applebome 1997; Horwitz 1999; Feller 2004). One post on the student newspaper website stated, "In my opinion, Professor Brophy is a advocate for all the forces now waging a war of cultural genocide against Alabama's history and traditions." Or, in one extreme example, the request for an apology is likened to terrorism:

The source of the University of Alabama Professor Alfred Brophy's anti-Southern cultural bigotry is not at all hard to trace. It is apparent if you consider the fact that his Ph.D. was awarded by those neo-Puritan monoculturists at Harvard University. . . . Brophy should be ashamed for promoting such hair-brained, hateful, prejudicial and divisive schemes as apologies for slavery. He should be especially so now when American soldiers are dying every day to protect us from fanatics who have exactly the same philosophy as the so-called "secret six." These were the six prominent Yankees who financed and supported that original American fanatic and terrorist named John Brown. By the way, at least four of those six were Harvard alumni. If Brophy or any other neo-Puritan wants apologies for past injustices let them start by apologizing for the policies and philosophies promulgated by Harvard that led directly to an unnecessary fratricidal war that killed 620,000 Americans and kept most Southerners (of all races) in an impoverished and subjugated condition for three generations.

The criticism of the faculty who sought the apology points to the importance of identity of those seeking the apology. As one anonymous discussant wrote about me, "I am sorry that your owner in Africa sold you to some white guy instead of to another african [sic]. There's your apology. Maybe that professor needs to learn a little of his own history." There was substantial interest in the racial and geographic identity of who was seeking the apology. Perhaps because the apology came from the beloved university, which represented Governor Wallace's stand in the schoolhouse door in the minds of so many, it was more meaningful than it would have been had it come from other institutions in the state, like the *Mobile Register* or the *Montgomery Advertiser*, two newspapers that were in existence before the Civil War.

Lessons for the Present

Yet the apology is about acknowledging the continuing guilt of an institution, which was intimately involved in slavery and its legacy of Jim Crow discrimination afterward. Much of apology is about truth and inclusiveness. It tells people who have been left outside history that they are to be included. It rebalances history, which is meaningful to many. Gwendolyn M. Patton wrote in response to a *Montgomery Advertiser* editorial opposing the apology:

I find your editorials devaluing the importance of an apology to descendants of African-Americans whose forebears were forced into slavery at the University of Alabama dehumanizing. I have traced my paternal family history from 1835. My forebears without a doubt were forced into slavery. An apology from the descendants and institutions who "owned" my ancestors would mean much to me. Much could come from this contemporary reconciliation as a pledge that present white descendants will not engage forever white-skin privilege of the horror of racism, exploitation, discrimination, injustice, inequality and the variations thereof that we still, unfortunately, experience today. (Patton 2004)

If we remember that alternative history, of violence and forced labor, then we will be more likely to question the current distribution of power. The process of obtaining an apology, which was built on an intense discussion of the university's relationship to slavery, and the aftermath of the apology provides an opportunity for on-going exploration of history and the meaning of that history. For apologies are part of a larger process of negotiating different understandings of the past held by divergent groups.

And one hopes that the discussion around the apology has increased the knowledge of history on the campus.

The credibility of the historians' account comes in part from providing complete and accurate accounts of what happened. They must give due process and adjudicate competing claims. It is critical to pay attention to competing claims, even if some of those claims are ultimately rejected. There are differences, of course, between an interpretation of history and what to do about that history. The former permits a relative consensus; questions about the latter, however, cannot be answered by historical facts alone.

In thinking about having apologies that are productive of harmony, we need to be sensitive to the current generation. The people who are alive today are, obviously, not the people who enslaved others. They may, however, be the beneficiaries of that enslavement; some are also the descendants of those who were enslaved. And even some of those who are arguing the fiercest against acts like the apology are themselves engaged in remembering the past. The League of the South, a neo-Confederate group, for example, celebrates Confederate history and seeks to effect a return to the values of the Confederacy, even as it opposes Congressional investigation of the history of slavery. Harmony and building something positive for the future is critical. But at some point, some groups are likely to be offended, for there are alternative understandings of history. Sometimes those understandings cannot be reconciled. One way of trying to minimize those taking offense is to have a history that is as complete and accurate as possible. Apologies for the past, though, are controversial precisely because they take a stand and they rebalance past, inaccurate histories. They are controversial because history and self-image have value. Apologies may also lead to calls for making atonement complete by other concrete acts, such as scholarships or changes in names of buildings, or actions to increase the presence of black students, staff, and faculty.

An apology functions to define us, as well as to send messages to others. It tells us about our current identity and makes a statement to those excluded from the University and to others about the past and the present, as well as those who are beneficiaries of that past. An apology is a part of how we remember our history and it is also an antidote to selective memory. And now we have a monument to the slaves who worked on the campus and are buried on it.

I would like to thank the participants in the UCIS conference on apologies for their help in revising this essay, especially Elazar Barkan, Mark Gibney, Rhoda Howard-Hassmann, and Niklaus Steiner, and Brown University's Slavery and Justice Committee, especially James Patterson, Seth Rockman, and Michael Vorenberg. Patricia Bauch first asked me to work on the University's history of slavery and then convinced me to continue working, when my interest waned. I am grateful to my colleagues at the University who planned and spoke in favor of the apology, including Greg Dorr, Lisa Dorr, Bryan Fair, Damon Freeman, Utz McKnight, Joshua Rothman, Amilcar Shabazz, George Williamson, and one person who asked to remain anonymous. Several leaders in the faculty senate made the apology happen, including Wythe Holt, John Mason, Robert Moore, and Matthew Winston. Mary Sarah Bilder, Mark Brandon, and Keith Wingate provided comments. Finally, and importantly, Rebecca Schwartz, John Montgomery, and Clayton Taylor provided excellent and timely research assistance.

References

Applebome, Peter. 1997. *Dixie Rising: How the South Is Shaping American Values, Politics, and Culture.* New York: Times Books.
Brophy, Alfred L. 2004. "University Right to Remember and Apologize." *Birmingham News*, April 25.
Clark, E. Culpepper. 1995. *The Schoolhouse Door: Segregation's Last Stand at the University of Alabama.* New York: Oxford University Press.
Clark, Kim. 2004. "Apology Fine, Reparations Not So Fine." *Crimson-White*, March 30.
Ellison, Ralph. 1995. "Going to the Territory." In *The Collected Essays of Ralph Ellison*, ed. J. Callahan. New York: Modern Library.
Emerson, Ralph Waldo. 1837/1983. "The American Scholar." In *Ralph Waldo Emerson: Essays and Lectures*, ed. Joel Porte. New York: Literary Classics of America.
Feller, David. 2004. "Libertarians in the Attic, or a Tale of Two Narratives." *Reviews in American History* 32 (2): 184–95.
Fuller, A. James. 2000. *Chaplain to the Confederacy: Basil Manly and Baptist Life in the Old South.* Baton Rouge: Louisiana State University Press.
Goldfield, David R. 2002. *Still Fighting the Civil War: The American South and Southern History.* Baton Rouge: Louisiana State University Press.
Grahn-Farley, Maria. 2004. "The Master Norm on the Question of Redressing Slavery." *De Paul Law Review* 53 (3): 1215–28.
Horwitz, Tony. 1999. *Confederates in the Attic: Dispatches from the Unfinished Civil War.* New York: Pantheon.
Manly, Basil. 1840. Diary of Basil Manly. Manly Family Papers, University of Alabama Hoole Special Collection Library.
Montgomery Advertiser. 2004. "Apology's Value Questionable." April 21.
Nott, Josiah. 1854. *Types of Mankind.* Philadelphia: Lippincott, Grambo.
Patton, Gwendolyn M. 2004. "Letter to the Editor." *Montgomery Advertiser*, May 3.
Quist, John. 1998. *Restless Visionaries: The Social Roots of Antebellum Reform in Alabama and Michigan.* Baton Rouge: Louisiana State University Press.
Sellers, James. 1953. *History of the University of Alabama.* Tuscaloosa: University of Alabama Press.

Chapter 8
The Role of Apologies in National Reconciliation Processes: On Making Trustworthy Institutions Trusted

Pablo de Greiff

This chapter is an effort to clarify the notions of reconciliation and apologies as well as their interrelationship. I have no intention of remaining at the level of either "aspirational claims" or descriptive or predictive statements. Above all, it is important to try to articulate accounts of why taking a certain course of action gives us reasons to believe that this will lead to certain consequences.

Apologies (on most credible accounts, accompanied by other measures), for example, are frequently defended as means to achieving reconciliation. As an aspiration, I find this largely unobjectionable. But it would be useful to understand the reasons underlying the expectation that this can in fact be the case. This paper, then, aims to provide an argument about the contribution that apologies can make to processes of national reconciliation that is more than an aspiration but retains some normative edge.

The word "reconciliation" continues to figure prominently in both the literature and the practice of transitional justice, despite the lack of consensus about what the term means or what achieving such a condition would require. In the first section, I articulate some of the constraints that a defensible conception of reconciliation must respect. In the second section, I provide a sketch of three deflationary conceptions of reconciliation, the last one of which understands reconciliation in terms of the achievement of a thin, civic trust. I then raise the question of the contribution that apologies can make to processes of reconciliation. I then argue for an essentially norm-affirming conception of apologies. Finally, I argue that the affirmation of norms that is required for reconstituting civic trust in the aftermath of violence calls for concrete actions that go beyond apologies, thereby showing the limits of apologies and the need to complement them with other transitional justice measures. However, since it is possible for post-authoritarian institutions to become *trustworthy* and nevertheless not be *trusted* in fact by citizens, I suggest that the acceptance of responsibility and the expression of regret characteristic of apologies may be what some citizens need to make the attitudinal change that allows them to grant their trust to those individuals and institutions who have earned it. Whether any of this will in fact obtain, that is, whether transitional measures will foster the sort of civic trust that I see as the essential part of a "reconciled" society, whether official apologies will actually help citizens grant their trust to trustworthy institutions, etc., are empirical questions which cannot be decided a priori. Indeed, experience suggests that we should have modest expectations at best.

Constraints

I begin by setting forth some of the constraints that a defensible conception of reconciliation must respect.

First, the primary domain of application of the conception of reconciliation offered here will not be the personal, but the civic or political.[1]

Second, I take as a non-starter what has been called "cheap" or "false" reconciliation[2]—efforts to use reconciliation either *as a substitute for justice*, or to come as close to that as possible.

Third, although it must be recognized that the achievement of reconciliation will involve efforts, expenses, and investments, I object to any understanding of the term that involves huge inequities in the distribution of such burdens, particularly, yet another transfer of responsibility from perpetrators to victims!

Fourth, I do not support conceptions of reconciliation that focus too heavily on wiping the slate clean. Even if (as it has not happened yet anywhere) there was a case of successful and exhaustive prosecutions, complete truth-telling, munificent reparations, and deep structural reforms, the slate still would not be totally wiped clean. Strictly speaking, it is impossible to go back to the status quo ante. Therefore, conceptions of reconciliation that emphasize an unqualified sense of closure, or that posit a comprehensive ideal of social harmony, are unrealizable, and also indefensible.

Fifth, conceptions of reconciliation that reduce the phenomenon to a psychological state, something akin to a "turn of mind," are unacceptable. The problem is compounded if such conceptions require attributes that are, according to most views of human beings, absolutely extraordinary. While some of us are willing to tolerate some degree of perfectionism, conceptions of reconciliation that do not require exceptional virtue amounting to sainthood will generate easier acceptance.[3]

Sixth, while the religious origins of a conception of reconciliation do not disqualify it, for a variety of reasons including multicultural convictions and applicability in different contexts, it is important to find a conception of reconciliation that can be articulated in terms that do not *depend* entirely on any particular set of religious beliefs.

Three Conceptions of Reconciliation

Given these multiple constraints (which do not form an exhaustive list), is there any room left for a conception of reconciliation? The following positions, all of them at least initially deflationary, seem plausible.

Reconciliation as a Reducible Idea

The first position amounts to saying that reconciliation is a complex but reducible concept, and that some of its essential components include the sorts of things that go into transitional justice policy, e.g., criminal justice, truth-telling, reparations, and institutional reform. Thus, a reconciled society is one that stems from achieving these goals.

It might illuminate this way of thinking about reconciliation to recall what Aristotle has to say about happiness (*eudaimonia* or human flourishing) in Book X.4 of the *Nicomachean Ethics*. Happiness is for Aristotle no mere emotional state, nor a fleeting and insignificant goal, but rather, the *summum bonum*, the best mode of being, the actualization of the potentialities of beings like us. Nevertheless, it is, he insists, "epiphenomenal," in the sense that rather than being a goal that one seeks in itself, it results from, or supervenes upon, living life in a certain way.

There are advantages to conceptualizing reconciliation in an analogous way. First, and contrary to what may be an initial appearance, this actually leads to a demanding conception of reconciliation. Just as for Aristotle happiness can only be experienced by living life in certain ways, reconciliation, one might say, cannot be achieved without achieving its preconditions. Presumably, this would entail, minimally, some degree of success, mere efforts not being sufficient, in punishing perpetrators, telling the truth, repairing victims, and reforming institutions. This is certainly much more stringent than a good part of the rhetoric on reconciliation bandied about both in the literature and in practice. Furthermore, since there is no need to argue that the elements of transitional justice mentioned above constitute a complete definition of justice, to the extent that this mode of thinking makes reconciliation dependent on justice and that "justice" can impose further conditions such as a modicum of distributive fairness, it is possible to make reconciliation even more demanding, all the while permitting a certain (defensible) reticence about the notion.

The significance of a demanding understanding of reconciliation should not be underestimated; it encapsulates the insight behind each of the constraints listed in the first section. As if this were not enough, considering reconciliation as a reducible concept also captures what seems to be a genuine difficulty that a good part of the literature on reconciliation seems reluctant to accept: there are very few things that can be done to promote reconciliation directly, that is, *independently of justice-related goals*, especially if the constraints under consideration are taken seriously. Within certain homogeneous religious contexts—for example, those where Christian beliefs are both widely and deeply shared—some of the constraints can be relaxed, opening avenues for pursuing reconciliation more directly, such as by trying to bolster the prevailing dispositions in favor of unconditional forgiveness. But in most contexts, whatever is meant by a "reconciliation policy" ultimately will not only require, but can largely be reduced to a set of "justice policies."

Obviously, it is impossible to think about any issue in a way that does not involve some costs. Perhaps this way of understanding reconciliation, although respectably reticent, is too reductionistic, and thus, in a way, paralyzing. It could be said that this way of conceiving the subject does not invite sufficiently imaginative exploration of the possibilities of promoting reconciliation on two different levels. First, at the level of individuals, this view generates two difficulties, one of which is particularly significant. In concentrating on objective conditions, this way of thinking about reconciliation neglects its subjective, attitudinal dimension. Furthermore, as a consequence of this neglect, it can be argued that this reduction captures none of the immensity of a richer understanding of the concept that Charles Villa-Vicencio describes in the following terms: "reconciliation carries within it what is perhaps an anthropological if not a primordial longing for wholeness . . . It suggests that humanity is incomplete to the extent that individuals and communities are alienated from one another" (Villa-Vicencio 2006: 4). The failure here is not only descriptive, but normative; this way of understanding reconciliation provides no basis for recommending the adoption of what many would have reason to think is a highly commendable attitude.

Second, some would argue that this way of understanding reconciliation is similarly uninspiring from a political or policy-making perspective, and that contrary to one of its premises, there *are* policies independent of justice measures that can be pursued explicitly pursuant to reconciliation, foremost among them, official apologies, to which I will return extensively below. Again, the failure here is not merely descriptive. In this case it is pragmatic—it leaves avenues of action unconsidered—and also, perhaps, conceptual: this position may involve conflating justice as both a necessary and a sufficient condition of reconciliation. It may be that justice is indeed a necessary condition of reconciliation, but that achieving reconciliation requires some additional steps, and about these, this position remains silent.

Some may find these difficulties with a reductionistic conception sufficiently severe to make it desirable to look for other ways of understanding reconciliation.

Reconciliation as Coexistence

Staying firmly within the domain of deflationary conceptions of reconciliation, it is possible to think about reconciliation in terms of the conditions of coexistence, and to insist that these conditions may go beyond the minimum requirements of justice, calling for something from individuals, namely, the willingness and capacity to assume a certain attitude toward their collective life.

A popular document on reconciliation, IDEA's *Reconciliation After Violent Conflict: A Handbook*, provides the following initial definition of the notion:

> At its simplest, [reconciliation] means finding a way to live alongside former enemies—not necessarily to love them, or forgive them, or forget the past in any way, but to coexist with them, to develop the degree of cooperation necessary to share our society with them, so that we all have better lives together than we have had separately. (Bloomfield 2003: 12)

Needless to say, much depends on how the terms of coexistence are defined. To give credit to the authors of the *Handbook*, they do not settle for a pittance, but argue that "Reconciliation is an over-arching process which includes the search for truth, justice, forgiveness, healing, and so on" (Bloomfield 2003: 12) and that coexistence is merely one of three stages of reconciliation. While this is actually too loose—I have doubts about including forgiveness as part of reconciliation—I focus on the fact that this way of understanding reconciliation also involves a change in attitude (Huyse 2003).

The attitude that is called for is described in various ways throughout the literature. The most frequent description is "looking for alternatives to revenge" (Huyse 2003: 20). In my view, what lies at the core of the attitude that gets labeled "coexistence" is best described in terms of an interruption. John Borneman approaches the point as follows: "Reconciliation I define not in terms of permanent peace or harmony but as a project of *departure from violence*" (Borneman 2002: 282). What reconciliation interrupts is something that resembles trauma-induced repetition compulsions, which make those who suffer from them prone to either repeat the scene of violence suffered—explaining the sense of many victims of being "locked in the past"—or desire the infliction of pain on the perpetrators—explaining why Villa-Vicencio, among others, speaks of reconciliation in terms of "interrupting the continuum between hatred and revenge" (Villa-Vicencio 2006: 12).

The adoption of this line of thought has its merits. Finding an alternative to revenge is no mean accomplishment, particularly in situations of great harm *and* of virtually no possibility of having claims to justice redeemed. Finally, and most important, since this view does not dispense with the institutional measures described in giving content to the reducible conception of reconciliation, but rather adds to them a reminder that reconciliation always involves an attitudinal change, it enriches what may have seemed a meager account of a complex notion.

Once again, however, there are some costs associated with this position. Critics will object that having started on the attitudinal route, it does not go far enough. To the extent that the conditions of "coexistence" can be satisfied in situations in which the predominant attitudes are "dormant hostility," it can be said that an account of reconciliation in terms of coexistence under-describes the sort of attitudinal transformation that would warrant the name "reconciliation" (Govier and Verwoerd 1997).

Thus, again, there might be those who find it reasonable to look for a richer conception of reconciliation, one that maintains institutional requirements, but that strengthens the attitudinal dimension, without violating the accepted constraints described above.

Reconciliation and Civic Trust

Perhaps it is the fact that trust is a richer conception than coexistence, but one that does not commit us to closure, that explains the fact that the literature on reconciliation is peppered with references to the notion of trust.

But because the references to trust are largely unexplained,[4] I first say a few words about the sense of trust at issue here (a); I then elaborate why this notion of trust helps in discussions about reconciliation (b), before proceeding, in the following sections, to explain why apologies may be thought to contribute to reconciliation understood in these terms, but also why they need to be complemented by other transitional justice measures.

(a) While trusting someone involves relying on that person to do or refrain from doing certain things, trust is not the same as predictability or empirical regularity. If that were so, the paradigm of trust would obtain in our relationship with reliable machines. That reliability is not the same as trustworthiness can be seen in our reluctance to say that we *trust* someone about whose behavior we feel a great deal of certainty but only because we both monitor and control it (e.g., through enforcing the terms of a contract), or because we take defensive or preemptive action (Thomas 1995). Trust involves an expectation of a shared normative commitment. I trust someone when I have reasons to expect a certain pattern of behavior from her, and those reasons include not just her consistent past behavior, but also, crucially, the expectation that among her reasons for action is the commitment to the norms and values we share. This explains both the advantages of trust and its risks: in dispensing with the need to monitor and control, it facilitates cooperation immensely; but as a wager that at least in part for *normative reasons* those we trust will not take advantage of our vulnerabilities, it ensures that we always risk having our expectations defeated.

Trust can be thought of as a scalar relationship, one that allows for degrees. The sense of trust at issue here is not the thick form of trust characteristic of relations between intimates, but rather, "civic" trust, which is the sort of disposition that can develop among citizens who are strangers to one another, but who are members of the same *political* community. True, the dimension of a wager is more salient in this case than in that of trust toward intimates, since we have much less information about others' reasons for actions. However, the norms and values that we assume we share with others and the domain of application of these norms and values are much more general.

Regarding civic trust, we have reasons to be interested in "horizontal" trust among citizens and also in the "vertical" trust between citizens and their institutions. How is the latter to be understood if trust cannot be reduced to mere empirical regularity, but involves something that is possible only among individuals, namely, an awareness of mutual normative reciprocity? Claus Offe offers the following explanation:

"trusting institutions" means something entirely different from "trusting my neighbor": it means *knowing* and recognizing as valid the values and the form of life incorporated in an institution and deriving from this recognition the assumption that this idea makes sufficient sense to a sufficient number of people to motivate their ongoing active support for the institution and the compliance with its rules. Successful institutions generate a negative feedback loop: they make sense to actors so that actors will support them and comply with what the institutionally defined order prescribes. (Offe 1999: 70–71)

Trusting an institution, then, amounts to knowing that its constitutive rules, values, and norms are shared by participants and that they regard them as binding (Tyler and Huo 2002).

(b) How does the notion of trust help us think about reconciliation? Before assessing advantages and disadvantages, it is necessary to flesh out the position a bit more:

Reconciliation, minimally, is the condition under which citizens can trust one another *as citizens* again (or anew). That means that they are sufficiently committed to the norms and values that motivate their ruling institutions, sufficiently confident that those who operate those institutions do so also on the basis of those norms and values, and sufficiently secure about their fellow citizens' commitment to abide by these basic norms and values.

What is so advantageous about thinking of reconciliation in this way?

First, this view makes clear that reconciliation involves, but is more than, a psychological state. It presupposes that both institutions and persons can become *trustworthy*, and this is not something that is merely granted but *earned*. This allows us to insist on the demanding character of the preconditions of trustworthiness (and hence of reconciliation). The question is, what can be done to make institutions trustworthy in the aftermath of violence? As I will argue below, it is not unreasonable to think that this would be more difficult in the absence of some criminal accountability, a lot of truth-telling, as much reparations as possible, and all plausible and necessary institutional reform. At the same time, the fact that this conception folds in a concern with attitudes addresses one of the problems that affected the conception of reconciliation as a reducible idea.

Second, the fact that trust is a scalar relationship makes it possible to graduate the corresponding conception of reconciliation in different degrees of "thickness," from the very formal, secular, or institutional, to the deeply personal, religious, or spiritual, thus addressing the concern that an account of reconciliation centered on the notion of coexistence is simply too meager.

Third, it seems that this understanding of reconciliation is capable of abiding by all the constraints mentioned above that have not been covered in the preceding remarks: a conception of reconciliation that hinges on the trustworthiness of institutions will not amount to "cheap" or "false" reconciliation; nor is it likely to lead to an inequitable burdening of victims; nor does it rest on the idea that the slate has been wiped clean. Indeed, strictly speaking, it does not require, although it may lead to, forgiveness.

Apologies and Reconciliation

The account of reconciliation in terms of civic trust, then, helps to clarify a notoriously fuzzy and contested notion. Here I will argue that it also helps to understand the intuitively appealing—but insufficiently explained—idea that apologies can further reconciliation. But since the notion of an apology is no clearer than that of reconciliation, it will be necessary to explain the way I understand this notion. To go about this task functionally at first, it would be useful to have a fuller picture of the condition that apologies are meant to help overcome—an "unreconciled" society. This turns out to be more difficult that one may think, for obviously there are no societies where *all* claims to justice have been solved, and this fact, on its own, cannot determine that a society is "unreconciled." Here the philosophical notion of "resentment" can play a useful role. As a first approximation, one can say that an unreconciled society is one in which resentment characterizes social relationships.

Margaret Walker, in a series of splendid papers (Walker 2004, 2006), has developed a conception of resentment based on P. F. Strawson's notion of a reactive attitude (Strawson 1968). On this account, resentment is not merely another name for generalized anger or other negative affective reactions, but rather, for a specific type of anger, one that attributes responsibility for the defeat, or the threat of defeat, of *normative expectations*. To illustrate the two main elements in this account by means of contrast, the reaction to misfortunes, including accidents great and small, can very well be anger, even deep anger, self-pity, etc., but properly speaking, should not be resentment, for what defeats my expectations is entirely fortuitous, and therefore no attribution of responsibility is plausible. Similarly, the reaction to the defeat of expectations that are based on preferences can be quite negative, but can not, properly, amount to resentment, for there is nothing to suggest that I have a right to have preference-based expectations met. Resentment, as Walker argues, "responds to perceived *threats to expectations based on norms* that are presumed shared in, or justly authoritative for, common life" (Walker 2004: 146, emphasis in original).

An "unreconciled" society, then, would be one in which resentment characterizes the relations between citizens and between citizens and their institutions. It is one in which people experience anger because their norm-based expectations have been threatened or defeated. Expectations concerning basic physical security, for instance, are not whimsical nor do they reflect mere preferences. The idea that the state is the final guarantor of physical safety is part of the core of the notion of the modern state. Threatening or defeating those expectations not just usually, but *properly*, leads to feelings of resentment among victims and others. This anger is more than blind rage or deep frustration; it is ineluctably intertwined with a claim about the validity of the threatened or violated norm, a claim which in turn generates an attribution of responsibility for the threats or the violations, and therefore, for the accountability of those who so acted.

There is a further aspect of this norm-based articulation of the notion of resentment that contributes to making it particularly useful for our purposes. It provides an illuminating account of a dimension of massive abuse that has to be kept firmly in mind when thinking about the prospects of reconciliation. Victims of torture—among other forms of abuse—report a sense of loneliness and isolation (Scarry 1987; Weschler 1998). Walker argues that resentment arises as a result of threats to and violations of not only norms, but also one's standing to assert or insist upon the validity of those norms. To the extent that the norms in question are those that define social, moral, or interpersonal boundaries, massive abuse can lead to a form of "normative isolation," of "demoralization" that can be seen clearly when one considers that the "accusing anger" that resentment constitutes is one that invites others to come to one's defense—an invitation that in these cases ordinarily goes unheeded. Hence the solitude of the abused:

> The human will to resist injustice runs deep, but to live in ongoing protest against one's exposure to indignity, subordination, exclusion, or violence is a heavy load to bear. It is difficult to sustain live normative expectations in the face of predictable violation, but especially so if one receives little confirmation for one's responses of resentment and outrage at bad treatment or insult. One is apt to be worn down or defeated without this support. (Walker 2006: 103)

So, how can an apology help to overcome resentment? Recent work on apologies bears the marks of a new and developing field, beginning with a lack of consensus about the semantics of the notion, and about the reasons why apologies are supposed to have an effect. A good number of accounts of apologies seem to mix the essential characteristics of an apology as a speech-act with the conditions of its success. The inclusion of the "performance of penance" (Goffman 1971: 113), the "express[ion] of concern for future good relations" (Orenstein 1999: 239), and most of all, the offer of repair as part of the essential components of an apology[5] reflect instances of this conflation. Using "Occam's razor," I suggest that a speech act is an apology if and only if it constitutes an acceptance of responsibility and an expression of regret.[6]

Just as there are different accounts of the essential characteristics of apologies, there are different accounts of how apologies work. Two of them are worth mentioning in this context.

The first one concentrates on the fact that apologies involve an exchange of power, as succinctly expressed by Aaron Lazare,

> what makes an apology work is the exchange of shame and power between the offender and the offended. By apologizing, you take the shame of your offense and redirect it to yourself. You admit of hurting or diminishing someone, and, in effect, say that you are really the one who is diminished—I'm the one who was wrong, mistaken, insensitive, or stupid. In acknowledging your shame you give the offender the power to forgive. The exchange is at the heart of the healing process. (Lazare 1995: 42)[7]

In this view, what is important is not only the redirection of shame in its own terms, but one of its consequences: it puts the offender in a position of vulnerability, and therefore redraws the balance of power with the offended, who is now in a position to either grant or withhold something the offender wants, the release that comes through forgiveness.

Originally having had the power to hurt, the offender now gives the power to forgive or not to forgive to the offended party. This exchange of humiliation and power between the offender and the offended may be the clearest way of explaining how some apologies heal by restoring dignity and self-respect. (Lazare 2004: 52)

While I do not doubt that there are some circumstances—especially face-to-face apologies—which are fittingly described in these terms, to make an exchange of *power* the cornerstone of an explanatory account of how apologies work stretches credibility. I am not sure that Queen Elizabeth's apology to the Maoris in New Zealand, or President Clinton's apologies to the victims of the Tuskegee experiments, or—to include non-state apologies—Texaco's chairman's apology for racial slurs are best described in terms of a redrawing of the balance of power between the offender and the offended.[8] There are two reasons why this account overestimates the significance of a power shift between the parties. First, it is not clear that an apology actually has as its end result the redrawing, to any important degree, of the balance of power between the relevant parties. This is particularly important in the case of institutional, official apologies, where the relationship between the offender and the offended is frequently asymmetrical (as in the three examples above). Second, even if one sets aside the effects of the apology and concentrates on what the account considers to be the relevant exchange—an apology for release—many of these instances may constitute examples of an offer one cannot refuse, if for no other reason than that the apology might be the only gesture on offer. If this is so, there are reasons to question the moral significance of the exchange.

The second account of how apologies work focuses on the fact that apologies are unthinkable in the absence of norms and values whose validity—despite the transgression—is reaffirmed in the act of apologizing. This is a view that can be constructed on the basis of Tavuchis's sociological approach to apologies in his *Mea Culpa* (although he does not offer an explanatory account of their effectiveness). Tavuchis argues that in examining a wide variety of apologies, the discernible common theme he found was "the violation of an unstated but consequential, moral rule" (Tavuchis 1991: 3). I find the reference to specifically moral rules unduly constraining, and Tavuchis himself eventually broadens the scope of his attention; but focusing on the fact that apologies reaffirm norms and values is fundamentally correct. In the most elaborate statement of this point in his book, Tavuchis writes:

Genuine apologies . . . may be taken as the symbolic foci of secular remedial rituals that serve to recall and reaffirm allegiance to codes of behavior and belief whose integrity has been tested and challenged by transgression, whether knowingly or unwittingly. An apology thus speaks to an act that cannot be undone but that cannot go unnoticed without compromising the current and future relationship of the parties, the legitimacy of the violated rule, and the wider social web in which the participants are enmeshed. (Tavuchis 1991: 13)

The point I want to make is not only that conceptually speaking an apology is unthinkable in the absence of a norm that the offender considers to be binding—a norm that is typically, although not always, shared with the offended—but that the reason why an apology may "work" is that it involves the affirmation of the validity of the norm.

However, recalling that part of our interest should lie in articulating accounts that give reasons to think that a certain action will have certain effects, it is worth insisting on the details of how it is, precisely, that an apology may further reconciliation. The answer should be clear enough; this account of the norm-affirming nature of apologies jibes with the account of resentment mentioned above. Thus, if an unreconciled society is one characterized by resentful relations, and if resentment is a response to the violation or the threatened violation of expectations based on norms, the reaffirmation of the validity of the (breached or threatened) norms can be expected to allay resentment, and in this way, to contribute to reconciliation. Furthermore, since a public, official apology can reaffirm the general validity of impersonal norms, there are also reasons to expect that it can address two of the phenomena that were mentioned in the account of resentment: that the breach of or threat to norms may produce resentment not only in those directly targeted by the offense; and that the breach or threat often produces a sense of solitude or demoralization in victims. As to the latter point, Lazare has argued that "by acknowledging that a moral norm was violated, both parties affirm a similar set of values. The acknowledgment re-establishes a common moral ground" (Lazare 1995: 42), and in so doing may also give assurance to victims that the offenses were not their fault, that they did not contribute to the provocation of the offenses (Lazare 2004), and, more generally, one can add, that their judgment about what is acceptable and unacceptable, judgment that systematic violence often intentionally targets, was reliable after all. For similar reasons, to the extent that communities can be defined in terms of allegiance to norms and values, and that apologies involve the affirmation of norms, apologies can have community-inducing effects.

I propose, then, that it is the norm-affirming function of apologies that helps us understand the potential contribution apologies can make to reconciliation. Whether that contribution takes place in any given instance, of course, requires empirical research. My interest does not lie in providing a general argument in defense of apologies, but first, in understanding how they can be thought to work.

The Limits of Apologies

Lest anyone think that despite my caveats I still think that apologies, on their own, can make a significant contribution to reconciliation, two (related) reminders are in order. First, although I have adopted a frugal understanding of the concept of apologies as an acceptance of responsibility and an expression of regret, there is a strong tendency in the literature to define the concept more expansively, including in the very definition elements such as the promise to forebear and the offer of reparations. Even if these expanded definitions confuse the essential characteristics of apologies with the conditions of their success, the tendency points toward a healthy reluctance to think that mere words, disconnected from the future of the sequence of interaction, can have important effects.

More compelling still is the reminder that, especially in the aftermath not of individual breaches of norms ("individual" in the sense that the breaches are carried out by isolated individuals and that they constitute relatively isolated, disconnected acts), but of massive and systematic human rights abuses, the recovery of trust in institutions requires not only that the basic underlying norms be legitimate, but also, that the institutions be effective in realizing those norms. Effectiveness cannot be achieved merely through the verbal reaffirmation of norms. This reveals the limits of apologies and the need to complement them with different transitional justice measures.

Arguably, transitional justice initiatives, singly and collectively, are meant to promote trust through action.[9] An effective *prosecutions policy* can contribute to the reconstitution of the trust of citizens in their institutions. At the most general level, law both presupposes and catalyzes trust among individuals and trust between them and their institutions. It can help generate trust *between citizens* by stabilizing expectations and thus diminishing the risks of trusting others. Similarly, law helps generate trust *in institutions* (including the institutions of law themselves) by accumulating a record of reliably solving conflicts, among other ways. But the accomplishment of these goals naturally presupposes the effectiveness of the law, and in a world of less than generalized spontaneous compliance, this means that law, although rational, must also be coercive. This coercive character at the limit entails criminal punishment.

Truth-telling can foster civic trust in different ways (de Grieff 2006b). Here I will concentrate on those citizens who are fearful that the past might repeat itself, whose confidence was shattered by experiences of violence and abuse. Their specific fear might be that the political identity of (some) other citizens has been shaped around values, dispositions, and attitudes that made the abuses possible and that might lead to violence again. If we are willing, however, to reflect upon the constitution of our identity and the character of our dispositions, we give those citizens who worry about our political identity, as well as those who worry about whether they can rely on people who may still carry dubious dispositions and attitudes, reasons to participate in a common political project. An institutionalized effort to confront the past might be seen by those who were formerly on the receiving end of violence as a good faith effort to come clean, to understand long term patterns of socialization, and in this sense, to initiate a new political project.

Reparations constitute for victims a manifestation of the seriousness of the State and of their fellow citizens in their efforts to reestablish relations of equality and respect. In the absence of reparations, victims will always have reasons to suspect that even if the other transitional procedures are applied with some degree of sincerity, the "new" democratic society is one that is being constructed on their shoulders, ignoring their justified claims. By contrast, if even under conditions of scarcity funds are allocated for former victims, a strong message is sent to them and others about their (perhaps new) inclusion in the political community. Former victims of abuse are given a material manifestation of the fact that they are now living among a group of fellow citizens and under institutions that aspire to be trustworthy. Reparations, then, can be seen as a method to achieve one of the aims of a just state, namely inclusiveness, in the sense that all citizens are equal participants in a common political project (de Greiff 2006a, 2007b).

Finally, most post-transitional *institutional reform* is motivated not just by the aims of increasing the efficiency of State institutions—understanding efficiency simply in terms of quantifiable output—but by the richer goals of relegitimizing the State and preventing the recurrence of violence. Vetting procedures, for example, can be seen as efforts to make the institutions of the State trustworthy by excluding from them people who in the past have breached the trust of the citizens they were meant to serve (de Greiff 2007a).

In the absence of measures such as these, we have no obvious reason to think that citizens will be willing to deposit their trust in the institutions of the State, independently of how profusely past violators may apologize. Indeed, in the absence of measures of this sort, the verbal reaffirmation of the underlying basic norms is bound to sound hollow. In their absence, then, apologies will not be able to bring about reconciliation, if this is a condition that involves civic trust.

And yet, just as apologies, on their own, are likely to be insufficient, it may be that these measures, without apologies, are themselves insufficient. Let us return to the idea that reconciliation is a rich and complex notion both because it rests on demanding institutional preconditions *and* because it makes reference to an attitude. The most that the promotion of particular transitional justice strategies leads to is an improvement in the *trustworthiness* of institutions (and fellow citizens). But that does not mean that citizens, particularly victims, will in fact *trust* those institutions (and their fellow citizens). For various reasons, both institutions and individuals may now be trustworthy and yet fail to gain the trust of others. Is there anything that can be done to make it more feasible for those who are still reticent to actually *grant* trust to those who have *earned* it? It seems reasonable to think that apologies may make a (modest) difference. While transitional justice measures of the sort mentioned above reveal the prospective reasons that warrant the claim to trustworthiness, it may be that an acceptance of responsibility and an expression of sincere regret for past breaches can help move victims and others who felt threatened in the past to make the critical attitudinal change. After all, to consider a norm to be binding is not simply a matter of unbending resolve to abide by its requirements in the future, but of experiencing regret (and taking appropriate corrective action) for past failures to abide by them.

Whether any of these measures have the results I have mentioned can only be determined empirically. I have no interest in predictions. I think all of us have good reasons to be interested in accounts that give us reasons to expect that if we follow a certain path of action, certain consequences will follow. Now, let us observe. Experience suggests we should be cautious, at best.

My gratitude to Eric Darko, Roger Duthie, Sarah Proescher, and Laetitia Lemaistre for research assistance.

References

Alter, Susan. 1999. *Apologising for Serious Wrongdoing: Social, Psychological and Legal Considerations.* Ottawa: Law Commission of Canada.
Bloomfield, David. 2003. "Reconciliation: An Introduction." In *Reconciliation After Violent Conflict: A Handbook,* ed. David Bloomfield, Teresa Barnes, and Luc Huyse. Stockholm: IDEA.
Boraine, Alex. 2000. *A Country Unmasked.* Oxford: Oxford University Press.
Borneman, John. 2002. "Reconciliation After Ethnic Cleansing: Listening, Retribution, Affiliation." *Public Culture* 14 (2): 281–304.
de Greiff, Pablo. 2004. "Reparations Efforts in International Perspective: What Compensation Contributes to the Achievement of Imperfect Justice." In *To Repair the Irreparable: Reparations and Reconstruction in South Africa,* ed. Charles Villa-Vicencio and Erik Doxtader. Cape Town: Dave Phillips.
———. 2006a. "Justice and Reparations." In *The Handbook of Reparations,* ed. Pablo de Greiff. Oxford. Oxford University Press.

———. 2006b. "Truth-Telling and the Rule of Law." In *Telling the Truths, Truth Telling and Peacebuilding in Post-Conflict Societies*, ed. Tristan Anne Borer. Notre Dame, Ind.: University of Notre Dame Press.
———. 2007a. "Vetting and Transitional Justice." In *Vetting as a Transitional Justice Measure*, ed. Alexander Mayer-Rieckh and Pablo de Greiff. New York: Social Science Research Council
———. 2007b. "Addressing the Past: Reparations for Gross Human Rights Abuses." In *Civil War and the Rule of Law: Security, Development, Human Rights*, ed. Agnes Hurwitz. Boulder, Colo.: Lynne Rienner.
Goffman, Erving. 1971. *Relations in Public: Microstudies of the Public Order*. New York: Basic Books.
Govier, Trudy and Wilhelm Verwoerd. 1997. "Trust and the Problem of National Reconciliation." *Philosophy of the Social Sciences* 32 (22): 178–205.
Huyse, Luc. 2003. "The Process of Reconciliation." In *Reconciliation After Violent Conflict: A Handbook*, ed. David Bloomfield, Teresa Barnes, and Luc Huyse. Stockholm: IDEA.
Lazare, Aaron. 1995. "Go Ahead, Say You're Sorry." *Psychology Today* 23 (1): 40–43, 76–78.
———. 2004. *On Apology*. Oxford: Oxford University Press.
Levi, Deborah L. 1997. "The Role of Apology in Mediation." *N.Y.U. Law Review* 72 (5): 1165–1210.
Méndez, Juan. 1997. "Accountability for Past Abuses." *Human Rights Quarterly* 19 (2): 255–82.
O'Hara, Erin Ann and Douglas Yam. 2002. "On Apology and Consilience." *Washington Law Review* 77: 1121–92.
Offe, Claus. 1999. "How Can We Trust Our Fellow Citizens?" In *Democracy and Trust*, ed. Mark E. Warren. Cambridge: Cambridge University Press.
Orenstein, Aviva. 1999. "Apology Excepted: Incorporating a Feminist Analysis into Evidence Policy Where you Would Least Expect It." *Southwestern University Law Review* 28: 221–79.
Scarry, Elaine. 1987. *The Body in Pain*. Oxford: Oxford University Press.
Strawson, P. F. 1968. "Freedom and Resentment." In *Studies in the Philosophy of Thought and Action*, ed. P. F. Strawson. Oxford: Oxford University Press
Taft, Lee. 2000. "Apology Subverted: The Commodification of Apology." *Yale Law Journal* 109 (5): 1136–60.
Tavuchis, Nicholas. 1991. *Mea Culpa: A Sociology of Apology and Reconciliation*. Stanford, Calif.: Stanford University Press.
Thomas, Laurence Mordekhai. 1995. "Power, Trust, and Evil." In *Overcoming Racism and Sexism*, ed. Linda Bell and David Blumenfeld. Lanham, Md.: Rowman and Littlefield.
Tyler, Tom and Yuen J. Huo. 2002. *Trust in the Law*. New York: Sage.
Villa-Vicencio, Charles. 2006. "The Politics of Reconciliation." In *Telling the Truths: Truth-Telling and Peace Building*, ed. Tristan Anne Borer. Notre Dame, Ind.: Notre Dame University Press.
Wagatsuma, Hiroshi and Arthur Rossett. 1986. "The Implications of Apology: Law and Culture in Japan and the United States." *Law and Society Review* 20 (4): 461–98.
Walker, Margaret Urban. 2004. "Resentment and Reassurance." In *Setting the Moral Compass: Essays by Women Philosophers*, ed. Cheshire Calhoun. New York: Oxford University Press.

———. 2006. *Moral Repair: Reconstructing Moral Relations After Wrongdoing.* New York: Cambridge University Press.
Weschler, Lawrence. 1998. *A Miracle, a Universe: Settling Accounts with Torturers.* Chicago: University of Chicago Press.
Wilson, Richard A. 2000. "Reconciliation and Revenge in Post-Apartheid South Africa." *Current Anthropology* 41 (1): 75–98.
Yamamoto, Eric. 1997. Race Apologies. *Journal of Gender, Race, and Justice* 1 (1): 47–88.

Chapter 9
Wrestling with the Past: Apologies, Quasi-Apologies, and Non-Apologies in Canada

MATT JAMES

Several purported instances of political apology in Canada share a consistent and perplexing tendency to deliver less than meets the eye. Two discoveries are particularly troubling. First, observers overestimate the scope and extent of Canadian political apologies for domestic human rights abuses. Second, the Canadian government has managed to extract unseemly political advantage from its participation in apology processes. These findings support Roger Daniels's Twainesque conclusion that "reports of an 'Age of Apology' have been . . . greatly exaggerated" (Daniels 2003: 10). But whereas Daniels bases his skepticism on the overwhelming absence of meaningful reparations in most cases, I suggest that many of what Daniels would dismiss as "uncompensated apologies" are deficient on broader grounds as well. Canada's underwhelming apologies reflect the advantages state authorities enjoy when the notion of political apology remains novel and ambiguous. Given this inequality of resources in the world of political apology, elaborate campaigns of self-interested strategizing by apology-seeking victims are required. We need to accept this reality while insisting that political apology has a moral core.

Criteria for an Authentic Political Apology

Nicholas Tavuchis identifies the distinctive moral core of interpersonal as opposed to political apology. An authentic apology conveys the offender's unambiguous and regretful willingness to own the consequences of his or her actions (Tavuchis 1991: 16). This requires wrongdoers to take full responsibility for their wrongdoing by acknowledging its wrongfulness and promising not to repeat it. It also means vesting in the wronged party the choice of forgiveness: a move that performatively reverses the logic of the offense, creating a space in which reconciliation might begin.

Tavuchis's concern to chart the moral core of interpersonal apology informs more recent and explicit discussions of political apology by legal scholar Martha Minow (Minow 1998), psychologist Janet Bavelas (Bavelas 2004), and legal scholar Susan Alter (Alter 1999). Five initial requirements of an authentic political apology can be distilled from this work: (1) naming clearly the wrong or wrongs in question; (2) taking responsibility for the wrong; (3) expressing regret; (4) promising nonrepetition; and (5) refraining from demanding forgiveness. These requirements add important detail to Tavuchis's primary focus on the conditions of authentic interpersonal apology.

But the unique genre of political apology calls for additional criteria to address reconciliation attempts involving collectivities. Tavuchis's separate discussion of "many-to-many" apologies stresses the importance of an official written record that allows group members on both sides to judge the reconciliatory work attempted in their names. A true many-to-many apology, writes Tavuchis, "is fashioned for the record and exists only by virtue of its appearance on record" (Tavuchis 1991: 102).

Like Daniels, some writers argue that reparations are also necessary to genuine political apology, noting that a delegated and institutionally mediated apology is one whose sincerity is uniquely vulnerable to doubt (Alter 1999). Reparations may thus help to satisfy Michael Cunningham's concern: that states "can presumably go around being sorry promiscuously about all sorts of things" (Cunningham 1999). Therefore, along with Tavuchis's emphasis on recording the apology, we can add reparations to the criteria for an authentic political apology.

Mark Gibney and Erik Roxstrom bring a similar focus on the moral core of apology to international relations (Gibney and Roxstrom 2001). Concerned to advance the development of customary international law, they argue that state apologies can provide a measure of historical consensus about particular wrongs, and furnish precedent-setting declarations of wrongful international conduct. Gibney and Roxstrom offer nine criteria, three of which add distinct, additional requirements to our emerging definition of an authentic political apology, and which appear useful in evaluating domestic as well as international apology. These criteria are publicity, ceremony, and consistency.

First, Gibney and Roxstrom argue that the apology must be adequately publicized in order to engage the community in whose name it is made. Second, they suggest that due attention to ceremony is necessary to lend the apology dignity and seriousness of purpose. This latter criterion may be particularly important given the alleged impossibility of conveying genuine collective remorse (Tavuchis 1991: 97). Finally, Gibney and Roxstrom stress that nations must be consistent in their apology output and behavior so as not to vitiate apology's norm-building potential (Gibney and Roxstrom 2001: 932).

The cumulative message of this literature is as follows. An authentic political apology: (1) is recorded officially in writing; (2) names the wrongs in question; (3) accepts responsibility; (4) states regret; (5) promises nonrepetition; (6) does not demand forgiveness; (7) is not hypocritical or arbitrary; and (8) undertakes—through measures of publicity, ceremony, and concrete reparation—both to engage morally those in whose name apology is made and to assure the wronged group that the apology is sincere.

These criteria serve at least four important functions. First, states can use them to help produce more meaningful apologies, which might enhance the long-run prospects for reconciliation between victim and perpetrator groups and their respective descendants (Alter 1999: 8–9). Three remaining functions of the criteria are of special interest here: (1) evaluating the robustness of particular instances of political apology; (2) distinguishing between qualitatively different instances of apology; and (3) evaluating the moral consistency of the cumulative apology records of particular states. I discuss Canada's main potential instances of political apology to judge their robustness, distinguish between qualitatively different types of cases, and evaluate the Canadian government's cumulative apology record.

The Cases

Closest to the criteria for authentic political apology is the prime ministerial statement that accompanied the Japanese Canadian Redress Agreement of September 1988 (Miki and Kobayashi 1991: 138–39). From 1942 to 1945, all persons of Japanese descent were removed from coastal British Columbia and interned in the province's interior. Hundreds of Canadian citizens were also "deported" to Japan, and homes, property, and businesses were seized without compensation (Sunahara 1981).

Some forty years later, with many Japanese Canadians watching from the visitors' gallery, Progressive Conservative Prime Minister Brian Mulroney rose in the House of Commons to offer "the formal and sincere apology of this Parliament" (Miki and Kobayashi 1991: 138–39). The apology is thus readily available as part of Canada's official record of parliamentary proceedings. After clearly naming and taking responsibility for the wrongs done—"the Government of Canada wrongfully incarcerated, seized the property, and disenfranchised thousands of citizens of Japanese ancestry"—Mulroney extended his "solemn commitment . . . that [such injustices] will never again be countenanced or repeated." The redress agreement also provided tax-free payments of $21,000 each to roughly 18,000 survivors, established a $12 million community development fund, and earmarked $24 million to create the Canadian Race Relations Foundation.

Thus, the apology to Japanese Canadians was properly recorded, named the relevant wrongs, accepted responsibility, led to some expression of regret, promised nonrepetition, observed considerations of publicity and ceremony, and provided reparations. However, when set against several Canadian quasi- or non-apologies, it appears somewhat arbitrary.

Next on a descending scale of conformity to the criteria is the January 1998 "Statement of Reconciliation" offered by the federal Liberal government to Canada's Aboriginal peoples (Learning from the Past, Stewart 1988). Under Canada's century-long residential schools policy, over 100,000 Native children were taken from their families and placed in coercive and alien settings that typically focused on cultural assimilation (Miller 1996). A federal advisory body, the Law Commission of Canada, concluded that the schools reflected "genocidal intent" in deliberately exposing Aboriginal children to "abuses perpetrated with the explicit goal of eradicating Native ways" (Claes and Clifton 1998). In addition to family separation and forced culture and language loss, over 12,000 survivors alleged in the *Baxter* class action suit that they were physically or sexually abused by the church personnel whom Ottawa charged with running the schools (Office of Indian Reservation Schools Resolution 2003) Canada's last residential school closed in 1986.

At a lunchtime ceremony in a government meeting room on Parliament Hill, Minister of Indian and Northern Affairs Jane Stewart sought to address this shameful past. Although Prime Minister Jean Chrétien was in Ottawa that day, he did not attend the ceremony. The event featured performances by Aboriginal singers and dancers, and concluded with Stewart presenting the Statement of Reconciliation, which she read aloud, in the form of ceremonial scrolls to five Native leaders (O'Neil 1998). The Statement of Reconciliation is not part of Canada's official parliamentary or legal record; it is merely posted on the Department of Indian and Northern Affairs website. Offered "on behalf of all Canadians," the Statement extended strong, though quite general words of regret about Canada's colonial legacy. Most notably, it declared that "we are burdened by past actions that resulted in weakening the identity of Aboriginal peoples, suppressing their languages and cultures, and outlawing spiritual practices." However, the Statement did not describe these actions in any detail, explain which institutions or policies might have been responsible for committing them, or indeed in any way "say sorry" for them.

The Statement then addressed the residential schools, acknowledging that they "separated many children from their families and communities and prevented them from speaking their own languages and from learning about their heritage and cultures." It also acknowledged Ottawa's role "in the development and administration of these schools." Next came the Statement's only explicit words of apology:

> Particularly to those individuals who experienced the tragedy of sexual and physical abuse at residential schools, and who have carried this burden believing that in some way they must be responsible, we wish to emphasize that what you experienced was not your fault and should never have happened. To those of you who suffered this tragedy at residential schools, we are deeply sorry.

Stewart concluded by announcing a $350 million "healing fund" to support the mental health needs of residential schools survivors.

With the important exception of Grand Chief Phil Fontaine of the Assembly of First Nations, the Native leaders present dismissed the Statement as an inadequate response both to Canada's unjust treatment of Aboriginal peoples in general and to the legacy of the residential schools in particular. The Statement did not admit that the purpose of the residential schools policy was forcibly to assimilate Aboriginal peoples (Barnsley 1998). Neither did it acknowledge the devastating, ongoing effects, including mental illness, alcoholism, and family breakdown, that can be traced back to the schools (Assembly of Frist Nations 1994). Perhaps most important, the Statement did not "say sorry" for either the intentions behind the policy or for any aspect of its effects beyond actual instances of physical and sexual abuse.

The initiative's sole reparative measure, the $350 million healing fund, was also inadequate. Although thousands of off-reserve and nonstatus Indians attended the schools, the fund was aimed almost exclusively at status Indians living on designated Indian reserves. Status Indians, that is, Indigenous peoples of Canada who are registered with the federal government as members of a First Nation, form the designated constituency of the Assembly of First Nations, whose leader accepted the Statement (O'Neil 1998). Therefore, because of vagueness about the character, scope, and impact of the wrongs in question, improper ceremony (as evidenced by the prime minister's absence), and inadequate reparation, the Statement of Reconciliation counts as a relatively robust quasi-apology.

Curiously, eight years earlier the governing Conservatives offered stronger words to a group whose treatment seems less egregiously unjust. From 1940 to 1943, approximately 700 Italian Canadians, roughly 1 percent of Canada's ethnic Italian population, were interned for their alleged leadership roles in Fascist organizations (Ramirez 1988). Many internees' bank accounts were frozen, and in some cases properties were seized that were never returned. No internee was ever charged with a crime (National Congress of Italian Canadians 1990). At a November 1990 luncheon cohosted by the Canadian Italian Business Professional Association and the National Council of Italian Canadians, Prime Minister Brian Mulroney said: "On behalf of the government and people of Canada, I offer a full and unqualified apology for the wrongs done to our fellow Canadians of Italian origin during World War Two" (Canada Office of the Prime Minister 1990).

Mulroney described in detail "the harassment and internment of Canadians of Italian origin under the *War Measures Act.*" He declared that "the indignity suffered by the Italian-Canadian community" was "deeply offensive to the simple notion of respect for human dignity and the presumption of innocence." He stated that the official silence about the internment had "become as much a part of the discrimination, and as much a cause for shame, as the original deeds themselves," and pledged that "never again will such injustices be inflicted." Some Italian Canadians voiced dissatisfaction with the ceremonial limitations of the banquet hall venue (Iacovetta and Ventresca 2000). Morover, the only printed record of Mulroney's words is the press release announcing the event, which does not belong to any legal or parliamentary record, and which is not even posted on the internet. Nevertheless, the prime minister named wrongs, took responsibility, stated regret, and pledged nonrepetition.

Mulroney also signaled reparations. On at least two prior occasions, he had promised to initiate collective negotiations on financial compensation with various redress-seeking groups. At the 1990 luncheon, he stated that his government would as "a matter of simple justice . . . begin discussions with representatives of the Italian-Canadian community . . . to discuss how best to symbolize our recognition of . . . discrimination . . . suffered at the hands of government." Yet three years later the Mulroney cabinet declared that no financial compensation would be offered to Italian Canadians (Sudlow 1993). The cabinet indicated shortly thereafter that the broader policy of negotiating compensation was under review ("Hefty Price Tag Delays Settlements" 1993).

Ottawa's handling of the matter satisfied no one. Critics, who argued that Mulroney's apology to the Italian Canadian community "publicly confirmed the validity of [a] laundered version of history" (Iacovetta and Perin 2000), noted that the internment targeted only suspected Fascist leaders, and that Fascist salutes and paraphernalia appear clearly in the inmates' own photographs of the camps. For their part, Italian Canadian leaders viewed the federal reversal on compensation as "insulting" (Sudlow 1993). Therefore, regardless of the appropriateness of Mulroney's initial words, his government's eventual approach created an offering whose reconciliatory potential is surely low: the retroactively downgraded quasi-apology.

Clearly inadequate from the standpoint of apology is the treatment of the Canadian Inuit known as the High Arctic exiles. During the 1950s, approximately 90 Inuit from Northern Québec were relocated 1,800 kilometers north in a deceitful and humiliating manner (Marcus 1992). Swayed by promises of better hunting opportunities, the Inuit, who had been receiving welfare payments, discovered after the fact that they had been sent north in a "rehabilitation" exercise whose purpose was to force them to resume a subsistence lifestyle in an environment harsher than any they had known. The Royal Commission on Aboriginal Peoples has also pointed to another motive: the desire to establish a human presence in Canada's sparsely populated far North to reinforce Canada's sovereignty there (Canada Royal Commission 1994: 162). Subsequent federal inaction compounded the injustice. The Inuit, who suffered hunger, cold, and loneliness in their exile, had been promised a voluntary relocation—yet a federal program offering funding and assistance for moves back south was not made available until 1988.

Several successive federal administrations refused to apologize. Instead, under a peremptorily named "Reconciliation Agreement," Jean Chrétien's Liberal government established a $10-million trust fund for the relocated individuals and their families in March 1996 (Canada Department of Indian and Northern Affairs 1996). The Agreement required the fund's beneficiaries formally to "acknowledge that they understand that in planning the relocation, the government officials of the time were acting with honourable intentions in what was perceived to be in the best interests of the Inuit at that time." In return, Ottawa admitted "that in part because of government planning and implementation, the Inuit encountered hardship, suffering, and loss in the initial years of these relocations." The Agreement also recognized "the contribution of the Inuit toward the enhancement of the Canadian presence in the North." Finally, Minister of Indian Affairs and Northern Development Ron Irwin observed that "such a major undertaking involving the movement of people would not be done in the same way today."

The Inuit "reconciled" under duress: the signatories, who had been demanding an apology for roughly a decade, relented to help "their aging elders . . . before they die" (Aubry 1996: A13). While the trust fund was undoubtedly welcome, Ottawa's treatment of the Inuit was disrespectful. The prime minister failed to attend a poorly publicized signing ceremony in Iqaluit, and the only written record of the Agreement seems to be an appendix to a press release which has been removed from the Indian Affairs website. The press release itself scolds the Inuit: "We cannot continue to dwell on the past, we must move on and concentrate on the future."

Thus, the High Arctic Relocation Reconciliation Agreement is characterized by a difficult-to-access written record, refusal to acknowledge wrongs, failure to take responsibility or state regret, an imposed requirement of forgiveness, and inadequate publicity and ceremony. The Inuit did elicit an oral statement of nonrepetition and significant financial reparation. But the absence of apology is jarring. The Parliamentary Standing Committee on Aboriginal Affairs, the Canadian Human Rights Commission, and Canada's Royal Commission on Aboriginal Peoples have all recommended a formal apology (Marcus 1992). By contrast, no advisory body has ever recommended an apology for the former Italian Canadian internees, let alone the entire Italian Canadian community. The disingenuous packaging of the settlement under the banner of "reconciliation," which designates what genuine apologies hope to effect, is also disheartening. The Inuit received an aggressively preemptive non-apology leavened by compensation.

More straightforward instances of non-apology are the unsuccessful redress claims of Canadians of Ukrainian and Chinese ancestry. Roughly 5,000 Ukrainian Canadians were interned during World War I, on the mistaken ground that their former status as citizens of the Austro-Hungarian empire made them national security threats (Morton 1974). The internment camps were punitive, inmates were exploited as uncompensated labor, and in many cases cash and valuables were seized and never returned (Luciuk 1988b), Although approximately 5,000 non-Ukrainians were also interned, including ethnic Bulgarians, Romanians, and Poles, only the more sizable and organized Ukrainian Canadian community has sought redress. In 2004 there remained one known internment survivor.

The Ukrainian Canadian Civil Liberties Association and the Ukrainian Canadian Congress seek official parliamentary acknowledgment of the injustices, various memorials, and a community development fund of approximately $1.5 million (the estimated, inflation-adjusted amount of the labor and valuables originally taken from the Ukrainian Canadian internees) (Ukrainian Canadian Civil Liberties Commission 2001). The federal government has erected two interpretive panels in Banff National Park in Alberta, while activists wish to see memorials at all 24 former internment sites. Although it would be inaccurate to say that Ottawa refuses to apologize for the internment, given that the community is not presently requesting an apology, the Ukrainian Canadian case still counts as an instance of non-apology (Mackenzie 1994).

Between 1985 and 1994, Ukrainian Canadian leaders did request an apology (Serge 1988). Two factors appear to have led to the changed position. First, the Conservative reversal on financial compensation in 1993 effectively shut down the collective redress negotiation process. The political climate for redress-seekers deteriorated further in December 1994, when the incoming Liberals announced that none of the groups involved would be offered financial compensation or apologies (Rinehart 1994).

Second, in summer 1994 the Ukrainian Canadian Congress was criticized for demanding what some saw as the exorbitant compensation sum of $30 million (Khan 1994). In an apparent response to both these setbacks, the Ukrainian Canadian Civil Liberties Commission reemerged with the significantly relaxed set of demands noted above. The Ukrainian Canadian Congress embraced the new demands in the late 1990s (Ukrainian Canadian Civil Liberties Commission 2001).

Since 1984, the Chinese Canadian National Council has sought financial redress and an official apology for the "Chinese head tax" and "Exclusion Act." Implemented at the rate of $50 in 1885, the tax was raised to $100 in 1900, and then to $500 in 1903. In 1923 it was replaced by a virtual ban on Chinese immigration to Canada, which remained until 1947 (Bolaria and Li 1985: 85–95). Although there were roughly 2,000 head tax payers alive when the redress campaign began in 1984, only a few survived in 2005 (Chinese Canadian National Council 1987).

Various harms can be traced to the legislation. The prohibitive cost of the tax fostered a system of indentured servitude, with labor contractors paying the price of admission to acquire indebted "clients" (Cho 2002). Furthermore, the legislation ensured that there would be virtually no second Chinese Canadian generation until the late 1970s (Bolaria and Li 1988: 94–95). This meant loneliness, psychological scars, and, for the few Chinese women who managed to immigrate, severe sexual and reproductive pressure. The legislation has also had the more long-term effect of hindering integration. As activists have complained, "the bitter legacy of the Canadian government's 62 years of legislated racism is a Chinese-Canadian community that is still seen as a new immigrant community" (Bolan 1995).

Despite two decades of lobbying, media work, demonstrations, and petitions, as well as a United Nations complaint and legal action under the Canadian Charter of Rights and Freedoms, the redress campaign has been unsuccessful (Dyzenhaus and Moran 2005). The Chinese Canadian National Council continues to seek an official apology, $23 million in compensation for surviving head tax payers and their immediate families (the amount collected under the tax without adjusting for interest or inflation), and an unspecified sum for anti-racism initiatives and community development (Chinese Canadian National Council 1987). This is the clearest Canadian case of a persistent redress campaign that has failed to secure any form of compensation, official acknowledgment, or apology.

The Implications and Utility of the Criteria

Using the criteria described above, I have gauged the apologetic rigor of the major Canadian cases. I treated the cases in descending order, distinguishing apology, quasi-apology, and non-apology. Moving down the list highlights a trend of increasing deficiencies in recording the relevant words, naming the wrongs done, taking responsibility, expressing regret, seeking forgiveness, and providing adequate ceremony and publicity. The appearance in what I have treated as an instance of non-apology of two final criteria, concrete reparations and a statement of nonrepetition, points up a slight exception to the linearity of the trend. This exception is the case of the High Arctic Inuit. Yet the Reconciliation Agreement counts as a non- rather than quasi-apology. The reparations and statement of nonrepetition appeared in isolation, unaccompanied by any of the core elements (naming wrongs, taking responsibility, and expressing regret) of an apologetic speech act itself.

The other case that partially diverges from straightforward descent down the criteria is Prime Minister Mulroney's statement to Italian Canadians. The statement itself was strong. However, Ottawa's subsequent reversal on reparations undermined the apology's sincerity and harmed the cause of reconciliation. I have therefore classified the Italian Canadian case as a quasi-apology. The Ukrainian and Chinese Canadian cases meet none of the criteria.

The considerable symbolic force of official state pronouncements, coupled with the historic novelty of watching a state assume an apologetic posture before people it has victimized, may lead observers to overestimate the scope and extent of political apologies (Bourdieu 1985). For example, several commentators cite Canada's Statement of Reconciliation to Aboriginal peoples as an instance of a vigorous apology for a range of past policies and actions that aimed to destroy a culture (Minow 1998; Thompson 2002; Cunningham 1999). Faring little better, I mistakenly described the Statement in an earlier work as an apology for "the past policy of forcing Native children to attend residential schools" (James 1999). The criteria thus seem helpful in dispelling the magical and potentially mystifying aura of the official apologetic state pronouncement. As we have seen, the only clearly named wrong (criterion 2) for which the Statement of Reconciliation took clear responsibility (criterion 3) and conveyed regret (criterion 4) was the sexual and physical abuse that occurred in residential schools.

This stress on textual scrutiny of potential instances of political apology suggests the importance of the first requirement for an authentic political apology: committing the apologetic words to an official written record. Several cases fall short on this criterion. Although words of apology have been extended to Japanese Canadians, Aboriginal peoples, and Italian Canadians, with the High Arctic Inuit receiving some mild phrases of "reconciliation," only the declaration to Japanese Canadians is recorded officially in permanent form. The Statement of Reconciliation to

Aboriginal peoples is posted on the internet but does not form part of an official legal or parliamentary record. Truly obscure are the High Arctic Relocation Reconciliation Agreement and Prime Minister Mulroney's words to Italian Canadians. Originally distributed as government press releases, they are now readily accessible only in the form of whatever fragments the major print media may have chosen to report at the time.

The record is not only important as the key basis from which to determine the apology's authenticity. It is also important because its permanency means that it will inevitably overshadow the more ephemeral apologetic speech act itself (Tavuchis 1991). A brief Canada-U.S. comparison helps make the point. In an interview conducted by historian Guido Tintori, Italian American redresss expert Lawrence DiStasi drew an unfavorable contrast between the "actual apology Italian Canadians obtained in Canada" and the Wartime Violation of Italian American Civil Liberties Act, which acknowledged but did not apologize for similar American injustices committed during World War II (Tintori 2001). But surely the contrast will eventually merit reversal. Memories of Mulroney's words will fade, the text itself will become increasingly difficult to find, and doubts about the actions and loyalties of at least some former internees may remain. For their part, Italian Americans will have a permanent, readily available, authoritative record stating that members of their community were victims of an officially acknowledged injustice. Thus, even the most seemingly fulsome state apology may ultimately prove less significant for victims of historic injustice than a more modestly worded— yet permanent and official—legal, congressional, or parliamentary declaration. This may be particularly true for groups concerned to elicit the "symbolic capital" of demonstrating conclusive success in clearing a once sullied name (Bourdieu 1986).

Attending to the record can also help identify elements that, in the interests of fidelity to the spirit of apology, ought not to be present at all. By helping to counter the immediate symbolic force of the state's apologetic speech act, this function testifies further to the importance of permanency of the official written record. The Japanese Canadian Redress Agreement is a case in point. Its apology component was robust; indeed, various apology-seeking groups cite it as the model utterance that their own experiences require (James 1999). However, as time leaves the immediate impact of Prime Minister Mulroney's unprecedented words behind and begins to favor the written record, different judgments may coalesce.

Tavuchis locates the moral core of apology in the act of conveying to the wronged a sincere and regretful willingness to own the consequences of one's wrongful actions. This moral core implies a requirement of humility, which Canada's apology to Japanese Canadians appears to violate. The apology was marred by partisan self-congratulation and nationalist oratory

148   Matt James

by the prime minister. Mulroney began ostentatiously, noting that he had raised the issue of Japanese Canadian redress "more than four years ago with the Prime Minister of the day." He then stressed how "the present government has sought . . . to put things right." Next, he praised Canada extensively as "a pluralistic society [of] respect [for] language . . . opinions, and religious beliefs . . . a tolerant people living in freedom . . . [who] celebrate our . . . multicultural diversity." This foray concluded with a rather unfortunate boast: "This is the Canada which our forebears worked to build." Mulroney's statement contains 13 lines addressing aspects of the political apology criteria, 12 describing the redress settlement, and 19 given over to partisan or nationalist rhetoric.

The imbalance may have been less palpable at the time of Mulroney's words. The unprecedented character of the occasion, the robustness of the apologetic utterance itself, and the historic novelty of the political apology genre—all might have combined to make the sheer phenomenon of apology the most overpoweringly salient fact. But this sort of impact inevitably wanes. Encountered on their own as a sidebar entry in a school textbook decades later, the actual words of Mulroney's apology to Japanese Canadians might not strike their audience as an attempt to atone for racist injustice. They might rather be absorbed complacently as a hymn to national virtue.

Summary and Conclusions

William J. Goode notes the occasional human tendency to shower certain entities with above-average esteem for what amount to sub-par performances (Goode 1978). This observation applies to the Canadian state's performance in the field of political apology. The Statement of Reconciliation to Aboriginal peoples, the prime minister's address to Italian Canadians, and even the apology to Japanese Canadians appear less vigorous when judged on the criteria elaborated in this chapter.

Weighing the main Canadian cases has not only highlighted what the criteria would identify as apologetic shortcomings. It has also exposed various attempts by the Canadian state to extract unseemly advantage from its participation in various apology processes that might otherwise have escaped notice. The federal government has used reparations without apology to impose counterfeit reconciliation on an oppressed and politically weak group (High Arctic Inuit). It has made "disappearing ink" acknowledgments of wrongdoing or harm that garner considerable immediate publicity and short-term political credit, but that may ultimately—because of their unofficial and impermanent form—contribute little to broader long-term public understandings of the injustices in question (Aboriginal peoples, High Arctic Inuit, Italian Canadians). Finally, by using an apologetic occasion to broadcast permanent evidence of purported Canadian virtue, Ottawa has sullied the earnestness of purpose that ought to characterize an official apology for official racism (Japanese Canadians).

These examples highlight an important benefit of the criteria: their role as a potential counterweight to the symbolic and temporal advantages that states appear to enjoy when it comes to the perceived scope and extent of their apologetic utterances. The criteria can also provide a rough basis for evaluating the moral consistency of a state's cumulative apology record. The Canadian federal government's apology record is morally inconsistent: the differences among the responses do not seem to correspond either to the magnitude of the injustices or to the extent to which those injustices may impose contemporary reconciliation responsibilities.

Japanese Canadians were victims of a harrowing injustice. With some 18,000 survivors and a victim community united strongly around the redress cause, Canada also faced serious reconciliation responsibilities. However, it is not obvious why the former students of residential schools—or indeed Canadian Aboriginal peoples in general—merit any less than the admittedly flawed, yet fully detailed, properly recorded, and in many respects ceremonially adequate apology given Japanese Canadians.

Neither does there seem to be any moral basis for the differences in treatment accorded Italian Canadians and the High Arctic Inuit. Surely a state-initiated relocation to harsh environs under a dubious and undisclosed rationale would warrant some form of apology to the unreconciled survivors, particularly given the Japanese and Italian Canadian precedents. A similar point can be made about Chinese Canadians. A racist head tax and immigration ban, injustices to which no other group was exposed, and which fractured, scarred, and stigmatized a community, would seem to demand some form of apologetic response. Perhaps one could defuse this objection by rejecting the notion of political apology itself. But Canada has not done this. Indeed, both Conservative and Liberal governments have at various times seen fit to offer words of apology or quasi-apology for historical injustices. Canada's apology record is morally inconsistent.

Moral inconsistency is not peculiar to the Canadian setting. Elazar Barkan suggests that processes resolved by "political negotiation" involving "social movements with political identities" will inevitably reflect the power of the victim groups concerned (Barkan 2000). This suggests that strategizing on the part of apology-seekers is crucial. Yet a focus on the moral core of apology might seem to proscribe strategy. For example, Tavuchis rejects Erving Goffman's view of impression management as an integral part of apology processes, arguing that it is a corrupting element that violates the essence of apology (Tavuchis 1991). My analysis has certainly embraced Tavuchis's concern to uphold the moral core of apology. I have argued that the criteria emerging from the new literature on the moral core of political apology are vital in compensating for the undue advantages that states may enjoy, and may seek to exploit, in apology processes.

But dealing with apology-seekers requires a different approach. If we focus only on apology as a moral process oriented toward reconciliation, it might seem that the victim's only legitimate role is to call for an apology and then silently await the state's response, perhaps spurning the recalcitrant offender who refuses. Discovering strategic, politically self-interested behavior by victims might provide an occasion for indicting the apology-seeking group, or even for rejecting the apparently corrupted genre of political apology itself. While it is right to judge the state's participation in apology processes on criteria that aim to uphold apology's moral core, victims are a different case. The imperative of self-interested strategizing by the historically oppressed and silenced may take us beyond questions of apologetic authenticity—but it should not be viewed as the uncovered "dirty secret" that discredits the notion of political apology.

Postscript

On June 22, 2006, Conservative Prime Minister Stephen Harper apologized for the Chinese head tax (http://www.canada.com/nationalpost/news/story.html?id=b902615e-3dfc-4fda-b843-feed3f45514f&k=37539). The apology was reasonably robust; the House of Commons setting ensured its official recording and provided solemnity and public engagement. Harper also named the wrongs, referring to "stigma and exclusion," familial separation, and poverty. He also accepted responsibility, conveyed regret, and promised nonrepetition. Harper noted that the injustices "were implemented with deliberation by the Canadian state," he expressed "sorrow over the racist actions of our past," and he undertook "to ensure that similar unjust practices are never allowed to happen." Criticisms can be made. While not explicitly demanding forgiveness, Harper was eager to "turn the page," claiming that the apology was "not about liability today [but] reconciliation." One could also speak of inadequate reparation: only living head tax payers or their surviving spouses are eligible for the package's $20,000 symbolic reparation payments. The apology also seems hypocritical given the Conservative government's policy of slashing expenditures on advocacy and social justice groups. In short, the apology fares better as a speech act than as a concrete instance of reparation. The more general question for future research is whether improvements on the speech-act dimension lead to positive results—or serve rather to mask inaction—on the concrete reparative dimension.

Thanks to Julie Fieldhouse and Rita Dhamoon for helpful comments on an earlier draft, Diane Vermilyea for research assistance, Rhoda Howard-Hassmann for kind encouragement, and the Social Sciences and Humanities Research Council of Canada for financial support (grant 410-2004-0301).

References

Alter, Susan. 1999. "Apologising for Serious Wrongdoing: Social, Psychological and Legal Considerations." Paper prepared for the Law Commission of Canada. http://www.lcc.gc.ca/en/themes/mr/ica/2000/html/apology.asp

Assembly of First Nations. 1994. *Breaking the Silence: An Interpretive Study of Residential School Impact and Healing as Illustrated by the Stories of First Nations Individuals*. Ottawa: First Nations Health Commission.

Aubry, Jack. 1996. "Inuit Receive $10 Million for Arctic Relocation." *Toronto Star*, March 8.

Barkan, Elazar. 2000. *The Guilt of Nations: Restitution and Negotiating Historical Injustices*. New York: W.W. Norton.

Barnsley, Paul. 1998. "Gathering Strength Not Strong Enough." *Windspeaker*, February 1.

Bavelas, Janet. 2004. "An Analysis of Formal Apologies by Canadian Churches to First Nations." Occasional paper 1, University of Victoria Centre for Studies in Religion and Society.

Bolan, Kim. 1995. "Chinese Group Asks UN to Act on Redress." *Vancouver Sun*, March 22.

Bolaria, B. Singh and Peter S. Li. 1985. *Racial Oppression in Canada*. Toronto: Garamond Press.

Bourdieu, Pierre. 1985. "The Social Space and the Genesis of Groups." *Theory and Society* 14 (6): 729–30.

———. 1986. "The Forms of Capital." In *Handbook of Theory and Research for the Sociology of Education*, ed. John G. Richardson. New York: Greenwood Press.

Canada Department of Indian and Northern Affairs. 1996. "High Arctic Relocation Reconciled." News release, March 28.

Canada Office of the Prime Minister. 1990. Notes for an Address by Prime Minister Brian Mulroney, National Congress of Italian Canadians and the Canadian Italian Business Professional Association, Toronto, November 4.

Canada Royal Commission on Aboriginal Peoples. 1994. *A Report on the 1953–55 Relocation*. Ottawa: Minister of Supply and Services.

Chinese Canadian National Council. 1987. *Minutes of Proceedings and Evidence* 11. December 8. Presentation to the House of Commons Standing Committee on Multiculturalism, Canada, House of Commons, Standing Committee on Multiculturalism.

Cho, Lily. 2002. "Rereading Chinese Head Tax Racism: Redress, Stereotype, and Antiracist Critical Practice." *Essays in Canadian Writing* 75: 62–84.

Claes, Rhonda and Deborah Clifton. 1998. "Needs and Expectations for Redress of Victims of Abuse at Native Residential Schools." http://collection.collectionscanada.ca/100/200/301/lcccdc/needs_expectationsredres-e/pdf/sage-e.pdf

Cunningham, Michael. 1999. "Saying Sorry: The Politics of Apology." *Political Quarterly* 70 (3): 285–93.

Daniels, Roger. 2003. *An Age of Apology?* Distinguished Speakers Series in Political Geography 7. Kingston, Ont.: Kashtan Press.
Dyzenhaus, David and Mayo Moran, eds. 2005. *Calling Power to Account: Law's Response to Past Injustice.* Toronto: University of Toronto Press.
Gibney, Mark and Erik Roxstrom. 2001. "The Status of State Apologies." *Human Rights Quarterly* 23 (4): 911–39.
Goode, William J. 1978. *The Celebration of Heroes: Prestige as a Social Control System.* Berkeley: University of California Press.
"Hefty Price Tag Delays Settlements." 1993. *Calgary Herald,* June 1.
Iacovetta, Franca and Roberto Perin. 2000. Introduction. In *Enemies Within: Italian and Other Internees in Canada and Abroad,* ed. Franca Iacovetta, Roberto Perin, and Angelo Principe. Toronto:University of Toronto Press.
Iacovetta, Franca and Robert Ventresca. 2000. "Redress, Collective Memory, and the Politics of History." In *Enemies Within: Italian and Other Internees in Canada and Abroad,* ed. Franca Iacovetta, Roberto Perin, and Angelo Principe. Toronto: University of Toronto Press.
James, Matt. 1999. "Redress Politics and Canadian Citizenship." In *The State of the Federation 1998/99: How Canadians Connect,* ed. Tom McIntosh and Harvey Lazar. Montreal: McGill-Queen's University Press.
Khan, Treena. 1994. "Group Wants Federal Redress." *Winnipeg Free Press,* August 7.
Stewart, Jane, Minister of Indian Affairs and Northern Development. 1988. Statement of Reconciliation: Learning from the Past. www.ainc-inac.gc.ca/gs/rec_e.html
Luciuk, Lubomyr. 1988a. Presentation to House of Commons Standing Committee on Multiculturalism, Canada. *Minutes of Proceedings and Evidence* 21, June 14.
———. 1988b. *A Time for Atonement: Canada's First National Internment Operations and the Ukrainian Canadians. 1914–1920.* Kingston: Limestone Press.
Mackenzie, Glen. 1994. "Redress Request Called Revenue Ploy." *Winnipeg Free Press,* August 10.
Marcus, Alan R. 1992. *Out in the Cold: The Legacy of Canada's Inuit Relocation Experiment in the High Arctic.* Copenhagen: International Work Group for Indigenous Affairs.
Miki, Royi and Cassandra Kobayashi, eds. 1991. *Justice in Our Time: The Japanese Canadian Redress Settlement.* Vancouver: Talon Books.
Miller, J. R. 1996. *Shingwauk's Vision: A History of Native Residential Schools.* Toronto: University of Toronto Press.
Minow, Martha. 1998. *Between Vengeance and Forgiveness: Facing History after Genocide and Mass Violence.* Boston: Beacon Press.
Morton, Desmond. 1974. "Sir William Otter and Internment Operations in Canada During the First World War." *Canadian Historical Review* 50 (1).
National Congress of Italian Canadians. 1990. "A National Shame: The Internment of Italian Canadians." Mimeo on file with author.
Canada Office of Indian Residential Schools Resolution. 2007. Negotiations update. http://www.irsr-rqpi.gc.ca/english/statistics.html
O'Neil, Peter. 1998. "Natives Say Ottawa's Apology May Sway Judges in Civil Suits." *Vancouver Sun,* January 8.
Ramirez, Bruno. 1988. "Ethnicity on Trial: The Italians of Montreal and the Second World War." In *On Guard for Thee: War, Ethnicity, and the Canadian State, 1939–1945,* ed. Norman Hillmer, Bohdan Kordan, and Lubomir Luciuk. Ottawa: Canadian Committee for the History of the Second World War. 71–84.

Rinehart, Dianne. 1994. "Ethnic Groups Denied Compensation." *Montreal Gazette*, December 15.
Serge, Joe. 1988. "Ukrainian Group Seeks Wartime Redress." *Toronto Star*, January 18.
Sudlow, Ron. 1993. "Italian-Canadians Reject Federal Offer." *Halifax Chronicle Herald*, May 29.
Sunahara, Ann Gomer. 1981. *The Politics of Racism: The Uprooting of Japanese Canadians During the Second World War*. Toronto: James Lorimer.
Tavuchis, Nicholas. 1991. *Mea Culpa: A Sociology of Apology and Reconciliation*. Stanford, Calif.: Stanford University Press.
Tintori, Guido. 2001. Interview with Lawrence DiStasi, "When Italian Americans Were Enemy Aliens." Altreitalie 22 (January–June 2001), http://www.altreitalie.org, last visited March 31, 2007.
Ukrainian Canadian Civil Liberties Commission. 2001. "Ukrainian Canadians Endorse Bill C-331." Media Release, April 5, www.uccla.ca/pressreleases/internment/press44.html

Chapter 10
Apology and Reconciliation in New Zealand's Treaty of Waitangi Settlement Process

MEREDITH GIBBS

When, in November 1995, Queen Elizabeth II apologized to the Tainui people for historical injustices committed during the colonization of New Zealand the event attracted worldwide media attention. She did so by personally assenting to legislation giving effect to a settlement package that included not only an apology to the Tainui, a major Maori tribe of the North Island, but also economic redress to the value of $NZ 170 million and the return of land of significance to the tribe. Three years later, in November 1998, the prime minister of New Zealand, the Honourable Jenny Shipley, spoke an apology to the South Island tribe Ngai Tahu for historical injustices at a formal Maori ceremony at Onuku Marae. This apology also attracted a large amount of media attention. The apology was also given official status by being included in an Act of Parliament, in both Maori and English. More recently, in July 2004, an apology ceremony was held at Otamatea Marae to formally mark a further apology by the New Zealand Crown for historical wrongs, this time committed against the Te Uri a Hau, a Maori tribe of the Far North. The current prime minster, the Honourable Helen Clark, and the minister in charge of Treaty of Waitangi negotiations, the Honourable Margaret Wilson, both attended the ceremony with the prime minister speaking the apology. This time, the event received much less media attention, perhaps reflecting the fact that such apologies have become somewhat commonplace in the New Zealand political landscape and the burgeoning of state (and non-state) apologies around the world.

While there are many critics of the current wave of apologies, I argue that the New Zealand experience suggests that apologies can make a difference and can be an important step in the process toward reconciliation between indigenous peoples and settler populations. I argue here that apology has played, and continues to play, a critical role in the nation's coming to terms with its colonial past. Apologies have featured in all settlements made to date for Maori grievances, and government policy indicates that this pattern will continue.

This chapter continues in three parts. First, I provide a brief background on New Zealand's Treaty settlement process and the Treaty of Waitangi. Second, I compare an example of New Zealand apology with some generally agreed requirements of apology and conclude that the apologies made in New Zealand's Treaty of Waitangi settlement process meet these requirements and thus are "genuine," insofar as state apologies can be genuine. In doing so, I examine several criticisms of state apologies in instances of historical injustice and explain how New Zealand has overcome some of these. I then consider why there seems to be a general acceptance of apology in New Zealand, arguing argue that four key factors contribute to national reconciliation. Finally, I sound a note of warning. Although the use of apology in New Zealand's Treaty settlement process points to successful steps toward reconciliation, recent developments call this outcome into question.

The New Zealand Treaty Settlement Process and the Treaty of Waitangi

New Zealand's Treaty settlement process (TSP) refers to a range of formal procedures whereby Maori who claim to have suffered prejudice as a result of Crown breaches of the Treaty of Waitangi, reach agreement with the government that an injustice requiring reparation did in fact occur, and negotiate appropriate redress to remedy the prejudice suffered.

The Treaty of Waitangi, signed in 1840, is a short document consisting of just a preamble and three articles. The precise meaning and application of the Treaty has been the subject of sustained debate, not least because it was signed in both English and Maori (with many Maori chiefs only signing a Maori version), where the English is not a direct, or accurate, translation of the Maori. Significantly, in Article I of the English version, Maori ceded full "sovereignty' to the Crown, but in the Maori version only *kawanatanga*, most often translated as "governance," was ceded. In exchange for ceding *kawanatanga* to the British, Article II reserved to Maori *tino rangatiratanga*, chieftainship, over their lands, homes, and other *taonga*, or "valuable possessions and attributes, concrete or abstract" (Biggs 1989: 308). In the English version this was worded as reserving to Maori their "full exclusive and undisturbed possession of their Lands and Estates Forests Fisheries and other properties which they may collectively or individually possess so long as it is their wish and desire to retain the same in their possession." From a Maori perspective the reservation of *rangatiratanga*, or chieftainship, in Article II would have signaled a guarantee of tribal sovereignty (Walker 1990). This crucial tension between the grant of "sovereignty" to the Crown in Article I of the English version and the retention of tribal *rangatiratanga* in Article II in the Maori version is central to contemporary debates about Maori Treaty rights. Thus, although a shared standard of justice is found in the Treaty, it is very much a negotiated justice (Gibbs 2002).

Despite the ambiguities and tensions inherent in, and arising from, the Treaty texts, the British Crown proclaimed its full sovereignty over the islands of New Zealand. The Treaty was regarded legally as "a simple nullity" (*Wi Parata v. The Bishop of Wellington* 1877) for much of New Zealand's history, leading to Maori dispossession, poverty, and ongoing disadvantage. In 1975, in response to decades of sustained Maori protest, the Waitangi Tribunal was established to investigate alleged Crown breaches of the Treaty, and to make recommendations to resolve well-founded Maori claims. Any individual or group of Maori who claim to be prejudicially affected by breaches of the Treaty may lodge a claim with the Waitangi Tribunal. In most cases, the Tribunal hears the claim and produces findings and recommendations using the Treaty as the shared standard of justice. Armed with the Tribunal's report, the Maori claimant group negotiates with the Crown, typically leading to a Deed of Settlement implemented by legislation.

New Zealand Apologies: An Example

In this section I examine the apology given to Ngai Tahu, a major tribe of the South Island, as an example of the type of apologies being given in New Zealand. Although the historical injustices suffered by the individual Maori tribes differ factually in their range and severity, the Ngai Tahu apology is characteristic in its style and form. Generally, New Zealand apologies are spoken by a minister of the Crown at a formal Maori ceremony, are written in both Maori and English, and are also formally enacted as part of legislation giving effect to settlements.

The Ngai Tahu Apology

The Ngai Tahu apology begins by acknowledging the generations of Ngai Tahu who have pursued the tribe's claims for justice since the signing of the Treaty of Waitangi in 1840. The apology concedes that the Crown acted unconscionably, and in repeated breach of the Treaty of Waitangi, in its purchase of Ngai Tahu lands, and subsequently in failing to ensure that Ngai Tahu was left with sufficient lands for its needs. The Crown also acknowledged that its failure to act in good faith deprived Ngai Tahu of opportunities to develop and kept the tribe in a state of poverty for several generations. The Crown apologized thus:

New Zealand's Treaty of Waitangi Settlement Process   157

The Crown expresses its profound regret and apologises unreservedly to all members of Ngai Tahu Whanui [the wider descent group of the tribe] for the suffering and hardship caused to Ngai Tahu, and for the harmful effects which resulted to the welfare, economy and development of Ngai Tahu as a tribe. The Crown acknowledges that such suffering, hardship and harmful effects resulted from its failures to honour its obligations to Ngai Tahu under the deeds of purchase whereby it acquired Ngai Tahu lands, to set aside adequate lands for the tribe's use, to allow reasonable access to traditional sources of food, to protect Ngai Tahu's rights to pounamu [New Zealand jade] and such other valued possessions as the tribe wished to retain, or to remedy effectually Ngai Tahu's grievances.

The Crown apologises to Ngai Tahu for its past failures to acknowledge Ngai Tahu rangatiratanga [chieftainship] and mana [tribal authority] over the South Island lands within its boundaries, and, in fulfilment of its Treaty obligations, the Crown recognises Ngai Tahu as the tangata whenua [people] of, and as holding rangatiratanga within, the Takiwa [tribal territory] of Ngai Tahu Whanui.

Accordingly, the Crown seeks on behalf of all New Zealanders to atone for these acknowledged injustices, so far as that is now possible, and, with the historical grievances finally settled . . . to begin a process of healing and to enter a new age of co-operation with Ngai Tahu. (New Zealand 1998)

THE REQUIREMENTS OF APOLOGY

An apology generally contains at least the following elements (Thompson this volume; Gill 2000; Taft 2000; Tavuchis 1991):

- The wrongdoer acknowledges to the victim her wrongful act and accepts responsibility for it;
- He feels regret, sorrow or remorse for the act; and
- She implicitly or explicitly promises not to commit a similar wrong in the future.

Does the apology to Ngai Tahu meet these requirements?

Acknowledgment of the wrong and acceptance of responsibility. Because the shared standard of justice between Maori and the Crown is sourced in the Treaty of Watiangi, any breach of the Treaty is an injustice requiring reparation (Gibbs 2002). By clearly acknowledging that it acted unconscionably and in breach of the Treaty of Waitangi, the New Zealand Crown admits in its apology that it acted unjustly. Furthermore, the Crown has explicitly accepted that it has a moral obligation to resolve Maori historical injustices (Office of Treaty Settlements 2002). But on what grounds does the current New Zealand government accept responsibility for wrongs committed by past administrations over which it had no control? And in what way are the current generation of Ngai Tahu people entitled to an apology and redress for injustices suffered by previous generations?

Philosophers have presented cogent reasons why current generations can, and should, take responsibility for the past that they inherit (Ivison

2000; Sparrow 2002; Thompson 2002). Some have argued that the problem can be dealt with by looking to the continuity of the state as an agent (Thompson this volume; Cunningham 1999). Along these lines, Cunningham argues that for injustices committed by governments "responsibility extends beyond the particular administration of the day and redounds to its successors" (Cunningham 2004). In the New Zealand situation, the latter approach is essentially how the problem has been solved. The parties to the Treaty of Waitangi were Queen Victoria and Maori chiefs. Although not envisaged by the Treaty, in 1863 the conventions of responsible government in Maori matters were transferred from the United Kingdom to New Zealand, and "the obligations of Her Majesty, the Queen of England, under the Treaty are now those of the Crown in right of New Zealand" (*New Zealand Maori Council v. A-G* 1994; Brookfield 1999). Therefore, the enduring notion of "the Crown" can clearly be established, and the present entity responsible for providing redress for breaches of the Treaty is the Crown in right of New Zealand, in practice the government of the day. When Queen Elizabeth II apologized to Tainui by assenting to the legislation containing the formal apology, she did so in her role as Crown in right of New Zealand. When the prime minister of New Zealand, or other ministers of the Crown, apologize, either verbally or by signing a written text of apology in a Deed of Settlement, they do so in their capacity as the New Zealand Crown.

Looking to the right of those living today to ask for, or receive, an apology or other reparation, in the context of injustices suffered by Maori, it can be argued that the tribe, or related kin-group, continues to exist. Whereas any Maori may bring a claim for breaches of the Treaty of Waitangi, in practice individuals have tended to bring claims on behalf of wider descent groups. Maori society, however, has always been dynamic, and the form and importance of different groupings within Maori society has changed over time (Ballara 1998: 336). Further, current Maori collectives may be constituted by a variety of legal means including trust boards, incorporated societies, Maori incorporations, and other corporate structures. Careful historical analysis will be needed to ascertain whether an entity making a contemporary claim has historical continuity with the unjustly treated Maori collective in question (Gibbs 2002). This approach has caused difficulty for more recent, mostly urban, groups of Maori that are not based solely on descent from one or more ancestors. There are also difficulties within historically continuous tribal groups regarding issues of representation and mandate of the contemporary manifestation of the tribe. While these issues continue to cause problems within the TSP, they are not insurmountable. Thus in the New Zealand context, the parties to apology are the New Zealand Crown and historically linked Maori tribes.

Expression of sorrow, remorse, or regret. But what about the next requirement of apology, that the offender feel regret, sorrow, or remorse for the wrongful act? The apology to Ngai Tahu states that the Crown "expresses its profound regret" and that it seeks atonement. What are we to make of this? How can a *state* experience feelings such as sorrow, remorse, and regret? If we accept that a state cannot feel these sorts of emotions, what does that mean for the notion of a "genuine" apology?

Tavuchis argues that apologies from the many, or collective apologies, have "little, if anything, to do with sorrow or sincerity but rather with putting things on the record" (Tavuchis 1991: 117). This is their power: "that it appears on the public record *is* the apologetic fact." In the legislation giving effect to the Ngai Tahu settlement the text of the apology is preceded by extensive preambles that set out a history of the injustices for which the settlement is intended to make reparation. This statement of history represents an agreed, brief version of the findings of the Waitangi Tribunal's inquiry into the tribe's claims. This, together with the apology, inscribes on the public, legislative record, the relevant history and the Crown's admission of wrongdoing.

Taking a different approach, Thompson (this volume) argues that in instances of state apologies it is not necessary that the officials performing the apology actually feel remorse or sorrow. Rather, she argues, a state apology requires "an appropriate moral motivation" and it is enough that citizens "recognize the responsibility of their state, as a transgenerational polity, to make recompense to victims for a history of injustice and disrespect" (Thompson this volume; see also Gill 2000). It is difficult to show definitively that such recognition exists generally within the wider New Zealand population. However, government policy regarding Treaty settlements acknowledges that historical breaches of the Treaty of Waitangi are injustices that require contemporary apology and redress (Office of Treaty Settlements 2002). That political parties in New Zealand and successive governments from the right (but not the far right), to the left and the Greens, endorse this moral obligation gives an indication of the breadth of support for the TSP across New Zealand society. Further, there is minimal vocal opposition to the giving of apology. Thus, on either approach, New Zealand apologies can be said to meet the second requirement.

Undertaking not to commit similar wrongs. Turning to the third requirement of apology, in what way does the apology to Ngai Tahu indicate that the New Zealand Crown will not commit similar injustices, or breaches of the Treaty of Waitangi, in the future? The apology clearly intends to aid reconciliation between the Crown and Ngai Tahu, speaking of "a process of healing" and of entering "a new age of co-operation with Ngai Tahu." These suggest, implicitly, that the Crown intends to abide by the Treaty of Waitangi in its future dealings with Ngai Tahu. This intention is backed up by many of the redress mechanisms contained in the settlement, which provide for institutional changes to ensure an active partnership between the Crown and Ngai Tahu in the management of conservation areas, species (particularly endangered species) of special significance to Ngai Tahu, and local resource management processes, for example.

Although the apology to Ngai Tahu appears therefore to meet the third criterion of apology, there is the issue of whether such promises can be relied on. Future governments can, after all, change them. As Thompson points out, states can, and do, make long-term commitments (Thompson 2002; see also Cunningham 2004). Indeed, international law depends on this. She argues in this volume that states can be seen as a "transgenerational polities in which members pass on responsibilities and entitlements from one generation to another." In this view, states *can* make genuine apologies, although, as Thompson points out, it is another matter whether they actually do. While apologies cannot *guarantee* that states will refrain from similar injustices in the future, Brooks suggests that without them "there would be greater concern, perhaps not just among the survivors, that those shameful acts might be repeated" (Brooks 1999: 4).

Perhaps because apologies act to affirm norms, they can help those wronged believe that the perpetrator will refrain from acting unjustly in the future. In the TSP, apologies and their settlement packages all confirm the binding nature of the Treaty of Waitangi as a just standard of conduct between the Crown and its Maori partners. As such they indicate the Crown's willingness to abide by the Treaty, and therefore act justly in the future. Indeed, I think that the implicit (and explicit) promises of a future relationship with the Crown based on the Treaty is a key reason why apologies are so important to Maori tribes and why apologies have been accepted by them. It is to the favorable reception of apology in New Zealand's TSP that I now turn.

Why Are New Zealand Apologies Accepted?

Apologies to Maori tribes for historical breaches of the Treaty of Waitangi have become standard practice in New Zealand's TSP. They continue to be accepted by Maori, as is evidenced by the recent ceremony to mark the apology given to Te Uri a Hau. Why do the majority of Maori, and the wider settler population in New Zealand, generally accept these apologies?

Healing

To focus again on the apology to Ngai Tahu, for many Ngai Tahu the apology was the most important part of the settlement package. Ngai Tahu acknowledged that in situations of injustice an apology "is always the first step in the healing process" and is necessary to remove a sense injustice (Te Runanga o Ngai Tahu 1997a: 30). Tipene O'Regan, principal Ngai Tahu settlement negotiator, described the Ngai Tahu claim as "a *taniwha* [spiritual being], a monster that has consumed our tribal lives down through the years as generation after generation has struggled for 'justice'," a *taniwha* that needed to be laid to rest if Ngai Tahu were to take control of its own destiny (Te Runanga o Ngai Tahu 1997b: 25, 27). Thus apologies are important because they are essential to the healing process that might ultimately lead to reconciliation.

RECOGNITION AND *Mana*

Significantly, the apology, together with the other aspects of the settlement package, signalled the Crown's acceptance of Ngai Tahu's *mana*, or tribal prestige, authority, and power. Smits argues, "in cases of historical mistreatment, the demand for apology is a demand for recognition of group identity" (Smits 2004: 3). She argues that the giving of apology for historical wrongs "confers the recognition of identity" and "establishes a new relationship between former victim and oppressor, of equal status." The recognition of group identity is particularly important in situations where the historical injustices have involved racist practices, often designed to wipe out a cultural group and to assimilate its members into the dominant culture. As such, "apology not only acknowledges the moral worth of the group at this time, but it makes clear that past treatment of the group was never morally justified" (Gill 2000: 23).

In the New Zealand context, the explicit recognition of tribal authority (*mana*) that apology confers is exceedingly significant and provides an important reason for their acceptance by Maori tribes. I have argued elsewhere that justice in the TSP requires the restoration of the tribe's *mana*, and any settlement that does not recognize and restore tribal *mana* would not be accepted by Maori tribes (Gills 2002). Documentation explaining the Ngai Tahu settlement clearly states that Ngai Tahu felt satisfied that the settlement reflected the Crown's recognition of Ngai Tahu and its *mana* (Te Runanga o Ngai Tahu 1997a). This appears to have been a important motivation for the tribe's acceptance of the settlement package.

The recognition of *mana* contained in New Zealand apologies is reinforced by substantive cultural redress mechanisms. For example, a key ingredient of the Ngai Tahu settlement was the renaming of New Zealand's tallest mountain from "Mt. Cook" to "Aoraki/Mt. Cook." Aoraki is one of the most revered of Ngai Tahu's ancestors, "who provides the *iwi* [tribe] with its sense of communal identity, solidarity and purpose" (New

Zealand 1998). The settlement also provides for the vesting of the mountain in the tribe, and, seven days later, for the subsequent gifting of the mountain by the Ngai Tahu people, back to the nation. As Ngai Tahu has acknowledged, this measure confirms the tribe's *mana*. The arrangement also provides for an ongoing role for Ngai Tahu in the management of the mountain, which lies in a national park, through a variety of mechanisms. The tribe recognized that these measures "Like the Crown Apology, . . . [are] a potent symbol of the new era that we are now entering" (Te Runanga o Ngai Tahu 1997a: 7).

The settlement also contains a range of other mechanisms all of which confirm Ngai Tahu's *mana* and lay the foundations for an ongoing relationship between the tribe and the Crown based on the Treaty. The settlement returned ownership of a number of significant sites to the tribe, or where ownership was not returned provided for an ongoing management role for the tribe; returned all the natural deposits of *pounamu* (New Zealand jade or greenstone, an ancestor of Ngai Tahu) to the tribe; contained mechanisms to ensure Ngai Tahu involvement in the management of particular native species and to allow for customary fishing; and instituted dual English/Maori place names in a variety of locations throughout Ngai Tahu's tribal area. Ngai Tahu were also given increased responsibility in environmental decision-making with designated seats on a variety of environmental and conservation boards, and statutory advisory status in certain circumstances. In addition to confirming and restoring the tribe's *mana*, these measures also signify the Crown's commitment to form a relationship with Ngai Tahu that respects the promises of the Treaty of Waitangi, thus furthering reconciliation.

Because of the vital element of recognition contained in state apologies, the status of the official giving the apology is crucial. If the performance of the apology is to confer the required recognition, and in the New Zealand context symbolize the *mana* of the tribe receiving the apology, it must also be attended with appropriate ceremony. As Tavuchis argues, "Attention and adherence to formalities is thus intimately linked to the group's honour and integrity" (Tavuchis 1991: 100). In the Ngai Tahu and Te Uri A Hau examples I note above, each involved a traditional Maori ceremony with the apology being given by the Prime Minister. Queen Elizabeth's performance of the Tainui apology is particularly significant from a Maori viewpoint. Just as the Treaty of Waitangi was a treaty between the queen and Maori chiefs, in this case the apology for breaches of the Treaty was an apology directly from the queen to the tribe. In other settlement apologies, the minister in charge of Treaty of Waitangi Negotiations has given the apology at a formal ceremony. Further, when legislation giving effect to the settlement and containing the written text of the apology is passed by Parliament, members of the relevant tribe are usually present. The speaker of the House of Representatives acknowledges their presence and many Parliamentarians' speeches are given in both Maori and English. In accordance with Maori tradition, tribal members sing traditional Maori *waiata* (songs) in support of speeches and the passage of the settlement legislation.

History and Memory

A further reason that apologies are accepted in New Zealand is because they function as a "response to testimony" (Smits 2004). By admitting the relevant wrong, the offender acknowledges the history of the victim (Barkan 2000; Cunningham 2004). This is essential where a nation's historical record has omitted its ugly past, and particularly so where injustices have gone unrecognized for generations. In Waitangi Tribunal hearings, tribes have an opportunity to tell their histories of injustice in a culturally appropriate setting (most hearings take place at Maori meeting houses), and many tribal members have benefited from the healing that may follow such truth telling. In undertaking research into historical grievances that cover almost all of New Zealand, the Tribunal has led the way in a recent revision of New Zealand history that has led to increased public awareness and debate about the nation's colonial past (Weyeneth 2001).

In the apology to Ngai Tahu, the Crown also clearly acknowledges the suffering of Ngai Tahu over time resulting from its failure to honor its Treaty obligations. This action again reinforces the victims' version of history and acknowledges a legacy of suffering. Thus, apologies also act as important instances of remembering. Waldron argues that the "determination not to forget is part of the moral respect we owe to human identity: the task of remembrance is bound up with the very being of community and individuality in the modern world" (Waldron 1992: 143). In this view, apologies function to "embody this remembrance." This aspect was especially important for Ngai Tahu because the tribe's long struggle for justice has "bonded [the tribe] together in a special way" shaping its tribal identity and organization (Te Runanga o Ngai Tahu 1997a: 5).

Compensation

All these factors have contributed to the acceptance of apologies in New Zealand. But critics may argue that apologies are still only words. Even with the acceptance of the political consequences that might flow from apologies, particularly from the recognition of the victim group, they come very cheaply to states. Cunningham argues that, because there are always problems with the sincerity of apologies, compensation can "provide a concrete and material test of the sincerity of the apology" (Cunningham 2004: 566). He argues that there is a "duty for [compensation] to be offered by the apologizing party," even if it is "only, or largely, symbolic." As discussed, New Zealand apologies have been given alongside substantive redress, including the return of significant land and resources, measures to restore cultural identity and authority, and mechanisms intended to lay foundations for just, ongoing relations between the state and Maori claimant groups. I have argued here that all of these factors have strengthened the recognition of tribal *mana* and identity in New Zealand apologies. Significantly, settlements have also included financial compensation.

While New Zealand settlements all contain a compensatory payment, the actual amount of these payments falls far short of full compensation for the lands and resources unjustly taken. For example, in the Ngai Tahu settlement the financial redress included payment of $170 million together with accumulated interest and rentals on certain Crown forestry lands, a deferred selection process allowing Ngai Tahu to purchase specified Crown properties under favorable conditions, and a perpetual right of first refusal to purchase certain surplus Crown properties. Both Ngai Tahu and the Crown acknowledged that the settlement quantum was less than what was required for full restitution. Indeed, Ngai Tahu had been advised that their claim was worth over $20 *billion* (Te Runanga o Ngai Tahu 1997a). Despite the fact that some Ngai Tahu believed that the settlement amount was too low and thus manifestly unjust, the tribe accepted it on the basis that the other financial measures noted above would allow the tribe to increase its net capital worth. Ngai Tahu acknowledged that to realize the potential of the settlement, and for this amount to be considered *sufficient* redress, the tribe would have to grow the value themselves.

In fact, Ngai Tahu has increased its tribal equity from approximately $200 million just after the settlement in 1998 to $315 million in June 2004, with almost half of this increase coming from Ngai Tahu's astute use of the deferred selection process contained in the settlement. As of June 30, 2004 the tribe had total assets worth $441 million. The tribe is now the second largest landholder, after the Crown, in the South Island and has substantial investments in a range of portfolios. Furthermore, the tribe realized a net surplus in the 2003/2004 fiscal year of $26.6 million; it distributed $14.7 million of that surplus to fund tribal programs and benefits such as educational scholarships and grants. These figures are all the more impressive when one considers that the tribe's net worth in 1990 was a mere $100,000 and tribal members were forced to mortgage their own homes to raise funds to finance the tribe's Waitangi Tribunal claim (Te Runanga o Ngai Tahu 2004).

Ngai Tahu now has an economic base from which to rebuild the tribe and its cultural life. Moreover, the tribe's strong financial position has increased its political power, particularly with respect to environmental and resource management matters in its traditional territory. At the time of the settlement the tribe recognized that the settlement "addresses much more than the economic aspects of Ngai Tahu's loss. Important, [it] includes redress items that clearly intend to acknowledge and affirm our *mana* as a people, and our *mana* over the landscape and resources of Te Wai Pounamu [the South Island of New Zealand]" (Te Runanga o Ngai Tahu 1997a: 6).

New Zealand Apologies and Reconciliation

The Crown's apology is fundamental to the [Ngai Tahu] settlement. It acknowledges the validity of the claims that our people have made over seven generations. It begins the positive process of rebuilding, whilst not forgetting the past. The Apology marks the end the grievance period. The healing process can begin. (Te Runanga o Ngai Tahu 1997a: 3)

As the apology to Ngai Tahu demonstrates, each of the elements of New Zealand Treaty settlements is crucial. The apology begins the healing process and recognizes tribal *mana*, authority, power, and identity. The element of recognition in the apology is reinforced by substantial cultural redress mechanisms and the acknowledgment and remembrance of the tribe's history of injustice. Significantly, the financial redress measures underpin the other settlement elements, providing an economic base for the tribe to move on from its grievances and take control of its own destiny. Thus, the apology, cultural redress, and financial compensation measures all validate each other.

Gill argues, "In offering the apology, the offender exercises the moral capacities that seems should be seem to have failed in committing the offence. After the display, the offender may be re-established as a more trustworthy and respectable member of the community" (Gill 2000: 24). In the New Zealand TSP, apologies not only serve to restore the *mana* of tribes, they also restore the honor of the New Zealand Crown. They have moral force through their (implicit and explicit) recognition of the standard of just conduct between the Crown and Maori Treaty partners, that standard of justice being found in the Treaty of Waitangi. New Zealand settlements contain many measures to lay the foundations for a partnership based on the Treaty and thus contribute to reconciliation processes.

But a note of warning is required. Although these measures point to a process of reconciliation taking place in New Zealand, let us not be too sanguine. The New Zealand government's recent extinguishment of Maori common law customary rights to the foreshore and seabed (New Zealand 2004) demonstrates that protecting indigenous rights in the face of majority demands continues to be elusive. This denial of Maori rights and clear breach of the Treaty of Waitangi casts doubt on the sincerity of the Crown's commitment not to commit further injustices, and thus calls into question the integrity of New Zealand apologies for historical wrongs and the TSP as a whole. Sparrow suggests that when sincere, apology "reaches back to the original events and changes their significance by placing them in a historical context which includes the later recognition of the wrong which has been committed. That history then becomes one of reconciliation instead of one of continuing injustice" (Sparrow 2002: 359). The New Zealand government's recent actions suggest that New Zealand's history is yet to become one of total reconciliation, despite the apparent success of the TSP and the apologies given by the New Zealand Crown for historical injustices to Maori.

Glossary

Aoraki	New Zealand's tallest mountain, ancestor of Ngai Tahu
kawanatanga	the exercise of governance
mana	authority, power, prestige
marae	traditional Maori meeting place
Ngai Tahu Whanui	the wider descent group of the Ngai Tahu tribe
pounamu	New Zealand jade or greenstone, an ancestor of Ngai Tahu
rangatiratanga	the exercise of chieftainship
takiwa	tribal territory
tangata whenua	people (usually Maori) of the land
taniwha	spiritual being, guardian, monster
taonga	treasures, valuable possessions, attributes
waiata	songs

References

Ballara, Angela. 1998. *Iwi: The Dynamics of Maori Tribal Organisation from c. 1769 to c. 1945*. Wellington: Victoria University Press.

Barkan, Elazar. 2000. *Guilt of Nations: Restitution and Negotiating Historic Injustice*. New York: W.W. Norton.

Biggs, Bruce. 1989. "Humpty-Dumpty and the Treaty of Waitangi." In *Waitangi: Maori and Pakeha Perspectives of the Treaty of Waitangi*, ed. I. H. Kawharu. Auckland: Oxford University Press.

Brookfield, Frederick M. 1999. *Waitangi and Indigenous Rights: Revolution, Law, and Legitimation*. Auckland: Auckland University Press.

Brooks, Roy L., ed. 1999. *When Sorry Isn't Enough: The Controversy over Apologies and Reparations for Human Injustice*. New York: New York University Press.

Cose, Ellis. 2004. *Bone to Pick: Of Forgiveness, Reconciliation, Reparation, and Revenge*. New York: Atria Books.

Cunningham, Michael. 1999. "Saying Sorry: The Politics of Apology." *Political Quarterly* 70 (3): 285–94.

———. 2004. "Prisoners of the Japanese and the Politics of Apology: A Battle over History and Memory." *Journal of Contemporary History* 39 (4): 561–74.

Gibbs, Meredith K. 2002. "Are New Zealand Treaty of Waitangi Settlements Achieving Justice? The Ngai Tahu Settlement and the Return of Pounamu (Greenston)." Ph.D. dissertation, University of Otago, New Zealand.

———. 2004. "What Structures Are Appropriate to Receive Treaty of Waitangi Settlement Assets?" *New Zealand Universities Law Review* 21 (2): 197–232.

Gill, Kathleen. 2000. "The Moral Functions of an Apology." *Philosophical Forum* 31 (1): 11–27.

Ivison, Duncan. 2000. "Political Community and Historical Injustice." *Australasian Journal of Philosophy* 78 (3): 360–73.

Mills, Nicolaus. 2001. "The New Culture of Apology." *Dissent* 48 (4): 113–16.

New Zealand. 1998. Ngai Tahu Claims Settlement Act.

———. 2004. Foreshore and Seabed Act.

New Zealand Maori Council v. A-G. 1994. 1 NZLR 513 (PC).

Office of Treaty Settlements. 2002. *Healing the Past, Building a Future: A Guide to Treaty of Waitangi Claims and Negotiations with the Crown.* 2nd ed. Wellington: Office of Treaty Settlements.

Smits, Katherine. 2004. "Identity Politics Redux: Apologies for Historical Injustice and Deliberation About Race." Paper presented at the New Zealand Political Science Studies Association 2004 Conference, Hamilton, New Zealand.

Sparrow, Robert. 2002. "History and Collective Responsibility." *Australasian Journal of Philosophy* 78 (3): 346–59.

Taft, Lee. 2000. "Apology Subverted: The Commodification of Apology." *Yale Law Journal* 109 (5): 1136–60.

Tavuchis, Nicholas. 1991. *Mea Culpa: A Sociology of Apology and Reconciliation.* Stanford, Calif.: Stanford University Press.

Te Runanga o Ngai Tahu. 1997a. *Crown Settlement Offer Consultation Document from the Ngai Tahu Negotiating Group.* Christchurch: Te Runanga O Ngai Tahu.

———. 1997b. *1997 Annual Report.* Christchurch: Te Runanga O Ngai Tahu.

———. 2004. "Ngai Tahu Announces Successful Year." http://lianz.waikato.ac.nz/PAPERS/Rob/Denial.pdf

Thompson, Janna. 2002. *Taking Responsibility for the Past: Reparation and Historical Justice.* Cambridge: Polity Press.

Waldron, Jeremy. 1992. "Historic Injustice: Its Remembrance and Supersession." In *Justice, Ethics, and New Zealand Society*, ed. Graham Oddie and Roy W. Perrett. Auckland: Oxford University Press.

Walker, Ranganui. 1990. *Ka Whawhai Tonu Matou: Stuggle Without End.* Auckland: Penguin.

Weyeneth, Robert R. 2001. "The Power of Apology and the Process of Historical Reconciliation." *Public Historian* 23 (3): 9–38.

Wi Parata v. The Bishop of Wellington. 1877. 3 NZ Jur (NS) 72 (SC).

Part III
International Apologies of States

Chapter 11
State Apologies Under U.S. Hegemony

CARLOS A. PARODI

This chapter examines the need for creating an international process of truth, justice, reparation, and reconciliation (TJRR) for confronting human rights violations with the participation of the United States as a responsible actor. The main thesis is that the creation of the TJRR process demands the transformation of fundamental principles governing international relations. The creation of an international TJRR would imply a major break with the existing global political economy characterized by U.S. hegemony. Under conditions of U.S. hegemony, not only is an international TJRR process not possible, but apologies "say very little, help understand very little, and change very little."[1]

The argument consists of the following steps. First, an apparent contradiction needs to be explained. If the thesis is that U.S. hegemony is an obstacle for the creation of an international TJRR process, what explains the creation of several national TJRR processes in Latin America in the last twenty five years? This section of the chapter reviews recent experiences in Argentina, Chile, El Salvador, and Guatemala of implementation of new methodologies for confronting human rights violations. The conclusion of the analysis is that the national TJRR processes preserved U.S. hegemony because, although its participation in human rights violations was acknowledged, the United States was not incorporated into the process as a responsible actor. Along the same lines, the next section discusses the specifics of the participation of the United States in Peru's national TJRR process. This case is particularly interesting because, in contrast to the previous four, a strictly national TJRR process without the participation of the United States as a responsible actor seems more appropriate.

U.S. Hegemony and Latin American Truth Commissions

The 1980s in Latin America were marked by several political transitions. Argentina and Chile experienced transitions from military to democratically elected governments. In El Salvador and Guatemala, political transition implied ending wars between the government and rebel forces. As a group, these transitions showed how the end of the Cold War was unfolding in Latin America. In each case, the political forces involved in the transition had to deal with human rights violations committed under the former military regime or during the war. A broad coalition saw the transition as an opportunity to charter a new course for the nation by taking a critical look to a past marked by massive human rights violations. Emblematic of such coalition was the phrase "¡NUNCA MÁS!": "never more" killings, disappearances, and torture.

The institutional responses implemented in each case have been subjected to extensive review and commentary (Hayner 2002). At the center of the debate is the question of the kind of justice that could be achieved in the context of a political transition. One group argues that the only adequate institutional response to mass human rights violations is the creation of Nuremberg-type trials. Anything less would constitute condoning impunity. This group praises Argentina's trials and is critical of institutional innovations like "truth commissions," which, they argue, shortchange justice for truth. Another group is critical of the "legalistic" approach to human rights violations and is sympathetic to institutional responses that embody different, non-legal forms of justice, such as restorative justice. In her comparative study of truth commissions, Priscilla Hayner explained that "it is partly due to the limited reach of the courts, and partly out of a recognition that even successful prosecutions do not resolve the conflict and pain associated with past abuses, that transitional authorities have increasingly turned to official truth-seeking as a central component in their strategy to respond to past atrocities" (Hayner 2002: 14). It is not my purpose here to review the pros and cons of truth commissions versus trials. Rather, my purpose is to discuss the extent to which the Latin American institutional processes created to confront human rights violations were critical of the international system and U.S. hegemony. The reason for this focus is straightforward: U.S. policies were responsible for the Cold War (at least in part), and the Cold War was responsible for military regimes and internal wars in Latin America that resulted in massive human rights violations. What follows is an analysis of four Latin American truth commission reports and their discussion of U.S. participation in human rights violations committed in their respective territories.

The participation of the United States is more or less acknowledged in Latin American truth commissions' reports, but within a nationalist approach to human rights violations where the United States is not treated as a responsible actor. In Argentina's report the participation of the United States in human rights violations appears in the text as part of the responsibility attributed to the Cold War in the implementation of the National Security Doctrine (NSD). The 1983 decree ordering trials for the members of the Military Junta stated "thousands were illegally stripped of their freedom, tortured or killed as the result of the implementation of fighting procedures inspired in the totalitarian National Security Doctrine" (Nunca Más 1984). Argentine generals trained by the United States in anti-subversive strategies implemented the NSD. These generals perceived communist totalitarianism as the major threat to the Western and Christian system of life. Although the report described the participation of the United States in human rights violations in Argentina, no international action was taken. Argentina did not call the United States to account for its responsibility in the "dirty war." On the contrary, since the mid-1980s, the core of Argentina's foreign policy has been the consolidation of a privileged alliance with the United States (Norden and Russell 2002).

Chile's truth commission also framed the participation of the United States within the context of the Cold War. According to the National Commission on Truth and Reconciliation, "the 1973 crisis may be generally described as one of sharp polarization between government and opposition" (Chilean National Commission 1991). The origins of such polarization are traced back to the Cold War, especially after the Cuban Revolution. The document is equally critical of parties of the left that believed in the path of armed revolution, and parties of the right that supported the use of weapons to impose their views. However, this dialectic was the local manifestation of a global ideological conflict. In response to the development of guerrilla *focos*, the United States started a counterinsurgency campaign in Latin America. "Just like the *focos*, such counterinsurgency was both local in nature in each country and centralized through a degree of coordination between all Latin American countries. The United States took charge of the overall coordination, and to that end it took advantage of the fact that generations of officers from the various Latin American countries were passing through its military training schools year after year." The report explicitly mentioned the participation of the United States in human rights violations. After the 1970 election of President Allende, "the United States immediately planned and engaged in a twofold policy of intervention in Chile's internal affairs: in October 1970 to prevent Salvador Allende from coming into power (the so-called 'track one'), and when that failed, to destabilize the new government economically ('track two')." Although the United States was prominently mentioned in the Chilean report, the Commission did not bring in the United States into the process of truth and reconciliation as a responsible actor.

The Report of the Commission on the Truth for El Salvador also makes a very brief reference to the fact that "the nation was a pawn in the East-West conflict" (Betancur, Planchart, and Buergenthal 1994). However, as Priscilla Hayner explained, the report was "criticized for failing to fully report on certain important aspects of the violence, such as the operation of death squads, and on *the role of the United States* in supporting the government forces" (Hayner 2002: 39–40, emphasis added). The self-imposed limitation of the Salvadoran truth commission went hand in hand with the neglect with which Washington treated migrant Salvadorans after the destruction caused by Hurricane Mitch in October 1998. Oblivious to U.S. responsibility in the civil war that engulfed El Salvador in the 1980s, and thus, of one of its major consequences: massive migration of Salvadorans to the United States, the U.S. Immigration and Naturalization Service determined in March 1999 that "approximately 1,600 Salvadorans and 300 Guatemalans faced immediate deportation" (*Prensa Libre* 1999). Keep in mind that the announcement was made at the time of President Clinton's visit to Central America that included the "apology" in Guatemala City.

On March 10, 1999, in the National Palace of Culture of Guatemala City, in the last day of a four-day visit to Central America, President Clinton said that the United States should not repeat the "mistake" of supporting "military forces or intelligence units which engaged in violent and widespread repression" of the kind described in the Report of the Commission for Historical Clarification (Clinton 1999). The official purpose of the presidential visit was to review the damage caused by Hurricane Mitch (October 26–November 4, 1998) and the progress in democracy, market reforms, and human rights by the governments of the region (Rubin 1999). The apology was not part of the official script. Although "Clinton's aides said the president had thought for some time about how to word his near-apology" (Babington 1999), he finally decided to apologize "reading from hand-written notes" (Latin American Working Group 1999). Clinton's words "startled and pleased nervous Latino politicians" (McGrory 1999). Guatemalan President Álvaro Arzú was so surprised with Clinton's words that his press aides said "they were unsure whether he would comment" (Babington 1999).

In the section "Conclusions and Recommendations," Guatemala's Commission for Historical Clarification (Comisión para el Esclarecimiento Histórico, CEH) affirmed that the "the movement of Guatemala towards polarisation, militarization and civil war" could not be understood exclusively as "national history" but also as "the result of the Cold War" (CEH 1998). The anti-communism "promoted by the United States within the framework of its foreign policy . . . demonstrated that it was willing to provide support for strong military regimes in its strategic backyard." This was a key factor "which had significant bearing on human rights violations during the armed confrontation." Anti-communism became the cornerstone of the National Security Doctrine, "first expressed as antireformist, then anti-democratic policies, culminating in criminal counterinsurgency." One of the most devastating effects of this policy was that state forces and related paramilitary groups were responsible for 93 percent of the violations documented by the Commission. However, even after providing evidence and explanation of U.S. participation in human rights violations, Guatemalans did not bring the U.S. into the process of truth and reconciliation, and certainly were not expecting the U.S. to apologize. The U.S. official interpretation was that genocide was committed for the most part between members of the same nation, an interpretation consistent with the nationalist framework prevailing in other truth commissions.

The case of Guatemala also demonstrates that in the context of hegemony, apologies are an instrument at the service of the powerful state's foreign policy. Reviewing the "spate of state apologies" of the 1990s, Mark Gibney and Erik Roxstrom were very critical of U.S. apologies and in particular of President Clinton's 1999 apology in Guatemala. Their conclusion was that "President Clinton's apology to the Guatemalan people says very little, it helps us to understand very little, and perhaps, it changes very little" (Gibney and Roxstrom 2001: 936). The authors questioned the United States for doing very little at transforming the wrongs it was apologizing for. "The biggest problem with state apologies is that the apologizing state wants it both ways: it wants credit for recognizing and acknowledging a wrong against others, but it also wants the world to remain exactly as it has been before the apology was issued." Reviewing more recent U.S. apologies, Mark Gibney and Niklaus Steiner in this volume argue that in the U.S. war against terror "apology has become a very useful political tool" and "a means of avoiding accountability."

Triumphalism Triumphant?

The above analysis shows that Latin American truth commissions acknowledged the participation of the United States in human rights violations committed in their respective national territories, but did not treat the United States as a responsible actor. The responsibility fell exclusively on national actors: Argentines killed Argentines, Chileans killed Chileans, and so forth. The end result was that responsibility for massacres was contained within state boundaries, thus effectively covering up the responsibility of the United States in local human rights violations. The international system was not questioned and the legitimacy of U.S. hegemony was preserved.

Latin American institutional responses to massive human rights violations resulted in part from political compromises specific to national historical circumstances and in part from the principles of the hegemonic system governing relations between Latin America and the United States. In other words, the 1980s and 1990s Latin American political transitions were local manifestations of the ending of the Cold War.

There is global consensus that the fall of the Berlin Wall and the dissolution of the Soviet Union marked the end of the Cold War. However, the mood with which the end of the Cold War was received varied around the world. One response was the attitude of triumphalism commonly identified with Francis Fukuyama's version of the "end of history." Triumphalists experience the end of the Cold War as the victory of the 'good' over the "evil" empire, and they exalt their virtues and condemn the principles and actions of the enemy.

The triumphalist mood can be found in the opening sentence of the National Security Strategy of the United States, published in September 2002: "The great struggles of the twentieth century between liberty and totalitarianism ended with a decisive victory for the forces of freedom—and a single sustainable model for national success: freedom, democracy, and free enterprise" (White House 2002). Sustained by the "faith in the principles of liberty, and the value of a free society," a triumphalist President Bush could proclaim: "We will champion the cause of human dignity and oppose those who resist it." Post-Cold War triumphalism has almost no sense of self-criticism. Nothing in themselves is questionable because they have defeated past enemies and now they are the ones responsible for dealing with the present and future enemies of the precious identity they protect.

Another example of post-Cold War triumphalism is Chile's General Augusto Pinochet. With the confidence of having done a great service to the world in defeating communism in Chile and successfully implementing market reforms, Pinochet decided in 1988 to gamble and called a plebiscite in which he proposed the continuation of his government. He miscalculated and lost the plebiscite. Elections were called for March 1990. Pinochet did not run but remained commander-in-chief of the army, a position he retained until 1998 when he was officially sworn in as Chile's first senator-for-life. General Pinochet, and many more who adored him, believed he was a national hero. Imagine the shock he must have felt when in October 1998 the London police told him, while lying on a hospital bed, that he was being detained at the request of a Spanish judge who wanted to interrogate him for crimes committed during his government!

This triumphalism contrasts with the sense of relief, anger, and pain felt by the millions of Chileans who said NO! to the dictator in the 1988 plebiscite. For them, as for millions in Argentina, Guatemala, and El Salvador, ending the Cold War was ending a hot and bloody civil war. Thus, a widespread reaction in these countries was more critical, less celebratory. Millions had been killed, tortured, or disappeared in the name of the Cold War. Under the guise of national security, governments violated human rights with impunity. People could get killed just for asking questions.

A comparison between the triumphalist and critical responses to the end of the Cold War helps to understand current political discourse. A triumphalist believes that the Cold War ended because "freedom, democracy, and free enterprise," with the United States as leader, defeated totalitarianism, communism, and statism. The dissolution of the Soviet Union and its satellite communist regimes in Eastern Europe demonstrated that centralized economies don't work and the "only sustainable model" is "free enterprise." In this new world, "the United States enjoys a position of unparalleled military strength and great economic and political influence" and "welcomes [the] responsibility to lead" in the "great mission" of saving "freedom" from "war and terror" (White House 2002).

Critics see ending the Cold War not as the victory of right versus wrong, but as the ending of a structural arrangement in which the use of violence to attain political goals was justified. From this perspective, ending the Cold War means the start of a long struggle to overcome principles, institutions, and practices that condone violence. For a triumphalist, the use of violence in the past against the enemy was justified, much as it is today against new enemies. Critics, on the contrary, call for an end of the cycles of *all* violence. Ending the Cold War means defeating U.S. triumphalism and beginning a global process of truth, justice, reparation, and reconciliation. With the U.S. embarked in a global war against terror, people working to end violence cannot expect to accomplish their goal only within their respective nations, without being critical of U.S. hegemony.

A significant difference between the triumphalist and critical responses to the end of the Cold War is their attitude toward the past. Triumphalism is associated with the idea of forgetting mistakes of the past. In the words of General Pinochet, "We must forget. And forgetting does not occur by opening cases, putting people in jail. . . . And for this to occur, both sides have to forget and continue working."[2] This attitude is in sharp contrast with the one expressed in the first paragraph of the decree law that created Chile's Truth and Reconciliation Commission: "the moral conscience of the nation demands that the truth about the grave violations of human rights committed in our country between September 11, 1973 and March 11, 1990 be brought to light" (Undersecretary of the Interior 1990).

The triumphalist attitude is an obstacle to ending the Cold War mentality that condoned, and continues condoning, violence. The triumphalist is blind to his own mistakes and celebrates his own virtues by doing more of the same he did in the past—but with a new justification. For a triumphalist, the exercise of "power without arrogance" has been "America's special role in the past, and it should be again as we enter the new century" (Rice 2000). Triumphalists believe that America should continue being true to its own self because that is the only way to fight the enemies of American identity. In the post-Cold War era, we are told, the enemy is not a single person or religion or ideology. Or, as the National Security Strategy proclaims, "In the war against global terrorism, we will never forget that we are ultimately fighting for our democratic values and way of life" (White House 2002).

In contrast, for a critic "the Cold War was a kind of tacit arrangement between the Soviet Union and the United States under which the U.S. conducted its wars against the Third World and controlled its allies in Europe, while the Soviet rulers kept an iron grip on their own internal empire and their satellites in Eastern Europe—each side using the other to justify repression and violence in its own domains" (Chomsky 1998). The dissolution of the Soviet Union did not make the use of force obsolete; on the contrary, it gave the United States more freedom to use military force to protect its interests.

In the United States, post-Cold War triumphalism went hand in hand with efforts across society to ideologically construct other enemies in order to justify a military force that was designed to fight the communist threat. Many fabricated the threat of Islamism to replace the threat of communism. The "green menace" replaced the "red menace" (Huntington 1993). Many others constructed the typical new threat as the "failed regimes" of Africa (Kaplan 1994). For Pentagon officials, the new threat was regional powers intent on acquiring weapons of mass destruction (WMD). For them, the general model of a threat became the "rogue state" ruled by an "outlaw regime" (Klare 1995: 27–28). Today, the common enemy is terrorism.

The fabrication of enemies is compatible with triumphalism because it is an ideological practice that glorifies the self by negating the "other." Triumphalism is about how the righteous "self" defeats the evil "other." For a triumphalist, the end of the Cold War was a one-time event (fall of the Berlin wall or dissolution of the Soviet Union). That chapter of history is closed; we won, they lost. Post-Cold War triumphalism encourages continuity with the past by avoiding facing the past and by fabricating new threats to continue justifying violence.

In contrast, a critical attitude sees the historical events marking the end of the Cold War as similar to the decision of an addict to stop using drugs. The decision is only the beginning of a long and painful process of withdrawal. From a critical point of view, the end of the Cold War is a moment for introspection, an opportunity to face our fears and change our mentalities and views about the other. A critical attitude calls for structural reform through introspection and dialogue with the "other." This critical attitude inspired the creation of truth commissions in Argentina (1983), Chile (1990), El Salvador (1992), Guatemala (1997), and Peru (2001).

National truth commissions have started a long process of structural transformation, but there are still several tasks pending. One key task argued here is the overcoming of truth commissions' nationalist framework. By framing human rights violations within the boundaries of the nation, truth commissions end up silencing the responsibility of the United States. The nationalist framework allowed the U.S. ambassador to Guatemala to comment after the public announcement of the commission's report, "I believe that the report's focus is appropriate, that these were abuses committed by Guatemalans against other Guatemalans— the result of an internal conflict" (Navarro 1999). Notice that these statements were made in spite of the fact that the U.S. funding and training of the Guatemalan army was publicly acknowledged.

The United States in Peru's Truth and Reconciliation Commission

So far, the chapter has demonstrated that Latin American TJRR processes, while questioning key factors of the Cold War period, preserved U.S. hegemony. Without questioning hegemonic international relations, national TJRR processes eventually lost their force. In their efforts at national reconstruction, Latin Americans responsible for advancing TJRR processes challenged power structures with different degrees of success. However, today, more than twenty years after the first Argentine process, much of the initial impulse seems almost gone. The jailed Argentine generals were set free, and President Saúl Menem approved an amnesty law he felt was needed in order to achieve the political stability required for his strategic alliance with the United States. In Chile, the persistent group of victims' families managed to keep pressure on retired general Augusto Pinochet, leading to his 1998 arrest in London and, in January 2005, to his being placed under house arrest for the second time. However, these events have taken place in the context of militant U.S. opposition to the International Criminal Court. In Guatemala and El Salvador, human rights conditions are as bad or worse today than at the time of their respective truth commissions.

The argument of this brief summary is that national TJRR processes will run out of steam if they do not incorporate the international dimension and, particularly, if the United States does not participate as a responsible actor. The argument is *not* that Latin American truth commissions were instruments purposely designed by the United States to preserve its regional hegemony. Certainly the United States, like many other groups, mobilized resources to influence Latin American TJRR processes. However, the United States was not capable of completely silencing the critical voices who demanded the end of the Cold War and its policies. Moreover, truth commission reports have been critical of U.S. Cold War policies, but stopped short of demanding the participation of the United States as a responsible actor in the TJRR process. Without this, specific acts—such as apologies—will remain suspicious instruments of U.S. hegemony.

Peru offers an interesting case in this regard. More than previous truth commissions, Peru's Truth and Reconciliation Commission (Comisión de la Verdad y Reconciliación, CVR) emphasizes that the main responsible actors for the violence were national and its main causes internal. The CVR's Final Report is forceful in the adjudication of responsibility to a broad spectrum of national actors such as the Communist Party of Peru-Shining Path (Partido Comunista de Perù-Sendero Luminoso, PCP-SL), state officials, peasant organizations, political parties, human rights organizations, the press, and the indifferent middle class. In its analysis of the causes of the violence, the CVR offered a combination of subjective and objective factors. Subjectively, the PCP-SL's "political will" was "decisive in the explanation of the initiation of the armed conflict," but not enough to account for its fast development. For the latter it is important to explain how such "political will took advantage of favorable circumstances, fed off of institutional weaknesses, took advantage of structural cracks, channeled certain demands and powerful frustrations, expressed certain popular imagination, and took roots in certain social groups and geographical settings" (CVR 2003).[3]

It is important to note that in its list of "actors of the conflict," the CVR does not include the United States, and in its discussion of objective causes of violence, international causes receive brief references, no systematic analysis. The purpose here is to correct this perspective. If the argument of this chapter holds, one should expect Peru's TJRR process to eventually lose force if the United States is not incorporated as a responsible actor.

Among members of Peru's CVR, there seems to be a resistance to the inclusion of the United States in the TJRR process. In the words of at least some of the members who were interviewed by the author, "Peru is not Guatemala."[4] What they meant was that, whereas the United States played a determinant role in Guatemala's violence, that was not case in Peru. Thus, not only was the United States not a main actor in the conflict, but demanding its participation could undermine the national TJRR process by encouraging national actors to cover up their responsibility by transferring blame onto this powerful external actor. It should be noticed that covering up responsibility is already taking place, even without the inclusion of the United States. Indeed, I will suggest that the participation of the United States as a responsible actor would make it *harder* for powerful national actors to hide their responsibility.

Fortunately, the CVR *Final Report* already provides valuable material for establishing the basis of the responsibility of the United States in human rights violations committed in Peru. Valuable information about the U.S. role in human rights violations can be found in subchapters dedicated to the Armed Forces and the two governments of Alberto Fujimori. In these subchapters, the *Final Report* presents information about the influence of "low intensity conflict" (LIC) strategies and training in the School of the Americas (SOA) on implementation of counterinsurgency strategies, as well as information about "negotiations" between Peru and the United States.

According to the CVR, the adoption of LIC strategies had several political implications. First, LIC strategies instrumentalized human rights education in order to "apply violence in a selective and psychologically conditioning manner" resulting "paradoxically in the closest that exists to terror." Avoiding human rights violations was a "collateral and secondary effect of the strategic restriction of the use of force. . . . Thus, at the same time that there is talk about human rights, members or supporters of subversive organizations are stripped of all their rights." Second, with the adoption of LIC strategies, the Reagan government "eliminated national development plans from their antisubversive policy." Third, in the work of counterintelligence, the concept of "collaborators" was substantially expanded. "It is plausible that identification of subversion collaborators include public officials, mayors and aldermen, doctors and teachers, as well as journalists, activists, and social organization employees who might be giving support to subversives. At the same time, it is clear that there is an extremely high risk of violating fundamental rights with these operations." Fourth, counterintelligence contributes to the militarization of society because "all the basic conditions within which the people's daily life unfolds are fields for counterintelligence action." Fifth, the broadening and deepening of counterintelligence "implies significant risks for the future of democracy" among other reasons because "the antisubversive armed forces tend to become a parallel and alternative government to the elected one." In the Peruvian context, "the predominance of special operations caused the emergence of a certain type of political-military power that conspired against democracy and finally subdued it." Sixth, counterintelligence "introduces a criterion for restricting force, alternative to the legal criteria." While the law regulates force through principles known to everyone, counterintelligence uses force in "a way that only the armed forces know the rules, while the enemy remains clueless." Seventh, for the purposes of counterintelligence "the detained insurgent must be stripped of all juridical protection." The interrogation manuals followed the teachings of the 1963 CIA manuals. "The basic rule is to impose on the prisoner the most strict isolation, depriving him of any reference about his surroundings.... He should not know where he is, nor where they are taking him, why he was detained, or the identity of his captors. The buildings described in the manuals are clearly clandestine prisons.... According to Human Resource Exploitation, detentions should be undertaken at dawn because it is the time when the individual is most passive."

Regarding the School of the Americas, the CVR said:

> According to our estimates, around 898 Peruvian officials took courses in the School of the Americas between 1980 and 1996. If we add to this the work done by North American military instructors, it is clear that counterinsurgency instruction had a wide reception. Moreover, we know of at least one joint counterinsurgency tactics exercise undertaken by the Armed Forces of Peru and the United States.[5]

The CVR further states that instruction in the SOA was done using manuals derived from "Project X," "the means used for storing experiences and resources developed during the Vietnam war."

The information provided by the CVR about "negotiations" between Peru and the United States is also quite revealing, but there is no overall assessment of the nature of the relationship. The *Final Report* describes economic, security, counternarcotics, democracy, and human rights aspects of the relationship between Peru and the United States, but without explaining their hierarchical ordering. The CVR does not offer an assessment of the net impact on human rights violations of U.S. policy toward Peru. According to the CVR, while the U.S. Congress was interested in human rights, the U.S. Executive was not:

> on 17 January 1992, the State Department "reluctantly" accepted the conditions imposed by Congress, as long as no effort was spared in order to reduce the flow of narcotics into the United States. The terms were communicated to Peruvian authorities, emphasizing the need of keeping a list of people in jail, and that aid would not include 10 million dollars for training three counterinsurgency Army battalions.

This statement portrays the ambiguity that characterizes the CVR analysis of the role played by the United States in human rights violations in Peru. What had a major impact on human rights violations in Peru: the United States anti-narcotics policy or the human rights conditionalities "imposed" by the U.S. Congress? What affected more the dynamics of violence in Peru: the LIC strategies or U.S. human rights foreign policy? The previous quote almost seems to imply that the United States was willing to put at risk the counterinsurgency strategy (by withholding military aid) if human rights conditions were not met. Certainly that was not the case because, as explained before, in the counterinsurgency strategy human rights were only one more instrument subordinated to the major objective of defeating the enemy. Actually, military aid was restored in March 1992.

A more critical evaluation of relations between Peru and the United States can be found in a book by Cynthia McClintock and Fabián Vallas (McClintock and Vallas 2003). The authors argued that in the 1990s, relations between the United States and Peru strengthened in three areas: security, market reforms, and antinarcotics policy. Cooperation in these areas, however, was done at the expense of sacrificing democracy and human rights. The authors stated that the U.S. lack of interest for democracy in Peru was not recent. On the contrary, it was a constant in the history of relations between these two nations. During the Cold War, the United States used the war against communism to justify support for authoritarian governments in Latin America. In the post-Cold War era, the support of authoritarian governments, like Peru's Alberto Fujimori, was justified as a means of securing the implementation of common bilateral policies in security, market reforms, and counternarcotics.

McClintock and Vallas do not accuse the United States of being directly implicated in human rights violations in Peru. They are emphatic in making the government of Alberto Fujimori directly responsible for murder, torture, and disappearance. Even further, they single out the president's main intelligence advisor, Vladimiro Montesinos, as the person directly responsible of ordering human rights violations.

> To most analysts, it was obvious that the mastermind of the abuses was Montesinos, operating through the Servicio de Inteligencia Nacional (SIN) and the Servicio de Inteligencia del Ejército (SIE, Army Intelligence Service). It was obvious also that Montesinos had spearheaded the Grupo Colina, the death squad that included both SIN and SIE members and was responsible for the massacres at Barrios Altos and La Cantuta. (McClintock and Vallas 2003: 155)

The importance of highlighting the responsibility of Vladimiro Montesinos is due to his links to the U.S. government. McClintock and Vallas indicate that cooperation between Montesinos and the Central Intelligence Agency (CIA) began in 1991 with counternarcotics campaigns. By that time, Montesinos was Fujimori's main intelligence advisor. The first significant joint project between Montesinos, the CIA, and the Southern Command of the U.S. army was the interception of small airplanes suspected of transporting cocaine. The program was kept secret until 1995 when it was announced to the public under the name "You fly, you die." In Peru, Montesinos was at the center in charge of SIN's antinarcotics office. He was the main contact for General McCaffrey, the antidrug czar, as well as General Wilhem, who headed the Southern Command. Mcclintock and Vallas charge that "During 1996–1998, this SIN unit was the recipient from the U.S. Department of State of approximately $200,000. . . . Also, the unit received at least $1 million in cash annually for a period of ten years from the CIA" (McClintock and Vallas 2003: 125). By this time there were well founded suspicions that Montesino himself was implicated in drug trafficking. And "In 1996, the notorious jailed Peruvian drug lord Demetrio Chávez Peñanerrera (dubbed "El Vaticano") testified in court the he paid Montesinos $50,000 a month for information on antidrug raids in 1991–1992" (58).

The CVR's structuralist or objective approach to the explanation of human rights violations also provides a valuable perspective for bringing the United States into the TJRR process as a responsible actor. As stated by the CVR, the Peruvian case demonstrates that fundamentalist organizations, like the PCP-SL, feed off of the weaknesses of post-Cold War democratic regimes. What needs to be added is that one of the major causes of this weakness is U.S. economic and security policies. Economically, Peru's emerging democracy had been weakened since the beginning of the 1980s by the foreign debt crisis and neoliberal restructuring packages determined by Washington's economic policies. The economic decline, together with the high price of cocaine resulting from U.S. consumption and anti-drug policies, encouraged the development of a global network of drug traffickers and the expansion of coca plantations among poor Andean peasants.

The war against drugs, even before the war against terrorism, exemplified the new shape of U.S. post-Cold War foreign policy. It would take only a few years for U.S. foreign policymakers to combine them into narcoterrorism. Peru was a leading example. While poverty and market forces were driving thousands of peasant families into the production of coca, the U.S. government was pressuring the Peruvian government to implement coca eradication campaigns, with the use of military force, if necessary. Under attack by their own government and exposed to the abuses of drug traffickers, Peruvian peasants sought the protection of the PCP-SL. The alliance with coca peasants gave the PCP-SL two key ingredients that fueled their rapid development throughout the 1980s. First, in exchange for protection, the PCP-SL charged a fee that gave them the financial resources to buy weapons and recruit frustrated urban youth whose best option was a dangerous police job that paid less than $100 a month. Second, the alliance with the peasants gave the PCP-SL a vast base of support communities, which was also helpful to retreat and hide from government attacks.

A serious TJRR process cannot be sustained in Peru in the midst of widespread poverty, racial, class, and gender discrimination, and existential uncertainty for the majority of the population; this much is known. The strategic alliance between the United States and Peru has resulted in the implementation of economic and security policies that maintain the structural foundations underlying poverty and discrimination, and thus violence. The CVR was aware of the importance of structural factors in explaining the violence of 1980–2000. However, by not making the United States a focal point of its work, the CVR allowed these structural causes—based in large part on U.S. hegemony—to remain firmly in place.

Conclusions

In the 1980s, Latin American truth commissions started local processes of truth, justice, reparation, and reconciliation that questioned the Cold War's structures and practices of violence. This chapter has argued that the continuation of the introspective and critical process of transformation requires the incorporation of the United States as a responsible actor. The absence of the United States from the Latin American TJRR processes has contributed to a post-Cold War triumphalism, now further reinforced by the war against terrorism.

In the final pages of the Introduction, the Final Report of Peru's CVR stated:

the Commission places its work within the framework of a world scenario that shows uncertain paths. Human rights culture and its supporting institutions are fragile and based on the consensus of States. In certain moments, like at the beginning of this century, fear of violence may generate a spiral of reprisals that can affect international legality and reduce the possibilities of strengthening the rights of nations and citizens of the world. (CVR 2003)

Along these lines, a crucial step to avoid the manipulation of fear to justify violence is the inclusion of the United States as a responsible actor in a global TJRR process. Outside such a framework, specific U.S. actions of participation in local TJRR processes will appear suspicious. In a context of U.S. hegemony, apologies (as in the case of Guatemala), support for local truth commissions (as in El Salvador, Guatemala, and Peru), and promises of financial aid for reparations programs (as in Peru) will be interpreted as instruments for maintaining hegemony.

References

Babington, Charles. 1999. "Clinton: Support for Guatemala Was Wrong." *Washington Post*, March 11.

Betancur, Belisario, Reinaldo Figueredo Planchart, and Thomas Buergenthal. 1994. "From Madness to Hope: The 12-Year War in El Salvador: Report of the Commission on the Truth for El Salvador," www.usip.org/library/tc/doc/reports/el_salvador/ tc_es_03151993_toc.html

The Case of Pinochet. 1995. http://cyber.law.harvard.edu/evidence99/pinochet/PPFFTTF.htm
Chilean National Commission of Truth and Reconciliation. 1991. *Report of the Chilean National Commission of Truth and Reconciliation*, www.usip.org/library/tc/doc/reorts/chile/chile_1993_toc.html
Chomsky, Noam. 1998. "The United States and the 'Challenge of Relativity'." http://www.zmag.org/chomsky/articles/9708-UD-relativity.html
Clinton, William J. 1999. "Remarks in a Roundtable Discussion on Peace Efforts in Guatemala City." *Weekly Compilation of Presidential Documents* 35 (10): 377–418.
Comisión de la Verdad y Reconciliation (CVR). 2003. *Comisión de la Verdad y Reconciliación: Informe final.* Lima: Comisión.
Commission for Historical Clarification (Comisión para el Esclarecimiento Histórico, CEH). 1998. *Guatemala: Memory of Silence: Report of the Commission for Historical Clarification: Conclusions and Recommendation*s. Guatemala: Commission for Historical Clarification.
Gibney, Mark and Erik Roxstrom. 2001. "The State of State Apologies." *Human Rights Quarterly* 23 (4): 911–39.
Hayner, Priscilla B. 2002. *Unspeakable Truths: Facing the Challenge of Truth Commissions.* New York: Routledge.
Huntington, Samuel. 1993. "The Clash of Civilizations." *Foreign Affairs* 72 (3): 22–50.
Kaplan, Robert D. 1994. "The Coming Anarchy." *Atlantic Monthly* 273 (2): 44–76.
Klare, Michael T. 1995. *Rogue States and Nuclear Outlaws: America's Search for a New Foreign Policy.* New York: Hill and Wang.
Latin American Working Group. 1999. *Of Truth and Apologies: The Guatemalan Truth Commission and the U.S. Role.* Washington, D.C.: Latin American Working Group, www.lawg.org/truth.htm
McClintock, Cynthia and Fabián Vallas. 2003. *The United States and Peru: Cooperation at a Cost.* New York: Routledge.
McGrory, Mary. 1999. "Apologies Are US." *Washington Post*, March 14.
Navarro, Mireva. 1999. "Guatemalan Army Waged 'Genocide', New Report Finds." *New York Times*, February 26.
Norden, Deborah L. and Roberto Russell. 2002. *The United States and Argentina: Changing Relations in a Changing World.* New York: Routledge.
Nunca Más. 1984. *Informe de la Comisión Nacional sobre la Desaparición de Persona*s. Buenos Aires: Nunca Más, www.desaparecidos.org/arg/conadep/nuncamas; nuncamas.html
Prensa Libre. 1999. "Inmigración: EE.UU por expulsar a guatemaltecos y salvadoreños ilegales." *Prensa Libre Guatemala.*
Rice, Condoleezza. 2000. "Exercising Power Without Arrogance." *Chicago Tribune*, December 31.
Rubin, James P. 1999. "Secretary Albright's Travel to Guatemala." U.S. Department of State Office of the Spokesman Press Statement.
Undersecretary of the Interior, Chile. 1990. Supreme Decree No. 355: Creation of the Commission on Truth and Reconciliation, edited by E. B. M. o. Justice.
White House. 2002. The National Security Strategy of the United States, http://www.whitehouse.gov/nsc/nss.html

Chapter 12
"Deliver Us from Original Sin":
Belgian Apologies to Rwanda and the Congo

PAUL KERSTENS

The Belgian state offered its apologies to Rwanda and Congo after two commissions of inquiry in the Belgian parliament. The Rwanda commission is officially known as the Parliamentary Committee of Enquiry in Charge of Research into the Genocide and the Murder of Ten Belgian UN Soldiers in Rwanda. It was established in January 1997 and presented its final report on December 6, 1997. The Lumumba commission, officially the Parliamentary Committee of Enquiry in Charge of Determining the Exact Circumstances of the Assassination of Patrice Lumumba and the Possible Involvement of Belgian Politicians, was established on February 24, 2000, and presented its final report on November 16, 2001. The report was discussed and accepted by the Belgian Parliament on February 5, 2002.[1] The apologies are linked to particular facts or events, namely the 1994 genocide in Rwanda and the assassination of Congo's first Prime Minister, but both are widely interpreted, in Belgium as well as in Rwanda and Congo, as affecting Belgian dealing with its colonial past, as well as with postcolonial realities.

The religious character of the title of this chapter may be disturbing, though it should be noted that the term "apologies" has a strong moral appeal. Apologies can be considered one of the stages resulting from reflections on past injustice, the others being recognition and reparation. Although the Belgian apologies did not result in reparation, at least not in the true sense of the word, they had a profound influence on Belgian politics, on the national and on the international level.

My approach to the Belgian apologies is ethnographic. I consider an apology to be a speech act, and I will focus on the speaking parties involved, their intentions, and the circumstances in which the speech act was uttered. Such an approach makes it possible to interpret the official apologies by the Belgian state, to understand their meaning and importance, and to define the differences between the two apologies.

Apology as a Speech Act

"Apology" is not a neutral word: it has strong personal and emotional connotations. An apology is a speech act between two individuals, during which there is a direct and even intimate contact between the partners, within a distinct hierarchical relationship. The speaker who apologizes asks to be forgiven; the other person has the authority to forgive or not. The purpose of the act is to restore a former relational equilibrium that may vary from strong bonds, as when apologies are exchanged between lovers, to mere indifference, as when they are uttered when bumping into a passerby on the street. The hierarchical relationship may be complex. A strong person may apologize to a weaker one to restore his or her "integrity" and preserve a higher position. The weaker person confirms the other's supremacy by accepting the apology.

"Apology" may also have religious connotations. People can ask God to forgive them for something they have done, or to forgive others who have done something to them. There is a kind of helplessness in these religious apologies. One appeals to a third party because it is impossible to apologize directly to the inflicted partner, or because one does not want to.

The term "apology" means "excuse," but it may also mean a plea or a defense. In his *Apology*, Plato pleads not for Socrates to be forgiven, but for him to be defended and rehabilitated. This ambiguity of the term "apology" is not present in the French, German, or Dutch language, where it is used solely as "defense" and not as "excuse," just as in ancient Greek "apologia," the source of the English word "apology." This semantic particularity should be taken into account in an analysis of apology as a speech act.

While particular speakers are involved and have explicit or implicit intentions, the speech act is also uttered in specific circumstances. These circumstances may provoke apologies or facilitate them, or they can prevent or exclude them. The reason people should apologize has to be established, either by themselves or by a third partner. Circumstances may oblige someone to apologize to someone else, while he originally did not feel the need to do so.

These characteristics of apologies as a speech act between two persons—speakers, intentions, and circumstances—are equally important when considering apologies between states.

Apologizer and Recipient: Belgium, Congo, and Rwanda

The relationship between the two partners, Belgium and Congo or Belgium and Rwanda, is largely defined by the colonial past.

Belgium is a small country, and a young country by western European standards. It gained its independence in 1830, although "independence" is not the right word. It might be better to state that it was created in 1830. At the beginning of the nineteenth century, characterized by romanticism and essentialism, "Belgium" was almost an avant-garde concept, as there was no underlying *ideal*. The unity of Belgian territory could not be traced to one history, one people, or one language. It was a political construction. While modern nineteenth-century nation-states such as England, France, Portugal, and the Netherlands were the heirs of empires that had ventured South, East, and West for centuries, Belgium did not have such a history.

King Leopold II was not content to be the master of a backwater country and reside in a small provincial town. A modernist, he put his country on the rails of industrialization and flourishing capitalism, and urbanized Brussels to become a metropole. His belief that the country needed a colony was connected with his idea of nation-building and his goals of industrialization and commercialization. These goals were also realized by an outspoken international extension of Belgian private enterprise. By the end of the nineteenth century, Belgian industrialists and bankers had become key figures in huge enterprises, such as the industrialization of Egypt.

Leopold considered the Belgian state and the city of Brussels to be personal projects. The État Indépendant du Congo—the Congo Free State—was quite literally a personal project: the Association Internationale du Congo, which was in charge of the project, was part of Leopold's private affairs, not controlled by the Belgian parliament. While Western colonization had largely been an affair of private commercial companies, only in Leopold's case was it a private affair of the head of state.

Due to international pressure, culminating in an international commission of inquiry into Leopold's exploitation of the Congo, the king was forced to cede his colony to the Belgian state in 1905. The fact that the Congo was no longer Leopold's property did not change much of the private character of the colonial enterprise. The state as such did not feel involved, the parliament did not pay much attention, and the idea of Belgium as a colonial power was not widespread. This differentiation between the metropole, which politically governed the colony, and the Congo, where the economic, administrative, and religious establishments ran the territory on their own terms, would become a rift and the basis of the double policy characterizing Belgian colonial and postcolonial politics toward the Congo.

Nevertheless, infrastructure in the colony developed steadily and Belgium became more and more engaged in it, especially after World War II, when uranium was discovered and made the Congo a strategic territory of world importance. Colonization, in the strict sense of the word, started only then. Belgian administrators and traders settled in the Congo with their families, and the second half of the 1950s saw the coming of age of a first generation of Belgians born and raised in the colony. One might say that Belgian consciousness as a colonial state was limited to a period of about twenty years, one generation.

Belgium was also given trusteeship of Rwanda and Burundi, as a kind of negotiated prize after Germany's defeat in World War I. The territory had been part of German East Africa, but was reassigned to Belgium by the Treaty of Versailles, whose conventions were ratified by the League of Nations in 1922. Rwanda and Burundi were officially considered occupied territory entrusted to Belgian administration, but Belgium was allowed to attach the territories' administration to the Belgian Congo. In practice, there was not much difference between colonization and trusteeship, and images of Rwandan *intore* dancers or of the Rwandan king were widely accepted as emblems of Belgian's African treasures.

However, colonization in the Congo differed from that in Burundi and Rwanda. Belgian strategies in the Congo were largely based on direct rule; Congo's administration and jurisdiction were manned by Belgian colonials. In Rwanda and Burundi, indirect rule was applied, as the territories were administered through a partly existing, partly created indigenous elite. As we will see, this does not mean that Belgium felt less involved in Rwanda and Burundi. Another difference is that the Belgian presence in Rwanda and Burundi was much less an economic one. Industry was very limited, almost nonexistent, and commercial transactions were largely based on cash crops such as coffee and tea. Their economic value cannot be compared to Congo's natural resources, ranging from diamonds, gold, copper, uranium, and nowadays coltan to rubber and precious woods.

While the partners in the exchange of apologies can be considered as the heirs of a colonial past, they do not embody this past. It is not the actual colonizer who asks the formerly colonized to accept apologies. It was the postcolonial Belgian government that in 2000 and in 2002 offered its apologies to the Rwandan and Congolese governments. This fact largely determines the nature and importance of the apologies.

In Belgium, a new government came into power in July 1999. It was *new* partly because the Christian Democratic Party was not included in the governing coalition. This party had dominated Belgian politics since World War II and had largely shaped official Belgian relations with its former colonies. It was also a new government because it was meant to embody different political principles. Guy Verhofstadt was the leader of the Flemish Liberal Party, which claimed to be the champion of the "New Political Culture." Belgium had gone through a series of crises that had deeply affected public opinion. The most important may be the Dutroux affair. Marc Dutroux kidnapped young girls to imprison them in the cellar of his house, abuse them, and murder them. Eventually he was discovered, and his last two victims were found alive. It soon became clear that Dutroux had not been stopped earlier because local and federal police forces were boycotting each other, and because Dutroux was well acquainted with some people working in the judiciary and police.

The affair brought about a massive mobilization of the Belgian population, known as the White March, when more than 300,000 civilians filled the streets, demanding transparency in Belgian politics and jurisdiction. The "New Political Culture" was its political answer. It would stand for transparency, good communication, a strong sense of accountability and responsibility, and an active and enterprising policy. The new minister of foreign affairs, Louis Michel, fit this picture perfectly. Profiling himself as a zealot for human rights, he took on the responsibility to put Central Africa high on the European political agenda.

In Rwanda, the Rwandan Patriotic Front (RPF) was in power. Its members were recognized as liberators by the United States and the United Kingdom, among others, because they had defeated the perpetrators of the 1994 genocide. But until 1999 the governments of Belgium and, even more so, France kept aloof and were reluctant to deal with their Rwandan counterpart. They doubted the legitimacy of an RPF government because it had come into power by military means. Furthermore, the RPF was identified as the instrument of the Tutsi minority to control the majority Hutu. Belgium and France had always been fierce defenders of the "Hutu" Habyarimana regime, which had close personal relations with Belgian politicians of the Christian Democratic Party, as well as with the Belgian king Baudouin (Saur 1998). The government was officially recognized, but diplomatic relations and bilateral cooperation were at an all-time low.

In Congo, political life was in turmoil. In February 2000, when the Lumumba commission was created, Laurent-Désiré Kabila was president of the (renamed) Democratic Republic of Congo. Kabila was an outcast. Already a rebel at the beginning of the 1960s, he had maintained his aura of nationalism and anti-imperialism when he came into power, and he was often described as a dictator by Western politicians. He was murdered on January 16, 2001, almost forty years to the day after Patrice Lumumba's assassination. His son, Joseph Kabila, was installed as the new president. Rather low-profiled compared to his father, and not continuing his father's ideological lineage to Lumumba, it did not take long for Joseph Kabila to gain the support of the Western powers. The country was almost constantly in a state of internal and international war that cost the lives of as many as four million civilians.

Intentions and Circumstances of the Rwanda Commission

The Rwanda commission was created in January 1997, under pressure of the relatives of the ten Belgian paratroopers serving under United Nations command who were murdered in Rwanda on April 7, 1994. Prime minister Jean-Luc Dehaene and his government were not keen on this commission of inquiry. Dehaene had been Belgian's prime minister at the time of the genocide, and that history was a delicate matter, as his Christian Democratic Party had actively supported President Habyarimana. King Baudouin had supported Habyarimana's plea for Belgium to send weapons and troops to Rwanda to support his regime when it was attacked by the RPF. Prime Minister Martens, a Christian Democrat, was forced by the Social-Democratic coalition partner of his government to limit Belgian intervention to humanitarian action. Habyarimana was killed in an assault on his plane on April 6, 1994, but the genocide had been prepared while he was in power.

Thus Belgium's governing parties would be scrutinized not only for the decision they made when the genocide began, but also for their actions during the period that immediately preceded it. Still, the Belgian government heeded the pressure of the relatives of the paratroopers, who were ardently lobbying in the political world as well as in civil society. A few years before, the government had been shaken by the White March in Brussels. Not responding to the relatives' call might provoke another mass demonstration against the political leaders. (The importance of this element is evident when one realizes that the conclusions of the Commission were given to the relatives of the paratroopers before being presented to the Belgian Parliament.)

Formally, the commission would only research Belgian political and military decision-making from November 1, 1993 until May 1, 1994. As soon as the commission started its work, however, it became clear that preceding decades, going back to independence and even before, could not be neglected, even if this period would not be included in the Commission's conclusions.

One of the major political decisions resulting from the commission's conclusions presented in December 1997 was that the Belgian government would no longer send troops to former Belgian territories, not even as part of United Nations missions. This decision is emblematic of Belgian's withdrawal from central Africa, where it had hitherto been one of the superpowers, together with France and the United States. The "new" minister of foreign affairs, Louis Michel, wrote the following about the politics of his predecessor: "Our politics concerning Africa were well on its way to become a politics of silence, of waiting, that was timid at least, if not fearful" (Michel 2003: 76).

The change of government in July 1999, however, would take things much farther. The new prime minister, Guy Verhofstadt, was widely perceived as the head of the Rwanda Commission, although he had acted only as its secretary. He had handled it in a very convincing and successful way, and this added much to his political grandeur. Also, this politician, who had never before taken on a strong African profile, declared himself profoundly shocked and shaken by the results of the Commission, and it became very much a personal commitment for him. This was also the case for Michel, who defended human rights and democratic values and proclaimed that the Belgian government should act actively as a peace broker in central Africa.

This emphasis on accountability, democratic values, and respect for human rights is typical of the international context. It explains not only the inflation of apologies by several Western states, but also the renewed interest of states in their own "undigested past." It is also present in large international conferences such as the World Conference Against Racism, Racial Discrimination, Xenophobia, and Related Intolerance in Durban in September 2001. The Belgian minister of foreign affairs played a key role in Durban, as Belgium held the presidency of the European Union at the time, and Louis Michel represented the Union at the Conference.

The apologies that resulted from the Belgian Commissions are a clear case of how the party that accepts the apologies confirms the supremacy of the "apologizer."

The Rwanda Commission resulted in two new major decisions under Verhofstadt's government: the enactment of what became popularly known as the "law on genocide" and the Belgian apology to Rwanda. The law on genocide, accepted June 16, 1993, made it possible for any person on Belgian soil to be brought to court if he or she was charged with genocide, even for actions that had not taken place in Belgium. This meant that Rwandans who had fled to Belgium after the genocide could be charged, arrested, and convicted in Belgium. The case of the "Four of Butare" was widely covered by the national and international press. Vincent Ntezimana, Alphonse Higaniro, Consolata Mukangango (Sister Gertrude), and Julienne Mukabutera (Sister Maria Kisito) were convicted for their participation in genocide. The law was a clear signal that Belgium would not allow perpetrators of the genocide to reside in Belgium, and that justice would prevail. However, some countries considered that matters had got out of hand when complaints were lodged against Israeli prime minister Ariel Sharon, American general Tommy Franks, and U.S. president George W. Bush. Months of political pressure, especially from the United States and Israel, including threats of economic sanctions and boycotting, forced the Belgian Parliament to change this law in such a way that it lost much of its meaning and power.

Prime Minister Verhofstadt went to Kigali in April 2000 to offer Belgian apologies to Rwanda. The final report of the Rwanda Commission had already been presented in December 1997, under the government of his predecessor Jean-Luc Dehaene, a Christian Democrat. In Kigali, on April 7, 2000, accompanied by a large delegation among whom were two ministers and the relatives of the murdered paratroopers, the prime minister stated that "my country, its political and military authorities, are responsible. Belgium was at the heart of the mission of the UN. It is under our eyes that genocide began" (*Le Soir*, April 8, 2000). He then offered Belgian apologies to Rwanda. Rwandan interim president Paul Kagame accepted and hailed the heroic gesture of the Belgian government which he considered to be sincere and brave because of "the opposition it may still provoke in your country."

Intentions and Circumstances of the Lumumba Commission

The origin of the Lumumba Commission is quite remarkable, as it was occasioned by the publication of *De moord op Lumumba*, by Ludo De Witte (De Witte 1999). The book garnered much attention when it was published, but it did not generate a demand from Belgian public opinion for a response by the Belgian political world. However, it did succeed in raising some questions in the political world itself, most specifically by some members of Parliament (MPs) belonging to parties that were included in Verhofstadt's "rainbow coalition," adhering to the "new politics." One of the first oral questions on this matter came from the Green Party's MP, Leen Laenens, who asked Louis Michel if it would not be appropriate to create some kind of Truth Commission on the Belgian colonial past, or a commission of inquiry to research whether the Belgian state was involved in Lumumba's murder. Michel's original answer was negative, but a few weeks later he agreed to form the commission.

The reasons for this change are political. First, such a commission would fit nicely with Michel's efforts to become a peace broker and a political heavyweight in central Africa, emphasizing respect for human rights and democratic values. The fact that the president of the Democratic Republic of Congo, Laurent-Désiré Kabila, liked to refer to Patrice Lumumba as a political relative, could turn the commission into a valuable political tool. The second reason is connected with Belgian internal politics. It was rumored that the far right party Vlaams Blok was also preparing a formal question about establishing such a commission. Michel did not want to answer positively to this question when it emanated from an anti-democratic party, but he also knew that by not responding he would raise a storm which would permit the far right to capitalize on the Lumumba question and on the general feeling of public disenchantment.

"Deliver Us from Original Sin"   195

Therefore, some members of the coalition parties decided to ask the government formally to establish the commission, which was agreed on February 2, 2000, a mere five months after the publication of De Witte's book.

The Commission was charged to research the exact circumstances that had led to the murder of Lumumba, and possible Belgian responsibilities therein. Patrice Lumumba, the first prime minister of the new independent Republic of Congo, was murdered on the night of January 17, 1961. Forty years later, research into this murder could still provoke heated public debate in Belgium. The reason is that Lumumba is one of the key figures in the failed decolonization of the Belgian Congo, a period that still is a trauma for an important part of the Belgian population. Belgian colonizers fled massively from the Congo, shortly after independence, leaving "their country" behind. They felt attacked, and many feared for their lives. The man who embodied everything they feared was Lumumba, who was said to preach hatred against all white people. When the Commission was established, it became clear that the Belgian colonial past might have been hidden, but it was still present in contemporary Belgium. When the Commission was asked to research not only the actual assassination, but also the circumstances that had *led* to the murder, this vivid trauma was reawakened.

The Commission concluded that the Belgian government held moral responsibility for the murder. Later, Louis Michel, in the name of the Belgian government, would drop the "moral" but accept "responsibility." The Commission also recommended further "research into the colonial and post-colonial era" in order to obtain wider scientific knowledge "that may assist in coming to terms with the past," a phrase that contains the verb *exorcise* in the original French text, to expresses the "coming to terms."[2]

When, during the debate in the Belgian Parliament, some MPs asked the government to formally apologize to the people of Congo, an MP of the far right Vlaams Blok shouted "and what about the apologies of the Congolese government for the harm Belgians had been done?" It was not a detached act. It can hardly be a coincidence that merely two months after the conclusions of the commission had been made public, and well before the debate in Parliament, a book was launched in which "colonists" related their stories about rape, murder, and destruction following Congo's independence (Verlinden 2002). During the months after the debate, the history of Belgian colonizers made its way into newspapers, radio, and television, after having been largely neglected for forty years.

The Belgian government did apologize to Congo. The foreign minister expressed his "profound and sincere regrets and apologies for the sorrow inflicted [on the people of Congo] by this apathy and cold indifference" (Braeckman 2002: 1). This gesture was widely considered as a brave act of a former colonizer that does want to confront its own past.

It seems, though, that it was perceived that way by "outsiders" rather than by Belgians or Congolese (Soudan 2002).

Results of the Rwanda and Lumumba Commissions

In order to measure the significance and importance of the Belgian apologies it is necessary to embed them in their overall effects, social as well as political.

Belgians in the Congo experienced a shock of decolonization shortly before and even more immediately after Independence Day on June 30, 1960. Most Belgian citizens in Congo had the impression that they were being chased out of "their" country. The majority fled in panic, without any pretense of handing over affairs to a new administration that had been scarcely provided for. Independence Day is emblematic of a deep rupture, a sharp discontinuity in Belgian history.

The shock of decolonization came much later in Rwanda. The Republic of Rwanda obtained its independence on July 1, 1962, and the transition was considered by Belgium to be successful. There was no rupture at all, and although power was handed over to a Rwandan president and government, relations between Belgium and Rwanda basically remained the same before and after independence.

This is remarkable, as the period preceding independence had been very violent, costing thousands of lives and forcing many more into exile. This violence, however, did not touch Belgium, because it was not directed against Europeans. Thus, it did not affect the picture of Rwanda as a model colony, nor did the continuous cycle of genocidal violence in the following decades.

The murder of the ten Belgian paratroopers on the morning of April 7, 1994, when the latest genocide started, was clearly an act of violence directed against Belgium. The murders directly affected several layers of Belgian society. Politicians were implicated for their support—political, financial, or military—of the regime that had perpetrated genocide. Science was questioned for founding an ideology of ethnicity in Rwanda. Catholic clergy were implicated for their almost unconditional commitment to Habyarimana, and corporations for their outspoken or silent support of politics and politicians.

The RPF, taking power in Kigali, marked this rupture in Belgian history. As had been the case in Congo when Lumumba became prime minister in July 1960, Belgium now felt "estranged" from Rwanda. The new leading class had not been raised in Belgian universities or coached by Belgian authorities. English, instead of French, was used by some people in the government and army. Some important Belgian nongovernmental organizations were refused entry to the country. The Belgian government retreated from the political scene, and its relations with Kigali were cool. The impression was that Anglo-Saxons, together with the Dutch, were moving in and had started to occupy Belgium's favorite territory.

The Rwanda Commission of the Belgian Senate confirmed that Belgium had failed completely in handling the crisis in spring 1994, but it was felt that this was emblematic of the failure of the "Belgian period" in Rwandan history as a whole. The actions of the Dehaene government were all aimed at retreat. Belgian soldiers would not operate in central Africa any more, not even under a UN flag, and Belgian policy on Africa would focus on countries other than Rwanda, Burundi and Congo.

Verhofstadt's government marked a change when it decided to turn its attention back to central Africa. In the case of Rwanda, the apologies of the Belgian government also meant that the RPF-dominated Rwandan government was now considered legitimate. Even if Belgian nongovernmental organizations (NGOs) (mostly of Roman Catholic origin) did not regain their former role, the Belgian state invested heavily in rehabilitation and development aid.

For some people, the Lumumba Commission did not live up to expectations, as it did not define *ad nominatum* the people responsible for the murder of Lumumba, although this had been one of the tasks the Belgian parliament had assigned the Commission. But the Commission did conclude that the Belgian government of that time had a "moral responsibility" because it had failed to prevent the assassination. Equally important are the conclusions that the Belgian government had violated international law when its military occupied the sovereign state in August 1960, and when it had intervened in Congolese national politics. The murder of Lumumba is not only associated with Belgian colonial failure, but also with Belgian postcolonial politics. Lumumba was the only political leader of the Congo to be democratically elected (until the time of writing in April 2005). The murder of Lumumba is also associated with the rise of President Mobutu, who during a reign of more than 25 years would ruin Congo, with Belgian support.

The effects for the Democratic Republic of Congo of Belgian government actions following the conclusions of the Commission were not as important as they had been for the Republic of Rwanda when Belgian apologies were offered. The political significance of the apology was limited to their being a tool for the diplomacy of Louis Michel in the region. The apology might have been much more important if Laurent-Désiré Kabila had still been president, because he claimed the heritage of Lumumba. In 2002, the political generation in Congo as well as in Belgium was no longer directly associated with the historical period. The apology was not needed to mark a new chapter in Belgian-Congolese political relations, as this new chapter had already begun.

The effects were limited for Belgian politics as well. The commission confirmed the image of the "new politics" of the Verhofstadt government, but it did not become a major mark in its history. The effects in Belgian society as a whole were much more important, because the colonial past once again became a major point of interest in public discussions. Books were published, television programs and radio series were produced, and it even entered the theater, such as in *Lumumba-bah* by Sam Bogaerts and Nadien Lavern. In several cases the books were apologetic, such as *Weg uit Congo* (Verlinden 2002) Also the Rwanda Commission occasioned apologetic works; for example, by the Belgian UN commander in Kigali in 1994, Colonel Luc Marchal (Marchal 2001).

Belgian Apologies as Speech Acts

We now return to the analysis of apologies as speech acts, in order to evaluate their meaning.

The status of the speakers is important. In both cases, the Belgian "apologizer" is not the entity directly responsible for the deplored action. The Belgian government assumes a responsibility, while it emphasizes at the same time that it is different from the government in power at the time of the acts. The speaker apologizes in the name of another who cannot or will not apologize.

In the case of the murder of Lumumba, the government in power in 1960 cannot apologize because it is not governing any more. Most of the politicians of that government are no longer alive, making it impossible for them to accept personal responsibility. However, the role of the present government as a speaker for the 1960 one is heavily contested. Descendants of politicians in charge in 1960, such as Mark Eyskens, son of Gaston Eyskens, prime minister, and Arnould d'Aspremont Lynden, son of Harold d'Aspremont Lynden, minister of African affairs, did not accept the Commission's conclusions and did not accept that the government should speak in their fathers' names. Many ex-colonizers were scandalized by the apologies, and proclaimed that they possessed much more authority to speak on these matters than a younger political generation.

In the case of Rwanda, the government in charge had not wanted to apologize. Jean-Luc Dehaene led the Belgian government during the genocide and when the commission of inquiry presented its results. The apologies followed two and a half years later, when a new government was in charge. Dehaene confirmed that "he would still take the same decisions" as in 1994, and Willy Claes, who had been minister of foreign affairs, stated that he did not understand "why Belgium should apologize" (Braeckman 2004).

The status of the partner receiving the apology is also complex. It was not so complex for the Lumumba case; with Kabila removed from the political scene, the two partners in the act of apology were clearly symbolic ones, only marginally related to the parties originally involved. For Rwanda, however, the role of "apologizer" was of the highest importance. The fact that Verhofstadt went to Kigali to present his apologies to the victims of the genocide, represented by President Kagame, implied that Kagame was considered a legitimate victim of the genocide. This is still contested, in Belgium as well as Rwanda, by people stating that the real victims are being neglected.

As for the hierarchical relations between the speaking partners and the way this affects the real meaning of the act of apology, it would be difficult to think that the acceptance of the apologies would confirm the supremacy of the "apologizer." Belgium is too much confronted with other parties in the region that are much stronger, to be able seriously to sustain an idea of supremacy. Such a claim would be rejected immediately by both the "apologized," the actual Congolese and Rwandan governments. Despite the fact that one of the speakers is rich and the other poor, the rich one depends on the poor's acceptance. The stakes are equal for the two partners.

In both cases, there were certain circumstances that compelled the establishment of the commissions of inquiry, and the conclusions of the inquiries called for apologies. The commissions had detected the errors and negligence of Belgian politics that caused highly detrimental effects for Rwanda and for Congo. Apologies were uttered only because the circumstances demanded this; in both cases there is no question of an act of apology emanating directly from the "apologizer" who, of his own initiative, pleads for forgiveness from the inflicted partner.

The Rwanda Commission clearly shows that circumstances may vary. While the conclusions of the Rwanda Commission did not provoke apologies in 1998, they did in 2000. The conclusions had not changed, but the change in political conditions made them more compelling.

The intention of the Belgian apology to Rwanda is clearly to restore relations between the two states. With the apology to Congo, this is not the case. Relations between Belgium and Congo may have been affected by the decision to establish the Lumumba Commission, as the new Belgian government was still in the process of redefining and reimposing itself as a peace broker in central Africa at the time, but the apologies had no effect. At the time they were uttered they had already lost their importance. Apologies presented by a Belgian government in the name of a former one with which it has very little affinity, and accepted by a Congolese government in the name of a former one in which it is only vaguely interested, must find their meaning on another level. One possibility is the religious level. When the Commission states in its conclusions that its work may help to "digest" a colonial past that is still "haunting" Belgian and Congolese people, the apologies uttered and accepted by younger generations may well be a call to be delivered from original sin. Another meaning may lie in the interpretation of "apology" as plea or defense. In this case, the "apologized" is of no importance. The apology is purely an affirmative act of the Belgian government and its new politics. What Congo may think of an apology of this kind does not really matter.

Apologies and Reparation

Apologies can be considered as one of the stages resulting from reflections on past injustice, the others being recognition and reparation.

While Belgian responsibility was clearly established in both the Congo and the Rwanda cases, it resulted only in the restoration of moral integrity, not financial compensation. Although both commissions were linked to a particular event, it is extremely difficult to measure the damage caused in financial terms. Still, there is some kind of "reparation" involved. The Rwanda apology resulted in the renewal of substantial aid from the Belgian government to Rwanda, to help rehabilitate the country and reorganize society. Belgium invested in logistics and in the Rwandan legal system. For the Lumumba Commission, the question is more complex. The Congolese government insisted on reparation, following the apologies, but later nothing was heard of this (Reuters 2002). Roland Lumumba, one of the sons of Patrice Lumumba, stated that he would lodge a complaint against the Belgian state and seek compensation. Because the Commission's conclusions clearly stated that the Belgian state had violated national and international law on several occasions, and that the Republic of Congo and/or Patrice Lumumba had been afflicted, there were sound grounds to do so. Another son, François Lumumba, refused to consider Roland a legitimate representative of the family. Both were present during the debate in Parliament, and it was during this debate that Louis Michel privately contacted some deputies with the idea to create a Patrice Lumumba Foundation to sustain democracy in Congo. In his final speech, Michel announced the establishment of this Foundation, and added that the Lumumba family would be involved in its administration. Later, the Lumumba family stated that they considered it as "an adequate answer of the suffering caused" (Timmerman 2002). Although it was not presented as such, one could consider this Foundation as a kind of reparation.

In the case of Rwanda, the element of recognition of the genocide was much more important. This still is a matter of debate in Belgium, and it is closely linked to the close relations of Belgian political and civil society with the Habyarimana regime. Recognition of Belgian passivity when genocide could still have been halted, and of the indifference of the international community to the enormous massacres, was also important. In the case of the Lumumba commission, the element of recognition is certainly present, but less so in Congo itself. In Belgium and in the Western world, the commission was heralded as recognition of direct Belgian meddling in national Congolese politics, and of contemporary Belgium as a society that would and could confront its colonial past. It is a recognition not necessarily of the colonial past, but of Belgium's courage in confronting that past

Conclusion

State apologies are a political strategy, but they still retain their personal and emotional connotations. In the Belgian case, it is not only a matter of one government asking another to accept apologies. Large parts of the population are directly involved, and there are personal relations and individual histories hidden behind the official political relations. Apologies may affect the population emotionally.

Therefore, when discussing the "Age of Apologies" it is important to consider every act of apology as a single speech act, where specific speakers are involved, with particular intentions and in particular circumstances.

References

Braeckman, Colette. 2002. "La Belgique s'excuse de la mort de Lumumba." *Le Soir*, February 6.
———. 2004. "Willy Claes: je ne sais pas de quoi la Belgique s'est excusée au Rwanda." *Le Soir*, March 31.
De Vos, Luc, Emmanuel Gerard, Philippe Raxhon, and Jules Gérard-Libois. 2004. *Lumumba: De complotten? De moord.* Leuven: Davidsfonds.
De Witte, Ludo. 1999. *De moord op Lumumba.* Leuven: Uitgeverij Van Halewyck. English *The Assassination of Lumumba.* London: Verso, 2001.
Marchal, Luc. 2001. *Rwanda, la descente aux enfers.* Bruxelles: Editions Labor.
Michel, Louis. 2003. *De as van het goede.* Antwerpen: Uitgeverij Houtekiet.
Reuters. 2002. "Congo vraagt herstelbetaling voor Lumumba." *de Standaard*, February 7.
Saur, Léon. 1998. *Influences parallèles: L'internationale démocrate-chrétienne au Rwanda.* Bruxelles: Editions Luc Pire.
Soudan, François. 2002. "Lumumba: une fierté belge." *L'intelligent Jeune Afrique* 2144, February 11.
Timmerman, Georges. 2002. "Belgisch excuus voor moord op eerste Kongolese premier." *De Morgen*, February 6.
Verlinden, Peter. 2002. *Weg uit Congo: Het drama van de kolonialen.* Leuven: Davidsfonds.

Chapter 13
Germany Faces Colonial History in Namibia: A Very Ambiguous "I Am Sorry"

Leonard Jamfa

Between 1904 and 1907, German colonial forces wrote one of the darkest pages of German history: the massacres of the Herero and Nama people in German South-West Africa (today Namibia), perpetrated in response to an organized resistance to colonial occupation that had resulted in the assassination of around 100 German settlers (Zimmerer 2001). On October 2, 1904, General von Trotha ordered that "Within the German boundaries, every Herero, whether found armed or unarmed, with or without cattle, will be shot. I shall accept no more women or children. I will drive them back to their people, or I shall order fire on them" (von Trotha 1904).

The brutality of the massacres allows historians to talk of genocide: a war of extermination, designed to annihilate a tribe. The Herero were encircled, leaving them with just one option, to flee to the Kalahari desert, where they massively perished from hunger and starvation. An estimated 60,000 to 70,000 people died. Of those who survived, 14,000 men, women, and children were imprisoned in concentration camps, where an estimated 7,700 died from maltreatment. Many were raped and tortured, some were used for scientific experiments, and those who survived were exploited in colonial plantations. Others were deported to other German colonies, where most of them died. At the beginning of the century, there had been an estimated 80,000 Herero, but only 15,130 were identified in the population census of 1911 ("Eine unbelastete Kolonialmacht?" 2004). The land, now "cleansed" of Herero, was ready for European economic exploitation. German settlers used Hereros as workers, under a regime of forced labor.

Since then, apology, reparation, and restitution have been a matter of great concern for the Herero people. Yet Berlin has paid very little attention to their claims. Helmut Kohl, in 1995 the first German chancellor to visit Namibia, did not say one word concerning the Herero genocide, and refused to meet a delegation of Herero elites. In 1998 during a visit to

Namibia, German president Roman Herzog acknowledged the crimes, but refused to apologize. He argued that the Herero had not been protected by international law at the time of the genocide, and that "too much time has passed for a formal apology to the Hereros to make sense" (Ngunjiri 2002). In March 1999, in response to numerous appeals by Herero elites for negotiations, an official of the German Foreign ministry stated: "We are aware of our moral and especially our historical obligation towards Namibia and the Hereros. Therefore, the Federal Republic maintains a comprehensive and unusually intensive developmental cooperation with Namibia" (Volmer 1999). In October 2003, during a visit in Windhoek, German foreign minister Joschka Fischer also refused a formal apology. In January 2004, when visiting Africa, Gerhard Schroeder did not include Namibia in the countries to be visited, and some commentators interpreted this as a way for the Chancellor to escape the Herero affair (Ayad and Benyahia-Kouider 2004).

Surprisingly, in August 2004 in Okakarara (Namibia), while attending the commemoration of the centenary of the Herero genocide, Heidemarie Wieczorek-Zeul, German minister for economic cooperation and development, expressed the deep regret of her state for the atrocities committed between 1904 and 1907 against the Herero and Nama. "We Germans," she said, "accept our historical, political, moral and ethical responsibility for the wrongs committed by our ancestors. May you, please, in the name of our 'common Father' forgive our deeds" (Wieczorek-Zeul 2004).

How should the sudden German change in attitude be understood? What significance can be attached to the German demand for forgiveness?

The German initiative took place in a very particular historical context characterized by two major facts. The first was the troublesome political situation in Southern Africa. This was mostly due to the deep social and racial inequality between blacks and whites that might easily dissolve into open confrontations in the countries of the region (Zimbabwe being a revealing example). The second was a lawsuit filed by the Herero elites in a U.S. court against the German State and three enterprises. This lawsuit was filed on September 19, 2001 in the U.S. District Court for the District of Columbia by the Herero People's Reparation Corporation and a group of individuals of Herero origin. The case is presently still pending.

This chapter analyzes the symbolic importance of Berlin's "apology" to the Herero and Nama people. Berlin may have been constrained to acknowledge the responsibility it had always rejected, and to open negotiations with the victims. But, by using the conditional tense in assessing the facts, by referring her demand for forgiveness to God ("our common Father"), and by disconnecting apology from reparation, as the Minister for Economic Cooperation and Development did on August 14, 2004,

Berlin acts according to realist principles (that is, national interest only), thus reducing greatly the symbolic importance of her gesture. To support this contention, I first present an overview of German management of its colonial legacy; next, I highlight the specificity of the statement made on August 14, 2004, and finally, I explain the insufficiencies of the German initiative.

Longstanding Refusal of Historic Responsibility

Berlin's historic lack of interest in Africa explains in part its present attitude to its colonial legacy. Only under pressure from German businessmen and a public opinion increasingly favorable to the colonial adventure did Chancellor Bismarck, in the nineteenth century, engage the Reich in the conquest of African territories (Austen 1985). This situation is understandable, as the German chancellor considered European affairs paramount. Only later was a colonial "policy" implemented. The German Colonization Society was created in 1882. Only in April 1884, that is, a few months before the opening of the Berlin Conference in which European states carved up Africa among themselves, was a sort of colonial roadmap conceived (Vidal 1900).

However, even if Germany's participation in colonial conquest was recent compared to other European powers, the German colonial empire in 1913 covered a geographical area of more than 2,707,000 km^2, in which 12,860,000 Africans and a considerable number of Europeans lived (Größe und Bevölkerung Unseren Kolonie 1938). The present Burundi, Rwanda, Cameroon, Namibia, Tanzania, and Togo later emerged from this territory as independent states, although German rule was replaced by Belgian, French, and British rule after the Germans were defeated in World War I. Apart from some very slight differences, the colonial policy of the Reich was similar in all its occupied territories, occupying African lands, using Africans as forced laborers, and taxing them. Logically, living in the era of apologies, one would have expected the German Republic to define a cooperation policy with all its former colonies, at least as far as the management of wrongs of the past is concerned. But this has not been the case.

"The Berlin Wall Is in the Mind" (Toulabor)

As if it were a psychological block, no great change has emerged in Berlin's attitude towards Africa in the postcolonial era. Gerhard Schroeder visited Africa six years after his election as Chancellor, in October 2003, but he visited none of the former German colonies. From December 10 to 16, 2004, the German Head of State, Horst Köhler, visited Africa, but none of the former colonies were included in his agenda. In fact, there is no particular German agenda for Africa. Thus, it is not surprising that the management of wrongs of the colonial period is not a matter of great concern in Berlin.

However, current African problems call for Germany to acknowledge its responsibility for apology, and eventually reparations. In addition to Namibia, where the massacre of the Herero is today a major aspect of domestic and external policy, the nation-building process in the former German colonial territories in general is strongly handicapped by the extreme poverty of the population, and the permanent tension among citizens of different ethnic groups. The cause of this situation can be located in part in German colonial policy. Several German international companies and the German State built their economic success through intensive economic exploitation of African human and natural resources. These companies are well identified, and the amount of their bloody profits can be estimated. In the Herero lawsuit in the U.S., for instance, Deutsche Bank and Woermann are two of those multinationals.

Moreover, the Herero and Nama genocide was perpetrated in response to an official German order, which no German government acknowledged until early 2004. How should the sudden German change in attitude toward the Herero and Nama genocide be understood? Why address an apology to the Herero, in Western Africa, yet not to the people of eastern Africa (in present-day Rwanda, Burundi, and Tanzania) who were also victims of German colonial troops?

The Specificity of the Namibian Case

To understand the position of Namibia in German foreign policy today, it is necessary to refer back to 1882 and the creation of the German Colonial Association. The main objectives of this Association were to promote the imperialist idea in German society; to campaign for the transformation of German protectorates into colonies; and to encourage German settlement in Namibia and East Africa. Today, of the 1,800,000 people in Namibia, 100,000 are white, among whom at least 25,000 are of German origin (CIA 2004). Germany's interest in Southern Africa, and the specificity of German-Namibian cooperation, has been primarily motivated by trade and the search for raw materials. Namibia is particularly important as a source of uranium and diamonds. But these existing historical and economic interests have not proven to be enough to motivate reconciliation with the aggrieved people. The political crisis in Zimbabwe, and the lawsuit in the U.S. District Court for the District of Columbia, explain Germany's recent changed attitude.

The Zimbabwean "Syndrome": Land Reform and the Risk of Brutal Removal of White Settlers

Berlin's initiative occurs when Southern Africa risks open confrontation between blacks and whites. Admittedly, post-apartheid South Africa gives the observer some reasons to hope for a bright future. But the white minority occupies the greatest part of the land, an obvious inequality which poses serious problems in an environment dominated by the crawling poverty of the large majority of blacks: 98 percent in Zimbabwe; 87.5 percent in Namibia; 98.7 percent in Zambia; 75.2 percent in South Africa (CIA 2004)

In Zimbabwe, after independence in 1980, the government embarked on a land reform project whose aim was to redistribute to blacks lands still occupied by the minority of white settlers. In the late 1990s, the land issue was still a matter of great concern, for land was still largely owned by white settlers. Under public pressure, the Zimbabwean government restarted land reform. In 1998, an agreement was signed between the governments of Zimbabwe and Great Britain, to provide financial support for land reforms. The World Bank promised to fund the project with $U.S.5 million. This program failed because of political mismanagement, lack of funds, and disengagement of external partners. London unilaterally interrupted its financial support, referring to lack of transparency in land allocations. The government of Zimbabwe then proceeded with unilateral expropriation of commercial farms owned by whites, creating a general climate of tension. A limit was crossed with the violent removal of some white farmers from their lands, in operations backed by the ruling elite

Land reforms could have been peacefully achieved had the 1979 Lancaster House agreements between the British and the incoming independent government been respected by all the parties involved, including local governments and international fund donors. Indeed, in the agreements that ended the Zimbabwean liberation war, Great Britain pledged to provide financial assistance for land redistribution. But it later did not respect the commitment. Furthermore, the Structural Adjustment Program of Bretton Woods institutions, followed by brutal curtailment of official development assistance, greatly limited the Zimbabwean regime's ability to redistribute land.

Consequently, the Zimbabwean "syndrome" has today invaded the whole of southern Africa, risking the reproduction in other countries of the bloody removal of rich white settlers from their farms by poor black populations. This threat is particularly real in Namibia, where land reform has always been a crucial matter of domestic policy. Even under South African administration (1919–1990), one of the main Herero claims was the return to their ancestral lands occupied by white settlers (Krüger and Henrichsen 1998: no page needed). Social inequality in Namibia has reached a critical point, due to the huge difference in standard of living between blacks who constitute the large majority of the population (87.5 percent) and whites (6 percent). As land possession is one important path to wealth accumulation, land reform has become the precondition for peaceful cohabitation between blacks and whites. This is an important challenge for the postcolonial Namibian ruling elite.

Equally, Berlin is preoccupied with land reform in Namibia, since it directly concerns German interest in protecting Namibian citizens of German descent. More than a thousand German-origin citizens occupy large tracts of land, and are among the main agricultural producers. An estimated 4,000 white farmers possess 44 percent of the land in a country where more than half the population live below the poverty line (World Socialist Web Site 2002).

In February 2000, when the "veterans' war" (invasion of white-owned land by veterans of Zimbabwe's war of independence) started in Zimbabwe, Namibian authorities did not firmly condemn the violent removal of white settlers. There are some indications that the former president, Sam Nujoma, did not disapprove of the Zimbabwean method of land management. Some members of the Namibian elite repeatedly drew Berlin's attention to the emergency need for land reform. According to Bishop Kameeta, "the injury of the land right, hurts the soul of humans. The re-establishment of land property right is, in turn, the re-establishment of the soul of the people" (Melber 2004). Some other members of the elite were more radical. In January 2004, a Herero high representative (and adviser to the paramount Chief) warned: "the younger generations do not have the patience of the oldest. If there is no agreement, they will probably take things in [their] hands. . . . What occurred to Zimbabwe could easily happen here" (Mburumba 2004).

All this demonstrates that the Zimbabwean crisis has influenced Namibia's internal situation. It is quite inconceivable today to consider the land reform process in Namibia without referring to the new political situation created by the veterans' war in Zimbabwe. The threat of propagation of the "syndrome" is taken very seriously by German authorities, as can be seen in the intensive cooperation agenda between Berlin and Windhoek, as well as in the activities of German political foundations since 2000. The Friedrich Ebert Foundation organized a workshop on land reform in southern Africa in 2003, and in 2004 organized a "reflection" to help the German public manage its colonial past.

The Lawsuit Against the German State and Private Companies

The decision to adopt judicial procedures was taken after Herero elites had failed on several occasions to obtain a negotiated arrangement from

Berlin. One of the most awaited occasions was the World Conference on Racism, Racial Discrimination, Xenophobia, and Related Intolerance held in Durban, South Africa, from August 31 to September 7, 2001. Here also, German authorities refused to present a formal apology.

On September 19, 2001, a group known as the Herero People's Reparation Corporation filed a lawsuit in Washington, D.C., against the German State and three corporations: Deutsche Bank; the mining company Terex Corporation, formerly Orenstein-Koppel Co.; and the shipping company Deutsche Afrika Linie, formerly Woermann Linie. The plaintiffs demanded $U.S.2 billion in reparations from the Federal Republic of Germany, and another 2 billion from the companies.

The decision to adopt judicial procedures in the resolution of the Herero problem had been taken a few years earlier. In 1998, Chief Kuiama Riruako attempted to file suit in the International Court of Justice (ICJ) in the Hague. His attempt was rejected, as only states can utilize the ICJ. The choice of the American court was motivated by the Alien Tort Claim Act (ACTA) of 1789, which gives private parties (individuals or groups) the opportunity to obtain legal reparation for particular human rights abuses they have suffered, such as crimes against humanity, regardless of their citizenship. The settlement of Jewish reparation claims in the USA may also have influenced the Herero decision to approach the American court. In 1999, the (Jewish) Unified Claims Conference succeeded in obtaining reparations from some Swiss banks. In summer 2003, a $U.S.6-billion Holocaust slave labor settlement was approved, funded jointly by the German government and a consortium of German and American corporations (Sebok 2001).

The Herero people, however, were not supported in their lawsuit by the Namibian government, whose official position is neutrality. The Government contends that all Namibian tribes were victims of colonial hardship. Therefore, supporting a claim introduced by a single group might appear unfair. Moreover, the South-West Africa People's Organization (SWAPO), the ruling party since independence, is largely controlled by the Ovambo, the dominant ethnic group in Namibia (50 percent), whereas the Herero constitute a minority (8 percent), mostly in opposition.

Despite the lack of government support for the Herero, after their claim for reparation became a judicial matter Berlin started what could be considered "serious" negotiations. Two factors affected its change in attitude. First, the settlement of the Holocaust reparation claim in the United States was based in large part on the ATCA, suggesting the possibility that the Herero claim, also rooted in the ACTA, might be successful. Second, even if the massive violation of fundamental human rights that occurred during colonialism was not considered illegal at the time, those crimes conformed neither to natural law, nor to the moral standards of that same time. The colonial decision-makers understood the true nature of their act. German chancellor Bülow, for instance, described the brutality against the Herero and Nama as contrary to "Christian and human values," an act that rendered the German Empire ineligible to be a member of the family of "civilized nations" (Kämmerer and Föh 2004). Furthermore, the genocide was debated in the German Parliament at the time, and condemned. This demonstrates that the colonial officers were conscious that they were committing a crime.

As Kammerer and Föh state, it is very difficult to use today's international law to settle precolonial and colonial injustices. Nevertheless, current international law could be used to address past crimes, should the interpreter adopt an evolutionary approach to legal instruments. Indeed, in its Advisory opinion in 1971 on South Africa's presence in Namibia, the ICJ asserted that "an international instrument has to be interpreted and applied within the framework of the entire legal system prevailing at the time of interpretation" (ICJ 1971). The ICJ relied not only on the law prevailing in 1919, when South Africa took power over Namibia, but also on the legal regime of the subsequent half-century. Despite the fact that the legality (or illegality) of historical events must be judged according to the law in force at the time they happened, "the continuing effects of these events can be judged by more recent standards" (Shelton 2004). In the Herero lawsuit against Germany, an evolutionary interpretation of international law may produce severe effects in Berlin: not only may this lead to the payment of a large amount of money for reparations for these crimes, it may open the doors to several claims. Thus, the German government is likely to pay serious attention to a Herero lawsuit based on ATCA.

It was only after the brutal takeover of white-owned lands in Zimbabwe, and the introduction of the lawsuit in the United States, that Berlin undertook the series of reconciliation initiatives which finally led to its "apology" on August 14, 2004.

A Very Ambiguous "I Am Sorry"

The year 2004 was the first time in the history of German-Namibian relations that a dignitary of ministerial rank took part in the commemoration of the massacre of 1904–1907. It was also the first time that a member of the German government expressed, in the name of her government, a request for forgiveness for the crimes committed against the Herero people by German colonial troops. The presence of the German minister of economic cooperation and development at the commemoration ceremony was extremely important. The symbolic importance of a request for forgiveness is augmented when presented by an authority of ministerial rank, especially on an issue as delicate as the Herero case.

However, the solemnity of Berlin's initiative is somewhat tarnished by three elements of the message: the use of the conditional tense; the reference to God; and the dictatorial attitude of the German government. This could delay the reconciliation expected by the German government.

The Use of the Conditional Tense

An apology is first of all a moral requirement. The more the victim feels the culprit's sincerity, the more valuable the apology. An apology can be considered serious only when culprit and victim share the same assessment of the facts. But the German minister did not describe the extermination war against the Hereros as genocide. She presented her state's "apology" for crimes which "would have been termed genocide, had it been today" (Wieczorek-Zeul 2004). The Herero people through their elites had asked quite clearly for an apology for the crime of genocide.

The minister also used the conditional tense (100 Jahre Herero-Aufstand 2004) highlighting Berlin's continual rejection of any phrasing that could be used as a basis for legal proceedings or reparation requirements. This rejection reduces the symbolic importance of the long-awaited August 14, 2004, gesture. Yet states neighboring Germany have taken riskier steps by offering solid bases for possible legal proceedings. The first article of France's 2001 law recognizing slavery as a crime against humanity clearly stipulates: "The French Republic recognizes on one hand that the transatlantic slave trade as well as the slave trade in the Indian Ocean; and on the other hand that slavery perpetrated against the populations of Africa, America, Madagascar and India as from the XV century, in America, the Caribbean, in the Indian Ocean and in Europe constitute a crime against humanity" (Law 2001-434, Art. 1). The law is written in the present tense. Another French law took a similar approach. The law of January 29, 2001 states that "France publicly recognizes the Armenian genocide of 1915" (Law 2001-70).

Similar to events in France, the inquiry commission created by the Belgian Senate in 1995 to investigate the Rwandan genocide, discussed in this volume by Paul Kerstens, highlighted the willingness of the Belgian state to face its colonial legacy. In the same way, by creating the Lumumba Commission in December 1999, Brussels clearly expressed its *mea culpa* to the Congolese people for Belgian responsibility in the assassination of their prime minister in the early 1960s.

Taking into consideration these cases, the use of the conditional tense by the German minister on August 14, 2004 is not likely to convince an observer of Berlin's willingness to face the atrocities of its colonial past.

The Reference to God

In the German message of "apology," the minister referred to God when she declared: "We Germans accept our historical, political, moral and ethical responsibility for the wrongs committed by our ancestors. May you, please, in the name of our common Father forgive our deeds."

For a believer, there is nothing reproachable in reference to God. However, the request for forgiveness by God in a speech addressed to the Herero suggests another interpretation; namely, the refusal to refer to the law as a reference point from which the actions of General Lothar von Trotha should be judged. Three months after her Namibian travel, Wieczorek-Zeul once more indicated the meaning of her message to the Hereros: "I asked in the name of the Federal Government and in the biblical sense (our common Father) for forgiveness for the crimes German colonialists committed towards the Herero people" (Wieczorek-Zeul 2004). Such an apology is not meant to have any legal import. Probably, the minister presented the "apology" in the name of "our common Father" in order to avoid words or expressions which could serve as a legal basis for financial reparations.

The Herero genocide was committed as a result of an act of government, not as a result of God's decision. Therefore, it would have been logical for the German minister to present her state's "apology" not in the name of "our common Father," but according to the "rule of the German state," the same rule which ordered the genocide. Therefore, the gesture of the German official on August 14, 2004, could not be considered a valid state apology.

A Feeling of Diktat: Berlin's Dictatorial Attitude

Berlin presented a dictatorial attitude to the discussion of financial reparations. By recognizing (even in the conditional tense) their historic responsibility for the massacre of the Hereros, and by expressing regret for it, German authorities took a significant step toward the normalization of relations between the Namibian and German states. Berlin has successfully undergone the stage of recognition of wrongs, necessary to any reconciliation process. But, by taking a directing attitude, by saying officially that she would not pay financial reparations, Berlin devalues its action. The culprit may not dictate to the victim the guidelines of a reconciliation process. Rather, it is the victim's privilege to take note of the sincerity of the apology, and to determine what is to be done. By indicating the guidelines of cooperation between the two parties, Berlin does not truly move away from the politics of domination.

Indeed, the German position has not changed on this point: German authorities consider their official development assistance to Namibia a form of financial reparation for colonial atrocities. As Namibia is the largest recipient of German aid, Herero people do benefit from German support. Therefore, in German eyes, there is no need for any special financial reparation program. The only thing Berlin could do is make sure that German financial assistance is properly distributed to all Namibian citizens, as Wieczorek-Zeul stated in an interview on September 26, 2004. "We carry responsibility for the whole Namibia. . . . Economic and financial co-operation also benefit the Herero. The remuneration of a given subpopulation it not at issue" (Wieczorek-Zeul 2004).

It is clear that Berlin disconnects "compensation" from "apology." Yet the expressions "I am sorry" and "reparation" should be understood as parts, elements of the unit "apology." "Reparation" is the determining part which confers substance to the apology. The phrase "I am sorry" alone, without financial reparations or compensations, does not constitute a valid apology. Wieczorek-Zeul took an important step by acknowledging the historical responsibility of her state. However, this "kindness" from Berlin has not prevented the Herero descendants from requesting financial compensation.

The Main Weaknesses of the German Initiative: The Absence of Institutions

There is a major limit in the German initiative: the weak institutionalization of the process, compared for example to the German-French and German-Polish reconciliation processes. This is not surprising, for Africa, as noted earlier, is not a priority to Berlin, and there are few institutions likely to sustain friendly cooperation between Germany and Namibia. So far, Berlin's words have been followed by a cultural center built with German funds, inaugurated on August 14, 2004, by Wieczorek-Zeul. This center is meant to maintain alive the memory of the German colonial period in Namibia.

By contrast, since the end of World War II, more than 1,000 treaties and many institutions of bilateral cooperation have been set up by the French and German authorities. Furthermore, more than 200 agreements and institutions of bilateral cooperation between Germany and Poland exist. In October 1991, the two states agreed on the creation of the German-Polish Reconciliation Foundation, designed to provide financial compensation to Polish citizens who were victims of the Nazi regime. Germany has also signed bilateral agreements with Belarus, the Russian Federation, Ukraine, and the Czech Republic, leading to the creation of the foundation Understanding and Reconciliation. The funds allocated to this foundation, nearly 500,000 Euro, were provided by the German government (German Foreign Ministry 2001). Also, a foundation named Remembrance, Responsibility, and Future was created in August 2000. Sponsored by the German state and industries for about 5.7 billion Euro, "The purpose of the Foundation is to make financial compensation available through partner organizations to former forced laborers and to those affected by other injustices from the National Socialist period" (Law 2000, Sec. II (1)).

Nothing similar has been undertaken for Namibia. Berlin presents its assistance program there as a form of compensation for historical crimes, and its commitment to maintain assistance as "institutionalizing" reconciliation. However, Berlin's financial flows seem particularly to benefit the German minority in Namibia. Berlin allocated 2,350,000 Euro to the first phase of land reform in Namibia, from January 2003 to December 2005. It is also difficult to justify use of German public revenues to purchase lands owned by South African settlers, as opposed to lands owned by Namibian citizens of German descent.

German assistance is also unlikely to benefit the Herero, because the Namibian ruling elite is essentially constituted of Ovambo, who oppose specifically targeting aid to the Herero and Nama. One may conclude that the main function of German official development assistance to Namibia is not the reparation of historical injustice, as it appears in some official discourses. Therefore, the argument of moral commitment toward Namibia for their particular common history has to be considered unimportant.

As noted above, the French Parliament adopted in 2001 a law recognizing the slave trade as a crime against humanity. The same law binds government authorities to some very precise actions: academic and research programs should integrate the teaching of colonial history in schools and universities (Law 2001-434, Art. 2), and French authorities should promote the idea in the international arena, the EU, the UN and other international organisations (Art. 3) Such an engagement is not yet foreseeable in the German Parliament. The symbolic importance of August 14, 2004, speech in Okarahara will remain at a very low level, since institutions of peaceful and friendly cooperation are the only objective criteria of a relevant "I am sorry."

Conclusion

By formally asking for forgiveness, Germany gave the victims of genocide a dignity they had always been refused. However, by referring to God in the message of apology, by using the conditional tense in the assessment of the facts, and by disconnecting reparation from apology, Berlin proves to be particularly unfair in the management of its historical legacy. Dealing with European victims of the Nazi regime, the German state issued a formal apology, provided billions in financial compensation, and created institutions which will hold alive their history. Dealing with the victims of the Herero genocide, nothing comparable has been done. One could even imagine a racist approach in the management of historical crimes by Berlin: "I am sorry" + "financial reparations" + "institutions" when it concerns crimes committed against Europeans; "I am sorry" + "nothing" when it comes to dealing with Africans.

Moreover, from a moral point of view it is generally the victim's privilege to estimate the amount and momentum of reparation. By mentioning clearly at the very beginning of the process its refusal to offer financial compensation, Berlin does not leave the victims the possibility to appreciate the sincerity of the act. Despite the recent change in German attitude, it is still not acceptable that the author of a crime retains the dominant position in a reconciliation process. As such, the German attitude is not likely to reinforce the symbolic importance of the August 14, 2004, gesture.

References

100 Jahre Herero-Aufstand: Annäherung im Konjunktiv. 2004. August 14. NTV-News. Online Edition, http://www.ntv-news.de/5413197.html

Austen, Ralph A. 1985. "Cameroon and Cameroonians in Wilhelmian Innenpolitik: Grande Histoire and Petite Histoire." In *L'Afrique et l'Allemagne de la colonisation à la coopération, 1884–1984: le cas de Cameroun*, ed. Alexandre Kum'a Ndumbe III, Acts of the International Symposium, One Hundred Years of African-German Relations 1884–1994: The Case of Cameron, Yaoundé, April 8–14. Yaoundé: Africavenir.

Ayad, Christophe and Benyahia-Kouider, Odile. 2004. "Namibie: les Hereros attendent des excuses allemandes." *Libération*, August 14.

Breackman, Colette. 2002. "Un combat légitime instrumentalisé par le régime: bataille pour la terre au Zimbabwe." *Le Monde Diplomatique*, May.

CIA. 2004. *The World Fact Book*. December 16. Washington, D.C.: Brasseys.

"Eine unbelastete Kolonialmacht?" 2004. http://www.africa anticolonial.org/downloads/herero_flugi.pdf

German Foreign Ministry. 2001. http://www.germanyinfo.org/relaunch/info/archives/background/forcedlabor2.html

Größe und Bevölkerung Unseren Kolonien. 1913. Hase u Koehler Verlag. http://www.jaduland.de/kolonien/index2.html

International Court of Justice (ICJ). 1971. Legal Consequences for States of the Continued Presence of South Africa in Namibia (South West Africa). Notwithstanding Security Council Resolution 276 (1970) ICJ, Advisory Opinion, June 21, 1971. ICJ Case Summaries. http://www.icj-cij.org/icjwww/igeneralinformation/ibbook/Bbookchapter7.HTM

Kämmerer, Jörn Axel and Jörg Föh. 2004. "Das Völkerrecht als Instrument der Wiedergutmachung? eine kritische Betrachtung am Beispiel des Herero-Aufstandes." *Archiv des Völkerrechts* 42 (3), September 2004.

Krüger, Gesine and Dag. Henrichsen. 1998. "We Have Been Captives Long Enough. We Want to Be Free: Land, Uniforms, and Politics in the History of the Herero in the Interwar Period." In *Namibia Under South African Rule: Mobility*

and Containment, 1915–1946, ed. Patricia Hayes, Jeremy Silvester, Marion Wallace, and Wolfram Hartmann, Athens: Ohio University Press.
Law 2001–70. 2001. (France). Relating to the Recognition of the Armenian Genocide of 1915. Signed January 29. http://www.armenian.genocide.org/Affirmation.154/current_category.7/affirmation_detail/html
Law 2001–434. 2001. (France). Recognizing the Slave Trade as a Crime Against Humanity. Signed May 21. Law on the Creation of a Foundation, "Remembrance, Responsibility and Future." 2000. (Germany). http://www.compensation-for-forced-labour.org
Mburumba Kerina, Tagesspiegel. 2004. 12.01. Online edition, http://archiv.tagesspiegel.de/archiv/12.01.2004/927661.asp
Melber, Henning. 2004. "Die Landfrage in Namibia—Vulkan vor dem Ausbruch?" *Zeitschrift Entwicklungspolitik* 18/19.
Ngunjiri, Philip. 2002. "Germany Refuses to Apologize for Herero Holocaust." *AOL Black Voices*, October 14. http://www.africana.com/articles/daily/index_20021014.asp
Sebok, Anthony J. 2001. "Slavery, Reparations, and Potential Legal Liability: The Hidden Legal Issue Behind the UN Racism Conference." *FindLaw*, October 9, 2001. http://archives.cnn.com/2001/LAW/09/columns/fl.sebok.racismconference.09
Shelton, Dinah. 2004. "The World of Atonement Reparations for Historical Injustices." *Miskolv Journal of International Law* 1 (2). http://www.uni-miskolc.hu/~wwwdrint/mjil2/20042shelton1.pdf
Toulabor, Comi. 1995. "Le mur-de-Berlin est dans la tête." In "L'Allemagne et l'Afrique," *Politique Africaine* 60, December. http://www.politique-africaine.com/numeros/060_SOM.HTM
Vidal, Edmond. 1900. *La politique coloniale de l'Allemagne en Afrique: conférence donnée à Alger en sa qualité de Secrétaire Générale de la Ligue Coloniale Française*. Algiers: Imprimerie Typographique et Lithographique S. Léon.
Volmer, Ludger. 1999. March. http://www.swagga.com/global.htm
Von Trotha, Lothar. 1904. http://www.deutsche schutzgebiete.de/von_trotha.htm.
Wieczorek-Zeul, Heidemarie. 2004. "Der Herero-Krieg—hundert Jahre danach. 1904–2004: Realitäten, Traumata, Perspektiven." November 19, Bremen (Germany). http://www.bmz.de/de/presse/reden/ministerin/rede20041119.html
World Socialist Web Site. 2002. http://www.wsws.org/francais/News/2000/aout00/19aout00_zimb1.shtml
Zimmerer, Jürgen. 2001. Deutsche Herrschaft über Afrikaner: Staatlicher Machtanspruch und Wirklichkeit im kolonialen Namibia. Münster: Lit.

Chapter 14
Words Require Action: African Elite Opinion About Apologies from the "West"

RHODA E. HOWARD-HASSMANN AND ANTHONY P. LOMBARDO

Apologies and Regrets from the West to Africa

Much of the literature about political apologies assumes that they are a necessary part of national politics; without apologies, wronged groups cannot reconcile themselves to life with those who harmed them. But are political apologies also a useful aspect of international relations? In the post 9/11 world, bitterness and despair cause support for terrorist activities, especially in former colonies that have not experienced economic growth. Africa is one such area: its desperate condition derives in part from the trans-Atlantic slave trade and colonialism; indeed, some argue that it also derives from post-colonial relations. Perhaps an apology from the "West" to Africa might lessen the likelihood of bitterness and despair, thus contributing to an international community in which there is moral equality among the different regions, and less likelihood of political resentment.

Does the "West," then, owe apologies to Africa? At a minimum, do the Western powers that traded in slaves or had African colonies—including the United Kingdom, France, the Netherlands, Germany, Spain, Portugal, and the United States— owe apologies? To date, there has been very little serious talk of apologies to Africa, and very few diplomatic events that suggest they might be forthcoming. Some Western states have acknowledged some of the damage they caused Africa, but few have formally apologized.

In 1999 during a visit to South Africa, Queen Elizabeth II spoke of the suffering endured by both whites and blacks during the Anglo-Boer War. She said, "We should remember with sadness the loss of life and suffering, not only of British or Boer soldiers, but of all those caught up in the war—black and white, men, women and children" (HM the Queen's Speech 1999). This speech was noted in the press as "regret," but there was no explicit apology (BBC News 1999a) Moreover, it cannot have been lost on black South Africans that despite the nod in their direction, the Queen's speech was primarily about an inter-European affair. Indeed, at the time of her visit South Africa's Xhosa King unsuccessfully called on her to apologize for British oppression of his people in the nineteenth century (BBC News 1999b).

In 2000, Jacques Chirac, president of France, rejected calls to apologize for France's use of torture during Algeria's war of independence forty years earlier. He claimed that to apologize would be simply to "re-open old wounds" (BBC News 2000). Looking to the more distant—and perhaps therefore less politically threatening—past, however, the French Parliament did pass a law acknowledging that slavery "is" a crime against humanity ("La République française reconnait que la traité negrière trans-atlantique . . . constituent un crime contre l'humanité" (Legifrance 2001). The French text used the word "reconnait" (from "reconnaitre," to recognize) thus acknowledging the crime but not apologizing for it: moreover, the use of the present tense suggests an unwillingness to take responsibility for the past. The French were also careful to refer to the slave trade in the Indian Ocean (carried out by Arabs) as well as the trans-Atlantic trade.

As Paul Kerstens discusses in this volume, Belgium apologized to Congo for its involvement in the murder of Patrice Lumumba, and to Rwanda for its lack of intervention during the 1994 genocide. And as Leonard Jamfa discusses, Germany offered an apology to the Herero people of Namibia for the genocide in the early twentieth century, although Jamfa does not consider that it fulfilled the criteria for a sincere apology.

At the World Conference against Racism, Racial Discrimination, Xenophobia, and Related Intolerance held in Durban, South Africa, in September 2001, several European states expressed their regret for their participation in the slave trade. "The British Government and the European Union profoundly deplore the human suffering, both individual and collective, caused by slavery and the slave trade," said the British minister for Africa, presumably speaking for both her own government and the European Union. The Netherlands minister for urban policy and integration of ethnic minorities expressed "deep remorse about enslavement and the slave trade" (United Nations 2001) But not all European states have yet been willing to offer apologies to Africa.

Outside Europe, both former president Bill Clinton of the United States, and the president at the time this chapter was written, George W. Bush, acknowledged that slavery and the slave trade were wrong. In a speech in Uganda in 1998, Clinton said "going back to the time before we were even a nation, European-Americans received the fruits of the slave trade. And we were wrong in that" (Clinton 1998a) But he did not explicitly apologize. Similarly, at a visit to Goree Island in Senegal in 2003, Bush stated that slavery had been a "crime," and quoted President John Adams, who called it "an evil of colossal magnitude." Again, however, Bush did not apologize (White House 2003) Nor did Clinton actually apologize for U.S. inaction during the 1994 Rwanda genocide, although in Kigali, the Rwandan capital, in 1998 he made a very eloquent speech to survivors claiming that "all over the world there were people like me sitting in offices, day after day after day, who did not fully appreciate the depth and the speed with which you were being engulfed by this unimaginable terror" (Clinton 1998b).

It is unclear whether the small, tentative steps to acknowledge and regret the harms perpetrated against Africa by Western powers will have any real impact upon international relations. Nor it is altogether clear that apologies might have any real meaning or impact within Africa, or to African citizens. Below, we assess what Africans themselves think of apologies.

Elite African Opinion

From June 2002 to March 2004 we interviewed 75 elite Africans, asking them whether they thought an apology was due to Africa from the West. Our interviews took place in various locales in North America and Europe. We defined as "African" anyone who was a citizen of any African country, regardless of "race," and we looked for individuals who were familiar with the debate on reparations to Africa, and were influential in their own societies. We interviewed 8 ambassadors to the United States, 23 academics, and 41 human rights activists and policy-makers from 26 countries. This sample included three members of the Group of Eminent Persons, established by the then Organization of African Unity in 1992 to pursue reparations to Africa. All but seven of the people we spoke with were either permanent residents of Africa, or had moved to North America within the preceding three years.

We refer to these Africans as "elite" because all of those for whom we obtained information on educational attainment had university degrees. Although elite, they were still close to their extended families, many of whom were still farmers in rural villages. Many had parents with little or no education. Our respondents were still conversant with traditional practices and customs, and were, tragically, all too familiar with economic decline and life-threatening illnesses.

Our sample is not statistically representative of all Africans, but there was a remarkably high degree of consensus among the people with whom we talked; without actions, they believed, words were meaningless. An apology that is merely symbolic is useless: it must be followed by material compensation. The consensus was based to a great extent on perceptions of massive material harm perpetrated upon Africa by the West, and upon Africa's urgent need for material assistance now. In part, though, it was also based upon the cultural ritual of apologies in our respondents' home societies.

Words: Acknowledgment and Apology

Apology and acknowledgment are not synonymous. In the former, there is a sense of remorse, regret, or sorrow that accompanies admission of a wrong. Within the act of apology, acknowledgment is implied: when an apologizer accepts fault, there is an implicit acknowledgment of participation in that fault.

Although in our interviews we asked about apology and acknowledgment as separate processes, most of the people we talked with did not distinguish the two. For example, a Kenyan finance manager with a nongovernmental organization said, "it would be very hard to pay back what we have lost over all those years. I think that they [the West] should acknowledge that, yes, this happened and probably apologize." Yet although apologies include acknowledgment, the reverse does not necessarily hold. One can stipulate that he or she was responsible for a wrong, but stop short of regretting it. A Tanzanian lawyer working with a human rights organization said, "acknowledgment does not necessarily mean an apology. Someone may acknowledge that I have done wrong [but] you may not apologize. So, I think the first stage should be acknowledging. From acknowledging then there should be apology and then the last area is how to start to resolve that, how to reconcile the problem."

Such statements give the impression that apologies and acknowledgments are intricately related processes, which must occur together to be meaningful. Indeed, many of our respondents maintained that apology and acknowledgment have similar functions. They believed that these symbolic processes carried various pragmatic consequences. One of the most important functions of apology and acknowledgment was that through them, the facts about wrongs committed against Africa could be set straight on the public record. A scholar from Congo spoke of the West's "debt of acknowledgment, a debt of gratitude for the fact that thanks to Africa, the West had its first industrial revolution." For him, the fact to be set straight was that historically, Africa had helped the West; the West had not helped Africa. Speaking with regard to colonialism, one Kenyan, a program officer with a human rights organization, said: "they [responsible nations] should not look at colonialism as an accident, they should not look at it as a small grief that they caused . . . but they should acknowledge that . . . those were wrong policies because of the harm that they cost to people who fell victims."

Numerous respondents stressed the need to make acknowledgments and apologies public. They wanted statements from government leaders, such as the Prime Minister of England or the President of the United States. To have an apology on the public record, our respondents hoped, would mean future relations between the West and Africa would be more equitable. For example, some were interested in greater African influence in major international decision-making bodies, such as the United Nations Security Council.

Our respondents also believed that acknowledgments of and apologies for past wrongdoing should be widely publicized within Africa, so that all African citizens would know of them. Without publicity, there would be no positive psychological effect on non-elite Africans; the scars stemming from historic harms still lingered in the African population, and acknowledgment and apology were necessary to heal them. A Togolese asserted that apology and acknowledgment could be "psychologically speaking, a healing process for both the offender and the person offended." "Somebody has to take a moral responsibility, and that will contribute to a psychological redress for the people who suffered," said a refugee from the civil war in Sierra Leone. Some of the people we talked with thought that through public apology and acknowledgment Africans could also gain a better understanding of their own history. A South African academic noted that apology might help change the "basic results of the colonial project . . . installing in the subject the . . . idea of them being inferior."

Our respondents also wanted to ensure that the harms perpetrated against Africa would stop. Guarantees of non-repetition of harms are a central feature of genuine apologies. As public, global expressions, it is thought, international apologies should necessarily constrain future behavior. For a Congolese activist, it was imperative to recognize past harms as wrong "because if it was not wrong that means it might happen again." For a South African student, acknowledgment meant that an offending nation could no longer ignore its past misdeeds: "if you behave as though you don't recognize . . . that your actions . . . had consequences in the past, then you can continue to disregard and behave as though there aren't consequences or as if you don't care about those consequences."

In sum, our respondents' comments demonstrate that acknowledgment and apology, although symbolic acts, also carry practical significance. Nevertheless, political reality made some respondents doubt the likelihood of an apology or acknowledgment from the offending parties. A Zimbabwean development officer with a Canadian organization said that while an apology would be a good thing, it "would probably be asking for too much. . . . When you hit somebody, you need to apologize, it's natural relations. But, because of the politics, maybe the African continent would be asking for too much." A South African who worked in a law clinic thought that apologies were unlikely, given global systemic racism: "I believe deeply that white lives . . . are more important to Western governments than black lives. . . . [T]he fact that they [the West] weren't willing to apologize for colonialism and they weren't willing to acknowledge the role of the West in underdeveloping . . . Africa . . . [is a] reflection of basically black lives and black people are not . . . as important as white lives and white people."

Political realities play an important role in the prospects for apology and acknowledgment as a starting point for reparations. There is little impetus for the West to apologize to Africa. Tavuchis argues that "an apology is emblematic of the offender's socially liminal, ambiguous status that places him precariously between exclusion (actual or threatened) and rehabilitation. . . . The crucial concern of an apology is . . . with the reclamation and revalidation of [the rights and obligations] enjoyed prior to the discreditable transgression" (Tavuchis 1991: 31). This definition implies the desire of the offending party to apologize to gain back social acceptance by the offended party; it implies that the offended has more power than the offender.

Such a definition, however, does not reflect the political reality regarding apologies to Africa. Another scholar from Congo put it, "We shouldn't deceive ourselves too much. States are not sincere . . . what counts is interest." In this situation, the offending parties, Western countries, possess power while the offended party, Africa, does not. The offended party seeks inclusion, not the other way round. An injustice may not always place the offender in a position in which he needs to regain acceptance.

A few respondents identified another obstacle to apology and acknowledgment, namely, the potential for legal ramifications. Jacob Ade Ajayi, a member of the Group of Eminent Persons, said, "Americans are always very wary of acknowledging because there's so much [to] leave them open to litigation and therefore they are not willing to acknowledge." Yet our respondents desired practical action beyond the simple words of a statement of apology. A Tanzanian lecturer said, "I am not interested in a verbal apology. I am interested in the economic apology." When asked how apologizing nations might demonstrate genuine repentance, one ambassador said, "I link the apology to . . . how they [former colonial powers] can come in and help with the general easement of the people. . . . That should show that they are committed and that their apology was sincere."

On the other hand, a small minority of respondents were of the view that apology itself was sufficient reparation. Another ambassador advanced his country's position:

If you feel that you have been wronged and someone says sorry, even if there's . . . nothing that follows that somehow it does help to feel like the person doesn't think, "Oh well, you know, we were just smarter than they were and we continue to be," . . . and, "to hell with them, you can suffer I don't care." You feel like the person realizes . . . we're all human and what happened we shouldn't ignore; it was wrong and we wouldn't want that [to] happen again.

Yet the majority of respondents strongly disagreed with this ambassador: for them, apologies must be accompanied by some form of material compensation. A Togolese activist said, "For the West, an apology would be to take concrete actions that could return Africans to their lost dignity." Viable and acceptable reparations required measures to address contemporary deprivation in Africa. Action beyond acknowledgments and apologies was imperative. Absent such measures, it would seem, most respondents might see Western apology as a "politics of gesture" (Cunningham 1999: 288) a method of assuaging white guilt without providing a concrete remedy. A number of respondents also felt that these material commitments, moving apologies beyond mere words, would make the reparations process more apparent to non-elite Africans. This belief stemmed in part from their interpretations of the social meaning of apologies within their own societies.

Apologies in African Societies

There is some question as to whether apologies can withstand intercultural differences. Different cultures may have different means of offering apologies. With this in mind, we asked our respondents how an apology might be offered within their own traditional societies. Usually, we framed this discussion by asking how a "big man," or chief, might apologize to a "small man" for an incident such as accidentally killing his goat or running over his bicycle.

Sometimes, we were told, a big man or chief would not apologize personally. He would, instead, apologize through an emissary. "If the chief destroys my bicycle the chief may send somebody in his council . . . to maybe pacify, maybe tell me what the chief did, it was a mistake, it was not intentional." Or he might visit the wronged individual at his hut, thus reversing traditional protocol, without actually making an apology.

In other cases, we were told that a big man or chief would indeed apologize personally. In fact, if there were witnesses to his misdeed, he might apologize in front of them, in front of village elders, or in front of the entire community. An Eritrean explained, "There is a committee in our village. . . . [It] meets . . . during evening or Sunday times or Saturday. . . . Then some people raise their voices and . . . they stand up and 'Mr. So-and-so had these problems, please apologize to him.' Then they force that person to acknowledge that wrongdoing of that person. And then publicly apologize." The symbolic, public aspect of the gesture was important, even if the word "apology" was not used. Said a Nigerian, "In Africa you don't live in isolation: everything you do, the community's affected. . . . The community would want to know the chief actually apologizes, so . . . he will have to do it publicly. . . . That alone is peace and tranquillity. And then he will take it a step further to replace the goat he killed."

In almost all cases, therefore, the wrongdoer would also offer material compensation: actions would speak as loudly as words. Sometimes, this material compensation was merely token: a particular item might stand for the apology. In one Togolese community "There are symbolic things to give . . . a ram, that's symbolic for us. A white ram . . . First, there is talking, and then the chief undertakes not to repeat, before everyone. And then he presents . . . a white ram to the assemblage." Here, the wrongdoer offers the gift to the entire village, as an act of public expiation.

Ordinary people, too, would be expected to offer compensation for a wrong, a Malawian activist told us.

> Yes, in Malawi, when somebody has wronged you . . . both of you . . . are taken before a chief, when a chief is settling that particular matter, and somebody has agreed that "Indeed, I happened to wrong this particular person, and I would like to apologize"; it is not only by word of mouth. The chief will say a little something. . . . He would say that maybe you should take maybe one goat, one goat or one cow, and give this particular person for the wrongdoing that you did.

In traditional society, what the chief or big man said was meaningless unless he also undertook to rectify a wrong. "Small" or ordinary men were also expected to rectify their wrongs. Although some of the rituals and symbolic goods described by our respondents may be new to readers of this chapter, the underlying premise of rectification should not be. Personal apologies are often considered hollow in Western society, without some form of follow-up gesture. Thus, there are no insurmountable cultural differences between what Westerners and Africans understand as a sincere apology. Our respondents' desire for financial compensation from the West, rather than only for "hollow words," is not outside Westerners' own realm of meaning.

Actions: Material Compensation

Since it was clear to us that the vast majority of our respondents thought apologies without material reparation were worthless, we asked them what kind of financial compensation they envisaged. Economic rehabilitation was by far the most pressing concern. Our respondents expressed a deep sense of abandonment. They could not understand why the West was willing to tolerate their overwhelming material suffering. Almost uniformly and without prompting, they told us that their priorities were health, education, transportation, and communications. Reparations were necessary to address basic human needs. "No apology is acceptable unless it is accompanied by development measures . . . to feed our people," said a Cameroonian. The most common request was for aid to education and health care services. For an Angolan, these areas were the "keys for development of society as a whole."

Our respondents also rooted their discussion of monetary reparations in the need for changes to how Africa participates—or does not—in the global economy. They were particularly interested in rendering international trade policies with Africa more equitable. "Does France trade with these [French-speaking African] countries truly as equal countries. . . . Are they equal? I think not. . . . There's a kind of colonialism that continues." To make trade equitable meant eliminating tariffs charged on African goods by Western countries, reducing subsidies to Western farmers for products that Africans could sell, and reducing foreign influence on prices of African exports. Many wanted help with African infrastructure, including money to build and repair roads and railways, and efforts to help communication within and from Africa. For example, a Kenyan development worker visiting Canada associated communication difficulties with unfair competition in the global economy:

> We do not tread on an equal footing. . . . [I]n Kenya to surf the Internet you pay a lot of money . . . therefore you limit the time that you surf the Internet but when I came to Canada it takes me a second to surf the Internet. . . . [It is] the same case with the telecommunications: the use of the telephone in Africa is very expensive . . . but here [Canada] it is very easy, very cheap.

Over half the respondents also supported cancellation of debts for loans from international lending agencies like the World Bank and International Monetary Fund. As a Kenyan with an education rights organization said:

> After all the injustices, and after African people . . . fought for their independence, that the West still has the audacity to claim that Africa owes them so much in terms of debts. . . . It is inhuman . . . if that person owes you money, and you went to ask for your money back and you found the person went without food. It is inhuman and immoral to insist that you must be paid for your money. So I see the reparations in terms of debts cancellations.

A Zambian with a human rights organization said, "We are indebted to the very people that colonized us. If anything at all, let them keep their money but we say, whatever we owe we bring it to zero. Then . . . we start from level ground." Stiglitz discusses "odious debts," which he defines as "debts incurred by a regime without political legitimacy, from creditors who should have known better, with the monies often spent to oppress the very people who are then asked to repay the debts" (Stiglitz 2003: 35, 42) In agreement with Stiglitz, some respondents noted that it was unfair that Africans should suffer for loans obtained by corrupt officials. A Nigerian professor at a Canadian university said "That is the problem. I don't trust any of the authorities to handle the money well. They have shown over and over that they are not to be trusted." Thus, some wanted debt cancellation to have conditions attached, to prevent a recurrence of government corruption or mismanagement.

Material Restitution as a Condition of Sincerity

We should not consider sincerity, remorse, and sorrow as embodied in the act of apology itself, but rather in the social actor's reaction to that act of apology. W. I. Thomas's classic sociological dictum, "If men [sic] define situations as real, they are real in their consequences," is instructive here: sincerity, remorse and regret exist more in the recipients' subjective definition of the situation than in the act itself. (Thomas and Thomas 1970: 572) One respondent from Niger said, "For me, the confession does not erase the injustice or the offence that the person has committed."

Our respondents agreed that there would be some value to verbal apologies. But for them to take apologies seriously, material reparation was of the utmost importance: apologies must be accompanied by reparations which would have real, pragmatic effect. Our respondents did not want the West to merely acknowledge past mistakes and apologize for them. Reparations were not understood only as measures for obtaining moral equality between Africa and the West. Instead, they called for reparations to create a better Africa: in short, to have Western help in developing the very continent the West had earlier underdeveloped.

The Africans we spoke to almost uniformly believed that Western powers and interests had caused both Africa's historic underdevelopment and its current economic weakness. Many also felt utterly used and abandoned by the West. These were reasonable and responsible people, many engaged in the struggle for human rights within their own societies, and well aware of the injustices that their own political and social systems had generated. They did not blame all problems in Africa on the West. Yet they could not understand why even when millions of lives were at stake, the West—and often the international community as a whole—cared so little for them. One Congolese scholar noted the millions of deaths in his country in the last few years, blaming the post-genocide, Tutsi-dominated government of Rwanda, supported in his view by Western powers. "The Rwandans are killing millions of people; they bury women alive. . . . Then they go and hide behind the international community, behind the United States. . . . So . . . they [the West] should react! As in the case of the Congo, why hasn't the international community reacted? It's because it is involved!"

International apologies operate much like interpersonal apologies: both attempt to fix ruptured relationships and effect reconciliation. In the case of apologies to Africa, however, we confront extreme power differences between the offending and offended parties. Thus, there is far less desire or need on the part of the offending party to effect reconciliation with the offended party, than is normal in a personal apology. Moreover, a "spontaneous" apology or acknowledgment from an offending country might leave it open to legal obligation. To deal with this problem, one approach might be to include acknowledgment and apology as part of an organized reparations settlement. If a world conference on reparations were convened to orchestrate a settlement between the West and Africa, and there were an agreement on material compensation, an apology could be offered without the threat of further legal obligation.

Material compensation occupies an ambivalent place in the reparations literature. For some, commitments beyond words are merely an optional part of reparations. Cunningham, for example, concludes that "the case for apology is most convincing on the grounds that it has the potential to improve relations between groups if the apology . . . is sincere and is acceptable to the recipients. . . . Reparations, in money or goods, may follow from this; but in practice reparation has occurred independently from apology" (Cunningham 1999: 291). Tavuchis likewise argues, "What is critical . . . is the very act of apology itself rather than the offering of material or symbolic restitution" (Tavuchis 1991: 22). On the other hand, Minow notes that "unless accompanied by direct and immediate actions . . . that manifest responsibility for the violation, the official apology may seem superficial, insincere, or meaningless" (Minow 1998: 116), and Barkan asks, "unless accompanied by material compensation or restitution, does not the apology merely whitewash the injustice?" (Barkan 2000: 323).

In the case of African-Western relations, the answer from our respondents is clear. Apology must be accompanied by action, by material compensation. Otherwise, the apology is indeed insincere and meaningless, a whitewash of past injustice. Rigby asserts that through apology, "opinion leaders can open up the symbolic space where victims and survivors can begin to cast the past in a new light, relinquishing the quest to settle old scores, and begin to focus on the future" (Rigby 2001: 188). Verbal apologies may indeed be a useful beginning, an opening up of space for dialogue. But for the people we interviewed, this was not sufficient. There must also be material compensation. Such compensation demands a complete renegotiation of Western-African relations, to assure that there will be no repeat of abusive treatment of Africa, and to assure good relations in the future.

This, however, is most unlikely to occur. History cannot be undone. The most that apologies can accomplish is recognition of past injustices, as in the French law on the slave trade, and aspirations for more concern in the future, as in President Bill Clinton's belated acknowledgment of American neglect of Rwanda. Acknowledgments of—even apologies for—the evils of the far distant past are weak measures, absent material restitution. It is perhaps better not to engage in the breast-beating of international apologies than to make gestures that recipients might regard as hypocritical empty words.

There is also the difficulty that there is no unified "West" with which Africa could negotiate. Not only the West, but also other countries, control and influence the International Monetary Fund and the World Bank, bodies that most of our respondents thought act in arbitrary, unfeeling ways toward Africa. The economic processes that affect Africa today are the consequences of many different decisions taken by many different bodies, including private corporations.

In the end, the world still consists of legally sovereign states. Their foreign policies will continue to be driven by national interest, not by international justice. As the recent refugee from Sierra Leone put it, "If you apologize to me, and you still practice unfair trade practices which continue to submerge me and become underdeveloped further, then where am I going?" Perceptions of insincerity from the West could well increase that political resentment that has created the new, post 9/11 international relations.

We thank Kristina Bergeron for her assistance in conducting 14 of the French interviews.

References

BBC News. 1999a. "Queen's Regret over Boer War." BBC News, November 10. http://news.bbc.co.uk/1/hi/world/africa/514608.stm
———. 1999b. "Xhosa Demand Apology from Queen." BBC News, November 8. http://news.bbc.co.uk/1/hi/world/africa/509169.stm
———. 2000. "Algeria: Chirac Rejects 'Torture Apology'." December 15. http://news.bbc.co.uk/1/hi/world/europe/107504.stm
Barkan, Elazar. 2000. *The Guilt of Nations: Restitution and Negotiating Historical Injustices.* New York: W.W. Norton.
Clinton, William. 1998a. Remarks at the Kisowera School in Mukuno, Uganda, March 24. http://clinton4.nara.gov/textonly/Africa/19980324-3374.html.
———. 1998b. Remarks to Genocide Survivors in Kigali, March 25. http://clinton6.nara.gov/1998/03/1998-03-25-remarks-to-survivors-rwanda.html.
Cunningham, Michael. 1999. "Saying Sorry: The Politics of Apology." *Political Quarterly* 70 (3): 285–92.
HM the Queen's Speech at the State Banquet in South Africa. 1999. November 10. http://www.etoile.co.uk/Speech/SA99Queen.html.
Legifrance: Le Service Public de la Diffusion du Droit. 2001. Loi no. 2001–434 du 21 mai tendant à la reconnaissance de la traité et de l'esclavage en tant que crime contre l'humanité." http://www.legifrance.gouv.fr/WAspad/Visu?cid=558011&indice=11&table=JORF&ligneD, accessed April 25, 2004.
Minow, Martha. 1998. *Between Vengeance and Forgiveness: Facing History After Genocide and Mass Violence.* Boston: Beacon Press.
Rigby, Andrew. 2001. *Justice and Reconciliation: After the Violence.* Boulder, Colo.: Lynne Rienner.

Stiglitz, Josef. 2003. "Odious Rulers, Odious Debts." *Atlantic Monthly* 292 (November): 39–45.
Tavuchis, Nicholas. 1991. *Mea Culpa: A Sociology of Apology and Reconciliation.* Stanford, Calif.: Stanford University Press.
Thomas, William I. and Dorothy Swaine Thomas. [1928] 1970. *The Child in America: Behavior Problems and Programs.* New York: Johnson Reprint.
United Nations. 2001. "Acknowledgment of Past, Compensation Urged by Many Leaders in Continuing Debate at Racism Conference." Press release, Rd/D/24, September 2. www.un.org/WCAR/pressreleases/rd-d24.html.
White House. 2003. "President Bush speaks at Goree Island in Senegal." July 8. http://www.whitehouse.gov/news/releases/2003/07/print/20030708-1.html.

Chapter 15
Colonialism, Slavery, and the Slave Trade: A Dutch Perspective

PETER BAEHR

Each national society has certain matters in its history of which it is not proud or about which views have changed from positive to less positive or even negative. In the city of Amsterdam stands a monument, erected in 1935, to the memory of General Van Heutz, a governor-general of the Netherlands East Indies. At the end of the nineteenth century, Van Heutz subjected the population of the province of Aceh in Northern Sumatra to Dutch rule by harsh military measures. Since then, views about his "accomplishments" have changed, and it was recently decided to rename the monument and dedicate it to the whole colonial period.

In modern times, such changes of view may lead to calls for public apologies. This chapter deals with two such cases involving the Netherlands. The cases deal with important events in the country's history that are nowadays looked upon with less than pride: colonialism in Indonesia and the slave trade and slavery. In these cases requests for official apologies on the part of the Dutch government have repeatedly been made, but not granted.

Colonialism in Indonesia

For hundreds of years, colonialism was seen as "business as usual": "colonialism and imperialism were the accepted political system of the time, and, like other government actions, were legal" (Barkan 2000: 416).

From the beginning of the nineteenth century, the Netherlands ruled a vast empire, which toward the end included the Netherlands East Indies, Surinam, and the Netherlands Antilles. During its history, calls were repeatedly made in the Netherlands for a more lenient and humanitarian way of dealing with the colonies, if not granting them self-determination or independence. These calls were not heeded, and became successful only after the Japanese occupation of the Indies, through the efforts of

Indonesian nationalists and because of considerable pressure exerted by the United Nations. The Netherlands parted in 1949 with the greater part of the Indies only with considerable reluctance. It held on to the western part of the island of New Guinea (Papua) until 1962, when it was forced to give up that as well. Surinam gained independence in 1975, while the Netherlands Antilles (and Aruba) retain until today the status of autonomous self-governing entities.

The first activities by Dutch traders in the East Indies date from 1619, when Jan Pieterszoon Coen founded the city of Batavia (now Jakarta). But the greatest expansion took place during the nineteenth century. Central Java was conquered during the Java War (1825–1830), in which some 200,000 Javanese perished, largely by starvation and disease (Kuitenbrouwer 2003). The longest colonial war took place in the province of Aceh in Sumatra (1873–1904), which the Dutch managed to conquer only with considerable effort. Some 70,000 Acenese died in combat and an unknown number perished by starvation and disease (Kuitenbrouwer 2003).

Historian Jurrien Van Goor argues that the Dutch acquired their colonies almost against their will. He speaks of a "reluctant imperialism" and notes that the Dutch were far too few in numbers to establish large human settlements in their colonies (Van Goor 1994). However, from an economic point of view, the Dutch were quite enthusiastic colonialists. For a long time, the East Indies was treated as an exploitation colony (Van Doorn 1995). During the nineteenth century, a Cultivation System (*Cultuurstelsel*)—an adaptation of an existing feudal system—was set up, which compelled Indonesian farmers to cultivate crops for the benefit of the Dutch. In the beginning of the century, profits from the Indies made up 20–30 percent of the national income of the Netherlands: as late as 1938, they made up 8 percent (Van Doorn 1995: 19).

It was only toward the end of the nineteenth century that voices began to be heard in the Netherlands that the country had a debt of honor (*ereschuld*) toward the people of Java, who had been ruthlessly exploited by the Dutch colonizers. Though not going so far as to argue in favor of self-determination, this debt of honor was expressed in both ethical and financial terms, asking for restitution of colonial surpluses to the people of Java (Locher-Scholten 1981: 51). As early as 1901, Queen Wilhelmina said in a speech that "the Netherlands, as a Christian nation, has a moral duty to fulfil toward the population of the East Indies" (Locher-Scholten 1981: 209–10). Exactly one hundred years later, a Dutch writer argued in favor of paying damages for works of art stolen from the colonies (*NRC Handelsblad*, January 9, 2001)

Thus, as much as the Dutch may have profited from their colonies, that profit was accompanied by a somewhat guilty conscience. According to the Dutch sociologist J. J. A. Van Doorn, perhaps none of the other colonial countries suffered as much as the Netherlands from "the incompatibility of colonial profit and colonial idealism" (Van Doorn 1995). By no means did this mean that self-determination, let alone independence, was under consideration. As late as February 1942, Dutch minister of foreign affairs Eelco van Kleffens rejected independence for the Indonesians, citing their "lack of governing gifts . . . as well as the necessity to protect them from deep-rooted deficiencies such as their love of gambling and nepotism, which made, at least for the Netherlands Indies, a guiding hand indispensable" (Kersten and Manning 1984: 142). There was also a feeling of pride about what had been achieved in the colonies, as expressed by a Dutch cabinet minister (Van Maarseveen) when sovereignty was transferred to the Republic of Indonesia in 1949:

The Indies were our pride. We had governed the Indies in a way that caused admiration everywhere and we had brought prosperity to the Indies, we had brought them the blessings of Christian civilization and Christian charity, we had trained the youth of the Indies in our schools and universities, we had sent them our best scientific and technical personnel and we were convinced that the Indies could not do without our leadership. We thought that we could count on the gratitude of the Indonesian people. (quoted in Fasseur 1985)

The Indonesian fight for independence after 1945 was seen as a rebellion that had to be suppressed. The declaration of independence by the Indonesian nationalist leaders Soekarno and Mohammad Hatta on December 17, 1945 came as an unwelcome surprise to the Dutch. An expeditionary force of some 120,000 men was sent overseas. The two Dutch military actions of 1947 and 1948 were called "police actions," meant to restore law and order in the colony (Van Goor 1994). The Dutch military were sent there, not as oppressors, but supposedly as liberators (Fasseur 1985). The Dutch even favored some form of gradual decolonization—on their terms. It is fair to speak of a "trauma of decolonization," a deeply felt sentiment of frustration about the loss of the Indies (De Jong 1986). In such an atmosphere there was little room for apologies.

Until very recently, the events of the years 1945–1949 remained controversial in the Netherlands. Around the turn of the present century, proposals were launched (and subsequently rejected) to hold a "national debate" to come to terms with the issue. The immediate cause for the controversy was the granting of a visitor's visa to a former Dutch soldier, Poncke Prinsen, who had defected to the Indonesian forces in 1948, subsequently had adopted Indonesian nationality, and become a well-known human rights activist in Indonesia (De Jong 1997). In 1969, another former Dutch military officer revealed in a television interview that, during the war of 1945–1949, Dutch military had committed atrocities against Indonesian civilians (De Jong 1986). The discussions on these issues and the emotions they entailed demonstrated that for the Netherlands the relationship with Indonesia had remained a very "special" one.

The debates in the Netherlands about Indonesia had several different aspects. The views people held on whether the Netherlands had taken the right position by trying to hold on to its colony from 1945 to 1949 were fundamental. Of a secondary nature were the debates about the position of Western New Guinea, a part of the colony that had been mostly ignored in the past, but gained prominence after it was excluded from the transfer of sovereignty in 1949, supposedly because of the different ethnic origin of its population, the Papuas. The real reason for the exclusion was that it made it possible to gain the required two-thirds majority in Parliament for the change of the Constitution to allow a transfer of sovereignty (Lijphart 1966). Next, there were important Dutch interests that wanted to continue or to reestablish close business contacts with their Indonesian counterparts. These clashed with representatives of non-governmental organizations that criticized the violations of human rights committed by the Suharto regime (Baehr 2002). The latter did not necessarily agree with development experts who wanted to use Dutch aid to further develop the Indonesian economy. All this was overshadowed by the actions of Moluccan nationalists. These nationalists, who were descendants of soldiers who had served with Dutch colonial forces in Indonesia and later been admitted to the Netherlands, undertook what now would be called "terrorist actions." Some Dutch civilians were killed in 1970, 1975, 1977, and 1978 in the nationalists' struggle for the creation of an independent Republic of the South Moluccans.

Against this background, a call for apologies arose on the eve of the official state visit by Queen Beatrix to Indonesia in 1995. This call was only expressed in the Netherlands. Nothing of the sort was heard from the Indonesian side. That is why the whole issue should be seen in terms of an internal debate within the Netherlands (with the Indonesians as undoubtedly interested and perhaps somewhat bemused observers). The Dutch government did not favor letting the Queen offer apologies to the people of Indonesia. Apologies for what? For three hundred years of colonial domination? The bloody subjection of Aceh by Dutch troops at the beginning of the twentieth century? The two military actions of 1947 and 1948? And apologies to whom? To the Government of President Suharto that was known for being responsible for a wide spectrum of human rights violations? To the Indonesian people as a whole? These questions were raised, but never satisfactorily answered.

In the eyes of many observers, the Dutch government added insult to injury, when Queen Beatrix did not begin her official visit to Indonesia on August 17, 1995, the day when Indonesia celebrated the fiftieth anniversary of its independence, but three days later, after having taken a "rest" in Singapore. The Dutch government had given in to organizations of veterans and people of mixed Dutch-Indonesian parentage, who viewed Indonesia as having gained its independence not in 1945, but on December 29, 1949, when sovereignty was formally transferred. The queen is said to have received a polite, but somewhat cool reception. The hoped for business deals that her entourage of Dutch business leaders were supposed to conclude did not occur. During an official dinner, on August 21, 1995, she said, "The separation between our countries has become . . . a long time process, that has cost much pain and bitter struggle. When looking back to that time, which now lies almost fifty years behind us, it makes us extremely sad that so many perished in that struggle or bear its scars during their entire life" (*NCR Handelsblad*, February 26, 2000). The "sadness" referred to both parties. No apologies were offered. Commentators expressed their disappointment over what they considered a missed opportunity to finally come to terms with the past (De Jong 1997).

Only in 2000 did calls to offer formal apologies to Indonesia really take force. It became known that Prime Minister Wim Kok, during an official visit to Japan, intended to ask the Japanese government for apologies for invading the Netherlands Indies in 1941 and for the suffering of Dutch subjects in Japanese camps. On February 21, 2000, Japanese prime minister Keizo Obuchi offered his apologies to Dutch war victims (*NRC Handelsblad*, February 21, 2000). According to editorial comments in the Dutch quality newspaper *NRC Handelsblad*, this meant that Kok for his part should offer his apologies for Dutch wrongdoing in its former colony. It would also offer an opportunity for the Netherlands to recognize that the Republic of Indonesia in fact had existed since December 17, 1945 (*NRC Handelsblad*, February 16, 22, 2000). The debate was continued by the historian Ido de Haan, who referred to the fact that Dutch troops serving as occupation forces in Indonesia had destroyed people and their possessions for the maintenance of Dutch power. If the Japanese government was asked to apologize to the Dutch, then there was even more reason for the Dutch to apologize to the Indonesians for their own "imperialist past":

After the [Indonesian] declaration of independence, the Netherlands has for a number of years denied the sovereignty of the Indonesian state and tried by the use of force to restore its colonial power. That [was] a violation of the principle of national sovereignty. For this the Netherlands might as well offer its apologies. (De Haan 2000)

On February 25, 2000, Prime Minister Wim Kok announced that he was willing, during a future visit to Indonesia (which never transpired), to publicly apologize for Dutch activities during the colonial period. He said that he would have no problem to make clear to President Wahid that what had happened under Dutch responsibility was regrettable. He did not clarify whether such apologies would refer to the entire period of Dutch colonialism, to the war in Aceh, to the Cultivation System, or only to the 1947–1949 "police actions." According to Kok, the Netherlands could express its regrets "in the same wording" as Japan had apologized a week before: "We must not apply double standards" (*NRC Handelsblad*, February 26, 2000). However, a few days later, faced with criticisms from veterans' organizations, Kok mitigated his wording:

> What should absolutely not happen is that many people, who through their presence [in Indonesia] have done their work in a sound and correct way and who often look back at that time with great problems, now would be indirectly told that there was some criticism about their presence. [He did not want that such people] who, posted by the Netherlands, have assumed the responsibility, would now after, so many years, be confronted with their guilt complexes. (*NRC Handelsblad*, March 2, 2000)

Kok's announcement met with mixed reactions. The Indonesian government let it be known that it did not need such expressions of regret. Poncke Prinsen, on the other hand, was satisfied: "For this we have always waited. I would be very happy, if it would now really happen" (*de Volkskrant*, February 28, 2000). But others were less happy. Leiden University professor Cees Fasseur, who had been secretary of a commission that had looked into possible excesses committed by Dutch military in 1947–1949, commented that the Dutch had never behaved as badly as the Japanese: "The Japs [sic] have carried on much worse. There are gradations to be distinguished in bad behavior. The Dutch have never been guilty of committing genocide" (*de Volkskrant*, February 28, 2000). He thought that the Indonesians were not waiting for apologies by the Dutch. Nor were veterans interested in expressions of regret. The chairman of the Veterans Platform thought that apologies would mean that thousands of military men buried in Indonesia would be treated with contempt. He also considered apologies injurious to living veterans, because they had only participated in a war that had been decided [by higher authorities] (*de Volkskrant*, February 28, 2000). The widow of the Dutch commanding general during the "police actions," Mrs. Spoor, wrote an open letter to Prime Minister Kok, in which she protested against expressions of regret toward Indonesia, which she considered as "misplaced":

> With a declaration of regret, you show that you have little knowledge of what was built up in Indonesia by the Dutch, before and after the Second World War and the sufferings of the Dutch, Indonesians and Chinese who wanted to cooperate with us.... We try to think as little as possible about the disasters of those years and remember the good things of the country and the population which we loved. You and many young people ... open up old wounds with those who still remember—a group that is dying out. (*de Volkskrant*, March 2, 2000)

An editor of the Amsterdam quality paper *de Volkskrant* devoted a full page to the problem of offering apologies. He concluded:

Apologies are an aspect of the much broader problem of how a society must look at its past. In the case of crimes against humanity, adjudication of the guilty ones under international law is of far greater importance than offering apologies. Furthermore, paying damages is of more avail to the victims than offering cheap apologies—cheap in a literal as well as figurative sense. (De Bruin 2000)

With this discussion, the public debate about offering apologies to Indonesia came to an end, and has not been revived. Neither Prime Minister Wim Kok nor his successor Jan Peter Balkenende, have paid an official visit to Indonesia, nor have they offered formal apologies.

Slavery and the Slave Trade

Slavery and the slave trade are nowadays considered among the worst violations of basic human rights. The idea that one person can own another flouts the fundamental principle of human dignity. Nevertheless, present-day society has found it difficult to come to terms with this heritage of the past or to decide on any form of reparation (Du Plessis 2003). Why is that so? Elazar Barkan has well summarized some of the reasons:

Among the issues is the dilemma concerning the nature of the groups involved. Who are the victims and who ought to be compensated—descendants of slaves? All blacks? What of those of mixed race? In addition, who are the perpetrators: descendants of slave owners? All whites? The society in general? (Barkan 2000: 97)

In the Netherlands, mainly persons of Surinamese or Antillean origin—descendants of former slaves—have repeatedly raised the issue of offering apologies and/or compensation.

In 1769 a Dutch ship's doctor wrote in the introduction to his handbook on the slave trade: "I just want to observe that there are many companies, who would seem to be not permitted, if there was not a particular advantage to be gained. Witness the slave trade, which because of the advantage it brings to the traders, can be absolved from illegality" (Oostindië 1999). Profits from the slave trade were sufficient to set aside any moral objections. The Constituent Assembly of 1798 opposed abolition on pragmatic grounds, in particular, lack of finances (Kuitenbrouwer 2003). When the Netherlands finally abolished the slave trade in 1807, this was not of its own free will, but under strong pressure from Britain, which during the Napoleonic wars had occupied Surinam and Curaçao (Oostindië 1999) Slavery itself was abolished by the Netherlands only in 1863, long after Britain (1834) and France (1848).(That late date was due to the lack of a strong movement for abolition, plus a considerable degree of stinginess. More than hundred years later, after Surinam had acquired its independence, sentiments to come to terms with the past were widely expressed. A call to pay damages to former slaves was heard:

> In the case of slavery—the greatest colonial crime—there is the burden that slaves were never offered any form of compensation for their suffering. And that, while the Dutch state did pay compensation to the slave owners[!] . . . There has never been a *beau geste* toward the victims of Dutch crimes against humanity. . . . It has never been said: sorry. (Arion 1999)

Others pleaded for apologies and for a monument for the victims of slavery:

> Erecting a monument to the memory of slavery should not be restricted to a one time "erecting event," but must be the starting point for a wide discussion and integral approach, directed toward schooling, training and education of the Afro-Surinamese. But also autochthonous Dutch must know this black page in their history. The monument must be the recognition that the slave trade and slavery are an integral part of Dutch history in the period of the Golden Age [seventeenth century]. The Dutch must be made sensitive to what has happened, in order to understand something of the problems of the Afro-Surinamese in the Netherlands. (Marshall 1999)

The discussion about offering apologies and/or compensation to the descendants of the slaves received renewed impetus with the approach of the United Nations World Conference against Racism, Racial Discrimination, Xenophobia, and Related Intolerance held in Durban, South Africa, August 31–September 7, 2001. At the request of the government, the (official) Advisory Council on International Affairs submitted a report (Advisory Council on International Affairs 2001). The Council considered, mainly for practical reasons, that reparation payments of the kind used in the past to settle accounts between States, were "not suitable ways of compensation" for historical practices of slavery and colonialism:

> such an approach would present considerable practical and legal difficulties. First of all, there is the concern that this kind of reparation payments, which are awarded to States and governments, would not benefit the actual victims or their descendants. Yet even if the compensatory measures were to be victim-oriented, there would still be questions about who is and who is not entitled to compensation for injustices committed in the past, and which States or other legal entities should be obliged to contribute to the compensatory measures. (Advisory Council on International Affairs 2001: 18)

Instead, it recommended measures aimed at achieving a more just distribution of wealth and natural resources at both the national and international levels for the benefit of the descendants of slaves, particularly through the realization of equal rights in the socioeconomic field, such as education, employment, and health care (Advisory Council on International Affairs 2001). The government had not asked about the possibility of offering apologies to the victims and their descendants, and the Council did not mention that possibility.

Four organizations of Surinamese and Antilleans reacted negatively to the report. In a statement called "Reflection of the Black Community" they rejected it, because the Council had consulted none of them and had "perhaps for political reasons" leaned too much toward views held by the European Community without taking into account the views of the black community. They asked the Government not to sign in Durban any "restrictive agreements" with regard to the problems of slavery and to begin talks, immediately after the Durban conference, with that community and with the governments of Surinam, and the Antilles and Aruba. The chair of one of the four organizations, the National Platform Slavery Past, added somewhat cynically (as well as erroneously) that the Advisory Council consisted of the descendants of slave owners, white civil servants: "We don't want personal financial compensations for the victims.... We think rather of a fund for historical research into slavery, in order to correct Dutch history books" (*Leids Dagblad* 2001).

The government decided, as did the other Western European governments, not to take up the matter of compensation in Durban. At Durban, a Dutch cabinet minister expressed his "deep remorse" about slavery and the slave trade, without explicitly mentioning the Netherlands. He recognized that in the past "great mistakes" had been made and expressed the hope that revised historiography would provide new generations with more objective information (Foreign Affairs to the Second Chamber of Parliament 2001). He then paid a five day visit to Surinam "to be informed about the slavery of the past and to invite the Surinamese President to attend the unveiling of the national monument to the memory of slavery in Amsterdam." According to a newspaper report, there was little interest in the subject in Surinam (*NRC Handelsblad*, September 19, 2001).

The national monument was unveiled in Amsterdam on July 1, 2002, in the presence of the Surinamese ambassador to the Netherlands. It is intended as a symbol of recognition of the Dutch past of slavery and as a monument of honor to the struggle for freedom of the slaves in the Dutch colonies. A local citizens' committee that organizes a yearly commemoration distanced itself from the monument, which it considered "too much an initiative of the Dutch Government." It demanded that the government and the parliament should send Queen Beatrix to Surinam and the Netherlands Antilles "to ask for forgiveness for all the suffering that the state had inflicted on the Surinamese and Antillean nations." A Surinamese cabinet minister, speaking at a "gathering of reflection" in The Hague, saw a direct link between the period of slavery and the present economic underdevelopment of Suriname. For that reason he put a financial claim to the Dutch Government (*NRC Handelsblad*, July 1, 2002).

At the Durban conference, compensation was sought for colonialism and slavery as crimes against humanity. According to a spokesman for the European Union, the final declaration agreed at Durban "amounted to an apology" ("In Durban EU Agrees to Apology for Slavery" 2001). Theo van Boven, in commenting on the final declaration adopted at Durban, referred to subtle and hair-splitting distinctions between "expressing remorse" or "presenting apologies," it being felt by legalistic minds that the latter term might open the door for compensatory demands (Van Boven 2001). The Netherlands government did not go farther than expressing its "remorse". It has never offered apologies for the slavery past.

Conclusions

In the words of Van Doorn, "The Indies were the sun in which the Dutch nation basked. The loss of the Indies could only be experienced as the definitive sunset" (Van Doorn 1995: 5). That is one of the reasons the Netherlands found it difficult to part with the greater segment of its colonial empire. Another reason was that it meant the definitive end of Dutch aspirations to be a major power in international relations. What remained was a relatively small country in Western Europe—economically wealthy, but politically powerless. For many Dutch people that recognition was difficult to accept, the more so as many of them saw the Indonesian nationalist leaders, Soekarno and Hatta, as traitors, having chosen the Japanese side during the Second World War.

At the same time, there was also a widely felt sentiment of responsibility in the Netherlands to what was happening in the former colony. A sizable amount of development aid was directed toward Indonesia: "The paternalism of ethical policy [was] replaced by the paternalism of development policy" (Van Doorn 1995: 39–40). The Dutch remained strongly divided about Indonesia until the end of the twentieth century. Those on the political left felt embarrassed about the colonial past and showed themselves in favor of offering apologies for what had happened. Those on the right were proud of what had been achieved and saw no need whatsoever for apologies. Faced with these antagonistic views, the government tried to steer a middle course, without great success. This middle course limited the government's freedom of action and resulted in not offering formal apologies, though it had that intention—some fifty years after Indonesia gained its political independence.

The presence in the Netherlands of almost 300,000 persons of Surinamese and some 125,000 of Antillean origin serves as a daily reminder of both the colonial and the slave past. The subject of offering apologies and/or paying compensation has been brought up by some of the descendants of these slaves. The issue has, however, never had the impact it has in the United States. In the Netherlands, it has caught the interest of only a relatively small group of people and so far, not become a hot political issue. Interest increased somewhat at the time of preparation for the Durban conference, but since then it has again lost its impact. The reason for this is probably that most people seem to be aware of the considerable practical problems of paying compensation after so many years have gone by. To offer "empty" apologies—apologies without financial compensation—seems to hold little attraction for anyone.

These two cases deal with events that many people now tend to consider "historical wrongs." Yet they were not seen so at the time they occurred. The question remains whether and to what extent present generations should apologize or even pay compensation for such events. In the cases of colonialism in Indonesia and the slave trade/slavery, the Dutch were themselves among the main perpetrators.

If there is such a thing as doing "historical justice" and if that means offering apologies by the State for past misdeeds, this is not what has happened in the cases dealt with in this chapter. In the case of the relations with Indonesia, the possibility of offering apologies was entirely a domestic Dutch political affair. No apologies were expressed, as many of the Dutch people who could still remember the colonial past, were of the opinion that the Dutch had been wronged and that the Netherlands had been unjustly forced to part with its colonial empire. The Indonesians had shown little appreciation for all that had supposedly been accomplished on their behalf by the Dutch during the colonial period. For others, it was all a matter of a time long ago that they could hardly remember. Moreover, many people felt there was little reason to offer apologies to the Suharto regime, that was itself guilty of systematic human rights violations.

The time of slavery and the slave trade was even longer ago than most Dutchmen were able or willing to remember. The proponents of the idea of offering apologies were Surinamese and Antillean descendants of the slaves, amounting to a minority of the Dutch population. Finally, there were the practical problems of offering apologies to whom, with what financial consequences.

I thank Fred Grünfeld and Joop de Jong for their comments.

References

Advisory Council on International Affairs. 2001. *The World Conference Against Racism and the Right to Reparation.* Advisory Report 22. The Hague: Ministry of Foreign Affairs.

Arion, Frank Martinus. 1999. "Een 'Beau Geste'." In *Het Verleden onder Ogen*, ed. Gert Oostindie. The Hague: Uitgeverij Arena/Prins Claus Fonds.

Baehr, Peter R. 2002. "On an Equal Footing? The Netherlands and Indonesia." In *Human Rights in the Foreign Policy of the Netherlands*, ed. Peter R. Baehr, Monique C. Castermans-Holleman, and Fred Grünfeld. Antwerp: Intersentia.

Barkan, Elazar. 2000. *The Guilt of Nations: Restitution and Negotiating Historical Injustices*. Baltimore: Johns Hopkins University Press.

De Bruin, Willem. 2000. "Excuus!" *de Volkskrant* (Amsterdam), March 4.

De Haan, Ido. 2000. "Eis van Excuses aan Japan is Misplaatst." *NRC Handelsblad*, February 22.

De Jong, Joop J. P. 1986. "De Nederlands-Indonesische Betrekkingen, 1963–1985." *Internationale Spectator* 40 (2): 130.

———. 1997. "Een Inktzwarte Bladzijde in de Geschiedenis: Nederland en de Indonesische Kwestie 1945–1950." In *Oorlogsdocumentatie '40–'45: Achtste Jaarboek van het Rijksinstituut voor Oorlogsdocumentatie*. Amsterdam: Rijksinstituut voor Oorlogsdocumentatie.

Du Plessis, Max. 2003. "Historical Injustice and International Law: An Exploratory Discussion of Reparation for Slavery." *Human Rights Quarterly* 25 (3): 624–59.

Emmer, Pieter C. 2000. *De Nederlandse Slavenhandel 1500–1850*. Amsterdam: De Arbeiderspers.

Fasseur, Cees. 1985. "Het Verleden tot Last: Nederland, de Tweede Wereldoorlog en de Dekolonisatie van Indonesië." *1940–1945 Onverwerkt Verleden?* Utrecht: HES.

Leids Dagblad. 2001. "Hollandse Slavenbezitters Waren Extreem Wreed." August 24.

"In Durban EU Agrees to Apology for Slavery." 2001. *International Herald Tribune*, September 8/9.

Kersten, A. E. and A. F. Manning, eds. 1984. *Documenten betreffende de Buitenlandse Politiek van Nederland, 1919–1945*. Periode C, dl. IV. The Hague: Nijhoff.

Kuitenbrouwer, Maarten. 2003. "Colonialism and Human Rights: Indonesia and the Netherlands in Comparative Perspective." *Netherlands Quarterly of Human Rights* 21 (2): 206.

Lijphart, Arend. 1966. *The Trauma of Decolonization*. New Haven, Conn.: Yale University Press.

Locher-Scholten, Elsbeth. 1981. *Ethiek in Fragmenten: Vijf Studies over Koloniaal Denken en Doen van Nederlanders in de Indonesische Archipel 1877–1942*. Utrecht: HES.

Marshall, Edwin. 1999. "Een Nederlands Monument voor de Slachtoffers van Slavernij." In *Het Verleden onder Ogen*, ed. Gert Oostindië. The Hague: Uitgeverij Arena/Prins Claus Fonds.

Van Boven, Theo. 2001. "World Conference Against Racism: An Historic Event?" *Netherlands Quarterly of Human Rights* 19 (4): 380.

Van Doorn, J. J. A. 1995. *Indische Lessen: Nederland en de Koloniale Ervaring*. Amsterdam: Bert Bakker.

Van Goor, Jurrien. 1994. *De Nederlandse Koloniën: Geschiedenis van de Nederlandse Expansie, 1600–1975*. The Hague: SDU.

Chapter 16
Is Japan Facing Its Past? The Case of Japan and Its Neighbors

ELIZABETH S. DAHL

The theme of this volume gives rise to an important question: Are only Western states apologizing for various historical wrongs? One only need look at news stories from Asia to see that interstate apologies also are a frequent issue in non-Western countries.[1] While such apologies are more frequently demanded than received, they seem to be an important part of Asian cultural dynamics (Matsuda and Lawrence 2001). In particular, the most controversial case in Asia has to do with the question of whether Japan has come to terms with its behavior during the Asia-Pacific War.[2]

The case of Japan also is useful in consideration of the question whether the "age of apology" represents a positive shift in terms of international values or not. Would even a long-standing issue—that of Japan's lack of a satisfactory state apology to its neighbors—be subject to this effect?

Another particular riddle about the case of Japan has been that, as a cultural group, the Japanese tend to apologize frequently in daily life.[3] Why, then, has it been so difficult for the Japanese to grant "full and sincere" apologies to their neighboring states for Japan's past imperial and colonial policies? Indeed, this chapter explores the broader question of why apologies for past wrongs are so contested.

In analyzing the case of Japan apologizing to its neighbors, an interdisciplinary approach will be utilized as issues of history, culture, and language are intertwined and therefore are of importance in developing a conflict resolution perspective. Communal apology is interpreted here as one means of promoting conflict resolution and reconciliation among states. While it is important to note that apologies rarely stand alone as a method of conflict resolution—financial reparations are often requested and tendered—apologies may have transformative potential if done with care.

For the purposes of this chapter, I focus on empirical analysis rather than normative evaluation, following Max Weber's model of separating the two to promote more systematic analysis.[4] I will explore the "configurational causality" of the case—the unique combination of processes and transactions that produced this current state of affairs for Japan and its neighbors (Ragin 2000: 42)— presenting a brief historical discussion of Japan's interactions with Korea and China since the late 1800s and how war and related trauma have worked to undermine trust between Japan and the victimized states.

The Case of Japan

With the onset of the influential Meiji restoration period in Japan in 1868, Japan embarked on a period of Westernization in which the roles of the emperor and military both were increased in importance. In a few years, Japan invaded China and Korea on the noble pretexts of reacting against the incursions and colonialism of the Western powers in Asia and of liberating the colonies, although, in effect, it perpetuated colonialism (Honda 1999: xxv). By 1876, the Japanese navy had forced Korea to open its ports to trade, and, once the Russo-Japanese war ended in 1905, Japan declared Korea its protectorate. Eventually, Japan embarked on a policy of assimilating Korea, using education as its main vehicle of indoctrination (Rhee 1997: 8-9).

As for China, the time period of most salience here is 1937–1938, when Japanese forces attacked Nanjing and surrounding areas over a period of three months—the event commonly known as the "Nanjing Massacre" or "Rape of Nanking" (Honda 1999). While soldiers' behavior during wartime is a frequent problem, Japanese troops are alleged to have been particularly bloodthirsty during the Nanjing Massacre. One partial cause of this destructiveness was the Japanese army's lack of adequate supplies, which led to house-to-house searches, situations prone to escalation into violence (Fujiwara 1999). Also, Japanese troops allegedly were stung by their military losses to Chinese soldiers, whom they otherwise considered inferior (Gibney 1999).

Indeed, Frank Gibney notes that the identity and practices of the Japanese armed forces were particularly important. With the Meiji Restoration of 1868, a new imperial identity was forged in order to undermine the power of remaining shoguns. The emperor was at the center of this project, and he was surrounded by a militarist effort to build up Japan's armed forces.

Japanese forces were designed above all to be loyal to the emperor rather than any democratic authority, so any infractions were met with corporal punishment. This hierarchy was one that permitted violence against those considered to be in a lower position. Thus, while most of Japan was democratic, the armed forces were not. In fact, as time went on, civilian control of the government was eroded by a number of attempted coups d'état which frightened politicians away from challenging military decisions. Instead, militaristic nationalism promoted Japanese expansion into other regions of Asia.

Women, it also should be noted, were not given much in the way of rights in Japan, particularly in rural areas—and such places supplied many of the men for the Japanese imperial forces. Meanwhile, foreign women were considered to be ranked even lower in this social hierarchy, which leads to consideration of the gendered aspects of the war.

Gendered Dynamics

One of the most difficult issues to discuss is that of the allegations of mass rapes of Chinese women by Japanese soldiers. As in other cases involving allegations of mass rape, the topic itself is emotion-laden and contested. Uncomfortable exchanges emerge between "hysterical" narrative accounts and cold, "rational" refutations based on printed reports and statistics.

In terms of feminist discussions of rape as a weapon of war, Jan Pettman notes that "Bodies, boundaries, violence and power come together in devastating combinations" (Pettman 1996: 101). Indeed, "rape is an aggressive and humiliating act," intended to be a demonstration of masculine power and a symbolic annihilation of the enemy (Stiglmayer 1994: 84). Some scholars have speculated that rape may be based, paradoxically enough, on a fear of not appearing "masculine" or powerful (Hague 1997: 56).

Moreover, Cynthia Enloe raises an important question: Who is the "ultimate target" of rape's intimidation? (Enloe 1993: 121). Most likely, the answer is that *both* men and women are intended to be the victims—both are "rendered by the rape, into an inferior position as feminine" (Pettman 1996: 100). This interpretation gains credence when considered alongside Gibney's observation.

> Many years after the Massacre . . . I found a quantity of the condoms regularly issued by the army to its soldiers. On the wrapping of each was a picture of a Japanese soldier charging with the bayonet. The caption below read simply *Totsugeki*—"Charge!" That little piece of paper told a lot about the Rape of Nanjing. (Gibney 1999: xx)

This theme of annihilation is related to "ideas concerning women in war as symbols of the nation—as 'ideal patriotic mothers' or as 'enemy whores'" (Corrin 1996: 92). Women often symbolize a nation's honor (Yuval-Davis 1997). Thus, the transgression of a woman's sovereign boundaries—whether of a person's body due to murder and/or rape, or of the "body politic" by some act of infringement and/or violence—is an issue of great harm and humiliation to the larger community.[5] Another gendered aspect of this conflict was that, in Korea and elsewhere, the Japanese imperial forces systematically set up "comfort stations" (*ianjo*) which provided local "comfort women" as sex slaves for their troops to use. While it should be noted that the original motivation of the Japanese generals was pragmatic, in order to prevent further rapes of local women, the euphemism "comfort women" is an ironic one (Tanaka 1999). Many of these women were teenagers, abducted or recruited under false pretenses, and often were subject to gang rape by soldiers. It is estimated that over 100,000 women of different nationalities were forced to be "comfort women" for the Japanese troops (Hicks 1994). In short, issues such as these cannot help but inflame a conflict, hitting as they do at gendered understandings of pride, respect, and honor in community and nation.

However, one dynamic has shifted over time. In the past, Japanese men were the ones who shaped and controlled domestic debate of the war. Recently, women have begun to take part in these important debates. Most notably, many former "comfort women" have come forth to speak on their own behalf.

Even so, some commentators have pointed out that even this indication of agency is problematic. For example, Dai Sil Kim-Gibson presents a pained account of her meetings with several former "comfort women." In it, she questions whether the women have been doubly objectified, being seen now merely as stereotyped victims rather than full-fledged human beings with other chapters to their lives (Kim-Gibson 1997: 259). Ueno Chizuki also expresses the concern that, given the prevalence of the "virgin/whore" dichotomy, only those comfort women who are viewed as "pure" before being forced into sexual slavery feel free to come forward as "model victims" to make statements (Ueno 2004: 89).

While a controversial view, investigation into practically any case of conflict reminds us that there may be different plausible interpretations of a given incident, as portrayed in the film *Rashomon*. It is probably no mistake that this influential film—and its association with different representations of "the truth"—centers on allegations of rape.[6]

Thus, the problem remains: can the truth be revealed? Or will we have to rely on educated guesses, survivor testimony (sometimes decades after a particular incident is alleged to have taken place), and other difficult-to-quantify data? At the moment, I can only raise these important questions, noting that they have bedeviled Holocaust studies, for example, as well as Sino-Japanese relations given the small but vocal number of Japanese who believe that the "Rape of Nanking" never took place. "The facts" never speak for themselves—humans present and interpret them.[7] However, it is important to note that, in these and other cases, the prevalent interpretations of "the truth" of each event broke down according to association to a given state. These considerations must be factored into the following discussion of why Japan has not apologized to its neighbors as of yet.

Why No State Apology?

Despite some improvement, debate continues in Japan whether and how to apologize to its Asian neighbors. While several Japanese leaders have made apologies and statements of regret regarding Japanese wartime behavior, their gestures have not met with much domestic or international satisfaction. For one, such statements can interpreted cynically as trying to pave the way for expanding economic exchange between Japan and the state in question—an instrumental goal. A broader problem is that many Asian citizens (as well as former Japanese prisoners of war residing in the West) are concerned about Japanese lack of willingness to take full responsibility for its wartime actions. In 1995, Prime Minister Murayama, a socialist, attempted to give an official apology to commemorate the fiftieth anniversary of the end of the World War II. Unfortunately, he was unable to persuade conservative Diet members to issue a state apology, and was forced to apologize as an individual instead of as an official representative of the Japanese government (Tanaka 1998: 8). Soon thereafter, the Japanese Socialist Party lost control of the government, and the more conservative Liberal Democratic Party (LDP) returned to power. At a domestic level, the window of opportunity had closed.

Again, another puzzle is the fact that Japan has apologized more fully to certain states than to others (Landers and Lawrence 1998). In consideration of the dynamics at work, three aspects—cultural, geopolitical, and psychological—will be considered in order to explain why Japan's few statements of apology have been so underwhelming. While not perfectly separable, each interpretation will be explored in turn before evaluation.

Cultural Dynamics

Has Japan's culture inhibited its ability to apologize to its neighbors? Cross-cultural communication experts posit that cultural differences do affect the phenomenon of apologies. According to Barnlund and Yoshioka, "Even so limited an act as offering an apology, what prompts it, to whom it is offered, how it is offered, with what consequences, embodies underlying cultural assumptions and values" (Barnlund and Yoshioka 1990: 203).

At first glance, it is intriguing that Japan has not made a complete apology, as many outside observers note that, at an interpersonal level, Japanese tend to apologize frequently (Kristof 1998: 40–41). However, Japanese commentators perceive such situations with more nuance.

246   Elizabeth S. Dahl

The Japanese . . . tend to stress their own lack of power to control what they will do from now on—which is tantamount to an apology, in advance, i.e., an excuse. Indeed, the Japanese apology very frequently has, in itself, a ring of self-excuse, a result of the fact that the Japanese sense of guilt includes a considerable admixture of the sense of shame from the very beginning.[8]

Similarly, Barnlund and Yoshioka find that, among Japanese, apologies "usually elicited neutral or negative reactions, only restoring relations to what they were before the infraction and apology occurred" (1990: 204). Part of the reason for this negative association is the high value placed on maintaining harmony in Japanese interpersonal relations.

Going beyond questions of the cultural understandings of apology itself, it should be noted that apologies require boldness and some freedom of action on the part of the person who represents the collective body. With the Japanese internal negotiating style of *nemawashi*, or long-term and deliberate "behind-the-scenes consensus-building," not a lot of room is available for bold individual initiative (Zhao 1993: 5). For a matter as controversial as Japan's wartime behavior, efforts to address this issue probably have been stymied. Thus, cultural difference may be of significance in explaining why Japan has been so reluctant to apologize. General statements of regret have been issued, but not without contestation and lengthy negotiation.

Geopolitical Dynamics

One historical event that has served to increase the pressure on Japan to apologize to its neighbors has been the end of the Cold War and the subsequent change in geopolitical conditions. For one, the United States influence during the Cold War effectively circumvented much discussion of Japanese wartime atrocities.[9] Furthermore, reconciliation was made more of an active project with Japan's Western allies—and even then not all the atrocities were revealed. Clearly, Japan apologized more readily to the United States, Great Britain, and Australia (Henderson 1996).

Asia, however, was another matter. Some issues were dealt with at the time of the Tokyo War Trials, but not to the satisfaction of the victimized. With China, for example, Japan often refuses to compensate war victims on the grounds that such issues were resolved when diplomatic ties were established in 1972 (Reuters 2003).

Also, controversy periodically has been stirred up by visits by Japanese prime ministers to the Yasukuni Shrine to honor Japanese war dead (including those convicted as war criminals). Similarly, China and the Koreas issue protests in the wake of statements such as the one made by Education Minister Fumio in 1986, which indicated approval of Japan's imperialism.

Despite Fumio's subsequent removal, such issues indicate Japan's social turmoil over its wartime legacy.

Since the end of the Cold War, however, some progress has been made. In 1992 and 1993, the Miyazawa government admitted to official Japanese involvement in the creation and management of "comfort stations" designed for use by imperial soldiers. Also, it was admitted that most of the "comfort women" were forced into sexual slavery (McCormack 1997).

In another positive development, Japanese Prime Minister Keizo Obuchi apologized to South Korean Prime Minister Kim Dae Jung in a joint declaration regarding the 35-year colonial rule over Korea. However, part of the reason why the declaration was forthcoming was because Kim was not as insistent as the Chinese leadership as to its need for a full apology from Japan (Rozman 1999). Also, Kim had been cooperative in loosening the South Korean embargo on many Japanese products. These actions indicate that apologies may be more or less forthcoming depending upon the behavior of the recipient state.[10]

An additional factor that must be considered regarding the "age of apology" is that of the priorities (and relative ability to maneuver) of political leaders. Thus, perhaps the issue of interstate apologies has more to do with geopolitics and political leadership than a shift in values. Or, rather, it is a question as to whether international and domestic conditions can combine positively to create "windows of opportunity" for apologies.

Psychological Interpretations

Meanwhile, one may speculate as to why some Japanese refuse to acknowledge the reality and impact of Japan's imperialistic past. During the period of Japanese imperialism, many Japanese believed that their country was merely helping its Asian neighbors.

Over the past few decades, there has been a series of textbook controversies in which the Japanese Textbook Certification Committee deleted or sanitized references to the Nanjing Massacre—actions which inspired one of the original authors of these passages, Professor Ienago Saburo, to take legal action several times. Word of this censorship also provoked angry responses from China and South Korea.

As part of this debate, several rightist organizations—often led by Tokyo University professor Fujioka Nobukatsu—emerged in the 1990s with calls for a "positive history" of Japanese nationalism in the country's textbooks. Furthermore, Fujioka and his allies have objected to any inclusion in school textbooks of the treatment of the "comfort women" and other war crimes, as these cases do not promote "correct history" (McCormack 1997).

At the same time, however, it should be noted that, in the 1990s, steps were taken to begin to acknowledge Japan's wartime legacy. In addition to the gestures mentioned previously, now most Japanese history textbooks address Japan's wartime behavior, and some school districts—backed by the Teachers Union, feminist and labor organizations, as well as liberal representatives of Japanese media such as the *Asahi Shimbun* newspaper—have refused to use the controversial *New History* textbook written by one of the members of the ultranationalist Society for the Creation of a New History (Nathan 2004).

Another issue is that of direct responsibility. As happens in historical conflicts, the original victims and perpetrators are dying in increasing numbers. Some from younger Japanese generations have wondered why they should be made to apologize.

However, Nicholas Kristof points out that unless Japan comes to terms with its militaristic past and apologizes and compensates victims, it will not gain the trust and confidence of its neighbors (Kristof 1998). Imperial Japan still holds the primary place in Chinese and Korean political memory, and thereby restricts Japan from asserting itself militarily or even in terms of regional leadership, as its every move is surveyed with suspicion. In recent years, its movement toward increased international military involvement, inclusion of nationalistic symbols, and potential nuclear-state status has raised regional fears again (Dawson 1999).

Some Japanese protest that their country has apologized many times already for its actions in the Asia-Pacific War (Kristof 1998). After numerous demands for apologies, many Japanese have come to believe that China, North Korea and South Korea use the Asia-Pacific War to guilt the Japanese government into better deals. Thus, according to Kristof,

All sides end up dissatisfied: Chinese and Koreans complain that the prime minister is insincere and that his cabinet worships war criminals, while the Japanese fret that after 53 years they are still not allowed to mourn their war dead.
In 1995, then Prime Minister Tomichi Murayama did make a genuine effort to wrench a forthright apology from the Diet, but the result only undermined the party line on Japan's supposed contrition. Drafters of the resolution replaced the word "apology" with "*hansei*," and "aggressive acts" with "aggressive-like acts." Most troubling, legislators ascribed the acts in question to all countries, not just Japan. Even in this gutted form, only 230 members of the 511-seat chamber voted for the measure. (Kristof 1998: 40)

Kristof believes that there are signs that Japan may come to terms with its past, such as former Prime Minister Obuchi's apology to South Korea, and recent public opinion polls, which indicate that Japanese believe that Japan should show its contrition. Also, Japanese and other writers have made the discussion of Japanese atrocities less of a taboo. However, the veterans' lobby and right-wing forces continue to work against such measures.

Indeed, the vocal presence of such rightist elements and their desire for a "positive" Japanese history and identity perhaps reflects nostalgia for "simpler" times and the promise of renewed Japanese glory instead of appeasing other states. However, such an ethnocentric denial of history means that many Japanese citizens cannot learn from their state's mistakes.

Other examples of denial are plentiful in Japanese society. Some right-wingers assert that the "comfort women" were actually professional prostitutes who volunteered to work for the high pay of the imperial army. A similar argument is put forth by Fujioka's colleague, Nishio Kanji, as to the nature of the Japanese state. While Japan might have embarked upon "a slightly high-handed patriotic war" (*sukoshi omoigagatta aikoku senso*), it did not commit "crimes against humanity" as Nazi Germany did (McCormack 1997).

Another issue of contention is in regard to the number of persons killed in the Nanjing Massacre. While her book helped educate many about the "Rape of Nanking," Iris Chang provoked a backlash in Japan, due in part to her debatable assertion that 260,000–350,000 Chinese were killed (Chang 1997).[11] Furthermore, Chang's book contains a number of additional inaccuracies, ranging from doctored or mislabeled photos to her lack of knowledge of Japanese (Ikuhiko 1998).[12] In contrast, Honda Katsuichi's work (1999) is considered more reliable—based on testimony by Chinese and Japanese witnesses—and adds a Japanese journalist's voice to the consideration of the Nanjing Massacre. A relevant issue in all this is whether inside or outside pressure (or both) is most useful in promoting reconciliation processes.

In sum, of the three possible factors, I believe geopolitics seems likely to be determinant in restraining Japan from offering a formal state apology to its neighbors, although psychological and cultural dynamics do have significant impact. Given the interplay among different levels of analysis ranging from the macro to the micro, it is important to consider next the question of who is responsible for apologizing for and rectifying—as much as that is seen as possible—what has taken place.

Issues of Responsibility

Perhaps one of the most significant obstacles to be surmounted is the frequent sense of many Japanese that they are victims themselves. Of course, the Japanese suffered a horrible loss unique in history with the bombing of Hiroshima and Nagasaki. Given the state of the world today, it is important for Japanese citizens to continue to make known the horrors of nuclear weapons. At the same time, it is important to recognize that another historical legacy—that of Japanese imperialism—also has to be addressed.

This dual role of victim and perpetrator seems to be the legacy of nations and states the world over (consider the dynamics between the U.S. and Japan regarding Pearl Harbor versus the bombing of Hiroshima and Nagasaki). Unfortunately, it also seems to be a pattern that it is preferable to concentrate on one's own wounds rather than the wounds one has inflicted upon the other. National histories can contribute to this myopia by glossing over negative actions taken in the name of their state and focusing instead upon situations in which their own citizens have been victimized.

In bilateral relations, this situation can lead two sides to talk past each other, each paying primary attention to one's own injury—especially if the parties have caused each other's wound. Sometimes, the two sides will try to settle the question of which side "suffered more"—what I call a case of "dueling victimhoods." When such claims compete for the moral high ground, stagnation may result. Even when episodic controversies die down, these competing claims simply remain in the ether, ready to be redeployed at a moment's notice. Thus, there is a sense of trying to find "equivalence" for such events, as if there could be an objective moral yardstick to use in such conflicts.

As mentioned previously, some Japanese individuals have asserted themselves in the public arena to educate the populace as to the full extent of Japan's wartime activity. As such, they prove that some agency and ability to take responsibility is possible. Honda Katsuichi notes that he was a mere child when the Nanjing Massacre took place, "so of course I didn't know anything about it, and I don't bear any responsibility; but due to the censorship that prevailed during that period, Japanese adults were never told about it either" (Honda 1999: xxv). However, he states that, "as a Japanese journalist, I bear some responsibility for leaving the story unreported for such a long time. Expressing remorse to China is the task of the Japanese government."

Honda observes that Japan's postwar process was starkly different from Germany's, which went through more of a process of demonstrating remorse. In contrast, Japan's wartime atrocities were not discussed widely for several decades. While some information was revealed at the Tokyo War Crimes Trials, they were not reported widely (Honda 1999: xxv–xxvi). Moreover, many Japanese viewed the proceedings as "victor's justice," thereby discounting the available evidence.

Years later, when Honda was a reporter covering the Vietnam War, he began to ask himself whether Japanese troops had mistreated other people in the Asia-Pacific War the way American forces were mistreating the Vietnamese. Thus, he researched and wrote about the Nanjing Massacre "not as a means of apologizing to China but as a means of revealing the truth to the Japanese people" (Honda 1999: xxvi). For his efforts, Honda has received a number of threats in addition to many verbal attacks from rightists for his efforts to revisit Japanese history.

Nevertheless, Honda and other Japanese authors have continued to write extensively on the Nanjing Massacre and other issues related to Japanese war atrocities. Notably, Honda recently published an American edition of his central work on the Nanjing Massacre to provoke more "outside pressure" on the Japanese government, as he believes that it is the best way to achieve change in Japan.

Similarly, Fujiwara states that "Creating a clear picture of the war as a whole as we continue to shed light on the Nanjing Massacre is one of our duties as Japanese people" (Fujiwara 1999). However, much work still remains to be done. Beyond considerations of Hiroshima and Nagasaki, many people in Japan remain convinced that they were duped by their leaders into war—hence, they, too, are victims.

Points for Discussion

The issue of Japan's need to apologize to its neighbors is timely. Given Japan's militaristic history and the fears of China, the two Koreas, and other Asian states, the increasing discussion of Japan's possible rearmament indicates that more work will have to be done on this account.[13]

In summary, while a state's leaders may be constrained by both domestic and international forces from giving an apology, sometimes an opportunity will present itself. Acts of individual agency can do much to prepare the groundwork for an apology, so that intersubjective cultural and psychological change can occur. In the case of Japan, I am confident that—thanks in part to the courageous work of Honda, Tanaka, Wakamiya Yoshibumi, Ishida Jintaro, and other Japanese scholars—an apology will emerge someday. Together, they and others have made it more acceptable to talk about Japan's conduct in the Asia-Pacific War.

Along the same lines, the case of Japan provides many issues for us to consider given the themes of this volume. A few points can be raised here in the spirit of furthering our knowledge of apologies:

While it is understandable to want to avoid looking at debates over apologies, these situations can be quite telling in terms of what issues are perceived to be at stake. After all, *apologies (and, for that matter, non- or pseudo-apologies) do not take place in a vacuum.* Frequently aired grievances among the citizens of either the perpetrator or victimized state indicate that the conflict has not been addressed adequately.[14]

Apologies probably should be considered part of a process rather than a one-time event. Given the length of time and scope of harm that historical wounds have been endured, apologies and other conciliatory measures probably will have to be re-done from time-to-time in order to promote trust among the parties.

A process orientation also leads to reevaluation of the terms used to describe what takes place. For example, such terms as "restitution," "conflict resolution," and "reconciliation" connote a sense of completion and wholeness that may not be accurate or helpful. Instead, we may need to add the word "processes" after each of the above terms to indicate the contingent, dynamic element of what is taking place, or perhaps think in terms of "verbs" rather than "nouns" (Jackson 2004).

Across cases of communal conflict, apologies are neither necessary nor sufficient. Nevertheless, in specific cases, depending upon the situation, they may well be necessary and sufficient. The context at hand and the dynamics among the parties are what are of importance.

Hence, *apology's transformative power is not intrinsic.* Rather, there probably has to be a dynamic between the former aggressor and victim in which each acknowledges the pain and cost suffered by the other—although *not* in an equivalent sense that "we're all victims." Most attention tends to be focused on the victims' need for their pain to be acknowledged. Nevertheless, the tensions faced by aggressors (or bystanders) in trying to atone for their past actions also must be considered. Depending on the situation, perpetrators may have more to lose by giving an apology.

Similarly, the desire to reach "consensus" on apologies may prove illusory, especially in the short term. Even a century or two from now, pockets of deniers still may exist. Not all will participate in a cognitive shift. This recalcitrance is understandable when it is considered how difficult it is to acknowledge that one (or one's country) may be wrong. Nevertheless, over time, one hopes that the mainstream of society will have accepted that apologizing was necessary and appropriate.

If they are to occur, communal apologies probably will require deliberation and initiative. The public needs to be prepared by efforts from above and below to make a communal apology. Thus, apology-making needs to be placed on a conscious agenda, especially at the state level.

Even so, intersubjective understandings among the members of a given state can work to constrain the state's range of "possible" policy options at an interstate and regional level. In my own research, I have found that most "aggressor" states and institutions are reluctant to apologize—with a few notable exceptions, of course. While legal issues are often mentioned as inhibiting apology, something else also seems to be at stake, be it image, honor, or "face."[15] If this intuition is correct, it indicates that Abraham Maslow's hierarchy of needs may need to be revised, as national identity and other higher-order needs often seem to take precedence over "basic needs."

Some theorists have noted that apologies themselves are gendered interactions. For example, Deborah Tannen's work (1998) has indicated that there tends to be a gendered dichotomy in the interpretation of apologies at the interpersonal level of analysis. In many American contexts, women are socialized to be more self-deprecating than men.[16] Moreover, such figures as Miss Manners assert instead that "A social apology is not an admission of legal guilt, but a way of defusing tension" (Martin 2002). This sort of face-saving behavior can smooth over relations.

In contrast, Tannen indicates that, for many American men, apologies equal taking responsibility for having done something wrong. Also, apologies can leave one vulnerable—leaving one open to exploitation (Tannen 1998). While suggestive, this evidence needs to be explored further to see whether the findings hold true across cultures.

These concerns lead me to believe that *rationality* alone will not be the answer in leading us away from these common pitfalls. Despite the shared conviction of neo-realists and neo-liberals alike, reason alone usually has not been sufficient to steer us away from deleterious conflict. More takes place in international relations than rational calculation of national interest or assessment of relative capabilities in terms of tanks and bullets. There are nonmaterial issues that often trump these analyses.

Thus, instead of the question of whether there was a substantive shift in international morality in the 1990s, perhaps it is better to consider it an issue of shifting communal interpretations of what is possible and desirable. There may be moments of opportunity when geopolitical and moral issues seem to be in concert, and well-coordinated and skilled pressure can achieve positive ends. After all, a state's "national interest" is open to interpretation.

Last, it would be of benefit to consider whether a neo-Enlightenment model is the best or only way to address issues of historical wrongs. In the case of this chapter, all that I am able to provide here are highly contingent answers to some of the world's most daunting problems. After all, there is some agreement that the past needs to be addressed—otherwise historical grievances can be resurrected in the future as justification to engage in destructive conflict (Montville 1990). If ways can be found to begin a healing process, then our work will not be in vain.

I want to thank Patrick T. Jackson for his helpful comments, as well as James Mittelman and Paul Wapner for their thoughts on an earlier version of this chapter. This chapter is dedicated to the memory of Iris Chang, author of *The Rape of Nanking*. She was a fearless advocate of Japan taking responsibility for its actions during the Asia-Pacific War, and I hope that she now is at peace.

References

Barnlund, Dean C. and Miho Yoshioka. 1990. "Apologies: Japanese and American Styles." *International Journal of Intercultural Relations* 14: 193–205.

Chandrasekaran, Rajiv. 2000. "Indonesian Leader Apologizes." *Washington Post*, August 8.

Chang, Iris. 1997. *The Rape of Nanking: The Forgotten Holocaust of World War II*. New York: Basic Books.

Corrin, Chris, ed. 1996. *Women in a Violent World: Feminist Analyses and Resistance Across "Europe"*. Edinburgh: Edinburgh University Press.

Dawson, Chester. 1999. "Japan: Flying the Flag." *Far Eastern Economic Review* 12.

De Mente, Boye Lafayette. 1993. *Behind the Japanese Bow: An In-depth Guide to Understanding and Predicting Japanese Behavior*. Lincolnwood, Ill.: Passport Books.

Dower, John W. 1998. Foreword. In *Hidden Horrors: Japanese War Crimes in World War II*, ed. Yuki Tanaka. Boulder, Colo.: Westview Press.

Enloe, Cynthia. 1993. *The Morning After: Sexual Politics at the End of the Cold War*. Berkeley: University of California Press.

Fujiwara, Akira. 1999. "Commentary." In Katsuichi Honda, *The Nanjing Massacre: A Japanese Journalist Confronts Japan's National Shame*, ed. Frank Gibney. Armonk, N.Y.: M.E. Sharpe.

Gibney, Frank. 1999. "Editor's Introduction." In Katsuichi Honda, *The Nanjing Massacre: A Japanese Journalist Confronts Japan's National Shame*, ed. Frank Gibney. Armonk, N.Y.: M.E. Sharpe.

Gries, Peter Hays. 2002. *China's New Nationalism: Pride, Politics, and Diplomacy*. Berkeley: University of California Press.

Hague, Euan. 1997. "Rape, Power and Masculinity: The Construction of Gender and National Identities in the War in Bosnia-Herzegovina." In *Gender and Catastrophe*, ed. Ronit Lentin. New York: Zed Books.

Henderson, Michael. 1996. *The Forgiveness Factor: Stories of Hope in a World of Conflict*. Salem, Ore.: Grosvenor Books.

Hicks, George. 1994. *The Comfort Women: Japan's Brutal Regime of Enforced Prostitution in the World War II*. New York: W.W. Norton.

Honda, Katsuichi. 1999. *The Nanjing Massacre: A Japanese Journalist Confronts Japan's National Shame*. Ed. Frank Gibney, trans. Karen Sandness. Armonk, N.Y.: M.E. Sharpe.

Ikuhiko, Hata. 1998. "The Nanking Atrocities: Fact and Fable." *Japan Echo*, 47–60.

Jackson, Patrick T. 2004. "Hegel's House, or 'People Are States Too'." *Review of International Studies* 30 (2): 281–87.

Kim-Gibson, Dai Sil. 1997. "They Are Our Grandmas." *Positions: East Asia Cultures Critique* 5 (1): 255–74.

Kristof, Nicholas D. 1998. "The Problem of Memory." *Foreign Affairs* 77 (6): 37–49.

Landers, Peter and Susan V. Lawrence. 1998. "Sorry, No Apology." *Far Eastern Economic Review*, December 10, 21.

Martin, Judith. 2002. "Miss Manners." *Washington Post*, March 30.

Matsuda, Mari J. and Charles R. Lawrence, III. 2001. "The Telltale Heart: Apology, Reparation, and Redress." In *The Conflict and Culture Reader*, ed. Pat. K. Chew. New York: New York University Press.

McCormack, Gavan. 1997. Holocaust Denial à la Japonaise. Working Paper 38. Japanese Policy Research Institute, Encinatas, California.

Montville, Joseph V., ed. 1990. *Conflict and Peacemaking in Multiethnic Societies*. Lexington, Mass.: Lexington Books.

Nathan, John. 2004. *Japan Unbound: A Volatile Nation's Quest for Pride and Purpose.* Boston: Houghton Mifflin.
Pan, Philip P. 2000. "Taiwan Leaders Offers Apology to Key Rival." *Washington Post*, November 6.
Pettman, Jan J. 1996. *Worlding Women: A Feminist International Politics.* New York: Routledge.
Pomfret, John. 2003. "Offical Says China Erred on Outbreak: Rare Apology Cites 'Poor Coordination'." *Washington Post*, April 5.
Ragin, Charles C. 2000. *Fuzzy-Set Social Science.* Chicago: University of Chicago Press.
Reuters. 2003. "Million Chinese Sign Anti-Japan Online Petition." September 17.
Rhee, M. J. 1997. *The Doomed Empire: Japan in Colonial Korea.* Brookfield, Vt.: Ashgate.
Rozman, Gilbert. 1999. "China's Quest for Great Power Identity." *Orbis* 43 (4): 383–402.
Ruggie, John G. 1998. *Constructing the World Polity: Essays on International Institutionalism.* New York: Routledge.
Stiglmayer, Alexandra. 1994. "The Rapes in Bosnia-Hercegovina." In *Mass Rape: The War Against Women in Bosnia-Herzegovina*, ed. Alexandra Stiglmayer. Lincoln: University of Nebraska Press.
Struck, Doug. 2001. "In Japan, Victims' Families Expect a Personal Apology." *Washington Post*, February 27.
Tanaka, Yuki, ed. 1998. *Hidden Horrors: Japanese War Crimes in World War II.* Boulder, Colo.: Westview Press.
———. 1999. "Introduction." In Maria Rosa Henson, *Comfort Woman: A Filapina's Story of Prostitution and Slavery Under the Japanese Military.* Lanham, Md.: Rowman and Littlefield.
Tannen, Deborah. 1998. "Apologies: What It Means to Say 'Sorry'." *Washington Post*, August 23.
Tavuchis, Nicholas. 1991. *Mea Culpa: A Sociology of Apology and Reconciliation.* Stanford, Calif.: Stanford University Press.
Ting-Toomey, Stella, ed. 1994. *The Challenge of Facework: Cross-Cultural and Interpersonal Issues.* Albany: State University of New York Press.
Ueno, Chizuko. 2004. *Nationalism and Gender.* Trans. Beverley Yamamoto. Melbourne: Trans Pacific Press.
Washington Post. 2003. "World in Brief: WWII Toxic Gas Leaks, Sickening 36 in China." August 10.
Weber, Max. 1958. "Science as a Vocation." In *From Max Weber: Essays in Sociology*, ed. H. H. Gerth and C. Wright Mills. New York: Oxford University Press.
Yuval-Davis, Nira. 1997. *Gender & Nation.* Thousand Oaks, Calif.: Sage.
Zhao, Quansheng. 1993. *Japanese Policymaking: The Politics Behind Politics: Informal Mechanisms and the Making of China Policy.* New York: Oxford University Press.

Part IV
Apologies by Non-State Actors

Chapter 17
Papal Apologies of Pope John Paul II

MICHAEL R. MARRUS

In the world of public apologies for great historic wrongs, those articulated by Pope John Paul II on behalf of his Church of a billion people have a special resonance, for reasons both of style and substance. Solemnly intoned, with commitments to contrition and reconciliation on a cosmic scale, the pope's apologies speak for the ages, and his declarations of repentance reach across boundaries of time, race, nationality, culture, ethnicity and religion. Moreover, the pope apologized often. Luigi Accattoli, a correspondent for the Italian newspaper *Corriere della Sera*, identified ninety-four occasions on which John Paul II acknowledged wrongs committed by the Church or asked for forgiveness. "In twenty-five of these instances," Accattoli notes, "the Pope uses the expression 'I ask forgiveness' or its equivalent" (Accattoli 1998: xv). Moreover, John Paul II's apologies cover an extraordinary range of subjects—from wrongs committed centuries ago against free inquiry (the case of Galileo) to present-day failures that divide the Church or society at large.

From the standpoint of an institution claiming divine authority, the scope and significance of John Paul II's apologies are remarkable, as was his apparent willingness to assume responsibility on the part of all Catholics. Strikingly, the pope even drew attention to the divisions in Christianity itself—the blame for which lies partly, he insisted, with the Catholic Church. "Such wounds openly contradict the will of Christ and are a cause of scandal to the world," he declared. "These sins of the past unfortunately still burden us and remain ever present temptations. It is necessary to make amends for them, and earnestly to beseech Christ's forgiveness" (John Paul II 1994). In the Czech Republic, in May 1995, the pope called attention to religious persecution: "I, the Pope of the Church of Rome, in the name of all Catholics, ask for forgiveness for the wounds inflicted on non-Catholics in the course of the troubled history of these peoples" (Accattoli 1998: 145).

Sometimes the apologies have sprung not from actions, but from inaction: "we Christians have burdened ourselves with great guilt . . . by not standing up against injustice," he declared in Vienna, with unmistakable allusion to the compromises of Catholic Austria during the Third Reich. Catholics have not always been 'peacemakers,' he told an assembly at Assisi in 1986. "We have caused conflicts and we have not been able to make use of all the opportunities for dialogue and reconciliation; we have tolerated and even too readily we have justified wars" (Accattoli 1998: 145). Accattoli devotes a short chapter to the pope's confessions of shortcomings in dealing with the Mafia, arguing that the Church had remained silent when wrongs were committed: "how many wild grapes we have produced instead of good grapes!" he exclaimed in Calabria, citing a passage from the Book of Isaiah. "How many feuds and vendettas, shedding of blood, thefts, robberies, kidnappings, injustices and violence of every kind! . . . The Church and Christians have a duty to put themselves in the front lines of those who denounce injustices, and especially to cultivate a strong moral, social and political conscience" (Accattoli 1998: 202).

On many occasions John Paul II addressed the victimization of aboriginal peoples at the hands of Christians. "How could the Church," he asked in Santo Domingo in 1995, "forget . . . the enormous sufferings inflicted on the inhabitants of this continent during the period of the conquest and colonization? It is necessary to acknowledge in all sincerity the abuses committed due to the lack of love on the part of those persons who were unable to see the natives as their brothers, as children of the same Father." Missionaries, he told Inuit groups in Canada, "in their blindness, often saw your culture as inferior. . . . It is time for forgiveness, for reconciliation and for a commitment to building new relationships," he continued. Women, too, received an apology. "Women's dignity has often been unacknowledged and their prerogatives misrepresented: they have often been relegated to the margins of society and even reduced to servitude"; "if objective blame . . . has belonged to not just a few members of the Church, for this I am truly sorry" (John Paul II 1995).

Despite his infirmities, the pope quickened the pace and highlighted his apologies during the last phase of his pontificate. Following Jewish tradition at the dramatic high point of his visit to Jerusalem in the spring of 2000, the pope placed a message between the stones of the Western Wall, one of the holiest sites for Jews. "God of our fathers," his note said, "you chose Abraham and his descendants to bring your Name to the Nations. We are deeply saddened by the behavior of those who in the course of history have caused these children of yours to suffer and, asking your forgiveness, we wish to commit ourselves to genuine brotherhood with the people of the Covenant" (John Paul II 2000a). And the next year, in what was certainly a first for popes, the pontiff dispatched an omnibus e-mail apology for a long list of wrongs committed by Roman Catholic clergy in Pacific countries, from a laptop computer emblazoned with the papal coat of arms, and set up for the occasion in the Vatican's ornate Clementine Hall of the apostolic palace. According to one account: "Reporting on a Synod meeting in 1998, the eighty-one-year-old pontiff wrote that bishops from the South Pacific 'apologized unreservedly' for the 'shameful injustices done to indigenous peoples' in Australia, New Zealand and the islands of the South Pacific." The pope also referred to "sexual abuse by some clergy," which "has caused great suffering and spiritual harm to the victims" (BBC News 2001).

In what follows I examine how these apologies came to constitute a signature element of John Paul II's pontificate, and how they relate to other dimensions of self-assessment and self-understanding within the Catholic Church. I also assess how these statements fit within the apology genre, and suggest some important limiting characteristics, explainable within the particular context of Catholic theology and worldview.

John Paul II's Path to the Papal Apologies

Although from the early years of his pontificate John Paul II was interested in rectifying wrongs committed by the Church, his focus on apologies derived importantly from the mid-1990s and the vast program for the celebration of the new millennium, referred to within the Church as the Great Jubilee. Drawing on biblical tradition of the Jubilee years, this refers to the passage of 2000 years since the birth of Christ—a historic moment in which the pope mandated a particular emphasis on the confession and forgiveness of sins. First bruited in a memorandum to the cardinals in the spring of 1994, John Paul II then outlined his program for the Jubilee in an apostolic letter, *Tertio Millennio Adveniente*, in November of that year. For the Church, the pope explained, the Jubilee presented a great opportunity to come to terms with the past. The theme of the Jubilee, he made clear, was penance and reconciliation—previously acknowledged, to be sure, but now launched as a program and objective: "it is appropriate that, as the second Millennium of Christianity draws to a close, the Church should become more conscious of the sinfulness of her children, recalling all those times in history when they departed from the spirit of Christ and his Gospel and, instead of offering to the world the witness of a life inspired by the values of faith, indulged in ways of thinking and acting which were truly *forms of counter-witness and scandal*" (emphasis original). Concretely, the Church had to set right specific wrongs that Catholics had committed. "[The Church] cannot cross the threshold of the new millennium without encouraging her children to purify themselves, through repentance, of past errors and instances of infidelity, inconsistency, and slowness to act. Acknowledging the weaknesses of the past is an act of honesty and courage which helps us to strengthen our faith, which alerts us to face today's temptations and challenges and prepares us to meet them" (John Paul II 1994).

Dubbing this process "the purification of memory," John Paul II set the tone for a vast process of repentance. "As the Successor of Peter," he declared in the Papal bull inaugurating the Jubilee, "I ask that in this year of mercy the Church, strong in the holiness which she receives from her Lord, should kneel before God and implore forgiveness for the past and present sins of her sons and daughters" (John Paul II 2000b) "Purification of memory," moreover, also involved forgiving others. "Let us forgive and ask forgiveness," the pope proclaimed in March, 2000. "From the acceptance of divine pardon comes the duty to pardon and to make up with our brothers and sisters," he added, drawing particular attention to those who have wronged Christians in the past. "As the victims of these abuses forgave, so must we forgive. The Church of today and for all time feels the duty to purify the memory of those sad events from every sentiment of rancor or charge" (John Paul II 2000c).

John Paul II's millennial program of apologies derived importantly from the ecumenical and reforming impulse of the Second Vatican Council of the mid-1960s. Without that assembly, Accattoli observes, the mea culpas of the pontiff would not have happened (Accattoli 1998). Following those proceedings closely in Rome, the pope (at the time Karol Wojtyła, the young bishop of Kraków), heard Angelo Roncalli, Pope John XXIII, inaugurate a theme of earnest self-criticism on the Church's relationship with various Christian denominations and with other faiths. Wojtyła followed Roncalli's pathbreaking modification of Catholic liturgy on prayers considered offensive by Jews and Muslims. Roncalli's goal, and that of his successor at the Council, Pope Paul VI, was reconciliation, an objective that came to define what was for the Church an unprecedented call for apology. To that end, the latter appealed to representatives of non-Catholic Christian denominations in St. Peter's in September 1963: "If we are in any way to blame for [your] separation, we humbly beg God's forgiveness and ask pardon too of our brethren who feel themselves to have been injured by us" (Accattoli 1998: 22). And in the *Decree on Ecumenism*, issued the next year, the pope reiterated his appeal: "we beg pardon of God and of our separated brethren" (Accattoli 1998: 29).

As often with revolutionary transformation, the agents of change cloaked themselves in tradition, in this case the enduring structures of the Catholic faith. While not yet articulating full-blown apologies, Vatican II admitted wrongs done in the name of the Church, just as the Church was always "clasping sinners to her bosom," as the November 1964 Vatican II proclamation, *Luminum Genitum*, had it. And with confession, apologies could not be far behind. The sociologist of apologies Nicholas Tavuchis notes the obvious affinities between the two. Confession, of course, has particular "canonical and sacramental significance" in Catholicism. "Both the apology and the confession are critical, central moments within larger moral economies whose narrative phases are sequentially parallel," he observes. "Just as apology is bracketed by a call and forgiveness following a violation, so is confession by contrition and absolution" (Tavuchis 1991: 123). The path to John Paul II's apologies, in this perspective, followed a course defined by enduring structures of Catholic practice.

The Context of John Paul II's Apologies

A word now on the specific context of John Paul II's pontificate that links these many requests for forgiveness and may assist us in the analysis that follows. It is particularly pertinent to look for specific background circumstances in Karol Wojtiła's pontificate because of the prominence of his personal campaign for forgiveness.

Aware that acknowledging the faults of the Church was not only controversial but also susceptible to misinterpretation and even abuse, the pope commissioned a team of theologians to produce a lengthy report on the "purification of memory" in December 1999. Approved by Cardinal Joseph Ratzinger (now Pope Benedict XVI), then prefect of the Congregation for the Doctrine of the Faith and a guardian of theological orthodoxy in the Church, the report acknowledged the unprecedented character of John Paul II's millennial apologies. "In none of the Jubilees celebrated till now," the document observed, "has there been . . . an awareness in conscience of any faults in the Church's past, nor of the need to ask God's pardon for conduct in the recent or remote past. Indeed, in the entire history of the Church there are no precedents for requests for forgiveness by the Magisterium for past wrongs" (International Theological Commission 1999). No other pope, in short, had ventured down this path.

Why, then, John Paul II? Apologies, it has been said, come more easily with distance from the wrongs committed, and some observers maintain that John Paul II's posture as an outsider—the first non-Italian pope in more than 450 years and the first Slavic pope ever—may have distanced him from his predecessors and facilitated a critical vision on their leadership or administration. John Paul II had a new perspective on the history of the Church. "He was much less under the weight of that history," writes Accattoli. Moreover, as a *Polish* pope, Wojtiła came from a society disassociated from some of the principal wrongs attributed to the triumphant assertion of Catholicism. "In Poland there was no Counter-Reformation, accompanied by repression and a military search for Protestants. Freedom of conscience had been proclaimed there before any other place in

Europe. And there was no conflict between the Church and nationalism or between the Church and the laity" (Accattoli 1998: 45–46).

Another reason derives from a key element in John Paul II's pontificate: he was the most travelled pope in history, having visited more than 130 countries, and he visibly relished all of the attendant contacts with Catholics and non-Catholics. This travel linked with a much-discussed accompanying commitment to beatify and canonize. The pope created some 200 saints, and declared another 1,300 to be "blessed," and thus to have crossed the major hurdle on the way to that objective. The process of apology seeking was understood, along with beatification and canonization, as a part of the pope's broad effort to connect with the many communities he visited. John Paul II sought out aboriginal people in dozens of places, for example, and made a special point, when doing so, of confessing to responsibility for the evils committed against them. The pope regularly engaged Jewish spokesmen on these visits, and his acknowledgements of wrongs perpetrated by Catholics formed part of his itinerary.

John Paul II's apologies stirred opposition within the Church. Cardinal Giacomo Biffi of Bologna was one of the first to criticize the trend, publishing a book on the subject in 1995. Biffi objected not so much to the principle of apologies as part of the Jubilee, as to the extension of apologies beyond individuals to declaring communal responsibilities for past wrongs. Writing in the conservative Catholic periodical, *First Things*, Mary Ann Glendon of Harvard University worried about "the general problem of public expressions of contrition in the age of spin" (Glendon 1997). How would apologies be received? Would the pope's fine distinctions be understood and appreciated? "My own uneasiness has nothing to do with what the Pope has said, and everything to do with the way in which the expressions of regret he calls for may be manipulated by spin doctors who are no friends of the Church." Her problem, she made clear, was with "persons for whom no apology will ever be enough until Catholics apologize themselves into nonexistence."

"Is the Pope overdoing the apologies?" asked *American Spectator* senior editor Tom Bethell, echoing the fears of Catholic historian Paul Johnson. Bethell's fear was not only that the trend would "give aid and comfort to [the Church's] critics," but also "has the potential to sow theological confusion about the Church" (Bethell 2000). Johnson and others also objected that the identification of past wrongs constituted a historical anachronism—taking our own moral standards and applying them indiscriminately to the men and women of the past. "There is something repellent, as well as profoundly unhistorical, about judging the past by the standards and prejudices of another age," he wrote (Dulles 1998).

While the pope and his supporters responded energetically to these criticisms, his commitment to public apologies remained controversial.

Not everyone accepts, as the conservative Catholic writer Father Richard John Neuhaus puts it, that "the Church must cross the threshold of the millennium on her knees if she is to walk upright in the next century" (Neuhaus 1998). In what follows, I examine these apologies in conceptual detail, assessing their conformity to the requirements of apologies in other contexts and situations.

Analysis of John Paul II's Apologies

Rooted in Catholic principles of confession and absolution, John Paul II's apologies fit within a particular tradition, and should be understood accordingly. Cardinal Avery Dulles, a major American theologian, insists that the pope's apologies serve a distinctly religious goal. "There can be no holiness without conversion and no conversion without acknowledgement of an unworthy and sinful past.... Freed from unrealistic perfectionism, we can turn humbly to God with the realization that His forgiving love is the only true source of our security" (Dulles 1998). Fair enough, from the Catholic point of view. However, students of apologies on behalf of states or large institutions must also look at them from a more general perspective. I turn now to three essential questions on the apologies undertaken by Pope John Paul II: To whom were they made? On whose behalf? And for what?

To whom? In most of the instances to which we have referred, the pope apologized to God, not to victims or their descendants—or at least not directly to them. The victims were sometimes addressed, and were occasionally invited to hear the declarations of contrition which were obviously deeply felt and sincerely delivered. On the other hand, there was a palpable reluctance to engage too closely with the victims, particularly if the latter were not part of the Catholic community: "any human recipients" of apologies, said the Church's experts on the matter in a careful circumlocution, "above all if these are groups of persons either inside or outside of the community of the Church, must be identified with appropriate historical and theological discernment, in order to undertake acts of reparation which are indeed suitable" (International Theological Commission 1999). For the pope, the real dialogue was with God and not the victims. In this respect many would find the apologies of John Paul II an inadequate manifestation of the genre.

Tavuchis argues that "the bedrock structure of apology is binary": apologies are fundamentally *interactions* between the offenders and the offended—or those who claim to represent them (Tavuchis 1991: 46). Apology is a "social exchange," in which there is a generally understood transmission of a message from one party to the other. Critically, "apology is a relational concept and practice that necessarily requires an individual or collective Other to realize itself" (47). Apologizing to God makes sense from the standpoint of Catholic theology, to be sure, but for students of apologies God is a third party in the affair, who may just as easily get in the way of things than not.

To be sure, there may be a role for third parties in apologies—as facilitators, witnesses, adjudicators, registrars or assessors. However, bringing third parties into the arena can render apologies extremely problematic. The presence of third parties, Tavuchis believes, "typically militates against a mutually acceptable and morally satisfying resolution insofar as it interferes with the normal unfolding of the process or shifts the ground of discourse so as to include other issues" (1991: 50). Harvard law professor Martha Minow refers to the "communal nature of the process of apologizing": the encounter of apologizer and victim must be carefully balanced. "An apology is not a soliloquy," she insists. "Instead, an apology requires communication between a wrongdoer and a victim, no apology occurs without the involvement of each party" (Minow 1998: 114). Apologizing to God changes the binary structure, taking the apology out of the arena of a moral community and inserting it into a religious encounter which may be entirely foreign to victims or their representatives. These apologies seem much closer to the confessions of sins, with requests for absolution, than formal apologies—at least as commonly understood. Notably, the victims do not participate in the definition of the wrongs committed, and they have no real standing to *accept* the apology.

One may conclude, therefore, that John Paul II's apologies fit a Catholic framework in which apologies take place "in a quest for purification, reconciliation, and personal salvation," but they may, thereby, have failed to achieve an essential goal of apologies as a dialogue between two parties with the object of restoring a shattered community. One hesitates, at this point, to be too categorical. Typically, John Paul II spoke about issues that lay deep in the past, and his statements of regret were expressions of great sincerity and contrition. The victims, moreover, had often long since disappeared, and it is not entirely clear to whom, if not to God, apologies could be made. There is nevertheless something incomplete about an apology to a third party.

By whom? Having made an unprecedented—and some have said hazardous—commitment to apologies on behalf of all Catholics, Church authorities have been concerned about the authority to initiate and define these confessions of wrongs. Who should direct the "purification of memory"? asked the authors of *The Church and the Faults of the Past*, the document intended to give some programmatic structure to the pope's apologies associated with the Jubilee year. In reply, the theologians came down, reasonably enough, on the side of ecclesiastical authority. "This expression of regret," they say, "can be done in a particular way by those who by charism and ministry express the communion of the People of God in its weightiest form: on behalf of the local Churches, Bishops may be able to make confessions for wrongs and requests for forgiveness. For the entire Church, one in time and space, the one capable of speaking is he who exercises the universal ministry of unity, the Bishop of the Church 'which presides in love,' the Pope" (International Theological Commission 1999). The Vatican answered those who feared that the call to "purification of memory" might lead to a cascade of declarations of wrongdoing, launched by all manner of Catholic critics and malcontents, by reinforcing the role of ecclesiastical authority.

The pope and the bishops control the process, but there is an important distinction to be made about the source of the apology—on behalf of whom, or what, apologies are made. Repeatedly, in the polemics associated with historic wrongs attributed to the Catholic Church, those claiming to speak for victims have demanded that the Church acknowledge institutional responsibility, that is to say that the offending party be identified as the Church *as such* (Novak 1999) On this critical point, Church spokesmen have insisted, in a formulation that is close to the very center of Catholic thought, that the Church itself cannot err; "the church," understood in this ecclesiological sense, is holy, even perfect: "the community of the baptized, inseparably visible and operating in history under the direction of her Pastors united as a profound mystery by the action of the life-giving Spirit" (International Theological Commission 1999). In the Catholic view, the Church "as such" expresses a body of truths defined by divine revelation that have inspired its followers throughout history. It is those who *constitute* the Church, her "sons and daughters," who, at various times, have "sullied her face, preventing her from fully mirroring the image of her crucified Lord" (John Paul II 1994). Cardinal Dulles puts it this way: "the Church in its theological reality as the Body of Christ is sinless, albeit not without sinners."(Dulles 1998) Apologies, therefore, are on behalf of the sons and daughters, and represent admissions that Catholics have not lived up to their own teachings. "We humbly ask pardon for the part each of us has played in these evils by our actions, contributing to disfigure the face of the Church," John Paul II himself said (John Paul II 200b).

From a Catholic perspective, this distinction is eminently reasonable. David Novak makes the point that, insofar as the Church "as such" represents the teaching authority of the Church, its *magisterium*, apology for the Church "as such" is logically impossible: "*Magisterium* means teaching that calls upon the one taught to do something or believe something that is essential for the very existence of that person within the community for whom that teaching is authoritative. When the Church is understood 'as such,' then she cannot possibly apologize based on her own theological assumptions. For if the Church at this level were to apologize, that would presuppose a criterion of truth and right higher than the revelation upon which the Church bases its authority, the revelation that the Church claims as her own"(Novak 1999). Put less formally, to accept this demand those who believe in the Church as an ideal would have to surrender this commitment. In short, the Church would have to apologize itself out of existence.

Understandable as this distinction is as a way of expressing contrition, doing so on behalf of the "sons and daughters" may further weaken the force of what is intended by coming to terms with the past. To understand why, it is useful now to consider the object of John Paul II's apologies.

For what? Drawing on biblical precedent, the Vatican's theologians insist on the legitimacy of apologies on behalf of those who constituted the Church in other historical periods—sometimes, indeed, centuries ago. The pope, they claim, acts out of "intergenerational solidarity," when he speaks for Catholics, referring to the "solidarity that exists . . . through time and space because of their incorporation into Christ and the work of the Holy Spirit" (International Theological Commission 1999). "Intergenerational solidarity," of course, can be understood in both religious and secular terms. In the one case apologies come from the "People of God" or the "community of the baptized"; in the other, the platform for apology is political—"a self-governing society or community with the power to make laws for itself . . . and to make agreements with other such societies" (Thompson 2002). In both, those who make such apologies assume a moral obligation extending across generations to address past wrongs and, if possible, to help set them right. In the case of the pope, Catholics believe that he enjoys divine authority to act on behalf of the faithful who have gone before; in the case of presidents and other institutional leaders, their authority to apologize in this way is less widely accepted.

This said, the apologies of Pope John Paul II fit within a tighter framework than secular versions, deriving from the process described above whereby the pope addressed his appeals to God and sought forgiveness on behalf of Catholics for failing to live up to the teachings of the Church. Left out of apologies so conceived is not only the interactional element with the victim, but also willingness to contemplate something deeper than a straying from the path of clearly established truth. David Novak contends that apologies can be cheap. "It seems that everyone is apologizing for just about everything in the past these days," he writes. Instead, he commends to the Church "a process of profound introspection" an "act of repentance," designated by the Hebrew word for the latter: *teshuvah* (Novak 1999).

Without disputing Novak's appreciation of *teshuvah*, it seems to me that apology can indeed contemplate the kind of more thoroughgoing exercise that he favors. What counts is the intention. Apologies usually seek to set things right in social or communal terms. Apologies are likely to achieve this when the statement of contrition involves a commitment to examine deeply wrongs done and ponder whether the wrongdoers' belief systems might themselves have been responsible for the harm. After all, fidelity to established beliefs, particularly beliefs that are not shared by both parties, carries no special appeal to those who have suffered. From their standpoint, what matters is whether lessons have been learned, and whether there will be change.

Apologies, Janna Thompson proposes, "might be regarded as acts that look to the future rather than the past." She sets an ambitious agenda: "to bring about a reconciliation between communities, to facilitate healing, to improve relationships between groups, to demonstrate a determination to act more justly in the future, to build an interpretation of the past that descendants of victims and perpetrators can share" (Thompson 2002: xiv). Apologies, in this sense, are a work in progress. And progress, however incomplete, is a theme of this chapter. The apologies of Pope John Paul II, restricted as they were by their institutional context and limited by their theological framework, broke new ground, not only in identifying particular instances of wrongdoing, but in reaching out, albeit in a circumscribed way, to groups that had been wronged. Papal apologies can be more open-ended than confessing to God for a straying from established beliefs, and occasionally John Paul II went further. Whether the Church's apologies will continue to do so will depend on the progress of dialogue with affected groups, an inescapable part of the apology process, and one to which the pontificate of John Paul II made a significant contribution.

References

Accattoli, Luigi. 1998. *When a Pope Asks Forgiveness: The Mea Culpa's of John Paul II*. Trans. Jordan Aumann, OP. New York: Alba House.

BBC News. 2001. "Pope Sends First E-mail Apology." November 23.

Bethell, Tom. 2000. "Is the Pope Overdoing the Apologies?" *Beliefnet*. http://www.beliefnet.com/story/14/story_1458.html

Dulles, Avery. 1998. "Should the Church Repent?" *First Things* 88 (December): 36–41.

Glendon, Mary Ann. 1997. "Contrition in the Age of Spin Control." *First Things* 77 (November): 10–12.

International Theological Commission. 1999. *Memory and Reconciliation: The*

Church and the Faults of the Past. http://www.christlife.org/jubilee/essays/C_memoryandrec.html

John Paul II. 1994. *Tertio Millennio Adaveniente.* http://www.vatican.va/holy_father/john_paul_ii/apost_letters/documents/hf_jpii_apl_10111994_tertio-millennio-adveniente_en.html

———. 1995. *Letter of Pope John Paul II to Women.* http://www.vatican.va/holy_father/john_paul_ii/letters/documents/hf_jpii_let_29061995_women_en.html, p. 3.

———. 2000a. *Western Wall Prayer.* March 26. http://www.bc.edu/research/cjl/metaelements/texts/documents/johnpaulii/westernwall.htm

———. 2000b. *Incarnationis Mysterium: Bull of Indiction of the Great Jubilee of the Year 2000.* http://www.vatican.va/jubilee_2000/ocs/documents/hf_jpii_doc_30111998_bolla-jubilee_en.html, p. 11.

———. 2000c. *Homily of the Holy Father Asking Pardon.* http://www.christlife.org/jubilee/essays/C_memoryandrec.html

Minow, Martha. 1998. *Between Vengeance and Forgiveness: Facing History After Genocide and Mass Violence.* Boston: Beacon Press.

Neuhaus, Richard John. 1998. "The Public Square." *First Things* 82 (April): 60–75. http://www.firstthings.com/ftissues/ft9804/public.html, p. 7.

Novak, David. 1999. "Jews and Catholics: Beyond Apologies." *First Things* 89 (January): 20–25.

Tavuchis, Nicholas. 1991. *Mea Culpa: A Sociology of Apology and Reconciliation.* Stanford, Calif.: Stanford University Press

Thompson, Janna. 2002. *Taking Responsibility for the Past: Reparation and Historical Injustice.* Oxford: Polity Press.

Chapter 18
Rethinking Corporate Apologies: Business and Apartheid Victimization in South Africa

BONNY IBHAWOH

After the collapse of apartheid, a major task that confronted South Africa was how to redress the wrongs of the past in a way that ensures justice and yet fosters national reconciliation. Like other attempts at addressing historical injustices, one of the central concerns has been how to deal with the fluid categories of victims, beneficiaries and perpetrators. Much of the initial discussion on beneficiaries and perpetrators focused on the role of individuals and state institutions under apartheid. In recent years, attention has shifted to corporate responsibility and culpability for apartheid victimization. Three distinct approaches have become discernable—the criminal justice approach, the civil justice approach and the amnesty and reconciliation approach. With the establishment of the Truth and Reconciliation Commission (TRC), the government of Nelson Mandela opted for the amnesty and reconciliation approach.

As part of its mandate to investigate human rights violations during the apartheid era, the TRC investigated individual and systemic abuses of human rights but also to understand how various sectors of South African society engaged with apartheid. This included the role of business organizations under apartheid. It concluded that business was "central to the economy that sustained the South African state during the apartheid years." Local corporations benefited immensely from the exploitation and repression of apartheid particularly through the exploitative use of black labor. Transnational Corporations continued to do business with the apartheid regime in defiance of international sanctions. Motivated by profits, these corporations rationalized their engagement with the apartheid regime in terms of the "constructive engagement" arguments that shaped Thatcherite and Reaganite policies toward apartheid South Africa.

This chapter addresses the ways local and transnational corporations have addressed questions about their roles under apartheid within the framework of the amnesty and reconciliation approach. I examine the grounds on which these corporations have been held responsible for apartheid victimization and the related discourse on apology, restitution, and reconciliation.

The Age of Corporate Apologies?

Unlike state apologies, corporate apologies have been relatively underexplored in the discourse on apologies. Much of the discussion on corporate apologies has taken place within the narrow context of business ethics rather than human rights or international politics. Within the human rights discourse, corporate apologies have clearly taken a backseat in our preoccupation with state apologies. Some of the reasons for this are quite obvious. For one thing, corporations rarely apologize. If state apologies are uncommon and controversial, corporate apologies are even more contentious. The same reasons that make states reluctant to offer apologies, even when one is clearly deserved, are amplified when it comes to corporate apologies. Here, the primary concern is that by acknowledging wrongdoings and apologizing for them, corporations risk undermining their public image and credibility. Corporations are also often concerned that a public apology can open a floodgate of litigation and costly legal settlements. The assumption is that apologies create legal liabilities for the apologist and for this reason corporate attorneys routinely recommend against apologies.[1]

Although corporate apologies may not attract as much public and academic attention as state apologies, present trends suggest that they may become as important as state apologies. If the post World War II era marked the age of state apology as some have suggested, the coming decades may well signal the dawn of the age of corporate apologies. In an era of globalization, non-state actors like transnational corporations (TNCs) are beginning to wield unprecedented influence over the lives of millions of people around the world. In many developing countries, the economic power that TNCs command has a stronger impact on the lives of ordinary people than the political power of the state. In an era where the gross annual intake of Wal-Mart is more than the GDP of most countries, the power of the state over its citizens is being increasingly replaced by the influence of global economic institutions. We must therefore begin to think seriously not only about state apologies but also about corporate apologies.

Typology of Corporate Apologies

In discussing corporate apologies, I find it useful to distinguish three types of apologies—soft, hard, and radical. Soft corporate apologies are apologies rendered by corporations for their acts or omissions that may have fallen short of industry standards or public expectations but have not grievously harmed any particular person or group of persons. They are typically general apologies to consumers or the general public, which corporations are willing to offer because they are of low risk. They are often offered when there are no threats of litigation and minimal risk of long-term damage to profits, image, or credibility of the corporations.

These kinds of apologies are relatively common. Some examples: the broadcasting network CBS offers an apology for an artiste's "wardrobe malfunction" resulting in "unintentional nudity" during its Super Bowl broadcast; the sportswear company Nike apologizes for an advertisement that tended to be disparaging of disabled athletes; the energy giant Shell apologizes for being lax in its environmental standards; and McDonald's apologizes for stating that its French Fries are cooked in "100 percent vegetable oil" when, in fact, it uses flavoring derived from a beef source. These are all soft corporate apologies. For the corporations offering them, they are risk-free acknowledgments of improper behavior. To much of the public, they come across more as public relations exercises than as acts of genuine contrition.

The second type of corporate apology is the hard corporate apology. These are apologies offered in situations where the stakes are much higher. Corporate apologies are hard apologies when offered in situations where there is real risk of monetary loss and damage to corporate image. Instances of hard corporate apologies have been few and far between. Johnson & Johnson set the standard for this type of apology in the 1980s after news broke that some of its Tylenol capsules had been laced with cyanide. The company immediately alerted the public of the danger, issued an unequivocal public apology and followed by quickly pulling all capsules from the market—a move that cost it over $125 million. These kinds of apologies are rare because of the conventional wisdom that apologies are bad for business. Even where corporations have been willing to settle legal claims, they have backed away from making hard apologies.

The third type of apology—the radical corporate apology—is what I am concerned with in this paper. This arises when issues of gross human rights violations are involved. It arises when the acts or omissions for which a corporation apologizes are not merely about failure to meet industry standards and public expectations, but rather, about the *systemic* violation of the basic human rights of large groups of people. Radical corporate apologies are not about infringements on consumer rights. They are about violations of fundamental human rights. What is at stake when a corporation offers a radical apology is more that just corporate image or profit. It is sometimes the very survival of the company.

Unlike states, corporations usually do not find themselves in human rights situations that require radical apologies. States, not companies, are usually the primary violators of human rights on such a large scale. Where companies have been accused of gross human rights violations, it is often because they have had connections with a repressive government. The clearest example of this was during the post-World War II war crime trials where the board of the German corporation I.G. Ferben, which collaborated with the Nazi regime, was convicted of mass murder and slavery. Had the board of I.G Ferben chosen to apologize in this case, it would have been a classic example of a radical corporate apology.

Recent examples of radical corporate apologies come from South Africa. As part of its mandate to investigate human rights violations during the apartheid era, the TRC held public hearings on the role of business under apartheid. These "institutional" hearings explored the role of white business, black business, and labor during the apartheid period. It focused on such issues as culpability, collaboration, and involvement as well as the costs and benefits of apartheid to the business sector. The TRC found that business was "central to the economy that sustained the South African state during the apartheid years" (TRC 1999a: 18). It concluded that white-dominated South African corporations not only benefited from apartheid policies, but in some cases were also actively involved in apartheid policy making. While most corporations disagreed that their roles under apartheid amounted to gross human rights violations, many acknowledged their failures to "act quickly and adequately" to change the apartheid system. Others pointed out that they had, in fact, contributed to the democratic transition and social justice in nonpolitical ways and apologized for not doing more.

How far do these apologies go? Do they convey full acknowledgment and adequate contrition for the role of the corporations under apartheid? To address these questions, we must begin by exploring the historical links between apartheid and capitalism.

Apartheid and Capitalism

The relationship between capital and apartheid has been one of the recurring debates in South African political history. Two opposing schools of thought have emerged—the liberal and radical interpretations of the nexus between capital and apartheid (Davies 1979; Saunders 1998; Nattrass 1991).

The liberal school argues that since apartheid was essentially a political ideology founded on state interventionism in all sectors of the society, it conflicted with basic tenets of free market capitalism. Apartheid amounted to drastic state intervention in the functioning of the labor market and the strict state regulation of other sectors of the economy. It was therefore essentially a politically inspired but economically irrational intervention that stifled business, distorted the economy and undermined long-term productivity growth. Some proponents go even further to argue that apartheid was imposed on business against its will and interests (Moll 1991).

Opposed to the liberal interpretation is the radical school of thought which seems to have gained ascendancy in recent years. It holds that segregation and apartheid structured the process of class formation and underpinned corporate profitability by depressing black labor costs. Proponents argue that many of the basic laws of segregation and apartheid were introduced to create a cheap black labor force to benefit businesses drawn from the white minority (Nattrass 1999). Such opposing views of the relationship between business and the authoritarian state are evident in other contexts such as the debate over the relationship between German corporations and the Nazi government. While accused corporations and their leaders stressed their lack of power to influence state policies, most contemporary commentators argue that Nazi policies were in the interest of these corporations which had the power and relative autonomy to influence state policies (Gregor 1998).

In the case of South Africa, the end of apartheid and the establishment of the TRC in the 1990s seemed to have intensified this debate. The dominant positions that emerged at the TRC hearings on business and apartheid mirrored the opposing liberal and radical paradigms. In their submissions, several organizations opposed to the apartheid regime such as the African National Congress (ANC), the South African Communist Party (SACP), and the Congress of South African Trade Unions (COSATU) presented apartheid as a system of racial capitalism. They held that apartheid was beneficial for white business because it was an integral part of the system premised on the exploitation of black workers and the destruction of black entrepreneurial activity. They argued that although business as a whole benefited from the apartheid system, some sections of the business community, notably the mining and defense industries, benefited more than others (TRC 1999). In their view, these corporations were not just beneficiaries but were also active partners and collaborators in crafting and sustaining apartheid. For them the question before the TRC was not whether business was culpable in apartheid victimization, but rather, the extent of this culpability and the forms restitution should take.

In contrast, business organizations that operated under apartheid such as Anglo American Corporation, Old Mutual, South African Breweries, and South African Chamber of Business (SACOB) claimed in their submissions that rather then being beneficiaries, business was also a victim of apartheid. They argued that apartheid raised the cost of doing business, eroded South Africa's skill base and undermined long-term productivity and growth. By emphasizing the obstacles which the apartheid regime placed on their profitability, these organizations sought to cast themselves more as victims or "hostages" of the system than as partners or collaborators. For them, the essential question that may be asked of business is not whether it collaborated with apartheid, but rather, why it did not do more to hasten the demise of apartheid?

At the end, the TRC took the position that the culpability of business went beyond not doing more to end apartheid. Business, it held, was a major beneficiary and active supporter of the apartheid system. It distinguished between three different orders of business involvement with the apartheid regime: active collaboration in the construction of apartheid (first order involvement); supplying goods and services used for repressive purposes (second order involvement); and benefiting from the apartheid economy (third order involvement). While most businesses benefited from operating in a racially structured context, certain sectors such as the mining industry were more than just beneficiaries. They helped to "design and implement apartheid polices" (TRC 1999a: 58).

Corporations as Beneficiaries and Collaborators

Much of the discussion on business and apartheid has focused on the role of corporations as beneficiaries of apartheid's political and economic agendas. When it came to power in 1948, the white supremacist National Party (NP) pursued an economic policy that ran counter to the logic of free market capitalism. It promised drastic state intervention in the functioning of the labor and other markets, and strict state regulation of all sectors of the economy. However, once it assumed power, the party was able to balance its agenda of promoting Afrikaner economic ascendancy while at the same time facilitating overall economic growth. In the 1950s and 1960s, the South African economy grew more quickly than any other capitalist economy except Japan. Far from undermining economic growth, the NP's protectionist apartheid policies tended to foster corporate capitalism by creating the conditions for rapid accumulation (COSATU 1997). These economic gains were not limited to the early days of apartheid. For much of its history, apartheid was enormously profitable but profit-driven economic growth coincided with the deepening oppression and dispossession of the majority.

One organization that played a key role in the nexus between business and the apartheid state was the secretive Afrikaner Broederbond, whose agenda was the entrenchment of its vision of white supremacy in South African society (Asmal, Asmal, and Roberts 1997). The Broederbond spearheaded the Afrikaner economic movement of the 1940s. It set out to mobilize the savings of Afrikaner farmers and workers for nascent Afrikaner business and was behind the establishment of several corporations among which was Volkskas Bank in 1934. Through organizations like the Broederbond, Afrikaner business interests played a central role in the elaboration of the overall thrust of apartheid policy. For instance, the South African business lobby was crucial to the adoption of the labor and other racial practices at the core of apartheid. Afrikaner business remained extremely close to the NP right up till the very end of the Botha regime.

In his submission to the TRC, the South African economist Sampie Terreblanche stated that what South Africa needed after the "political TRC" was an economic TRC. He argued that the collaboration between business and apartheid created and promoted a context that led to the systematic execution of gross violations of human rights. This collaboration contributed to the emergence of an economic and a political structure, a culture and a system that gave rise to, and condoned certain patterns of, repressive behavior (Terreblanche 1997).

Apartheid policies created an environment that was particularly conducive for privileged white businesses. Repressive laws such as the Pass Laws restricted the mobility and negotiating power of black labor, while the Masters and Servants Laws made it a criminal offence punishable by imprisonment for black workers to break their contracts by desertion, insubordination or refusing to carry out the command of an employer. Breaches of contract by employers were, however, treated as civil offences. There were also laws like the "Influx Control Regulations" intended to redirect black labor from the cities to the farms to serve white commercial farmers and the Group Areas Laws intended to exclude black owned businesses from central business districts. This greatly benefited white-owned businesses that were insulated from potential competition from black entrepreneurs (ANC 1997).

The Big Three: Mining, Defense and Banking

The mining industry was a primary beneficiary of apartheid segregation and discrimination. It falls into the TRC's category of first order involvement with apartheid because, beyond simply benefiting from apartheid, the mining industry historically played a central role in laying the foundations of systematic racial oppression in South Africa. Its strategies included influencing legislation that forced black workers into the wage system; promoting state-endorsed monopolistic practices; and exploiting black labor and the brutal suppression of black workers and trade unions. Mining corporations like De Beers pioneered the prison-like compound system and the racialized contract labor system (COSATU 1997).

The exploitative use of black labor was central to the relationship between business and apartheid. In its submission to the TRC, the Congress South African Trade Union COSATU stated that the real content and substance of apartheid was the perpetuation of exploitative cheap labor system (COSATU 1997). Many business interests cooperated with the apartheid state in its measures to undermine and crush the trade unions. They took advantage of government interventions in the labor market and its decimation of black trade unions to drive down their labor costs. Real African industrial wages fell continuously between 1948 when apartheid was established until 1959. In the mining industry, African wages in 1969 remained below the level of 1896.[2] By keeping labor costs down, apartheid proved to be good for both domestic and trans-national white business involved in mining.

The defense industry was second only to the mining industry in terms of its corporate connections with the apartheid regime. The imposition of arms embargo against South Africa in 1960s led to the emergence of a locally based armaments industry, supervised by the state-owned Armaments Development and Production Corporation (ARMSCOR). By the end of the 1970s, ARMSCOR stood at the core of a new, indigenous military-industrial complex becoming South Africa's third biggest industrial group. With 60 percent of ARMSCOR's research and production contracted out to the private sector, almost all levels of the private sector were linked with the military through the armaments industry. These included the subsidiaries of virtually all of South Africa's major non-state conglomerates as well as a number of high profile multinationals such as IBM, Shell, Daimler-Benz, and many others.

Beyond these business links, some corporations were directly involved in the repressive activities of South African security agencies. Evidence revealed at the TRC hearings on the role of business showed there was extensive collaboration between business interests and the security agencies of the apartheid state. For example, apartheid spy and self-confessed letter bomb murderer, Craig Williamson, stated that certain banks provided apartheid intelligence officers with covert credit cards for covert operations.[3]

Transnational corporations, particularly international lending organizations, benefited substantially from doing business with the apartheid regime. Major Swiss banks such as Credit Suisse and its predecessor UBS played a key role in South African investments and gold marketing under apartheid. In fact, the chairman of UBS is reported to have described apartheid as "desirable" for business (TRC 1999b: 144). Swiss banks played an important role in propping up the apartheid regime during the sanctions years of the 1980s. After American banks such as Chase Manhattan cut back on their lending policies to the apartheid regime, the Swiss banks promptly came to the rescue, saving the regime from an impending debt crisis. While many countries (including the United States) were imposing sanctions on apartheid gold, the Swiss banks continued to import over half of the gold produced in South Africa (TRC 1999b: 145). Such was the concern about the financial ties between the Swiss banks and apartheid regime, even in Switzerland, that one Swiss parliamentarian stated:

> Let's be honest. Our businessmen just want to do business with South Africa at any price. And this policy is not a sound policy for our country internationally. One of these days it's going to come back and haunt us. (TRC 1999b: 145)

Yet, the links between apartheid and business were not limited to big transnational corporations. White-owned small and medium businesses, many of them owned by Afrikaners, also gained substantially from apartheid. Many of these small white-owned businesses moved into the trading vacuum created by the group areas removals of blacks in the 1950s and 1960s. It is estimated that white-owned commercial farms acquired an extra 106,000 hectares of farming land between 1960 and 1978 as a result of the dispossession of black farmers from black owned land outside the reserves (*Business Day*, October 29, 1997). There is also evidence that small-scale white farmers benefited from the use of black convict and child labor during the apartheid years (Marcus 1989).

Apartheid Reform and "Constructive Engagement"

Many businesses have attempted to rationalize their roles under apartheid by claiming that they supported reforms and played a role in bringing an end to apartheid. They point to successive recommendations by corporate representatives to the South African government to reform apartheid labor policies. For example, Harry Oppenheimer of the conglomerate Anglo American was a perceived opponent of certain aspects of apartheid. He stated in 1985 that the policies of the Nationalist Party had made it impossible to make proper use of black labor and called for reforms (*Financial Mail*, November 29, 1985). However, critics argue that businesses were only interested in superficial reforms of the apartheid system in order to guarantee its stability. They were much less interested in the total dismantling of white minority rule.[4]

Indeed, with growing international pressure on South Africa in the 1980s, business support for the apartheid regime began to waver. Concerns about debt repayment provoked a serious economic downturn and concerns began to be voiced within business circles about the slow pace of political reform. But in spite of these concerns, the business community was reluctant to "rock the profitable boat of apartheid" (COSATU

1997). Many of these businesses banded together in the 1960s to support the South Africa Foundation, which they used to promote what they considered the "bright and promising side" of apartheid to foreign politicians and industrialists. Like many supporters of "apartheid reform" and the policy of "constructive engagement" with apartheid, the foundation consistently opposed anti-apartheid sanctions and held several pro-apartheid political positions. Although it conceded that apartheid policies were intrinsically flawed, its position was that these flaws could be accommodated until changes were made.

This accommodationist approach was not limited to business. It was central to Reaganite and Thatcherite policies toward South Africa. In 1985, President Reagan famously stated that P. W. Botha's "reformist administration" had "eliminated the segregation that we once had in our own country". Even when the U.S. Congress voted for limited sanctions against South Africa in 1986, Reagan vetoed the sanctions. Congress eventually overrode his veto.

Although the corporations that made submissions to the TRC put up a spirited defense of their roles under apartheid, the position of the TRC at the end of its hearings was that business was central to the economy that sustained the South African state during the apartheid years, and as such, it bears some responsibility for apartheid victimization (TRC 1999).

Restitution and Reparation

Like other attempts at addressing historical injustices, one of the main challenges that the TRC confronted was how to deal with the fluid categories of victims, beneficiaries, and perpetrators. With regard to corporate responsibility for apartheid victimization, three main approaches have become discernable—the criminal justice approach, the civil justice approach and the amnesty and reconciliation approach, which the South African state opted for with the establishment of the TRC.

The criminal justice approach is premised on the relevance of the concept of the corporate war criminal to the South African situation. It draws on postwar trials such as the Tokyo trials of Japanese individual and corporate war criminals. The notable reference point is the Kajimi Gumi Company, which paid the Japanese Imperial army for the use of war prisoners and kidnapped Chinese civilians. Hundreds of Chinese slaves were bought in this way to work in mines owned by Japanese firms under dehumanizing conditions. Kader Asmal et al. have compared the plight of these Chinese slaves to those of South African prison laborers rented out to apartheid farmers (Asmal, Asmal, and Roberts 1997).

Although there is no evidence of widespread use of prison labor in apartheid's mining and industrial sectors, many corporations exploited apartheid's immigrant labor system to maximize profits. The conditions under apartheid's private and public industrial labor regimes were so deplorable that it raised concerns within the business community even during the heydays of apartheid. Directors of the mining giant Anglo American privately discussed the fear that their company would be remembered as the "I.G. Ferben of Apartheid," a reference to the company that, through slave labor, became the industrial backbone of the Nazi regime. The concept of the corporate war criminal in the South African context has been largely limited to academic discourse. It has not been seriously explored either by the South African government or by individual victims of apartheid.

Unlike the criminal justice approach, the civil justice approach has been extensively explored by victims of apartheid and those who claim to act on their behalf. As of 2003 at least four lawsuits, some in the form of class action suits, had been filed and instituted in the United States on behalf of the victims of apartheid.[5] The central argument behind these lawsuits is that the crimes of the apartheid regime—forcible removals, discriminatory labor practices based on race, imprisonment, torture, murders, and so on—were the direct or indirect result of corporate support (Ntsebeza 2003).

One such lawsuit was filed in 1994 against the Government of South Africa and major corporations seeking $10 billion for "genocide, expropriation and other wrongful acts" committed by the firms under apartheid. It also demanded another $10 billion from the post-apartheid government for "continuing to allow companies to exploit victims." Named in the lawsuit were mining firms Anglo-American and Goldfields, IBM and UBS Bank of Switzerland. Echoing the conclusion of the TRC, Ed Fagan, the American lawyer who launched the suit, argued that the case was winnable because "at the end of the day these companies were strategic partners of the apartheid government" (BBC 2004).

What has been clearly missing from both the criminal and civil justice approaches has been any serious talk about corporate apologies. The civil suits have been largely concerned with monetary compensation for the victims of apartheid, while the discussions about criminal justice have been more concerned with retribution. The slogan of proponents of the criminal and civil justice approach has been "No amnesty, no amnesia, just justice." But the South African government, eager to attract foreign capital, has distanced itself from these approaches to addressing the wrongs of apartheid (Rostron 2002). Instead, it has opted for the amnesty and reconciliation approach, which focuses not only on restitution but also on apologies as a means of healing the wounds of the past and moving the nation forward.

Truth, Apology, and Reconciliation

Apart from investigating gross human rights violations during the apartheid era, one of the mandates of the TRC when it was established in 1995 was to "consider amnesty for those who confess to political crimes and recommend reparations and rehabilitation of victims." Although apology was not specifically mentioned in the Promotion of National Unity and Reconciliation Bill which set up the TRC, it was assumed that confessions to political crimes and applications for amnesty would logically be accompanied with apologies. Apology and forgiveness was also an important part of the TRC's final recommendations. The Report outlined four interconnected steps necessary for national reconciliation. These include: restoring the dignity of victims and survivors; *acknowledgment of guilt and apology*; forgiveness, and finally, reparations and restitution (emphasis added).

In their submissions to the TRC, corporations and business organizations were reluctant to acknowledge guilt and offer radical apologies along the lines of the TRCs recommendations. Many of them disagreed that their roles under apartheid amounted to gross human rights violations. The financial corporation Old Mutual stated:

In principle, the mandate of the Commission which focuses on gross violations of human rights would almost certainly exclude Old Mutual from having to make any submission. (TRC 1999a: 21)

As far as most corporations were concerned, their purpose in participating in the TRC hearings was to promote understanding of their role under apartheid and explore areas where they failed to press for change at both political and organizational levels. It was not primarily to acknowledge wrong or apologize for human rights violations. Their failure to act adequately on the political front was regarded as an "error of omission." Failure to adjust employment and labor practices was regarded as "regrettable," but not amounting to gross human rights violations (TRC 1999a: 21).

However, some corporations specifically acknowledged their failures to "act quickly and adequately" to "change the apartheid system on the political front" and to "adjust employment practices" (TRC 1999a: 21). Anglo American Corporation accepted that it "could have been a better corporate citizen" and apologized for not doing more. The Development Bank of South Africa (DBSA), a major player in the apartheid economy, accepted that in supporting apartheid through providing development loans to homelands and by advising officials on policy, "the Bank was an integral part of the system and part and parcel of the apartheid gross violation of human rights." The Bank went further to apologize for this.

It is interesting, though not surprising, that corporations were willing to apologize for their omissions rather than their alleged acts of collaboration with the apartheid state. DBSA was perhaps the only corporation to offer a radical corporate apology along the lines of the typologies discussed earlier. Other corporations were content on offering soft apologies. In spite of the prominent role they played under apartheid, transnational corporations like the Swiss banks did not even bother to make submissions to the TRC.

Conclusion

The corporate apologies so far offered for apartheid victimization in South Africa can at best be described as superficial and ineffectual. Although the role of corporations under apartheid clearly demands radical apologies, the corporations that have bothered to offer any have only offered superficial apologies. Beyond apologies, many of these corporations have been equally reluctant to offer any form of voluntary restitution for their role under apartheid. In its final report, the TRC recommended the establishment of a Business Trust for the purpose of funding reparations to victims of apartheid.[6] Across the board, local corporations rejected the suggestion that they might help to fund the restitution process. Submissions to the TRC included objections that this would only encourage "a sense of entitlement and victimhood" (Rostron 2002). A similar international fund established in Switzerland to contribute to reconstruction and development in South Africa secured a commitment of less than 0.02 percent of the profits made by Swiss banks and investors in South Africa for each year during the 1980s (TRC 1999b: 142).

These positions of local and transnational corporations have raised concerns about the efficacy of the amnesty and reconciliation approach to really redressing the crimes and injustice of the apartheid era. Many have voiced concerns about "empty apologies and hollow reconciliation." If acknowledgment of wrongdoing and apology are the first steps toward reparations and reconciliation, it can be said that corporations have been reluctant to take that first step. At the end, the criminal and civil justice approaches may well be the only hope of getting corporations to take true responsibility for their roles under apartheid. Even at that, apologies extracted by legal action will have no more than pedagogical value. As other chapters in the volume have identified, such apologies are not always considered authentic and do not convey genuine contrition. Yet, such judicially ordered apologies, with all their limitations, may not be entirely out place in addressing corporate responsibility in apartheid victimization.

References

African National Congress (ANC). 1997. Submission to Special Truth and Reconciliation Hearing on the Role of Business. Johannesburg: South African Truth and Reconciliation Commission.

Asmal, Kader, Louise Asmal, and Ronald Suresh Roberts. 1997. *Reconciliation Through Truth: A Reckoning of Apartheid's Criminal Governance.* New York: St. Martin's Press.

BBC. 2004. "Mbeki Sued over Apartheid Era." June 21.

Bell, Terry and Dumisa Buhle Ntsebeza. 2003. *Unfinished Business: South Africa, Apartheid, and Truth.* New York: Verso.

Congress of South African Trade Unions (COSATU). 1997. Submission to the Truth and Reconciliation Commission Hearings on Business and Apartheid. Johannesburg: Congress of South African Trade Unions.

Davies, Robert. 1979. *Capital, State and White Labour in South Africa 1900–1960.* Brighton: Harvester Press.

Gregor, Neil. 1998. *Daimler Benz in the Third Reich.* New Haven, Conn.: Yale University Press.

Marcus, Tessa. 1989. *Modernizing Super-Exploitation: Restructuring South African Agriculture.* London: Zed Books.

Moll, Terence. 1991. "Did the Apartheid Economy Fail?" *Journal of Southern African Studies* 17 (2): 271–91.

Nattrass, Nicoli. 1991. "Controversies About Capitalism and Apartheid in South Africa: An Economic Perspective." *Journal of Southern African Studies* 17 (4): 654–77.

———. 1999. "The Truth and Reconciliation Commission on Business and Apartheid: A Critical Evaluation." *African Affairs* 98 (392): 373–91.

Ntsebeza, Dumisa Buhle. 2003. "Reparation, the Truth and Reconciliation Commission and Corporate Liability: The Unfinished Business." Presented at the first anniversary of the forming of Ngcebetsha Madlanga Attorneys, Johannesburg.

Patel, Ameeta and Lamar Reinsch. 2003. "Companies Can Apologize: Corporate Apologies and Legal Liability." *Business Communication Quarterly* 66 (1): 9–25.

Rostron, Bryan. 2002. "The Business of Apartheid." *New Statesman,* August 12.

Saunders, Christopher. 1998. *The Making of the South African Past: Major Historians on Race and Class.* Cape Town: David Philip.

Terreblanche, Sampie. 1997. Testimony Before the TRC During the Special Hearings on the Role of the Business Sector: South African Truth and Reconciliation Commission.

Truth and Reconciliation Commission of South Africa (TRC). 1999a. *Truth and Reconciliation Commission of South Africa Report.* Vol. 4. London: Macmillan.

———. 1999b. *Truth and Reconciliation Commission of South Africa Report.* Vol. 6. London: Macmillan.

Part V
The War on Terror

Chapter 19
Apology and the American "War on Terror"

MARK GIBNEY AND NIKLAUS STEINER

Given the way that "apology" has barged into the realm of international politics, perhaps it should not come as any great surprise that this phenomenon has come to occupy a central role in the "War on Terror." Until a few years ago, states were almost universally resistant to admitting any type of wrongdoing. Certainly, this fear of acknowledgment has changed markedly, and states (as well as many other entities) are now more willing to admit "wrongs" and to atone for them. Yet, state apologies continue to be sporadic events that seldom tell a complete or coherent story. More than that, however, these acts of acknowledgment and contrition have also proven useful in hiding larger truths.

One thing that emerges from our analysis of the War on Terror is that apologies are no longer to be confined to events of the past, which goes far in blurring any previous distinction between state apologies, on the one hand, and diplomatic demarches or admissions of fault. Instead, what seems to be emerging is an international norm whereby states (especially Western states) are expected to apologize for the commission of certain wrongs almost immediately after they occur, with the rush of apologies after the abuses at Abu Ghraib were publicly exposed serving as a case in point. Yet, what remains problematic is what wrongs prompt acknowledgment and apologies, but what wrongs do not—and in what manner this is carried out.

This relates to a second point, which is how the conduct of foreign policy and military affairs has appropriated the language and symbolism of apology. Oddly enough, perhaps, apology has been associated with virtually every aspect of the War on Terror—and here we are not even considering Saddam Hussein's own attempt to apologize before the onset of hostilities in his country for his earlier invasion of Kuwait, which set in motion the first Persian Gulf War. This includes the debate on America's preparedness against a terrorist attack; the manner in which the War on Terror has been carried out, particularly the abuses at Abu Ghraib but also the handling of civilian casualties; and finally, the present discussion of the justifications for invading Iraq. Yet, despite apology's omnipresence—indeed, in many respects because of it—many of the larger truths about the War on Terror remain hidden, and the demands for certain acknowledgments fiercely resisted. In that way, apology has become a very useful political tool. Acknowledgment has also become a way of not acknowledging and apology a means of avoiding accountability.

Yet, we are not completely cynical. Apologies can serve as a means of publicly acknowledging wrongdoing and showing empathy and respect for those harmed by our actions and most, if not all, of the apologies under discussion would meet this description. Still, our concern is that apology has come to be used more to obfuscate than to illuminate. What we attempt to do, then, is to shine some light on how the War on Terror has used (and misused) apology.

Ignoring the Terrorist Threat

> Your government failed you. Those entrusted with protecting you failed you. And I failed you. We tried hard but that doesn't matter, because we failed. And for that failure, I would ask, once all the facts are out, for your understanding and your forgiveness. (Richard Clarke, former U.S. government counterterrorism expert, March 24, 2004)

To our knowledge, Richard Clarke remains the only official of the United States government—past or present—who has apologized for government policies that left the country vulnerable to terrorist attack on September 11, 2001. Clarke, who was out of government service by this time, did so in a very dramatic way immediately prior to testifying before the September 11 Commission. What added to the poignancy of the moment is that Clarke addressed his apology directly to the families of the 9/11 victims present in the committee hearing room. An editorial the next day from the *New York Times* said of Clarke's apology: "It suddenly seemed that after the billions of words uttered about that terrible day, Mr. Clarke has found the one that still needed saying" (*New York Times* 2004a).

Perhaps the most impressive aspect of Clarke's apology is the manner in which it combines the political with the personal. Not only had the U.S. government failed to protect the deceased, but Clarke, personally, had failed as well. What Clarke's apology did was to give some meaning to these deaths. By his repeated use of the word "failure," Clarke's apology attempted to convey the idea that this tragedy might have been avoided. But his mission was not simply to assign blame. Rather, almost in a religious way, Clarke seemed to want to use these killings for our own salvation in the sense that the U.S. government would learn from the mistakes that it had made in the period leading up to September 11, thus averting another calamity.

For their part, however, the Bush administration has taken the opposite tack. Not only did National Security adviser Condoleezza Rice refuse to offer any kind of apology during the course of her testimony a short time later, but she and all of the other members of the Bush administration have resisted acknowledging any shortcomings in the country's preparedness that day. The reasons for this are both political and obvious.

The more interesting reaction to observe is that of the American public. A March 29, 2004, CNN/USA Today poll asked respondents "Who are you more likely to believe?" and the results showed that more people "believed" Rice (46 percent) than Clarke (44 percent)—which would seem to suggest that a majority of the public would be of the mind that there was no need to apologize for anything. There are several possible explanations for this. One might simply be that Clarke, a relatively unknown government bureaucrat before all this, was simply no match for a unified White House campaign that sought to portray him as not only being "out of the loop" on national security matters, but a political opportunist as well. Another explanation is that while an admission of government "failure" might have struck a responsive chord with the grieving 9/11 families, it might have had a much different meaning for the country at large, which remains fearful of additional attacks to this day. Related to this is the possibility that a fearful public simply refuses to believe that their government was not prepared—at the same time they have been willing to believe virtually everything else, contrary evidence notwithstanding, including the idea that Saddam Hussein was behind the September 11 attacks (see Marks, this volume).

Finally, there is the means by which Clarke issued his apology. By offering his remarks directly to the 9/11 families, his apology was apparently not interpreted as an apology to the broader American public—although the language he employed could easily have been interpreted that way. Related to that is the issue of Clarke's timing. While the unexpected apology made for exceptionally high drama, by issuing it at the same time that he was testifying before the Commission, his moral message (the apology) might easily have been drowned out by his political message that the Bush administration had downplayed the seriousness of the terrorist threat.

Abu Ghraib

I told him I was sorry for the humiliation suffered by Iraqi prisoners and the humiliation suffered by their families. (President George W. Bush, White House Rose Garden, May 6, 2004)

Certainly the most sickening images of the War on Terror have been the pornographic photographs of the humiliation and torture carried out by

U.S. military personnel at the Abu Ghraib prison in Iraq. The images were first aired on *Sixty Minutes II* on April 28, 2004, after CBS network had reached an agreement with the Bush administration to hold off showing the images for two weeks. The president's first public remarks on the matter were made on Friday, April 30, 2004, at which time he described the practices at Abu Ghraib as "abhorrent," and he expressed his "deep disgust" at these images. (As Susan Sontag 2004 has pointed out, the president's remarks almost seemed to indicate that the fault or the horror lay in the images themselves, and not in what they depicted.) The president went on to say that the mistreatment "does not reflect the nature of the American people." In addition, in a theme that some (but not all) members of the Bush administration have echoed repeatedly (although refuted by several government reports), the president set forth the defense that the abuses were merely the work of a "few bad apples," further arguing that the "actions of a handful of soldiers should not taint the tens of thousands who serve honorably in Iraq." Finally, Bush also pointed out that the investigation of this matter was moving ahead and that the transgressors would be dealt with appropriately.

What was said was not nearly as important as what was not said: Bush did not offer any apology. Several days later, in the face of rising world anger, President Bush essentially repeated this same message in an interview on Arab television. Once again, Bush sought to assure his Arab (and worldwide) audience that: "Our citizens in American are appalled by what they saw, just like people in the Middle East are appalled" (Stevenson 2004). And he went on to state: "We share the same deep concerns. And we will find the truth, we will fully investigate. The world will see the investigation and justice will be served."

Once again, however, all attention was focused on the president's continued refusal to apologize. This (purportedly) occurred the following day. At a White House Rose Garden ceremony where he was accompanied by King Abdullah of Jordan, President Bush recounted a private Oval Office conversation between the two: "I told him I was sorry for the humiliation suffered by Iraqi prisoners and the humiliation suffered by their families" (Bumiller and Schmitt 2004).

There are a host of questions about the Bush "apology." One is that there remains the question whether this particular apology—indeed, any apology at all—actually had been issued. All that is public is the president's rendition of a private conversation that may (or may not) have occurred. Few (if any) state apologies have been issued in such a manner. A second problem is timing. For a week, the president resisted every entreaty to apologize, and his resistance continued even after two members of his administration (Rice and Armitage) and two military leaders in Iraq (Kimmitt and Miller) apologized.

What is also problematic is that the apology was given to King Abdullah, the royal monarch of a neighboring country, and that it was not directed to the victims themselves or to the Iraqi people. Finally, to compound all of this, immediately after announcing that he had apologized, the president went on to say that he was: "equally sorry that people seeing these pictures didn't understand the true nature and heart of America." The problem, of course, is his attempt to equate these two "sorrows," as if the blow to America's self image was as egregious as the abuses themselves.

The American president is reacting because no American wants to be associated with any dehumanization now of the Iraqi people. We are deeply sorry for what has happened to these people and what the families must be feeling. It's just not right. And we will get to the bottom of what happened. (National Security Adviser Condoleezza Rice, in an interview with the Arabiya television network, May 4, 2004)

I think those photos show despicable acts. I couldn't be angrier about them. I couldn't be sadder about them. And, frankly, I couldn't be sorrier that some Iraqi prisoners had to suffer from this humiliation. (Deputy Secretary of State Richard Armitage, in an interview with Al Hurra television, May 4, 2004)

My army has been has been embarrassed by this. My Army has been shamed by this. And on behalf of my Army, I apologize for what those soldiers did to your citizens. (Brigadier General Mark Kimmitt, Baghdad, May 5, 2004)

I would like to apologize for our nation and for our military for the small number of soldiers who committed illegal or unauthorized acts here at Abu Ghraib. These are violations not only of our national policy but of how we conduct ourselves as members of the international community. (Major General Geoffrey Miller, Baghdad, Iraq, May 5, 2004)

As noted above, at the same time that President Bush was resisting calls for an apology, other members of his political and military team stepped forward and issued their own. What remains unclear is whether these other apologies had been cleared first by the White House and were attempts to cover for the president, or whether these were in the nature of more spontaneous and personal reactions to these atrocities.

Furthermore, there are odd features to several of these apologies. In terms of Condoleezza Rice, her statement about not wanting to be "associated" with this dehumanization might be read to mean that her real concern is the political embarrassment and fallout of being connected with this event, more so than the suffering of the victims. Likewise, Mark Kimmitt, spokesman for the American military in Iraq, refers to the "embarrassment" and "shame" suffered by the U.S. Army from these revelations, but makes no mention of the "embarrassment" and "shame" suffered by the prisoners themselves and their families. Finally, Geoffrey Miller, the commander of Abu Ghraib, is very quick to take up the line that only a "small number" of soldiers were involved in the Abu Ghraib abuses, although no investigation of this matter had as yet begun.

So to these Iraqis who were mistreated by members of the U.S. armed forces, I offer my deepest apology.... It was inconsistent with the values of our nation, it was inconsistent with the teachings of the military to the men and women of the armed forces, and it was certainly fundamentally un-American. (Secretary of Defense Donald Rumsfeld, testifying on Capitol Hill, May 7, 2004)

With the exception of the president himself, the most widely anticipated apology was one from Donald Rumsfeld. Almost as if he were reading from a script of a play, Rumsfeld delivered the apology that worldwide opinion and a domestic audience demanded of him. In doing so, Rumsfeld undoubtedly saved his position as Secretary of Defense. In terms of the language itself, the apology hits all the right buttons: the apology was directed to the Iraqi victims and in it Rumsfeld offers his "deepest apology." In addition, as a means of assuaging his congressional critics, Rumsfeld also acknowledged that: "I failed to recognize how important it was to elevate a matter of such gravity to the highest levels, including the president and the members of Congress."

Yet, Rumsfeld's apology shows us something else. What it shows is how apology can be appropriated as a political tool and how "acknowledging" can serve as a means of doing just the opposite. For one thing, it is now known that Rumsfeld had been fully aware of the abuses at Abu Ghraib for quite some period of time before the program was aired but there is no mention of this in his apology, nor had any investigation been initiated. Second, it is also now known that the abuses at Abu Ghraib were not an aberration. Rather, these harsh interrogation practices had started at Guantanamo Bay, Cuba and had then "migrated" to Afghanistan and from there to Iraq. Yet, there is no acknowledgment of this lineage. Furthermore, Rumsfeld offered his apology as one who was several steps removed from any of these practices. Yet, several government reports, including the Schlesinger Report and the army's Fay/Jones Report, concluded that Rumsfeld had personally authorized many of these harsh interrogation practices. The point is that absolutely none of this is ever acknowledged in the apology.

Another problem with Rumsfeld's apology, like so many others, is the manner in which it seeks to minimize what had taken place at Abu Ghraib, namely, torture, which is defined under international law as: "any act by which severe pain or suffering, whether physical or mental, is intentionally inflicted on a person for such purposes as obtaining from him or a third person information or a confession." Note that in his apology, Rumsfeld refers to "mistreatment." Later in his testimony, when asked whether torture had taken place, Rumsfeld replied: "I don't know if the—it is correct to say what you just said, that torture has taken place, or that there's been a conviction for torture. And therefore I'm not going to address the torture word." The point is that torture *did* take place at Abu Ghraib. To continue to avoid dealing with this issue is to continue to deny the truth itself.

The final issue is accountability. Apologies should help to begin the process of establishing accountability, not serve as a means of replacing it. Yet, there has been almost no accountability for the practices at Abu Ghraib and one important reason for this is that apology has come to be equated with accountability, when at times the two might actually work in opposition to one another.

> The president has expressed an apology on behalf of the nation. I will reinforce that apology. We are devastated by what happened at Abu Ghraib. We apologize to those who were abused in such an awful manner. (Secretary of State Colin Powell, at a meeting of Arab leaders in Jordan, May 16, 2004)

The final apology by a member of the Bush administration that we will look at is Secretary of State Colin Powell's effort. The apology is noteworthy in several respects. One is that while his deputy (Armitage) issued an apology almost immediately after these images entered the public domain, inexplicably enough, Powell waited for nearly two weeks. What is also puzzling about Powell's apology is that it was directed at a group of Arab leaders who were meeting in Jordan, and thus, it was not directed or personally delivered to the individuals who suffered from the abuses. Finally, Powell states that "We are devastated by what happened at Abu Ghraib." Yet what Powell misses is that American devastation is beside the point. What matters—or at least what should matter—is the devastation of the victims themselves and the Iraqi people.

> I would like to apologize to the Iraqi people and to the detainees. I want to apologize to the Army, to my unit, to the country. I want to apologize to my family. I let everybody down. This is not me. I should have protected the detainees. I shouldn't have taken that picture. I've learned a huge lesson: you have to stand up for what is right. (Specialist Jeremy C. Sivits, at his court martial proceedings, Baghdad, May 19, 2004)

In our view, the most sincere apology in this entire affair was that of Jeremy Sivits during the course of his court martial proceedings. As background, Sivits had played a relatively minor role in the Abu Ghraib abuses. He was accused of escorting an Iraqi detainee to the cellblock where the mistreatment was occurring, handing him over to a group of soldiers as they violated other detainees and taking a photograph of a pile of naked and hooded Iraqi men. Sivits pleaded guilty to four charges including dereliction of duty. For this, but also for agreeing to testify against other soldiers, Sivits was given a sentence of one year and ordered expelled from the Army.

Much like Richard Clarke, Sivits personalizes his behavior and his acceptance of responsibility. While Clarke had referred to the "failures" of the government and his own role in those failures, Sivits uses more common language: he had "let everybody down." More than that, Sivits catalogs who this "everybody" is: his Army unit, his family, himself, his country, but most important of all, the detainees and the Iraqi people. Sivits claims that he has learned a "huge lesson," and perhaps he has. We question whether anyone else could make this same claim.

Casualties of War

While the abuses at Abu Ghraib received instant worldwide attention, very little has come to be known about some of the other forms of suffering of the Afghan and Iraqi people. In that way, while many Americans would have a fairly good idea of how many U.S. soldiers have been killed in the fighting in Iraq, there has been only sporadic attention given to Iraqi and Afghan casualties—civilian or military. This, of course, is a failure on the part of the U.S. government but it is also a condemnation of the media as well.

Our focus, however, is on apology and it is interesting to observe how this has come into play on this issue. In Afghanistan, President Bush has refrained almost totally from acknowledging civilian casualties. One exception to this occurred in July 2002 after an American bombing raid had killed 40 civilians and wounded 100. This particular tragedy, which received worldwide attention primarily because it was determined that a wedding ceremony had been bombed, prompted President Bush to contact Afghan President Hamid Karzai (Bumiller 2002). According to White House spokeswoman Claire Buchan, the president termed the bombing a "tragedy," and he called "to express his sympathies to those whose loved ones lost their lives." Bush apparently also told Karzai: "Any time innocent life is lost we're sad." Although there was no "apology" as such, the call is itself a form of acknowledgment of wrongdoing. The larger point, however, is that this is one of the few times where the president has publicly acknowledged Afghan civilian deaths.

It is interesting to compare this (non)response with the deaths by "friendly fire" of four Canadian soldiers in the Spring 2002. Responding to Canadian political pressure, President Bush apologized privately to the Canadian prime minister and he publicly reissued this apology few days later: "I want to say publicly what I told Jean Chrétien the other day—about how sorry I am that Canadian soldiers lost their lives in Afghanistan. It was a terrible accident" (Krauss 2002). Beyond this, during their court martial proceedings (in which they were eventually exonerated), the American pilots issued their own personal apologies to the families of the Canadian soldiers. The point is that while hundreds if not thousands of Afghan civilians have been killed by American forces during the course of the fighting—with virtually no acknowledgment and apology—the deaths of four Canadian soldiers elicited both a private and a public apology from President Bush, as well as apologies by the soldiers involved in the tragic event. Or to put this matter another way, are the deaths of Canadian soldiers somehow more tragic than the deaths of Afghanis?

Iraq, on the other hand, has been a completely different matter. Beginning in 2003, U.S. officials instituted a program to provide monetary compensation for civilians (or their surviving family members) who had been killed or injured or had their property destroyed. The *New York Times* describes the compensation program this way:

Twice a week, at a center in Baghdad, masses of grief-weary Iraqis line up, some on crutches, some disfigured, some clutching photographs of smashed houses and silenced children, all ready to file a claim for money or medical treatment. It is part of a compensation process devised for this war. (Gettelman 2004)

Ironically (or perversely) enough, these restitution payments are accompanied by a brief apology from an American official. The *Times* headline sums up U.S. policy this way: "For Iraqis in Harm's Way, $5,000 and 'I'm Sorry'."

It is difficult to know what to think of such actions. On the positive side, the compensation scheme should be applauded in the sense that it provides at least some money for those who now have to try to cope with the death or injury of a family member or the loss of a house or to help pay for medical costs. Moreover, there is a symbolic value in the offer of financial compensation, as there is in the apology itself. On the other hand, there is something grossly unsettling about Iraqis getting in line, filing a claim and having money handed to them—accompanied by the most perfunctory apology imaginable. Do the same officials who hand out the cash also issue the apology—or has the American military saw fit to segregate these functions?

This is not to suggest that the U.S. government is not "sorry" about these tragedies or at least does not consider them "unfortunate." Nor does this mean that the U.S. has not done everything in its power to attempt to minimize civilian casualties and harm, although the ever-rising numbers would seem to suggest otherwise. The larger point is that as a nation we somehow believe that saying "We are sorry" to some Iraqis who have been harmed in the course of fighting means that we do not need to say "We are sorry" to the Iraqi people, generally, for the cruel and incompetent way in which the war and the ensuing occupation have been carried out. And in believing this we are decidedly wrong.

The Justifications for the War in Iraq

It's hard to imagine how the commission investigating the 2001 terrorist attacks could have put it more clearly yesterday: there was never any evidence of a link between Iraq and Al Qaeda, between Saddam Hussein and Sept. 11. Now President Bush should apologize to the American people, who were led to believe something different. (*New York Times* 2004b)

Apology has also been invoked in the ongoing debate relating to the justifications for extending the "War on Terror" into Iraq, with the most prominent example of this quoted above. Not only has the president resisted doing so, but his administration has maintained its spirited defense for the war, notwithstanding the absence of any weapons of mass destruction and despite any evidence that Iraq played any role in Al Qaeda's attack on the United States on September 11, 2001—the twin towers of justification for invading Iraq in the first place.

We make two points, which at first glance might seem internally inconsistent. The first is whether the *Times* has gone far enough. That is, if the president is to apologize for invading Iraq on what now appears to be completely faulty intelligence, such an apology should not only be directed at the American people, as the editorial suggests, but it should be particularly aimed at the Iraqi people as well. After all, American casualties pale in comparison to Iraqi casualties.

The second point relates to the danger of marrying apology to present political discourse. While we are sympathetic to the *Times* call for an admission of fault, one of our concerns is that the demand for an apology raises the stakes in such a way that it might have just the opposite effect politically. One of the things that is most remarkable about the apologies phenomenon is the way in which individual-level behavior—the act of apologizing—has been extrapolated to the behavior of states. But perhaps it is wise to carry this analogy one step further. Much like the petulant person who resists apologizing as a matter of principle, although it is invariably difficult to discern what this principle happens to be, could it be that states act in a similar fashion? Which is to say that the debate concerning acknowledgment and apology might have become so central that the Bush administration finds it necessary (politically) to stay the course of *not* apologizing. What this would also mean, of course, is that the interests of the Iraqi people would become little more than a sideshow. But perhaps they always have been this.

Conclusion

Scholars writing on the apologies phenomenon have described it in transformative terms. Elazar Barkan has expressed the idea:

Despite the oft-contentious debate, the principle of apology is increasingly accepted. At the very minimum these apologies lead to a reformulated historical understanding that itself is a form of restitution and become a factor in contemporary politics and humanitarian action. (Barkan 2000: xxix)

In many ways we share this sentiment but in other ways we do not. What we have explored here is the manner in which apology has stormed into the political discourse of the War on Terror. Unlike previous state apologies, which offered some sense of perspective on the past, what we are experiencing now is a form of almost immediate analysis and instant apologies—and from all levels of government as well. What might be positive about this is that states are willing to admit certain wrongs and to do so immediately. On the other side, powerful states continue to dictate what they are willing to acknowledge. Because of this, powerful states have used apology as a means of acknowledging certain truths—which has proven to be a very useful way of ignoring other, larger truths.

References

Barkan, Elazar. 2000. *Guilt of Nations: Restitution and Negotiating Historic Injustice.* New York: W.W. Norton.
Bumiller, Elisabeth. 2002. "Bush Offers Karzai Sympathy on Dead." *New York Times,* July 6.
Bumiller, Elisabeth and Eric Schmitt. 2004. "Bush Apologizes for Iraq Abuse; Backs Rumsfeld." *New York Times,* May 7.
Gettelman, Jeffrey. 2004. "For Iraqis in Harm's Way, $5,000 and 'I'm Sorry'." *New York Times,* March 17.
Krauss, Clifford. 2002. "Canada and U.S. to Cooperate in Inquiry on Bombing." *New York Times,* April 29.
New York Times. 2004a. "Assessing the Blame for 9/11." March 25.
———. 2004b. Editorial, "The Plain Truth." June 17.
Sontag, Susan. 2004. "Regarding the Torture of Others: Notes on What Has Been Done—and Why—to Prisoners, by Americans." *New York Times Magazine,* May 23.
Stevenson, Richard W. 2004. "Bush, on Arab TV, Denounces Abuse of Iraqi Captives." *New York Times,* May 6.

Chapter 20
The Fourth Estate and the Case for War in Iraq: Apology or Apologia?

JONATHAN MARKS

This chapter contains an account of apology and an argument for apology that is somewhat different from many of the other papers in this collection. My account is not premised on a violation of fundamental human rights or other legal wrong, and the case I make for an apology does not arise from the conduct of a state actor or from circumstances that may be more comfortably observed in the rear-view mirror of historical analysis. I argue for apology by members of a class of actors, the American media, who have—to varying degrees—failed to critique administration statements. In a deliberative democracy, this is a crucial failure of responsibility. Although the focus of my analysis is the media's coverage leading up to the war in Iraq, I also critique some of the coverage following the commencement of hostilities that served to reinforce impressions created by prewar coverage. Disturbingly, a number of studies suggest a causal relationship between widely held public misperceptions about prewar Iraq and exposure to media coverage. In particular, the media served to create or uncritically reinforce the mistaken impression that there was a material link between Saddam Hussein and Al Qaeda, and that Iraq had weapons of mass destruction (WMDs). The Bush administration repeatedly told the American people that the danger came from so-called "rogue states" such as Iraq that had both weapons of mass destruction and links to terrorists to whom they might provide such weapons. Clearly, the executive branch must bear responsibility for making misleading statements. However, I will argue that the American media also had a responsibility to test the Bush administration's claims regarding Iraqi WMDs and Al Qaeda links, to report factual inconsistencies, and to remind us of previous inconsistent statements by members of the administration. In addition, they should have given due weight to opposing views on the case for war, including those who argued that the invasion of Iraq would be a violation of the most fundamental norm of international law.

To date, only a few members of the print media have acknowledged the shortcomings in their prewar coverage of Iraq. Such acknowledgments have at best been in the form of a muted *mea culpa*, and at worst an *apologia*: a defense or justification of the wrongdoing. This paper performs just one biopsy—but in my view an important one—which reveals a systemic pathology that must be treated. Palliative treatment requires the admission of wrongdoing and the expression of regret. But a lasting cure depends on measures being put in place to ensure that these failures cannot and do not recur.

The Duties and Responsibilities of the Media

The power of the press has long been recognized. Long before the onslaught of visual media with fast-moving graphics and dramatic soundtracks, Edmund Burke observed that while there were three estates in the British Parliament, in the reporters' gallery there was "a Fourth Estate more important than they all" (Carlyle 1993 [1841]). When Alexis de Tocqueville turned his critical eye to the fledgling republic, he similarly noted that "after the people, the press is nonetheless the first of powers" (De Tocqueville 1969 [1850]). In a deliberative democracy, the power of the press is protected not simply for the benefit of those who write, but also for the benefit of those who might read what is written. Article 19 of the Universal Declaration of Human Rights, which protects the right to freedom of expression, provides that the right includes the "freedom . . . to seek, receive and impart information and ideas through any media." Moreover, as Article 19 of the International Covenant on Civil and Political Rights makes clear, the exercise of the right "carries with it special duties and responsibilities." Although the draftsmen of that provision appear to have been concerned that the media should not make defamatory statements or divulge material that might threaten national security, the essential responsibilities of the press encompass broader concerns.

This was made clear by the Supreme Court in the Pentagon Papers case, in which the U.S. government invoked national security concerns when it unsuccessfully sought to restrain publication of the contents of a classified study of U.S. policy on Vietnam. Justice Potter Stewart observed:

> the only effective restraint upon executive policy and power in the areas of national defense and international affairs may lie in an enlightened citizenry - in an informed and critical public opinion which alone can here protect the values of democratic government. For this reason, it is perhaps here that a press that is alert, aware, and free most vitally serves the basic purpose of the First Amendment. For without an informed and free press there cannot be an enlightened people (*New York Times v. United States* 1971)

In his separate opinion, Justice Black expressed similar concern and invoked the notion of media responsibility:

Only a free and unrestrained press can effectively expose deception in government. And paramount among the responsibilities of a free press is the duty to prevent any part of the government from deceiving the people and sending them off to distant lands to die of foreign fevers and foreign shot and shell.

He also commended the *New York Times* and the *Washington Post* for their "courageous reporting" and noted that "In revealing the workings of government that led to the Vietnam war, the newspapers nobly did precisely that which the Founders hoped and trusted they would do." As we shall see, the coverage leading up to the war in Iraq was far from courageous and would not have impressed Justice Black.

Dissent, Disclosure, and the Role of the Press

A free press is a vital part of any deliberative democracy. At one time, a discussion of the importance of a free press might have taken as its starting point the concerns of John Stuart Mill and Alexis de Tocqueville about the "tyranny of the majority" (Mill 1869; De Tocqueville 1969 [1850]). However, twentieth-century psychologists have contributed enormously to our understanding of conformity and decision-making (Sunstein 2003).[1] One phenomenon identified in recent experiments is often described as "social cascades," of which there are two varieties.

The first might be called *descriptive or factual cascades*. These result when people rely on and follow or reiterate others' descriptions of the world, their express or implied statements about *what is*. This may mean, at its simplest, agreeing with others that one line on a piece of paper is longer than a second one when both are the same size. Alternatively, it may mean agreeing with others that there are weapons of mass destruction in Iraq when, in fact, there are none. The second category of cascade might be called *normative cascades*. These occur when people rely upon and follow the apparent views of others about *what ought to be* (for example, whether the United States should invade Iraq without authorization from the United Nations Security Council). Clearly, the two types of cascade may go hand-in-hand. In the U.S., a cascade reinforcing a description of the world in which Iraq had WMDs and links with Al Qaeda contributed to a normative cascade supporting the invasion of Iraq.

Both cascades may result from a number of factors. Some people may have or be perceived to have more or better information, in which case others will be inclined to follow them. A perceived *information differential* may have been a factor in the case of the alleged Iraqi WMDs. When Secretary of State Colin Powell made his presentation to the Security Council on February 5, 2003, he undoubtedly sought to reinforce the view that his administration had access to persuasive intelligence information that the rest of us did not. A second factor is an actual or perceived *expertise differential*. This may arise when some are perceived as being better qualified to interpret the data available to others. (Again, Powell's presentation purported to offer a definitive—but subsequently discredited—interpretation of ambiguous intelligence reports.) Another factor may be an actual or perceived *confidence differential,* where those who describe the world or how it ought to be appear so confident that they may lead us to doubt our own views. A fourth factor is *reputational concern*. Although we may believe that others do not have better information or greater expertise than we do—and that they have no reason to be more confident—we follow them because we fear social persecution. This was at the heart of Mill's concern about tyranny of the majority. Although all four factors may play a role in either type of cascade, information and expertise differentials are likely to play a greater role in descriptive cascades, while confidence differentials and reputational concerns are more likely to feature in normative cascades.

As Cass Sunstein notes, *disclosers* (who convey new information) and *dissenters* (who present alternative opinions) may prevent or interrupt cascades (Sunstein 2003). In particular, disclosers may offer important antidotes to descriptive cascades, while dissenters may provide a powerful countervailing force in the case of normative cascades. Although editors and journalists are, of course, human and therefore susceptible to cascades themselves, the media can and should strive to play an important role in ensuring that cascades—particularly those based on questionable information—do not occur, by conveying new information (or alternative descriptions of the world) and by giving voice to alternative views. As we shall see, this is what most of the media failed to do when dealing with Iraq's alleged WMDs, links with Al Qaeda and the case for war. By side-lining alternative accounts and views, the media reinforced perceptions of disclosers and dissenters as *contrarians* whose views were not to be relied upon.

The Failure of the Media and the Impact on Public Perception

Evidence of Misperceptions

In October 2003, the University of Maryland's Program on International Policy Attitudes (PIPA) published a report on misconceptions relating to the war Iraq (PIPA 2003). Based on seven nationwide polls of 8,634 Americans conducted between January and September 2003, the report indicated that 60 percent of Americans were laboring under one or more of the three following misconceptions:

(i) that evidence of links between Iraq and Al Qaeda had been found;
(ii) that weapons of mass destruction had been found in Iraq; and
(iii) that world public opinion favored the U.S. going to war with Iraq.

This was just one of a number of polls conducted in 2003 that revealed important public misconceptions. In another disturbing example, 69 percent of respondents to a *Washington Post* poll in August thought that Saddam Hussein was either "very likely" or "somewhat likely" to have been "personally involved" in the terrorist attacks of September 11 (*Washington Post* 2003).

The relationship between these misconceptions and the respondents' principal news sources was starkly revealed by a large subset (3,334) of the PIPA respondents who were asked to identify their main news source. Of those who identified Fox, more than 80 percent had one or more misconceptions, with 45 percent having all three. The figures for four other television news sources (CBS, ABC, CNN, and NBC) were better than those for Fox, but still poor: 55 to 71 percent had one misconception, while 12 to 15 percent had all three. Print media (identified as an aggregate category) appeared to be less misleading: 47 percent of those whose main news source was print had one or more misconceptions, 9 percent had all three. But those who relied on NPR and/or PBS as their main news source were least likely to be misled: only 23 percent had one or more misconceptions, while a mere 4 percent had all three.

While demographics and respondents' party identification may have played some role, these factors alone cannot account for the misperceptions. For example, the average rate of misperception (across all 3 issues) among Republicans who principally relied on Fox was 54 percent, while the rate for Republicans who relied on PBS and/or NPR for news was 32 percent. All respondents were asked how closely they followed the news about Iraq. It was most striking, the report noted, that the more closely Fox viewers followed the news, the *more* likely they were to have misconceptions.

Although the report does not claim that these misperceptions created domestic support for the war in Iraq, there is undoubtedly some correlation between the exposed misconceptions and the respondents' support for the war. Of those with no misperceptions, only 23 percent supported the war. In contrast, 53 percent of those with one misperception, 78 percent of those with two misconceptions and 86 percent of those with three misperceptions supported the war in Iraq. This is consistent with the view I have already expressed, that descriptive cascades—regarding alleged Iraqi WMDs and links to Al Qaeda—may bolster normative cascades, in this case favoring war.

These misperceptions were not short-term aberrations. In a further PIPA poll carried out in March 2004, more than half of the respondents

The Fourth Estate and the Case for War in Iraq   303

(57 percent) still believed Iraq was "directly involved" in carrying out the September 11 attacks or had given "substantial support" to Al Qaeda. Almost half of respondents (45 percent) mistakenly believed the U.S. had found "clear evidence in Iraq that Saddam Hussein was working closely with the Al Qaeda organization." When asked about WMDs, 60 percent of respondents thought that Iraq had actual WMDs before the war or a "major program for developing them."

One might have thought that these misperceptions could not have survived the publication of reports by the Senate Select Committee on Intelligence and the 9/11 Commission. On July 7, 2004, the Select Committee concluded that the claims made in the CIA's National Intelligence Estimate (October 2002) regarding Iraqi WMDs were overstated and/or were not supported by underlying intelligence (Senate Committee on Intelligence 2004; Butler et al. 2004). Two weeks later, the 9/11 Commission found no evidence of a "collaborative operational relationship" between Iraq and Al Qaeda, "Nor . . . evidence indicating that Iraq cooperated with Al Qaeda in developing or carrying out any attacks on the United States" (National Commission 2004). However, a third PIPA survey in August 2004 suggested that much of the American public believed otherwise: 50 percent of respondents still believed that prewar Iraq was involved in the 9/11 attacks or was giving substantial support to Al Qaeda and 54 percent believed that Iraq had WMDs or a major WMD program. For many, these misconceptions endured through the November 2004 presidential election and beyond (Harris Poll 2005).

The Sources of and Reasons for the Misperceptions

A number of critiques and studies have recently explored the flaws in the media coverage that contributed to the misperceptions outlined above.

Media practices. The media provided *amplification* of administration claims by reporting them in front-page and "top-of-the-news" stories (Moeller 2004). For example, President Bush's claim on May 30, 2003, that WMDs had been found in Iraq was reported on the front page of the *Washington Post* the following day with the headline "Bush: 'We Found' Banned Weapons." Such *stenographic reporting* has drawn particularly vocal criticism from Michael Massing (Massing 2004a, b; Massing et al. 2004). Similarly, in their Iraq coverage a number of TV networks, most notably Fox News, used banners adopting the administration's euphemistic name for the war ("Operation Iraqi Freedom") or implicitly affirming the association between Iraq and Al Qaeda ("War on Terrorism") (Kull 2004). One analysis of 300 editorials in response to 15 national addresses made by President Bush between September 2001 and May 2003 revealed that the media "consistently amplified the words and ideas of the President and other administration leaders" (Domke 2004). These included a "binary zero-sum conception of the political landscape" (e.g., good versus evil and security versus peril, the first of which was only challenged in two of the 300 editorials) and claims that dissent was unpatriotic and a threat to the nation. Many media outlets became "passive transmitters" rather than critical filters of the administration's messages. This permitted *delegation of agenda-setting* to the administration (causing, for example, the threat posed by Russia's "loose nukes" to fall off the radar while the administration made a case for war in Iraq) (Moeller 2004).

In addition, the media gave little play to subsequent refutations of the administration's claims (e.g., regarding the alleged discovery of WMDs in Iraq) and often failed to challenge misleading representations by the administration. Similarly, evidence and analysis supporting or reflecting alternative perspectives tended to be buried. Notably, the media's respectful approach to claims by the administration was not applied to the statements made by officials of international bodies when they were not supportive of the case for war. This was most clearly demonstrated by the coverage of the inspections process and statements made to the Security Council by Dr. Hans Blix, head of UNMOVIC (the UN biological and chemical weapons inspection team) and Dr. Mohamed El-Baradei, head of the International Atomic Energy Agency (responsible for monitoring Iraq's alleged nuclear activities). While front page stories in the New York Times, for example, focused on Iraq's reluctance to cooperate with weapons inspectors, the paper buried on page A10 the main article concerning Dr. El-Baradei's January 9, 2003 statement that "no evidence of ongoing prohibited nuclear or nuclear-related activities has been detected" (Massing 2004a). Shortly thereafter, the *New York Times* headlined Dr. Blix's criticisms of Iraqi compliance on the front page, while his positive statements to the Security Council on January 27, 2003—"access has been provided to all sites we have wanted to inspect and with one exception it has been prompt" and "Iraq has on the whole cooperated rather well"—were buried in the heart of the paper. (Although buried articles may still be read, good placement can signal the importance of the issues being discussed or views being expressed, as every journalist jockeying for front page coverage knows well. Similarly, poor placement may have the opposite effect.)

The reluctance to express views that did not support the war even applied to earlier statements made by *members of the Bush administration* when they downplayed the threat posed by Iraq. Michael Moore's film *Fahrenheit 9/11* was the first occasion on which most Americans were given the opportunity to hear statements to this effect made by Colin Powell and Condoleezza Rice before September 11. These statements were not hard to find. A twenty-minute search on the State Department website revealed at least six statements in February 2001 alone in which Secretary Powell expressed the view that Saddam Hussein was being contained by sanctions and/or was not a threat to America.[2]

Techniques that gave prominence to pro-war voices continued and may have intensified after hostilities in Iraq began. Fairness and Accuracy in Reporting (FAIR) conducted one notable study of 1,617 on-camera news sources appearing in Iraq stories between March 20 and April 9, 2003, on the evening newscasts of six television networks. This revealed that viewers were six times more likely to see a pro-war source than an anti-war one and, among American guests, the ratio of pro- to anti-war increased to 25:1. These sources were far from representative. While only 3 percent of U.S. guests represented or expressed opposition to the war, more than one in four Americans opposed the war (Rendall and Broughel 2003).

Even more importantly, the media focused on the case for war as a pure policy issue rather than discussing the international legal implications. As the Scottish satirist Armando Iannucci observed in his *London Daily Telegraph* column, "the presentation of the attack on Iraq by all the main television networks as a "War on Terror" helped to sidestep the questions of the legality of a war that's so far uncovered no weapons of mass destruction" (Iannucci 2003). The legality of the war was clearly an important question. As the 1946 Nuremberg Tribunal emphasized, initiating war in violation of international law is "not only an international crime; it is the supreme international crime differing only from other war crimes in that it contains within itself the accumulated evil of the whole."

Although the legal debate cannot be recapitulated here, it should be noted that the vast majority of international lawyers in the United States (not to mention the larger global community of international lawyers) considered the invasion of Iraq to be a violation of international law.[3] However, the legality of the impending war was rarely discussed in the media, and any analysis or discussion of the issue that did take place was usually kept brief. Howard Friel and Richard Falk have noted that in none of the 70 *New York Times* editorials on Iraq between September 11, 2001, and March 21, 2003, were the words "UN Charter" or "international law" used (Friel and Falk 2004).[4] This author's search of the editorial pages of the Washington Post during the six months leading up to the Iraq war revealed some discussion of international law in an Iraqi context. However, the editors preferred to focus on whether Iraq was violating international law instead of considering whether the imminent attack would be lawful.

It may also have been of interest to the American people that while the Bush administration was publicly emphasizing the alleged threat posed to the United States by Saddam Hussein, this was not the basis upon which it justified the invasion to the United Nations. The letter from John Negroponte, then U.S. ambassador to the UN, to the Security Council dated March 20, 2003, contained five substantive paragraphs that sought to justify the use of force by the U.S. in Iraq. All five paragraphs emphasized Iraq's failure to comply with Security Council resolutions. Only the penultimate sentence of the fifth paragraph made any reference to self-defense. Even there, no special threat to the United States was cited and the claim was tied to the defense of the international community as a whole (Negroponte 2003). Thus, while the Bush administration was making out a case for war at home based upon self-defense, it was making the case to the international community on the grounds that it was entitled to act as 'global policeman'. One cannot but wonder what the impact would have been if the press had taken the trouble to draw out this inconsistency. The American public would surely have been somewhat more reluctant to support a war that put American lives at risk principally in the name of global vigilantism.

Reasons for media practices. Some critics attribute the media failure to "the inverted pyramid style of story telling . . . leading stories with the most 'recent' and most 'important' information by the most 'important' newsmakers" (Moeller 2004a). Susan Moeller has observed that this practice "single-handedly ensured that the administration's perspective on issues of national security and intelligence would lead the news—as long as the White House came out with a new message for each news cycle"(Moeller 2004a). Less charitable is Michael Massing's claim that the behavior of the media is due to "pack mentality" (Massing 2004a). One might argue that journalists and editors were themselves victims of descriptive and normative cascades. However, their susceptibility is less excusable than that of the general public. The media had access to many sources of conflicting information and competing views that were anxious to be heard.

One professor of journalism has observed that "the Bush administration benefited from a U.S. news media that gave it the benefit of the doubt in a matter unprecedented in the post-Vietnam post-Watergate era," and that "the typically inquisitive approach of journalists towards government was dropped—at least for a period of time" (Domke 2004). Many in the press (notably, CBS's Dan Rather and Fox News anchor Neil Cavuto) openly said they did not believe it was their role to be unbiased or to challenge the administration either in the run-up to the war or during the war and the beginning of the occupation (Kull 2004). The comments of Dan Rather (to whom I shall return later) are particularly noteworthy:

> I want to fulfill my role as a decent human member of the community and a decent and patriotic American. And therefore, I am willing to give the government, the president and the military the benefit of any doubt here in the beginning. . . .

I'm going to do my job as a journalist, but at the same time I will give them the benefit of the doubt, whenever possible in this kind of crisis, emergency situation. Not because I am concerned about any backlash. I'm not. But because I want to be a patriotic American without apology. (Jensen 2003)

Writing in the *British Journalism Review* in 2004, Christian Christensen observed that "In the current U.S. media environment, unquestioning patriotism is a virtue, while sceptical critique is a vice" (Christensen 2004). Although some journalists realized that patriotism and journalistic critique were not incompatible or mutually exclusive (Baker 2002) and others were conspicuous for their healthy skepticism regarding the WMD claims, these were a distinct minority. It is clear that the administration sought to encourage a suspension of critique, an approach typified by John Ashcroft's now infamous declaration addressed to civil rights advocates who "scare peace-loving people with phantoms of lost liberties":

Your tactics only aid terrorists for they erode our national unity and diminish our resolve. They give ammunition to America's enemies and pause to America's friends. They encourage people of good will to remain silent in the face of evil. (CNN 2001)

Ironically, it was statements like these that encouraged people of good will to remain silent! In a recent candid admission, CNN's leading war correspondent, Christiane Amanpour, expressed the view that "the press self-muzzled" and acknowledged her own network was among those that exercised self-censorship (Johnson 2003). Although such self-censorship may also have been motivated by concerns about ratings, hate-mail in response to critical coverage and fear of being branded as 'traitors' or 'liberals' by other media outlets, these can hardly excuse the media's failure to critique the case for war (Massing 2004a).

The Harm Caused and the Opportunity Costs

Each public misperception created and/or exacerbated by the media coverage leading up to the war in Iraq was clearly "harm" in and of itself. A deliberative democracy requires the electorate to be informed, not misled. The failure of the media can undermine the entire democratic process by preventing informed deliberation. The absence of such deliberation may have implications beyond the decision to go to war in Iraq. The results of the second PIPA study suggested that voters who were mistaken about Iraq's alleged possession of WMDs or support of Al Qaeda (and those who believed that experts agreed with them on these points) were significantly more likely to vote for the president in the November 2004 election. Apparently, this was because their views on these issues affected their perception of the president's honesty. Moreover, such perception may have been "even more powerful than party identification as a predictor of voting": those who said they believed the president was honest were more than 20 times more likely to vote for him than those who had doubts about his honesty or did not answer the question. Misperceptions affecting impressions of probity may therefore compromise elections in a manner that extends well beyond the issues to which the misperceptions relate.

It may be impossible to demonstrate conclusively that a more critical media would have prevented Congress from authorizing the president to use force in Iraq or would have prevented or discouraged the president from exercising that authority. But those possibilities similarly cannot be excluded. Moreover, the media clearly fueled the drive to war, the costs of which may be even more catastrophic than those that have materialized thus far. One expert, Graham Allison, has argued that if a terrorist nuclear attack occurred in the United States, Russia—whose enormous nuclear arsenal is vulnerable to theft—would be top of the list of potential suppliers, followed by Pakistan (where there are continuing links between security services and Al Qaeda) and North Korea ("the most promiscuous weapon proliferator on earth"). In Allison's view, Saddam-era Iraq "would not even have made the top ten." While the administration focused on Iraq, North Korea was given time to accelerate its own weapons programs. And, by failing to discover WMDs in Iraq, the U.S. has compromised its own credibility and damaged the reputation of its intelligence community (Allison 2004). A further opportunity cost has been highlighted by Stephen Flynn. He has observed that "Although the CIA has concluded that the most likely way [WMD] would enter the United States is by sea, the federal government is spending more every three days to finance the war in Iraq than it has provided over the past three years to prop up the security of all 361 U.S. commercial seaports" (Flynn 2004). If the media had been more critical of the case for war and emphatic about the need for more security measures at home, these vulnerabilities might already have been addressed.

Apology or Apologia?

There has been a dearth of media apologies for news coverage leading up to the war in Iraq. In print media, there have been a few admissions of error or wrongdoing and expressions of regret, the two commonly-agreed constituents of an apology. However, there has been no real commitment to alter the practices that led to the failure in the first place. Nor is it clear that any steps have been taken to ensure that mistakes are not repeated. Admissions have generally been articulated in a manner that seeks simultaneously to defend or justify the failings of the author's publication and, for that reason, they are closer in nature to an *apologia* than a true apology.

On May 26, 2004, an editorial in the *New York Times* admitted that the editors had

> found a number of instances of coverage [during the prelude to the war and into the early stages of the occupation] that was not as rigorous as it ought to have been. In some cases, information that was controversial then, and seems questionable now, was insufficiently qualified or allowed to stand unchallenged . . . Articles based on dire claims about Iraq tended to get prominent display while follow-up articles that called the original ones into question were sometimes buried. In some cases there was no follow up at all. (*New York Times* 2004)[5]

One example of coverage the editors found wanting was the discussion of the usefulness of the infamous aluminum tubes in making nuclear fuel. Doubts about the utility of the tubes for that purpose were "buried deep," 1,700 words into a 3,600-word article on September 8, 2002. Five days later, when *Times* reporters learned that the tubes were the subject of debate among the intelligence agencies, these misgivings appeared deep in an article on page A13. It was not until January 9, 2003, when the evidence was challenged by the International Atomic Energy Authority, that the *Times* finally gave voice to skeptics. However, this report appeared on page A10 although the editors acknowledged "it might well have belonged on Page A1."

Four days after the publication of this self-critique, the *Times* published an article by Daniel Okrent, then its "Public Editor" (whose task was to represent the interests of readers). He was more brusque in his critique, observing that the *Times* had published "breathless stories built on unsubstantiated 'revelations'" about WMDs. He also drew particular attention to an article by James Risen entitled "CIA Aides Feel Pressure in Preparing Iraqi Reports," which was "completed several days before the invasion and unaccountably held for a week." Okrent further notes that the article "didn't appear until three days after the war's start, and even then was interred on Page B10" (Okrent 2004).

The *Times* editors did not formally apologize for their shortcomings. Instead, there was an oblique admission of error and expression of regret:

> Looking back, we wish we had been more aggressive in re-examining the claims as new evidence emerged or failed to emerge. . . . We consider the story of Iraq's weapons, and of the pattern of misinformation, to be unfinished business. And we fully intend to continue aggressive reporting aimed at setting the record straight. (*New York Times* 2004)

The tone here is both defiant and defensive. The apparent undertaking to "continue aggressive reporting" appears to suggest that the reporting of the Times up to this point had been aggressive; this is somewhat at odds with the admissions made earlier in the same editorial. It is also far from clear that the editors' undertaking demonstrates any commitment to make systemic changes that would prevent the paper from making similar mistakes in the future. In a further critique of the performance of the *New York Times*, Massing rightly criticizes the paper for its initial reluctance to run the story of the abuse of prisoners at Abu Ghraib, citing the paper's coverage during the two week period leading up to its May 10, 2003 *mea culpa* (Massing 2004b).

It took the *Washington Post* a little longer to consider its coverage. On August 12, 2004, Howard Kurtz, a staff writer, responded to critics who said "the media, including the Washington Post, failed the country by not reporting more skeptically on President Bush's contentions during the run-up to war" (Kurtz 2002). Kurtz noted that "The *Post* published a number of pieces challenging the White House, but rarely on the front page" and acknowledged that the paper's coverage "despite flashes of groundbreaking reporting, in hindsight looks strikingly one-sided at times." Kurtz quotes his colleague, *Post* Pentagon correspondent Thomas Ricks, who similarly observed that "Administration assertions were on the front page," while "Things that challenged the administration were on A18 on Sunday or A24 on Monday." Executive editor Leonard Downie, Jr., admitted: "This was a mistake on my part." Assistant managing editor Bob Woodward also admitted: "We did our job but we didn't do enough, and I blame myself mightily for not pushing harder." As with the *New York Times*, however, there was no formal apology. Liz Spayd, assistant managing editor for national news, insisted the *Post*'s "overall record" was "strong." When she asked herself whether she wished the *Post* had "pushed harder and deeper into questions of whether [Iraq] possessed weapons of mass destruction," her reply was unequivocal: "Absolutely." But does she feel that she owes her readers an apology? "I don't think so."[6]

Although PIPA's studies suggest that television networks are generally more culpable than their print counterparts, members of broadcast media have been even more reluctant to carry out an introspective analysis of their prewar coverage. And those that have done so have failed to apologize. On July 25, 2004, at a Harvard panel discussion, Dan Rather was asked to look collectively over his "journalistic shoulders" and consider what could have been done better in the run-up to the war in Iraq. Rather appeared to acknowledge the shortcomings of the press: "One of the things we could have done is ask more questions, with more follow-up questions, in an effort to get more direct answers." But he was far from unreservedly repentant:

Look, when a president of the United States, any President, Republican or Democrat, says these are the facts, there is heavy prejudice, including my own, to give him the benefit of any doubt, and for that I do not apologize. (Rather 2004)

In an ironic twist, Rather did end up apologizing—in essence, for *failing* to give the president the benefit of the doubt—but it had nothing to do with the war coverage.[7] The apology followed his reliance (during a *60 Minutes* program) on documents concerning President Bush's National Guard record in the Vietnam era that CBS was unable to authenticate. Having initially defended the documents (CBS 2004), Rather issued an apology on his evening broadcast: "I want to say personally and directly I'm sorry," he said, adding, "This was an error made in good faith." Andrew Heyward, the CBS News president, also said: "We should not have used them. That was a mistake, which we deeply regret" (Rutenberg and Zernike 2004).

Disturbingly, following the CBS apology, the network decided to postpone *until after the election* a report that was to have detailed how the administration relied on false documents when it said Iraq had tried to buy yellowcake uranium from Niger (Rutenberg and Zernike 2004). A CBS spokesman claimed that it would be "inappropriate" to air the report so close to the election.[8] This is an issue on which the electorate should have been well-informed prior to the 2004 election. But having been stung once, CBS reverted to its default position: don't critique the government!

Conclusion

According to a recent epidemiological study in *The Lancet* (Burnham et al. 2006), hundreds of thousands of Iraqis have suffered violent deaths since the war began in March 2003. To hold the American media responsible for these fatalities and for the deaths of thousands of Americans—not to mention the many more maimed or injured—in a war that might not have proceeded without the media's acquiescence may appear to stretch the chain of causation and lay disproportionate blame on the American media. But the media must at least share responsibility, and the pool of demonstrable victims of their failure is arguably greater than those directly involved in the conflict. All Americans are victims of that failure and, consequently, the failure of the country's deliberative democracy. For although an increasing number of Americans have resorted in frustration to foreign news sources—such as the *Guardian* or the BBC website—or to weblogs for alternative perspectives, traditional print and broadcast media are still the principal news sources for most Americans. As a result the media caused or contributed to—or at the very least acquiesced in—cascades of misinformation that they had the power to challenge and, in some cases, perhaps correct. The media had access to credible alternative views and sources of information that were not available to the general public. They had a duty to share that information and those views with the American public, but they often buried that material or suppressed it.

There has been little in the way of apology from members of the media.

Few journalists or editors have recognized that their constituency was their readership or their audience—not the president or their board of directors—and that they seriously failed their constituency. Although the first step should be a clear admission of responsibility and expression of regret, a meaningful apology requires something more. Members of the media must commit to preventing the recurrence of the mistakes in their prewar coverage. They must also carry out systemic reforms to ensure that claims made by the administration—whether in the course of domestic or foreign policy and whether in times of peace or a time of war—are subjected to critical analysis rather than mere stenographic reportage. These steps are necessary if "news"—particularly broadcast news—is to become more than mere "(mis)infotainment." One famous American journalist recently remarked that "the quality of journalism and the quality of democracy go hand-in-hand" (Moyers 2004). When there is only one superpower, it is not only democracy at stake: global peace and security are riding on the diligence of America's journalists.

References

"Agora: Future Implications of the Iraq Conflict." 2003. *American Journal of International Law* 97 (3): 553–642.

Allison, Graham. 2004. "How to Stop Nuclear Terror." *Foreign Affairs* (January/February).

Asian Wall Street Journal. 2004. "Guess Who's a GOP Booster?" September 24.

Baker, Russ. 2002. "Want to Be a Patriot? Do Your Job." *Columbia Journalism Review* (May/June).

BBC. 2004. *BBC Statements in Full,* January 29. http://news.bbc.co.uk/2/hi/uk_news/politics/3441869.stm

Burnham, Gilbert, Riyadh Lafta, Shannon Doocy, and Les Roberts. 2006. "Mortality After the 2003 Invasion of Iraq: A Cross-Sectional Cluster Sample Survey." *The Lancet* 368: 1421–28.

Butler of Brockwell, Lord (Chairman), John Chilcot, Lord Inge, Michael Mates, and Ann Taylor. 2004. *Review of Intelligence on Weapons of Mass Destruction: Report of a Committee of Privy Counsellors.* Ed. House of Commons. London: Stationery Office.

Carlyle, Thomas. 1993 [1841]. "Lecture V: The Hero as a Man of Letters: Johnson, Rousseau and Burns." In Carlyle, *On Heroes, Hero-Worship, and the Heroic in History,* ed. Michael K. Goldberg. Berkeley: University of California Press.

CBS. 2004. "CBS Defends Bush Memos." September 14. http://www.cbsnews.com/stories/2004/09/15/politics/main643541.shtml

Christensen, Christian. 2004. "For Many, British Is Better." *British Journalism Review* 15 (3): 23–28.

CNN. 2001. "Ashcroft: Critics of New Terror Measures Undermind Effor." December 7. http://archives.cnn.com/2001/US/12/06/inv.ashcroft.hearing/

De Tocqueville, Alexis. 1969 [1850]. *Democracy in America.* Ed. J. P. Mayer and Max Lerner, trans. George Lawrence. New York: Doubleday.

Domke, David. 2004. "A Matter of Faith: The White House and the Press." *Nieman Report* 58 (2): 68–70.
Flynn, Stephen E. 2004. "The Neglected Home Front." *Foreign Affairs* (September/October).
Friel, Howard and Richard Falk. 2004. *The Record of the Paper: How the New York Times Misreports U.S. Foreign Policy*. New York: Verso.
Harris Poll. 2005. Harris Poll on Iraq, 9/11, Al Qaeda and WMDs, released on February 18, 2005. Available at www.prneeswire.com (last accessed February 28, 2005).
Iannucci, Armando. 2003. "Last Ditch." *Daily Telegraph*, May 16.
Jensen, Robert. 2003. "Dan Rather and the Problem with Patriotism: Steps Toward the Redemption of American Journalism and Democracy." *Global Media Journal* 2 (3).
Johnson, Peter. 2003. "Amanpour: CNN Practised Self-Censorship." September 14. http://www.usatoday.com/life/columnist/mediamix/2003–09–14-media-mix_x.htm
Kull, Steven. 2004. "The Press and Public Misperceptions About the Iraq War." *Nieman Report* 58 (2): 64–66.
Kurtz, Howard. 2002. "The Post on WMDs: An Inside Story." *Washington Post*, August 12.
———. 2004. "New Republic Editors 'Regret' Their Support of Iraq War." *Washington Post*, June 18.
Marks, Jonathan H. 2006. "9/11 + 3/11 = 7/7 = What Counts in Counterterrorism." *Columbia Human Rights Law Review* 37 (3): 559–626.
Massing, Michael. 2004a. "Iraq: Now They Tell Us." *New York Review of Books* 51 (3).
———. 2004b. "Unfit to Print?" *New York Review of Books* 51 (11).
Massing, Michael, Dana Milbank, and Gordon Michael. 2004. "'Now They Tell Us': An Exchange." *New York Review of Books* 51 (6).
Massing, Michael, James Risen, Judith Miller, and Robert G. Kaiser. 2004. "'Now They Tell Us': An Exchange." *New York Review of Books* 51 (5).
Mill, John Stuart. 1869. *On Liberty*. London: Longman and Green.
Moeller, Susan D. 2004a "The President, Press and Weapons of Mass Destruction." *Nieman Report* 58 (2): 66–68.
———. 2004b. "Media Coverage of Weapons of Mass Destruction." College Park: Center for International and Security Studies at Maryland.
Moyers, Bill. 2004. *Now with Bill Moyers*. Public Broadcasting Service, December 17.
National Commission on Terrorist Attacks upon the United States. 2004. *The 9/11 Commission Report: Final Report of the National Commission on Terrorist Attacks upon the United States*. New York: W.W. Norton.
Negroponte, John D. *Letter dated March 20, 2003 to the Security Council President from Ambassador Negroponte*. United States Mission to the United Nations 2003. http://www.un.int/usa/03iraqltr0320.htm
New York Times. 2004. "The Times and Iraq." *New York Times*, May 26.
New York Times v. United States, 403 U.S. 713 (1971).
Okrent, Daniel. 2004. "The Public Editor: Weapons of Mass Destruction? Or Mass Distraction." *New York Times*, May 30.
Program on International Policy Attitudes (PIPA). 2003. October 2003. http://65.109.167.118/pipa/pdf/oct03/IraqMedia_Oct03_rpt.pdf
Rather, Dan. 2004. Harvard Panel Discussion, July 25. Transcript available from www.ksg.harvard.edu/presspol/News_Events/Press_and_Election04.pdf (last accessed February 28, 2005).

Rendall, Steve and Tara Broughel. 2003. "Amplifying Officials, Squelching Dissent: FAIR Study Finds Democracy Poorly Served by War Coverage." *FAIR*, May/June.

Rutenberg, Jim and Kate Zernike. 2004. "CBS Apologizes for Report on Bush Guard Service." *New York Times*, September 25.

Senate Committee on Intelligence. 2004. *Report on the U.S. Intelligence Community's Prewar Intelligence Assessments on Iraq.* http://intelligence.senate.gov/iraqreport2.pdf

Sunstein, Cass R. 2003. *Why Societies Need Dissent.* Cambridge, Mass.: Harvard University Press.

Washington Post. 2003. "Washington Post Poll: Saddam Hussein and the Sept. 11 Attacks." http://www.washingtonpost.com/wp-srv/politics/polls/vault/stories/data082303.htm

Notes

Chapter 4. Apologies: A Cross-Cultural Analysis

1. For a useful overview, see Weyeneth (2001); Trouillot (2000).

2. Others have also expressed concern about government use of symbolic apologies in lieu of paying compensation. For example, Kathleen Gill writes: "it should certainly not be used as a substitute for compensation or as part of an attempt to avoid compensating victims" (Gill 2000: 23). Similarly, Martha Minow has argued: "Perhaps most troubling are apologies that are purely symbolic, and carry no concrete shifts in resources or practices to alter the current and future lives of survivors of atrocities" (Minow 1998: 112). For a more sympathetic view, see the superb essay Govier and Verwoerd (2002).

3. Fraser (1981) suggests that will be challenging to distinguish between the genuine and ritual apology.

4. The real question is whether there is a homeomorphic equivalent to sincerity in other worldviews. Sugimoto's comparative analysis of sincerity and *sunao* is fascinating: sincere and *sunao* are similar but not identical notions (Sugimoto 1999: 52–55).

5. "the payment of reparations is an apology that takes a distinctly material form" (Weyeneth 2001: 18).

6. See, for example, Blum-Kulka, House, and Kasper (1989); Coulmas (1981).

7. One dissertation in the field of interlanguage pragmatics, for instance, focuses on the misuse of apologies by Koreans who assume they can simply transfer Korean apology strategies to English. See Kim (2001); also Cordella (1991); Suszcynska (1999).

8. A joke underscores this finding. A sociological study of four countries is underway. The researcher begins in Poland with the question: "Excuse me, sir, what is your opinion of the recent shortage of meat in Warsaw?"; the Pole replies: "What is meat?" The researcher goes to Texas and asks the question "Excuse me, what is your opinion of the recent shortage of meat in Texas?"; the Texan answers: "What is a shortage?" The researcher goes to Russia and poses the question "Excuse me, what is your opinion of the recent shortage of meat in Moscow?"; the Russian responds: "What is opinion?" Finally the researcher goes to Israel and asks the question, "Excuse me, what is your opinion of the recent shortage of meat in Israel?"; the Israeli answers: "What is excuse me?" The informant for the joke was Professor Alan Dundes, February 1, 2005.

9. But see Fuentes-Mascunana (1998). Her provocative essay, after analyzing apologies in twenty Tagalog short stories, raises the question as to whether apology is "language universal" meaning that all apology acts are accompanied by an expression of responsibility or if they are language specific because expressions of responsibility vary by culture (22). Her findings were consistent with those of another scholar, Maria Bautista (1979), who also found that the "speaker's choice of an apology formula is patterned."

10. See, for example, Tukatsu and Takechi (1995); Field (1995).

11. The American view of apology is that words are empty; a ritual apology is insincere and therefore meaningless. The popular children's game called Sorry may reflect the notion that apologies involve strategy.

12. Court-ordered apologies are problematic for this same reason and may also violate the right against compelled speech. For a fascinating study of court-ordered apology in Korea, see Choi (2000).

13. Govier and Verwoerd contend that an apology that does not satisfy victims may be "defective." They mention a practical solution which is "to consult victims and seek their assistance in drafting the apology" (2002: 156).

Chapter 5. Elements of a Road Map for the Politics of Apology

1. For the most thorough compilation of state apologies see the website created by Rhoda Howard-Hassmann, http://political-apologies.wlu.ca

2. Historically, perpetrators have often seen themselves as victims. For example, in the context of German anti-Semitism and Nazism, see Burrin (2005), chap. 3. For Rwanda, refer to Mamdani (2001).

Chapter 8. The Role of Apologies in National Reconciliation Processes: On Making Trustworthy Institutions Trusted

1. This requires two caveats: first, as I will point out below, there is an inescapable personal dimension of reconciliation; second, to take the distinction between the personal or individual and the broader civic or political does not in itself entail that reconciliation has to be entirely reconceptualized in each of those two different spheres (or in the intermediate spheres of the family, small groups, professional associations, etc.). There are advantages to conceptions that could be applied consistently across the individual/social divide, as is argued also in Govier and Verwoerd (1997).

2. Qualifiers used by Alex Boraine (2000) and Juan Méndez (1997) respectively.

3. Archbishop Tutu, in discussing reconciliation, claimed, "I believe that we all have the capacity to become saints" (quoted in Wilson 2000). This is an admirable conviction, whose truth status I do not want to dispute here. However, one would hope to be able to articulate a conception of reconciliation that does not depend upon such a claim, especially not on taking the claim as if it were an empirical proposition.

4. The exception is Govier and Verwoerd (1997), already cited.

5. In addition to Goffman (1971) and Orenstein (1999), the following authors include the offer to repair as an essential component of apologies: Wagatsuma and Rossett (1986); O'Hara and Yam (2002); Alter (1999).

6. Other authors who follow this tack are Tavuchis (1991); Taft (2000); Levi (1997).
7. Lazare (2004) elaborates this position.
8. Eric Yamamoto (1997) provides what he calls an "apology catalog." It is a revealing exercise to go through these lists considering how many of the examples fit the description of an exchange of power; in my view, not many, at least not in any strong sense.
9. I have made this argument in more detail in de Greiff (2006). This is a massive study of reparations programs undertaken by the International Center for Transitional Justice, including case studies, thematic papers, and basic documents.

Chapter 11. State Apologies Under U.S. Hegemony

1. Paraphrasing Mark Gibney's and Erik Roxstrom's description of President Clinton's 1999 apology to Guatemala, Gibney and Roxtrom (2001).
2. Statement made on September 13, 1995, two days after the 22nd anniversary of the military coup. The Case of Pinochet (1995).
3. I am using the electronic version of the *Informe Final* published in the webpage of the Comisión de la Verdad y Reconciliación del Perú; http://www.cverdad.org.pe/. The references are from Part 2, Chapter 1.
4. Interviews with Carlos Iván Degregori and Carlos Tapia in Lima, Peru, July 2003.
5. A footnote indicates that the exercise took place in Chiclayo, August 1–25, 1989, with the "participation of 276 Peruvians and 232 Americans."

Chapter 12. "Deliver Us from Original Sin":
Belgian Apologies to Rwanda and the Congo

1. An English summary of the final report ("Summary," "Introduction," "Conclusions") is published on the Belgian parliament website, www.lachambre.be/kvvcr/pdf_sections/comm/lmb/summary.pdf; www.lachambre.be/kvvcr/pdf_sections/comm/lmb/introduction.pdf; www.lachambre.be/kvvcr/pdf_sections/comm/lmb/conclusions.pdf. The team of scientific experts who worked for the Commission published a book summarizing the complete report, De Vos et al. (2004). A French version will follow.
2. Rapport, Enquête parlementaire visant à déterminer les circonstances exactes de l'assassinat de Patrice Lumumba et l'implication éventuelle des responsables belges dans celui-ci, DOC 50 0312/006–007, Bruxelles, Chambre des représentants de Belgique, November 16, 2001, 844.

Chapter 16. Is Japan Facing Its Past? The Case of Japan and Its Neighbors

1. Consider the following twenty-first-century headlines: "Taiwan Leader Offers Apology to Key Rival" (Pan 2000); regarding SARS: "Official Says China Erred on Outbreak: Rare Apology Cites 'Poor Coordination'" (Pomfret 2003); regarding the *Ehime Maru* collision with an American submarine: "In Japan, Victims' Families Expect a Personal Apology" (Struck 2001); "Indonesian Leader Apologizes" (Chandrasekaran 2000).

2. I am using the term "Asia-Pacific War" instead of "World War II" because Japan's wartime actions go beyond the time period generally considered to be World War II.

3. Apologies are discussed in most books on how to understand the Japanese, such as De Mente (1993).

4. While it may be problematic to make fact/value distinctions, it is practical at times to do so, especially concerning analysis of such a contested subject as communal apologies (Weber 1958).

5. Furthermore, there are indications that this concern with the nation as the "body politic" is gendered as "the nation" often is depicted as the feminized "motherland" while militarized masculine images are representative of "the state."

6. Much as with other human rights violations, there will be those who believe that it is possible and essential to "uncover the truth"—stances that signal a neo-Enlightenment project theoretical basis. For the purposes of this chapter, however, I am not "searching for the truth" of what took place in each case because what "really happened" is (1) of less relevance to my research question than the predominant "intersubjective" interpretations of the events, (2) difficult if not impossible to ascertain, and (3) politically contested. I must credit Patrick T. Jackson for distilling these points. "Intersubjective" means that, for a given group, some aspects are shared in terms of general outlook or "worldview," beyond individuals (Ruggie 1998).

7. As further evidence of the possible range of interpretations of events, consider that, in the months following author Iris Chang's apparent suicide, conspiracy theories have emerged in Chinese internet chat rooms that she actually was murdered due to her pursuit of justice for the Nanjing Massacre.

8. From psychiatrist Takeo Doi, as quoted in Tavuchis (1991: 40).

9. For example, the cover-up of such issues as Unit 731 was due to the U.S. desire to glean the scientists' findings on biological warfare. See Dower (1998).

10. An important dynamic of communal apologies is that official leaders may have expended a great deal of political capital domestically to generate an apology to the victims. If the apology is not received graciously or is rejected, it may harm the domestic standing of the political leader.

11. Some observers speculate that China has inflated its official estimates of the numbers of Chinese war dead from 10 million to 35 million and for those killed during the Nanjing Massacre from 42,000 to 300,000, in part to assert that more people died in the Nanjing Massacre than from the dropping of the bombs on Hiroshima and Nagasaki. See Kristof (1998: 42).

12. Unfortunately, while designed to be moderate, fact-checking analyses and debates over "the numbers" often have an emotionally distant tone—which almost seems to anger Chinese more than outright denials of the Nanjing Massacre. See Peter Hays Gries's discussion of an incident involving Hata Ikuhiko and Iris Chang (Gries 2002).

13. To this day, cases emerge that cause trouble for Japan, such as the discovery of vats of Japanese poison gas that sickened and killed Chinese people (*Washington Post* 2003).

14. However, "closure" is a Western concept and therefore may not travel across all cultures. Actually, I also am skeptical of its usefulness in Western settings.

15. Given this evidence, there is support for the claim that issues of "saving face" go beyond Asian contexts (Ting-Toomey 1994)

16. Some feminists and assertiveness proponents advise women not to apologize so frequently, interpreting it as unhealthy self-abasement and blame taking.

Chapter 18. Rethinking Corporate Apologies: Business and Apartheid Victimization in South Africa

1. However, some recent studies have suggested that apologies generally do not constitute evidence of guilt and that, in fact, they sometimes have positive consequences for the apologists. For a fuller discussion see Patel and Reinsch (2003).

2. For a more detailed discussion of the role of the mining industry under apartheid see TRC (1999a: 33–36).

3. For a detailed discussion of this and similar cases of collaboration between the business community and apartheid's security agencies see Bell and Ntsebeza (2003).

4. This position of the business community toward the apartheid "reform" is well illustrated by a statement made in 1985 by Sir Michael Edwards, former chairperson of British Leyland, in which he urged the South African government to address the threat of growing international sanctions by "sensible representation but without the trauma of one-man one vote." See *Financial Mail*, September 6, 1985, 16.

5. Apartheid lawsuits in the United States have been made on the basis of the Alien Tort Claims Act of 1789, which gives aliens in the United States a legal right to sue anyone in U.S. courts for wrongs committed anywhere in the world. The cases that have been brought up so far rely on counts of conspiracy, aiding and abetting, unfair and discriminatory labor practices, gross violations of human rights, and unjust enrichment.

6. Other proposals made by the TRC for ways in which the business community could generate funds for reparation and restitution included: a wealth tax; a one-time levy on corporate and private income; a 1 percent "donation" by companies listed on the Johannesburg stock exchange of their market capitalization; and a retrospective surcharge on corporate profits. The main criticism of the TRC's recommendation is that its restitutive measures are not proportional to the different levels of corporate involvement which it acknowledged in its report. All accumulated wealth was regarded by the TRC as deserving of restitutive taxation. For a comprehensive study of this aspect of the TRC report see Nattrass (1999).

Chapter 20. The Fourth Estate and the Case for War in Iraq: Apology or Apologia?

1. Although I am indebted to Sunstein for drawing the material together and for his insightful analysis, I have modified his taxonomy of social cascades and offer my own elaboration of causal factors. See also Marks (2006).

2. Full texts of all Secretary Powell's statements are available from www.state.gov

3. For a selection of views on the legality of the war, see Agora (2003).

4. This book—published after the first draft of this chapter had been completed—makes a number of points also made here.

5. Compare the far more comprehensive 14,000-word *mea culpa* on May 11, 2003, for the editors' failure to spot the fabrications of one journalist, Jayson Blair.

6. Martin Peretz, publisher of the *New Republic*, similarly doubted that his magazine owed its readers any apology, adding dismissively, "These apologies are silly." See Kurtz (2004).

7. Some readers may find it more ironic—and disturbing—that the only unreserved media apology came from the BBC (2004) for its critical coverage of the British government's case for war.

8. Remarkably, this decision coincided with the public endorsement of President Bush by the CEO of Viacom, CBS's parent company. See *Asian Wall Street Journal* (2004).

Contributors

PETER R. BAEHR studied political science at the University of Amsterdam and Georgetown University. He was Professor of International Relations at the University of Amsterdam and Staff Director (later member) of the Scientific Council for Government Policy, an advisory body to the Dutch Government. Later he became Professor of Human Rights at the Universities of Leyden and Utrecht. At Utrecht he was also Director of the Netherlands Institute of Human Rights (SIM). He is now honorary Professor of Human Rights at Utrecht University and Editor-in-Chief of the *Netherlands Quarterly of Human Rights*. Recent publications in English include *Human Rights: Universality in Practice*, *Human Rights in the Foreign Policy of the Netherlands* (with Monique Castermans-Holleman and Fred Grünfeld), *The Role of Human Rights in Foreign Policy* (with Monique Castermans-Holleman), and *The United Nations: Ideal and Reality* (with Leon Gordenker).

RICHARD B. BILDER is Foley & Lardner-Bascom Emeritus Professor of Law at the University of Wisconsin-Madison. He was educated at Williams College, Cambridge University, and Harvard Law School and served for some years as an attorney in the Office of the Legal Adviser of the U.S. Department of State. Among other positions, he has served as Vice-President, Honorary Vice-President, and Counselor of the American Society of International Law; member of the Board of Editors of the *American Journal of International Law*; on the Executive Board of the Law of the Sea Institute; as Chair of the International Courts Committee of the American Bar Association and Committee on Diplomatic Protection of the International Law Association; on U.S. delegations to international conferences; and as an arbitrator in international and domestic disputes. He is the author of *Managing the Risks of International Agreement* and of a number of articles and other scholarly publications in international and foreign relations law.

ALFRED L. BROPHY is Professor of Law at the University of Alabama. He received a Ph.D. from Harvard University and a J.D. from Columbia University. He writes in the areas of property, reparations, and history of law. His publications include *Reconstructing the Dreamland: The Tulsa Riot of 1921—Race, Reparations, Reconciliation* and *Reparations: Pro and Con.*

JEAN-MARC COICAUD heads the United Nations University (UNU) Office at the United Nations in New York. Previously he was a Senior Academic Officer in the Peace and Governance Programme of UNU in Tokyo (1996–2003). From 1992 to 1996 he served in the speechwriting team of UN Secretary-General Boutros Boutros-Ghali. A former fellow at Harvard University, he held appointments with the French Ministry of Foreign Affairs and the European Parliament (financial committee). He has also taught at the University of Paris I-Sorbonne, Harvard University, the New School for Social Research, and Keio University (Tokyo). He earned a Ph.D. in political science-law from the Sorbonne and a Doctorat d'État in Philosophy from the Institut d'Études Politiques of Paris. He has published widely on issues of international legitimacy, international ethics, and international relations. His recent and forthcoming publications include *Beyond the National Interest* and, in Japanese, *The Politics of International Solidarity.*

ELIZABETH S. DAHL teaches political science at the University of Nebraska-Omaha. She received a Ph.D. in international relations in 2006 and an M.A. in international peace and conflict resolution from American University in 2000. She also obtained an M.A.R. with a concentration in ethics in 1995 from Yale Divinity School. Her dissertation, "Navigating Crises in Sino-American Relations: Apology, Nationalism, and Historical Memory," analyzes the debates over apologies regarding the 1999 NATO bombing of the Chinese embassy in Belgrade and the 2001 EP-3 surveillance plane collision near Hainan island. Her research interests are issues of conflict and reconciliation in East Asia.

PABLO DE GREIFF is Director of Research at the International Center for Transitional Justice (ICTJ) in New York. He holds degrees from Yale University (B.A.) and Northwestern University (Ph.D.). Formerly Associate Professor of Philosophy at the State University of New York at Buffalo, where he taught ethics and political theory, he is the editor of seven books, including *Global Justice and Transnational Politics* and Jürgen Habermas's *The Inclusion of the Other.* He is also author of articles on transitions to democracy, democratic theory, and the relationship between morality, politics, and law. He has been Laurance S. Rockefeller Fellow at the Center for Human Values, Princeton University, and a recipient of a fellowship from the National Endowment for the Humanities. At the ICTJ, among other projects, he directed a large-scale project on reparations, *The Oxford Handbook of Reparations*. He is working on a book entitled *Redeeming the Claims of Justice in Transitions to Democracy*.

ELEANOR BRIGHT FLEMING is a Senior Lecturer in the Department of Political Science at Vanderbilt University. She holds a Ph.D. in political science from Vanderbilt University, with a dissertation, "Sisters Speak: A Multicultural Theory of Democratic Inclusion." She qualified at the Master's level in political theory and American politics, and possesses a B.A in political science and African American studies. Her research interests are multiculturalism, black political thought, feminism, and democratic theory. She is the recipient of numerous academic awards, and has served as an intern with *Journal of Politics*. She is an active participant in civil society organizations in her home city of Franklin, Tennessee.

MICHAEL FREEMAN is a Research Professor in the Department of Government, University of Essex. He was a founder-member, and for many years Deputy Director, of the University of Essex Human Rights Centre. He was Chair of the Human Rights Research Committee of the International Political Science Association, 1997–2000. He has been a member of Amnesty International since 1977 and was Chair of its British Section, 1986–88. He teaches political theory and human rights, and has published widely on various topics in these fields. He is author of *Human Rights: An Interdisciplinary Approach*. He has lectured on human rights in more than 20 countries, from China to Brazil.

MEREDITH GIBBS is a lawyer at Blake Dawson Waldron, Melbourne. She holds a B.A. and L.L.B. (Hons) from Australian National University and a Ph.D. from Otago University. She is Barrister & Solicitor of the Supreme Court of Victoria, Australia, and until recently was Senior Lecturer in Law in the School of People, Environment & Planning at Massey University, New Zealand. Her research specializes in reparative justice, New Zealand's Treaty of Waitangi settlement process, Indigenous rights to natural resources, and environmental law. She has worked professionally in both New Zealand and Australia as a solicitor, resource management lawyer, and policy analyst in commercial legal practice, for a nonprofit conservation organization, and for a Maori authority. Her publications have appeared in *World Development*, *Society & Natural Resources*, *New Zealand Universities Law Review*, *New Zealand Journal of Environmental Law*, and *Brookers Resource Management*.

324   Contributors

MARK GIBNEY is Belk Distinguished Professor at the University of North Carolina-Asheville. He holds a Ph.D. from the University of Michigan and a J.D. from Villanova University School of Law. His publications have appeared in such journals as *Human Rights Quarterly*, *Harvard Human Rights Journal*, *Fletcher Forum of World Affairs*, and the *Harvard International Journal of Press/Politics*. His latest book is *Five Uneasy Pieces: American Ethics in a Globalized World*.

RHODA E. HOWARD-HASSMANN is Canada Research Chair in International Human Rights at Wilfrid Laurier University and a Fellow of the Royal Society of Canada. She is also a Senior Research Fellow at the Centre for International Governance Innovation in Waterloo. Her more recent books are *Human Rights and the Search for Community*, *Compassionate Canadians: Civic Leaders Discuss Human Rights*, and *Economic Rights in Canada and the United States* (coeditor with Claude E. Welch, Jr.). In 2006 she was named the first Distinguished Scholar of Human Rights by the Human Rights Section of the American Political Science Association. Her current research is on reparations for Africa. With funding from the Canada Foundation for Innovation, she has also established a website database of political apologies, http://political-apologies.wlu.ca

MATT JAMES received his B.A. from Queen's University, Ontario, and his M.A. and Ph.D. from the University of British Columbia. He currently teaches in the Department of Political Science at the University of Victoria. A student of social movements, constitutionalism, and citizenship, he is presently conducting a multiyear research project that studies reparations movements as a window on Canadian citizenship and social movements in an era of neo-liberalization. He is the author of *Misrecognized Materialists: Social Movements in Canadian Constitutional Politics*. He has also published on reparations in the *Canadian Journal of Political Science* and in the recent edited books *Critical Policy Studies* and *Multiculturalism and the Welfare State*.

LEONARD JAMFA (Moise Léonard Jamfra Chiadjeu) was born in 1969 in Cameroon and started his university studies at the Faculty of Law and Economics of the University of Yaounde, Cameroon (1989–1997). He then studied at the University College of Federalist Studies of Aosta, Italy (1998), at the Diplomatic Academy of Vienna (1998–1999), and at the Centro Internacional Bancaja para la Paz y el Desarollo, Spain (2000). He holds a Ph.D. in Political Science from the University of Kassel, Germany (2003). He is currently a postdoctoral research fellow at the Philosophisch-Theologische Hochschule Sankt Georgen in Frankfurt. He is also Chairman of the nongovernmental organization African Development Initiative.

JIBECKE JÖNSSON is a doctoral researcher in the Department of Political and Social Sciences of the European University Institute in Florence. Previously, she was a program assistant at the United Nations University Office at the United Nations in New York. She holds an M.Phil. in International Relations from the Institut d'Études Politiques s, for which she conducted research and fieldwork on the reconciliation process in Bosnia and Hercegovinia. She earned her B.A. (Hons) in Politics and International Relations from the University of Kent at Canterbury and the Institut d'Études Politiques/ Université Pierre Mendès France in Grenoble. While at the International Service for Human Rights, Geneva, she published various articles in the *Human Rights Monitor*.

PAUL KERSTENS studied Dutch and English literature and linguistics at the University of Antwerp, and African languages and cultures at Ghent University. He worked as an assistant of MP Leen Laenens for the Lumumba commission of the Belgian Parliament. He is now a Ph.D. student of Professor Janos Riesz at the University of Bayreuth. He also works at KVS, the Royal Flemish Theatre in Brussels, co-ordinating Green Light, a group of professional artists of African origin, and collaborating on the project, The Unknown Congolese. He has participated in several international conferences and has published articles on African literatures and on the Belgian colonial heritage in French and Dutch. He is also the secretary-general and founding member of the association BeCAME (Brussels Centre for Africa in a Multicultural Europe).

ANTHONY P. LOMBARDO is a doctoral candidate in the Health and Behavioural Sciences Program, Department of Public Health Sciences, Faculty of Medicine, University of Toronto. He received his Master of Arts degree from McMaster University, where his thesis, "Reparations to Africa: Examining the African Viewpoint," explored African opinion toward reparations and investigated the prospects and challenges for a social movement for African reparations. He is senior author (with Rhoda E. Howard-Hassmann) of "Africans on Reparations: An Analysis of Elite and African Opinion," in *Canadian Journal of African Studies*. His doctoral research will focus on aspects of health promotion and behavior related to HIV/AIDS. He is the recipient of a Canada Graduate Scholarships Doctoral Scholarship (Social Sciences and Humanities Research Council of Canada, September 2004–September 2007) and a Studentship Award (Ontario HIV Treatment Network, September 2006–September 2008). His article "Anatomy of Fear: Mead's Theory of the Past and the Experience of the HIV/AIDS 'Worried Well'" was published in *Symbolic Interaction* in 2004.

JONATHAN H. MARKS is Associate Professor of Bioethics, Humanities and Law at Pennsylvania State University and a barrister at Matrix Chambers, London. He is a former Greenwall Fellow in Bioethics at Georgetown University Law Center and Johns Hopkins University Bloomberg School of Public Health. He has taught law and policy courses on U.S. counterterrorism measures after 9/11, and on the war in Iraq at a number of universities in the U.S. and Europe, including the University of North Carolina Chapel Hill Law School, the University of Augsburg, and the Woodrow Wilson School of Public and International Affairs at Princeton University, where he was Director of a Policy Task Force on "Lawful Responses to Terrorism After September 11." His publications span a number of fields, including international law, environmental law, public health, and human rights. His current research explores the relationship between law and ethics and the tensions between the protection of human rights and public health. He obtained his M.A. (Jurisprudence) and B.C.L. from Oxford University.

MICHAEL R. MARRUS is Chancellor Rose and Ray Wolfe Professor Emeritus of Holocaust Studies at the University of Toronto. He has been a visiting fellow of St. Antony's College, Oxford, and the Institute for Advanced Studies of the Hebrew University of Jerusalem, and a visiting professor at UCLA and the University of Cape Town. He is the author, among other books, of *The Politics of Assimilation: French Jews at the Time of the Dreyfus Affair, Vichy France and the Jews* (with Robert Paxton), *The Unwanted: European Refugees in the Twentieth Century, The Holocaust in History, Mr. Sam: The Life and Times of Samuel Bronfman*, and *The Nuremberg War Crimes Trial, 1945–46*. He was a member of the international Catholic-Jewish historical commission to examine the role of the Vatican during the Holocaust.

CARLOS A. PARODI, economist and political scientist, is graduate director of the Department of Politics and Government at Illinois State University, where he teaches Latin American politics, human rights, and international political economy. His first publications were about the relationship between transnational corporations and the state in Peru. His latest book is *The Politics of South American Boundaries*. He is now working on a book manuscript about the politics of truth commissions in Latin America.

ALISON DUNDES RENTELN is Professor of Political Science and Anthropology at the University of Southern California, where she is Director of the Unruh Institute of Politics. A graduate of Harvard University, she has a Ph.D. in Jurisprudence and Social Policy from Boalt Hall at Berkeley and a J.D. from the USC Law Center. Her publications include three books, *International Human Rights: Universalism Versus Relativism*, *Folk Law: Essays in the Theory and Practice of Lex Non Scripta*, and *The Cultural Defense*, and numerous articles. She was a core member of the Law and Culture Working Group of the Social Science Research Council (U.S.) and worked with the United Nations on the treaty to protect the rights of persons with disabilities. She also served on the California Committee of Human Rights Watch and several California civil rights commissions.

NIKLAUS STEINER is Director of the Center for Global Initiatives at the University of North Carolina-Chapel Hill. He earned his Ph.D. in Political Science at Northwestern University; his research interests include refugees, nationalism, and national identity. His publications include *Arguing About Asylum: The Complexity of Refugee Debates in Europe*, *The Problems of Protection: UNHCR, Refugees, and Human Rights* (coeditor with Mark Gibney and Gil Loescher), and *Regionalism in the Age of Globalism* (coeditor with Lothar Hönnighausen, Marc Frey, and James Peacock). He is currently writing an undergraduate textbook on international migration and citizenship.

JANNA THOMPSON is a Reader and Associate Professor in the Philosophy Program at La Trobe University, Melbourne. She is a graduate of University of Minnesota and Oxford University and has taught in the UK as well as Australia. She is the author of *Taking Responsibility for the Past: Reparation and Historical Injustice*, *Justice and World Order*, and other books and articles on intergenerational and international justice, environmental ethics and topics in political philosophy.

Index

Abdullah (king of Jordan), 290, 291
Aboriginal populations, apologies to, 3, 31, 32, 40–42, 73, 101–4, 260–61, 264. See also Australia; Canada; Great Britain; New Zealand
Abu Ghraib, apology for, 289–94
Acknowledgment (as not apologizing), 85–86, 288, 292, 297
Alien Tort Claims Act, 208–9, 281
Allende, Salvador, 173
Al Qaeda, links to Saddam Hussein, 298–303, 307–8
Amanpour, Christiane, 307
Amstutz, Mark, 72, 73
American public, misperceptions regarding "war on terrorism," 301–2
Annan, Kofi, 89–90
Apologia, 299, 308–12
Apologies: acknowledgment of harm, 3, 5, 32, 43, 54, 72, 99, 157–59, 219–21; African culture, 222–23; and atonement, 97–101, 118; cultural context, 7, 61–76; and dispute settlement, 26–27; examples, 14–17; future-oriented, 43, 57, 69, 100; genuineness of, 5, 21, 32, 40–44, 61–62, 68, 78, 85–86, 137–39, 157–60, 225–27, 251–53; and group harmony, 70–71; and healing, 160–61; historical contexts, 47–60; humiliation (of oneself), 61, 147–48; institutional reform, 133, 212; legal ramifications, 17, 28–29, 66–68, 70–71, 272; moral inconsistency, 148–50; and new international order, 2, 4, 241; and normalization of crime, 86–87; personal, 4, 6, 24, 288, 294; political, 31, 34–38, 40–44; process of, 223–27, 251–52, 269; and publicity, 220; reaffirmation of values, 130–31; reasons for and against, 24–27; reestablishing trust, 132, 134; relationship between giver and receiver, 1, 2, 14, 25–26, 78–80, 84–85, 129, 188, 199, 211, 214, 221, 225; religious significance, 57, 71, 188, 199–200, 265, 288; remedy under international law, 17–19; remorse, 159; resentment, 128–29; respect for victim, 87–88; "saving face," 68–69; self-reconciliation, 80; social exchange, 129, 137, 265–66; temporal dimensions, 6, 77–78, 259, 268; trust, 6–8, 121, 125–27, 132–34; truth telling, 132; the "unforgivable," 6, 82–85; "unreconciled" societies, 128, 131; written record, 138, 146–47. See also International apologies; Justice; Reparations
The Apologist (novel), 26
Argentina, Truth Commission, 89, 172–73
Aristotle, 122
Armitage, Richard, 25, 290, 291, 293
Ashcroft, John, 307
Australia: Aboriginal population, 40–44, 101–4; federal government refusal to apologize, 102; Sorry Day, 41, 102–3, 106; Stolen Generation, 73, 101–4

Barkan, Elazar, 1, 149, 226, 235, 296–97
Barnlund, Dean and Miho Yoshioka, 245–46
Barry, Brian, 52–54, 58

Beatrix (queen of the Netherlands), 232–33, 237
Beld, Ton Van den, 48–49
Belgium: colonial past, 188–90, 196; law on genocide, 193; Lumumba Commission, 187, 194–201; Rwanda Commission, 187, 192–94, 196–201
Benedict XVI (pope), 263
Birney, James, 111
Bittker, Boris, 96–97
Black Manifesto, 96
Blair, Tony, 31, 37, 50
Botha, P. W., 277, 280
Brooks, Roy, 54
Burke, Edmund, 299
Bush, George W., 17, 67, 105, 217, 289–91, 294, 303

Canada, apologies of: Japanese Canadians, 139–40, 147; aboriginal populations, 103, 140–41, 146; Italian Canadians, 141–44, 147; High Arctic exiles (Inuit), 142–44; Ukrainian Canadians, 144–45; Chinese Canadians, 145, 150
Cascades, social, 300–302, 311
Catholic Church: aboriginal populations, 260; Brothers and Sisters of the Church, 266–68; confession, 262–64; God, apologies to, 265–66; Jews, 3, 260; Jubilee movement, 261, 263; Mafia, 260; omissions, 259–60; opposition to apologies, 264–65; Pacific states, 260–61; Second Vatican Council, 3, 262; Teshuvah, 269; women, 260; World War II, 3, 260
Central Intelligence Agency, U.S. (CIA), 183
Chang, Iris, 249
Chicac, Jacques, 217
Chigara, Ben, 56
Chile, Truth Commission, 58, 89, 173, 177
Chinese Embassy, bombing of, 5, 16, 20, 25
Chrétien, Jean, 140, 143
Clinton, Bill, 5, 15–16, 21, 23, 25, 31, 37–38, 105, 130, 174–75, 217, 226
Clark, Helen, 154
Clarke, Richard, 288–89, 294
Cold War, 173, 175–79
Colonialism, 3, 7, 31, 51, 88, 187–90, 196–97, 220, 224, 260. *See also* individual countries

Congo, as Belgian colony, 189–90
Corporations, apologies of: collective responsibility for slavery, 100; concern with legal liability, 272; dearth of, 272; lawsuits against, 281; Swiss banks, 278, 283; typologies, 272–74; under apartheid, 282–83; under Nazi regime, 274–75, 281
Crimes against Humanity, 83–85
Cunningham, Michael, 138, 158, 163, 226

Daniels, Roger, 137–38
De Grieff, Pablo, 57, 58
Dehaena, Jean-Luc, 192, 194, 197
Derrida, Jacques, 83
De Tocqueville, Alexis, 300
Development Assistance, 58, 212–13, 223–24
Digeser, Peter, 36
Diplomacy, and apologies, 5, 27–29, 45–46
Distributive justice, 5, 46–47, 54
Donnelly, Jack, 52, 58
Dundes, Alan, 62, 63, 315 n.8
Du Plessis, Max, 50

Ehime Maru incident, 16–17, 24, 67
Elizabeth II (queen), 130, 154, 158, 162, 216
Ellison, Ralph, 113
El Salvador, Truth Commission, 173
Enloe, Cynthia, 243
Ex gratia payments, 19, 26

Fairness and Accuracy in Reporting (FAIR), 305
Forgiveness, 5, 36, 57, 71–72, 79, 83–84, 124, 129–30, 137, 188, 262
France: Algeria, 217; slave trade, 217
Fraser, Malcolm, 103
Fugimori, Alberto, 181, 183

Germany: absence of institutions, 212–13; atrocities in Namibia, 202; conditional tense, 210; colonial and postcolonial policy, 204–5; God, reference to, 211; lawsuit in U.S., 203, 205, 208–9; reluctance to apologize, 202–15; World War II, 78–79, 81; "Zimbabwe syndrome," 206–7
Gibney, Frank, 242–43

Gibney, Mark and Erik Roxstrom, 2, 19–24, 43, 88, 138–39, 175
Gill, Kathleen, 165, 315 n. 2
Govier, Trudy, 35–36
Govier, Trudy and Wilhelm Verwoerd, 34, 316 n. 13
Goldstone, Richard, 56, 59
Great Britain: Boer war, 216; Irish potato famine, 31; Maori, 154, 157–60; Poland, 46
Guatemala, 15, 21, 23, 31, 37; Truth Commission, 174–75
Guilt, forms of, 6, 78–79

Harper, Stephen, 150
Hayner, Priscilla, 172, 174
Herron, John, 102, 103
Hickson, Leticia, 65–66
Holocaust, 3, 78
Honda, Katsuichi, 251
Howard, John, 31, 35, 41
Human dignity, 99–101
Human rights, 47–48, 50–53, 58, 61, 70, 77–78, 83, 99–100, 106, 181–82, 184, 232, 239, 271–74, 277, 282
Humanity, recognition of, 99–100
Humor, cultural differences of, 63–64
Hussein, Saddam, 287, 298, 305

Intergenerational justice, 5, 6, 35–36, 38–40, 99
International apologies, 6–7, 13, 14
International Court of Justice (ICJ), 16, 23
International diplomacy, 14–17
International law: apology as formal remedy, 17; customary, 2, 13, 19–23, 138; invasion of Iraq as violation of, 305–6; "satisfaction," 18–19, 24, 29; soft law, 23
International Law Commission, 14, 17, 18, 26, 29, 33
Internationally wrongful act, 18, 20
Iraq war, justifications for, 296
Islamic culture, 71–72

Japan: apologies within culture, 64–68, 86, 241, 246; colonial practices, 242–43; "comfort women," 8, 73, 82, 243–45, 247, 249; difficulties in apologizing, 245–49; Hiroshima and Nagasaki, 249; lack of sincerity in apologies, 86; Nanjing massacre, 242, 244, 247, 249–51; South Korea, 247; textbook controversies, 247–48; victimhood, 249–50; Yasukuni Shrine, 246–47
Jaspers, Karl, 78–79
John II (pope). *See* Catholic Church
Justice: and apologies, 46–60, 90 intergenerational, 5, 38–40, 47–57, 99–100, 268

Kabila, Joseph, 191
Kabila, Laurent-Désiré, 191, 194, 197, 199
Kagame, Paul, 194, 199
Karzai, Hamid, 294
Keating, Paul, 40, 41
Keizo, Obuchi, 247–48
Kimmitt, Mark, 290–91
Kohl, Helmut, 202
Kok, Wim, 233–34
Kristof, Nicholas, 248
Kymlika, Will, 51–52

LaGrand decision (ICJ), 16, 22
Lazare, Aaron, 1, 64, 71, 129, 131
Leopold II (king of Belgium), 189
Low intensity conflict (LIC), 181, 182
Lumumba, Patrice, assassination of, 187, 194–95, 198
Lumumba Commission, 187, 191, 194–98, 200–201, 210

Mana (recognition), 161–63
Manly, Basil, 111–12
Maoris, apologies to, 154–67. *See also* New Zealand
Marović, Svetozar, 45–46
Massing, Michael, 306, 310
McClintock, Cynthia and Fabián Vallas, 183, 184
Media: CBS News, 273, 290, 306–7; Fox, 302–3; in democratic society, 299–301; and public misperceptions of "war on terror," 301–3; support for invasion of Iraq, 303–8
Memory, 48, 163
Menem, Saul, 179
Michel, Louis, 192–95, 197, 200
Mill, John Stuart, 300
Miller, David, 48–50
Miller, Geoffrey, 291

Minow, Martha, 57, 71, 138, 226, 266, 315 n. 2
Monterinos, Vladimiro, 183–84
Mulroney, Brian, 139, 142, 146–48

Nader, Laura, 70–71
Namibia, land reform, 206–7
Nanjing Massacre, 8, 242–44, 247, 249–51. *See also* Japan
National Security Doctrine (NSD), 173, 175
National Security Strategy (NSS), 176, 178
Negroponte, John 306
Netherlands: colonial policy, 229–35; slave trade, 235–38
New York Times, 296, 300, 305, 309–10
New Zealand: Tainui, 154: Ngai Tahu, 154–66; Te Uri a Hau, 154
9/11 Commission, 303
Non-Western states, need for apologies, 88–89
Normative expectations, 128
Novak, David, 267–69
Nozick, Robert, 49–50
Nuclear Test Case (*Australia and New Zealand v. France*), 23

Paglia, Camille, 53
Parekh, Bhikku, 52
Personal narrative, 4
Peru, Truth and Reconciliation, 179–85
Pinochet, Augusto, 176–77, 179
Powell, Colin, 67, 293, 300–301, 304–5
Primoratz, Igor, 49
Pueblo incident, 15, 26

Rainbow Warrior, 15, 20, 24
Rather, Dan, 306–7, 310–11
Rawls, John, 46–47, 49, 50, 52, 54
Realism, 37, 45
Reconciliation, 8, 120–11, 154–55
Reagan, Ronald, 280
Remedial Justice, 19
Remembrance, 33
Reparations, 32–34, 46–47, 50, 54–57, 72–73, 95–98, 133, 137, 141–42, 150, 163–66, 187, 200–201, 212–13, 221–23, 225–27
Resentment, 6, 7, 128
Restitution, 18, 62
Rice, Condoleezza, 289–91, 304

Robinson, Randall, 96–98
Rumsfeld, Donald, 292
Rwanda, 5, 21, 23, 218; relationship with Belgium, 187–94, 196–98
Rwanda Commission (Belgium), 187, 192–94, 198–99, 210
Rwandan Patriotic Front (RDF), 191, 196

School of the Americas, 181, 182
Schroeder, Gerhard, 203–4
Serbia, apologies by, 45–46
Shelton, Dinah, 19
Sivits, Jeremy, 293–94
Slavery, 5, 7, 31, 50, 51, 53, 72, 85, 88, 216, 217; need for national apology, 95–108; lawsuits based on, 98; Southern Baptist Church, apology of, 104; Clinton-Bush "near" apologies, 105, 217
Social movements, 3, 4
Social recognition, 4
South Africa: Afrikaner Broedarbond, 276–77; apartheid and capitalism, 274–76; Congress South African Trade Union, 278; constructive engagement, 271, 279–80; Truth and Reconciliation Commission, 1, 4–5, 58, 79, 276, 280–83
Statement of Reconciliation (Canada), 140–41, 146, 148
State responsibility, 14, 17, 19
Stewart, Jane, 140, 141

Tannen, Deborah, 253
Tauvchis, Nicholas, 130–31, 137, 147, 149–50, 159, 162, 221, 226, 262–63, 265–66
Thompson, Janna, 49, 50, 57, 58, 159, 160, 269
Torpey, John, 1
Treaty of Waitaugi (New Zealand), 155–60, 162, 165–66
Truths, 4, 32, 56, 117
Truth Commissions, 8, 56, 58, 89, 179
Tully, James, 51, 152, 154
Tuskegee experiment, apology for, 104–5, 130
Tutu, Desmond, 316
Tutwiler, Henry, 111

United Nations, apologies for Rwanda and Srebrenica, 89–90

United Nations Conference on Racism (Durban), 85, 193, 208, 217, 236–38
United Nations Convention on Genocide, 101
United Nations Security Council, 300
Ubunta, 5
United States: absence in Latin American truth commissions, 171–86; Abu Ghraib, 289–94; Canadian soldiers, death of, 294; civilian casualties, 294–95; Guatemala, 16, 21, 23, 31, 37–38; Japan (*Ehime Maru*), 16–17; Japanese Americans, 97, 101, 104–5; Native Hawaiians, 31, 104; Rwanda, 15, 21, 23; Tuskegee experiment, 104–5, 190
United States Senate Select Committee on Intelligence, 303
Universal Declaration of Human Rights, 99
University of Alabama, 6, 109–19; buildings named after slaveowners, 111–13; faculty apology for slavery, 112–13; opposition to apology, 113–17; *Montgomery Advertiser*, 116–17
University of Maryland, Program on International Policy Attitudes (PIPA), 301–3, 307, 310

Verhofstadt, Guy, 193, 194, 197, 198, 199
Vienna Convention on Consular Relations, 16
Vienna Convention on the Law of Treaties, 22
Villa-Vicencio, Charles, 123, 124
Von Trotha, General, 202

Waddle Scott, 17, 24, 67–68
Waldron, Jeremy, 33, 54–55, 57–58, 163
Walker, Margaret, 128–29
War on terrorism, 8, 287–314
Washington Post, 300, 302–3, 310
Weber, Max, 241
Western imperialism, 53, 57
Western states, meaning of apologies, 1–2, 4, 7, 88–90
Westley, Robert, 99
White March, 191, 192
Wieczorek-Zeul, Heide-Marie, 203, 209–12
Wierzbicka, Anna, 62–63

Zimbabwe, 5, 206–7, 209

Acknowledgments

We are extraordinarily grateful for the tremendous support—financial and otherwise—provided by the United Nations University (UNU). This project would never have become a reality without it.

We wish to thank Yoshie Sawada, Programme Administrative Assistant in the Peace and Governance Program of UNU, Tokyo, for her administrative support throughout the project. We also wish to thank UNU Senior Vice-Rector Ramesh Thakur and Scott McQuade, head of UNU Press. Moreover, we are indebted to the Center for Global Initiatives at the University of North Carolina at Chapel Hill (formerly the University Center for International Studies). We especially want to thank Kim Glenn, Narvis Green, and Galina Zilberter, who were instrumental in co-coordinating the conference in October 2004 that spawned this book.

Michael Lisetto-Smith, assistant to Rhoda Howard-Hassmann at Wilfrid Laurier University until August 2006, was responsible for sending out the memos and information that kept all authors and editors on track. We thank him very much for his punctilious attention to this project. James Gaede and Gregory Eady, also assistants to Rhoda Howard-Hassmann, were student editors for this project. We thank them for their care and attention to referencing, style, and all the myriad details that are important to a book. Without the assistance of all three of these fine Canadians, the task of editing would have been much more difficult. Rhoda Howard-Hassmann thanks the Canada Research Chairs program the funds to pay her assistants.

Three anonymous reviewers provided comments on the manuscript, for which we are very grateful, as we also are to the diagnostic editor of University of Pennsylvania Press, for excellent advice.

Finally, as editors, we thank all our authors for their participation in this project and their willingness to revise their chapters several times.

www.ingramcontent.com/pod-product-compliance
Lightning Source LLC
Chambersburg PA
CBHW030106010526
44116CB00005B/114